The New Houseplant

Bringing the Garden Indoors

The New Houseplant

Bringing the Garden Indoors

ELVIN McDONALD

Macmillan Publishing Company
New York

Maxwell Macmillan Canada
Toronto

Maxwell Macmillan International
New York   Oxford   Singapore   Sydney

Frontispiece: Miltonia, or pansy, orchid. Photographed at the Phipps Conservatory in Pittsburgh, Pennsylvania.

Text and photographs copyright © 1993 by Elvin McDonald

Macmillan Publishing Company
866 Third Avenue
New York, NY 10022

Maxwell Macmillan Canada, Inc.
1200 Eglinton Avenue East
Suite 200
Don Mills, Ontario M3C 3N1

Macmillan Publishing Company is part of the Maxwell Communication Group of Companies.

Library of Congress Cataloging-in-Publication Data
McDonald, Elvin.
    The new houseplant : bringing the garden indoors / Elvin McDonald.
      p.   cm.
    Includes index.
    ISBN 0-02-583126-7
    1. House plants.   2. Indoor gardening.   I. Title.
SB419.M38   1993
635.9'65—dc20   92-22292
                                                        CIP

Macmillan books are available at special discounts for bulk purchases for sales promotions, premiums, fund-raising, or educational use. For details, contact:

Special Sales Director
Macmillan Publishing Company
866 Third Avenue
New York, NY 10022

10 9 8 7 6 5 4 3 2 1
Printed in the United States of America

I DEDICATE THIS BOOK TO
MY FATHER, MY CHILDREN, AND
ESPECIALLY
ELEANOR HEPBURN NOALL
AND
HUGH FRASER NOALL

Contents

Five

Six

Seven

Eight

Nine

Overleaf: Bouquets of cut seasonal flowers such as Narcissus 'Soleil d'Or' *bring stimulating changes and scents to the house garden. The succulent blue-green rosettes of* Echeveria glauca *form a vertical garden in the background.*

Introduction
Validating the Houseplant

Only last week—early November 1991—my next-door apartment neighbor said to me as we rode the elevator together, "I just heard that houseplants clean up the indoor air. Now I'm going to go out and buy some fresh plants and really try to learn how to care for them. If only I'd known this when my husband was smoking."

It is worth noting that this scientific finding from the National Aeronautics and Space Administration, made public in the popular press in 1984, took seven years to reach the awareness of a fortysomething person who appears to be uncommonly intelligent and is probably as with it and well-read as anyone around. Her lament about the smoking husband subtly brings up what detractors have said about the NASA findings, that the public is being misled into thinking that all we need to do to clean up the air we breathe, cigarette smoke included, is to add a few houseplants. This is of course not true, nor has it ever been so claimed. All things being equal, however, each and every healthy plant has some beneficial impact on the air around it. As much as ten years before NASA said it, guests who came to my apartment regularly remarked on how "clean" the air felt or smelled, or how "buoyant" the atmosphere was. Such irony cannot escape me, that all the while my next-door neighbor, whose kitchen has shared a common wall with mine for nearly twenty years, had no idea what houseplants were about.

Coincidentally, also last week, in the mailroom of my building, another neighbor announced to me that he had gotten rid of all his living plants and replaced them with silk ones. Considering that this man's parents were lifelong florists, I was surprised that he would do this and said so. "I want to be able to take trips without worrying about who's going to water the plants," said he, with a certain pique at my response. "Well, I'm sorry," I said ("annoyed" would have been more truthful), "but silk plants are lifeless and collect dust. Living plants help purify the indoor air; every room needs its quota." End of conversation. In the interim I've calmed down. Living plants aren't for everybody.

Curiously, these encounters with my neighbors—neither of whom knew of my work on this book—sum up well where we are with houseplants today. Some individuals are discovering that plants are more than pretty things to brighten a dark corner, while others are still disconnected from the dynamic circle of life represented by each and every living plant. Those of us who may have been passionate indoor gardeners for a long while have much to share with others, which is really the premise for this book. While I wrote best-selling books on houseplants in the 1960s and 1970s, this one starts off from where we are today, at the outset of what could be the greatest craze yet for houseplants and indoor gardens. The first one, over a century ago, was fed by the increasing availability of better quality glass, central heating, and running water, not to mention such inventions as the steam engine, typewriter, telephone, and telegraph that speeded communications and facilitated as never before the dissemination of exotics.

Break the sill habit. Observe how light enters and crosses the interior of the room and select and situate plants accordingly. Here, in my New York apartment living room, I have painted the walls terra-cotta color and added a bamboo cane arch on which are tied—espaliered—the branches of weeping fig and pleomele. The desired effect is an inviting garden path instead of a soldier row of plants pressed against the windows.

Now we accomplish more in less time by Fed-Exing, faxing, word processing, and talking on the telephone as we walk or drive along, but in the last analysis it will be our growing awareness of the benefits of gardening in general that will feed this new appreciation for bringing nature up close, into the interior spaces where we live and work. Our new celebration of the houseplant will grow in the main from a vast army of relatively young gardeners who become hooked on the outdoor experience and feel bereft in any situation without living flora.

My next-door neighbor who is now going to go out and buy plants and apply to them a new kind of devotion also represents a vast crowd who at one time or another may have invested a sizable amount of money in "plantscaping" or "interiorscaping," because it was trendy and seemed the right thing to do, not because they understood plant life. The new houseplant I am talking about communicates plainly. It says

- I am living.
- I am inherently beautiful.
- I want to live well because the healthier I am, the better job I can do refreshing the air you breathe.
- I am a respectable necessity, neither luxury nor fad.

Since we spend ninety percent of our time indoors, and the indoor air is often two to five times more polluted than the air outside, one hardly needs a license to go out and spend money on thrifty, living indoor plants.

Another factor is the age-old belief that gardening in itself is beneficial therapy. I once saw engraved on a sign by a garden's entry,

> *The most difficult thing*
> *to carry into a garden*
> *is tension.*

I like the thought but find it works better for me if the source of the tension is deliberately put down—or at least acknowledged—before entering the garden. Plants and gardens demand our attention, and maybe some sweat,

The kitchen counter fluorescent-light garden was a surprising and unexpected bonus when I bought my new home in Houston, Texas. There are two 40-watt generic tubes, one cool white, one warm white. They burn about sixteen hours daily. This is an ideal place to grow seeds, root cuttings, nurture miniature plants, and create a gardenscape of one's own. I have added a wood statue surrounded by miniature African violets, a background of olive tree and purple basil, miniature azaleas, a small flowering guzmania that seems relatively huge, 'Graham Stuart Thomas' rose in a bud vase, a clove of garlic, squash, and assorted family pictures.

but they also miraculously help relieve the stresses of life, often at once giving us food for the table, the soul, the neighbors, and—if outdoors—some furred and feathered friends. The notion that a radish cannot be hurried through a fax machine says it all. Sowing the seeds, first opening the packet, then committing them to the earth, is a hopeful act of letting go.

BREAK THE SILL HABIT

What is singularly impressive to me about this subject is that there are in the world vastly more households where a garden can be grown indoors—one living plant is a beginning—than there are households accompanied by sufficient earth to garden outdoors. The new houseplant is about breaking the sill habit and becoming a gardener indoors who seeks and experiences the benefits and rewards of gardening outdoors.

Houseplants have been important to me for most of my more than fifty years. Around age ten a book on houseplants by Montague Free, who was for thirty-one years horticulturist at the Brooklyn Botanic Garden (BBG), fired my enthusiasm, as did numerous magazines of the period. I joined the American Begonia Society and learned of Logee's Greenhouses in Connecticut. This was long before UPS 2nd Day, but the Logee family already had a half century of experience in packing plants for travel via the U.S. mails. I will never forget the first parcel I received from Logee's, how each plant was so carefully wrapped that not a leaf was broken or bruised, even after traveling all those miles to the Oklahoma panhandle. (My mother and I smoothed out the newspapers used for packing and caught up on the Connecticut news.) Today when I visit Logee's the first whiff of air inside the greenhouse instantly transports me back to opening that carton of treasures from a place very far away, at least in 1947 miles.

My most intense experiences as an indoor gardener have occurred in the last couple of decades, since I moved to a modern high-rise apartment in New York City. A decade of gardening indoors convinced me that if I accomplished nothing else in my life, I must work a season as an outdoor gardener, a dream come true in 1985 at the BBG. All through these years my friends C. Z. Guest and Larry Power also provided me a place to garden outdoors in the country, with greenhouse collections of orchids and amaryllids, begonias, and woody plants from warm-temperate climates for me to lavish my attentions on weekend visits, like a doting grandparent. At first when I started work as a gardener at the BBG, I expected to lose interest in my apartment garden. But no, the experience of gardening outdoors and in various greenhouses and slathouses fired and renewed enthusiasm for my very own garden which for more than twenty years has been confined entirely to an apartment.

Only a few feet from the word processor, in the walk-in closet for what was intended as the master bedroom,

Besides terra-cotta and other earthy colors, those we associate with the coastal tropics—clear seawater turquoise, white beach sand—get on well with most plants, flowers, and a variety of pots and pot covers. Wicker and other porch furniture has a similar affinity for helping turn a collection of plants into a house garden. Instant seasonal color can be added with packs or small pots from the retail marketplace or one's own home nursery. Three gerberas in four-inch plastic pots are arranged in each eight-inch clay saucer, which gives them a natural setting and expedites their care.

is my closet light garden, three shelves each measuring two by four feet and lighted by two or four 40-watt fluorescent tubes that are turned on when I get up, and off as I am turning in, sixteen- or seventeen-hour days as a rule. A timer is set for eight-hour maintenance "days" when I am out of town.

The closet garden occupies only eight square feet and stands about five feet tall, yet here I have found peace and sustenance daily—and often nightly. When my children were in the process of leaving home I often woke in the night with anxiety attacks. The problem went away when I realized that I could stop fretting, stop tossing and turning, and just get up and start gardening. The great thing about a light garden is that you can turn on the lights whenever you want to and there's usually no other human around to care whether or not you're dressed or have peat moss on your nose. Many a dawn I have been found happily potting, pruning, and staking—all in a big-city apartment with not a single square inch of gardening space outside. By the way, the closet light garden is the starting place for all kinds of seedlings and cuttings that are driven to the country as soon as they are able to graduate from my rather closely hovered-over kindergarten and fend for themselves.

HOUSEPLANT READING

Houseplant books per se, having been published for well over a hundred years, are so legion as to be found at garage sales and flea markets. Essential reading that has helped shape and motivate me as an indoor gardener begins with *Garden in Your House*, written by Ernesta Drinker Ballard and first published by Harper & Row in 1958; it was reissued as *Growing Plants Indoors* in 1971 by Barnes & Noble as a quality paperback. A slim and pithy successor from Ernesta, appropriately entitled *The Art of Training Plants* (Harper & Row, 1962; paperback from Barnes & Noble, 1974), sums up most efficiently how both Eastern methods—Chinese penjing, Japanese bonsai—and Western—espalier, topiary, tree-form standard—can be applied to containerized plants. In this same era I was also friends with Bernice Brilmayer and singularly impressed with her work on begonias, which culminated in a book, *All About Begonias* (Doubleday, 1960), and vines, *All About Vines* (Doubleday, 1962), models for their time that have also managed to stay in my personal collection.

The bible I have turned to for houseplants more than any other is *Exotica* (Scribner's, 1985), the work of Alfred Byrd Graf, a man after my own heart. He has traveled the world photographing plants and has published the pictures together with informative text in large buckram-bound books, each successive edition growing heavier by the pound. My friends and New York City neighbors the Elberts, Virginie and George, have also followed this romantic path, integrating travel with the study of plants

This is my order in chaos, a small cut-leaved philodendron trained as a twelve-inch wreath growing from a six-inch plastic pot inside a green-painted wicker basket that came with a two-inch-deep waterproof saucer in the bottom. The tranquility belies the location, nine stories above one of New York City's busiest and noisiest streets.

and foods and living for brief periods in other parts of the world, then returning home for intense seasons of growing, cooking, and writing. Their book *Foliage Plants for Decorating Indoors* (Timber Press, 1989) is a tour de force in which many of the plants pictured were grown by them in an Upper West Side Manhattan apartment.

Another indoor gardener whose books I study is Charles Marden Fitch. He is a photographer and educator who gardens indoors in windows, under lights, and in a home greenhouse at every available opportunity. Over the last decade or so he has produced volumes devoted to houseplants, gardening under lights, orchids, and miniature roses, each containing ideas, inspiration, and specific cultivation information that make them worthwhile reading.

I also want to call your attention to the writings of James McNair and the books he produced early on in the Ortho series, those about houseplants and container gardening that date from about 1975 to 1985. James was houseplanting when he first arrived in New York in the 1960s. A subsequent move to California fed all his right instincts about bringing the garden inside. One of my favorite photographs shows edible sprouts he grew in petri dishes, dating from a house James rented in Hollywood in the late seventies, and where he helped me put together enough bowl gardens to produce a book called *Decorative Gardening in Containers* (Doubleday, 1978).

Latest on my reading list for understanding the new houseplant are two books by Tovah Martin, horticulturist at Logee's. The first is entitled *Once Upon a Windowsill* (Timber Press, 1989), a history of indoor gardening, replete with evocative woodcuts, wisdom about gardening, and a unique view of social history. Second is *The Essence of Paradise* (Little, Brown, 1991), which is all about fragrant plants for indoor gardens. On a recent springtime visit to Logee's, I found Tovah in the early morning preoccupied with her goat Titania's edema—which can be a problem for geranium leaves, too—and advanced pregnancy. While I took pictures of plants, Tovah ran back and forth from the barn filling orders, supervising in the shipping room and no doubt thinking about her next writing assignment. Near the end of this particular day, Tovah and I set up our chairs on a grassy slope

Plants that go dormant part of every year are especially welcome in a house collection, Dioscorea macrostachya, *for example, with its persisting boldly carved caudex and warm-season heart-shaped leaves. Since the needs and appearance of such plants can change radically, sometimes overnight, they become signals for what needs doing next, probably some rearranging and maybe the addition of new plants to take the active growing spaces of those placed in the dark or at least dim recesses for a rest.*

behind the house and talked houseplants. Tovah hopes that her books will inspire us to make windowsills into indoor gardens and predicts we will see more design indoors, employing garden furniture, fountains and other water features, and accessories more usually associated with the outdoors. "Indoor plants can be arranged as sensitively as those in a garden. Every plant also has an ideal way to be grown, some make perfect hanging baskets, others tree-form standards. The greatest rewards come to the indoor gardener who is not afraid to experiment. Just because you don't know the name doesn't mean the plant won't be a winner for you."

Another artist in our midst whose work is notably honest and enlightening is Ken Druse, my successor as garden editor at *House Beautiful* magazine and the author of *The Natural Garden* and *The Natural Shade Garden* (Clarkson Potter, 1989 and 1991). Before Ken moved to Brooklyn he lived in a SoHo, New York City, loft, with a rooftop greenhouse accessed via a spiral stair. When we first became friends Ken had just written a small paperback about houseplants, *The Month by Month Guide to Indoor Gardening* (Popular Library, 1977). No mention of it is made in his current glossy and beautifully photographed books but if you find a copy, waste no time making it your own.

HOW TO USE THIS BOOK

Some gardening books are meant to be read from cover to cover while others are designed as references. I hope you will use *The New Houseplant* both ways. The first three chapters are about setting and maintaining the stage, the fourth contains the cast of major and minor

The mystique of the garden is as elusive as our individual experience, yet certain elements alone or together are of themselves more evocative of being in a peaceful garden than one might think. The purity of freshly cut white Dutch hyacinths in an old galvanized watering can on an antique wire garden seat—the scene could be anywhere, indoors or out, and most of us find it romantically irresistible. Certain flowers are so associated with fragrance that we smell them almost by suggestion—hyacinth, jasmine, rose, honeysuckle, freesia—yet the real thing plays a definite role in the therapy of gardening.

Prunings from the outdoors, such as these crotons that grow prodigiously around the Golden Lemon, a resort in the eastern Caribbean on the island of St. Kitts, when put in a deep vase of water can last indoors in a decorative way for days, weeks, or almost indefinitely. Being able to combine plants and flowers with favorite treasures—artworks, glassware, fabrics—is a privilege of the house gardener.

characters, and the remaining introduce specialty plants and training procedures, solutions to problems, and where to find additional information, plants, supplies, and fellow houseplant growers. If you need to find a plant in a hurry, look in the index. The very seasonal flowering houseplants, which tend to be short-lived, are included in Chapter 2, while the vast majority will be found in Chapter 4, each with other members of its botanical family.

When I proposed the title for this book, *The New Houseplant*, it was the first time I had ever consciously put the two words together as one. My earlier book was *The World Book of House Plants*. This volume, however, makes a discovery: Houseplant, one word, carries more weight than house plant, two words. NASA has validated

the concept and the house garden awaits. There is more to the idea of being a house gardener or to house gardening than we seem ever to have gotten from earlier notions of indoor gardening.

Houseplanting is about having living, regenerative horticulture all through your home, through your life. Touches of nature, blossoms, leaves, berries, fruit, fresh and dried flowers. Leafy and succulent plants, seasonal bulbs, flowering branches snatched from winter's grip, smells of the earth. Of course when all of this is carried inside from the outdoors or from sundry growers, yes, there will be spiders, flies, moths, caterpillars, slugs, wasps, and all manner of creatures that hang out with plants. Mostly there awaits the excitement of having plant life all around, in the most intimate spaces and rooms in which we live and work, treasuring the dynamism of an ongoing, hands-on involvement with these extraordinary living creatures.

Last year, while researching the chapter on roses for the book *Gardens of the World* (Macmillan Publishing Company, 1991), these words written by Theophrastus, who died approximately 287 B.C., jumped off the page when I found them quoted in an old book; they express my sentiments precisely: ". . . consider how the torch of life is passed from plant to plant through the medium of small cuttings." Where roses are concerned, it is possible for us to grow a rosebush descended directly from those the Empress Josephine grew at Malmaison around the year 1800. Where houseplants in my apartment garden are concerned, the cuttings or offsets or seeds or young plants from which they have grown have come to me from dozens of different suppliers and individuals, many of whom are no longer gardening in this realm. I am myself a grandfather, so thoughts of passing torches from one generation to another fit comfortably with me as well as my garden.

—*Elvin McDonald*
New York City, December 1991

Postscript and Acknowledgments

In the slightly more than six months since I wrote the introduction I have transplanted myself to Houston, Texas, in what was apparently a favorable sign of the moon. Friday, January 17, 1992, at 5:30 P.M., having earlier in the day delivered the manuscript and photos for this book to Macmillan, I drove away from the apartment building on East 57th Street in New York that was for twenty years to the day my gardening laboratory, in a car packed with books, pictures, the Macintosh, forty-three plants too special to be left behind, and some personal effects.

Five hours later, at a motel in Glen Burnie, Maryland, I understood more vividly than ever before why plants and gardening are so important to me. Temperatures outside were below freezing, so I hastily moved the plants into my room. Having collapsed on the bed while using the telephone I soon realized that in front of me and all around, on tables, the floor, the sink counter, were my most cherished plants.

The upheaval represented in producing a cross-country move while simultaneously writing a five-hundred-page manuscript had taken its toll, and without thinking, I found myelf on my feet practicing plants as therapy, taking each plant in turn and attending to its needs, watering, showering, grooming, staking; yes, I do travel with pruners, a couple of stakes, some twist ties, and a motel room can make a surprisingly efficient garden work center.

I can't begin to acknowledge or thank all the individuals who have helped me write and photograph this book, although many are mentioned in the text. I can express my deepest appreciation to Macmillan editor Pam Hoenig for editing the manuscript in a caring, involved way that is no longer supposed to exist in commercial publishing. Thanks also to her assistant, Justin Schwartz, who displays similar respect for the work at hand.

On a continuing basis I have always to thank my agent, Carla Glasser; David Glasser, lawyer; Anne Stewart Fitzroy, accountant; Hila Paldi, a method trainer, also an avid gardener and seed starter; Arthur Wooten, shiatsu massage practitioner; Richard Lewin at Jay Dee Camera in New York; longtime companion Bill Mulligan and our mutual friend, Linda Yang, neighbor, gardener, and journalist; Betsy Kissam, for *Plants & Gardens News* for the Brooklyn Botanic Garden, with whom I shared numerous office plants for six years; and finally, my sister, Beth McDonald, friend, correspondent, and, as she says, the only other person who can claim the same parents, Lillian Elizabeth King and J. D. McDonald.

Seasonal flowering plants such as this tree-form standard azalea bring change and color to the house garden. This one includes a braided Ficus benjamina *underplanted with* Peperomia obtusifolia *and a low shelf with* Chlorophytum comosum 'Variegatum' *(variegated spider plant).*

chapter one

The Basics: What Houseplants Need to Grow

A vast number of houseplants survive indoors in the same lighting conditions, temperatures, and general air quality that suit human needs and preferences. Houseplants also require watering, fertilizing, grooming, occasional repotting, and treatment against an opportunistic insect or slug. In return for this, houseplants improve the quality of life in a given space and also contribute their share of waste which, fortunately, is completely organic and can be converted to an ingredient for a future potting mix.

LIGHT FROM SUN AND ELECTRICITY

All plants need light, though it doesn't make much difference whether this is generated by the sun or from electricity—or both. In any given situation, the amount of light available is the first consideration in growing healthy plants. Even the kinds which are seemingly indifferent to the intensity and duration of light respond to ideal lighting. For example, the Chinese evergreen (*Aglaonema modestum*) will exist on pebbles and water in a dim corner or in front of a sunny window. However,

when it is grown in humusy, moist soil and filtered light, the result is a healthier, more vibrant plant.

Since I wrote a book on the subject, *The Complete Book of Gardening Under Lights* (Doubleday, 1965; Popular Library, 1974), and have continued to popularize fluorescent-light gardening, it may come as a surprise that I am ambivalent about installing other kinds of lighting such as metal halide or mercury vapor as the sole source of light for extensive indoor plantings. In terms of energy consumption and conservation I can justify efficient fluorescent lights for gardening; beyond that, I know there are exceptions, but mostly it might be better to remodel or move in order to gain sufficient sunlight for the desired houseplants.

Flowering houseplants need more light than those grown exclusively for foliage. Situate indoor gardens of flowering plants where they will receive direct sunlight part of each day in the fall and winter months. Except in the South, windows facing east, southeast, and south are preferred locations. Growers in such Sun Belt states as Florida, Louisiana, Texas, New Mexico, and Arizona may find southern and eastern exposures too bright for flowering plants, except cacti and other succulents. In these areas, daylong light from northern windows or partially shaded south-facing locations will give satisfactory results with many flowering houseplants.

Vast numbers of plants will grow indoors in the same conditions humans enjoy. Learn the basic care needed by each plant you wish to grow and then position it accordingly in your house. Large leafy plants or trees, like the 'Massangeana' dracaenas in the foreground of this picture, are often more adaptable to interior spaces with bright light, while flowering types and those allied with cacti and other succulents, such as the screw pine standing on a pedestal behind the piano, need varying amounts of direct sun. A beautiful-leaved calathea lives fulltime in a clay rabbit on top of the piano in bright, indirect light while hardy chrysanthemums set in woven baskets on the floor will be rotated back to full sun when flowering finishes.

During the darkest days of winter, there is little chance of having indoor plants harmed by too much sun. A possible exception occurs where winter snow comes early and stays late. A friend in Minnesota says that rays of sun on snow bounce back through her house windows, admitting up to a third more light than if the ground were bare. With constant snow cover it is possible to flower begonias and African violets in a window facing north. By the same token, if you have north windows that face a white-painted building, the reflected light can be put to work serving the needs of indoor plants.

Observing the quality and duration of direct sun or merely bright light that reaches an interior space is the first step toward situating plants intelligently. A casual acquaintance asked my advice about his ailing plants. When I asked him which way his windows faced, he answered without hesitation, "The street." I laughed but couldn't be helpful without more specific information.

Here is a quick way to understand indoor window light and how it is generally described by indoor gardeners: Take a pencil and sheet of paper. Draw four circles, each about an inch across.

Shady. Color in one circle entirely and label it "shady." This applies to north-facing windows in general and to any that may be constantly shaded by tall buildings or evergreen trees.

Semishady.   Next color in two thirds of a circle and label it "semishady." This applies to east windows and, depending on the circumstances, to some facing south and west as well.

Semisunny.   Color in one third of a circle and label it "semisunny." This applies to west-facing windows.

Sunny.   Leave the fourth circle open and label it "sunny." This applies to unobstructed windows facing south. All my apartment windows faced south, but a tall building across the street blocked enough sun for me to consider my indoor garden "semisunny."

It is also useful to watch how light changes in a given space from morning to evening. The wall and floor immediately to the side of a window can be much darker than areas within the room where some rays of sun may shine directly for part of each day. Even with a light meter it is not always possible to foretell how a given plant will respond. There are infinite variables, including latitude, local weather and average number of sunny days, time of year, and how recently the window panes have been cleaned.

One thing certain about indoor gardening is that most plants need more rather than less light. Some that adapt and grow well without direct sun are spathiphyllum or peace lily, aglaonema or Chinese evergreen, aspidistra or cast-iron plant, sansevieria, pothos or epipremnum, scindapsus, nephthytis or syngonium, trailing philodendron, and dracaenas having plain green leaves.

How can you tell if a plant needs more light? This question has no short, easy answer. Plants are indeed like people—complex living organisms. If a plant is otherwise healthy and well cared for, it can tolerate poor light better than a plant that is suffering from too much cold or heat, lack of humidity, soil that is too dry or too wet, too much or not enough fertilizer, or an attack of bugs. In recalling the symptons of light-starved plants I have known, I am reminded that in nearly all instances other stresses were also present. As you read my descriptions of plants suffering from poor light, keep in mind that lack of light may be only part of the problem.

Leaf drop.   This is one of the most common symptoms having to do with insufficient light, yet it is also perfectly natural for older leaves eventually to die—that

The direction a window faces does not necessarily reveal the kind of light it receives. An apartment building across the street from mine turned my south-facing windows into a half-sunny exposure. Here the season is fall and I have set in motion a variety of plant-training projects, including topiary and espalier, featuring Deacon geraniums, rosemary, passiflora, and hedera ivies. Spathiphyllum, flowering in the foreground, does best without direct sun except for brief periods.

is how we get trees. But when a houseplant loses a substantial number of leaves—half or more within days or a week or two—lack of light may be the cause.

Pale new leaves.   This description fits some normal growth. Podocarpus and many philodendrons have new leaves that are naturally paler than the older ones. However, when pale new growth fails to grow out into the normal color and size, more light may be needed.

Pale old leaves.   This is often a symptom of poor light, but usually other problems are present as well, such as lack of water. Not all plants wilt visibly when too dry; some just turn pale or develop a lackluster appearance. Foliage plants starved for nutrients may also appear pale. Air pollution or an infestation of spider mites can also contribute to overall paleness. Too much light can also fade or bleach out older leaves.

Polka-dot angel-wing Begonia maculata *var.* wightii *blooms summer and fall in a room that opens onto a terrace and rose garden at C. Z. Guest's Long Island home. Important to the begonia's radiant health at that northern latitude are several hours of direct sun, fresh air movement, temperatures of 60° to 80°F, a growing medium watered generously that is permitted only to dry slightly at the surface, and regular applications of fertilizer. In spring pruning out the tallest branches that have previously bloomed, then repotting or top-dressing, encourages strong basal shoots for this year's flowering.*

Brown leaf tips and margins. When the extremities of leaves turn prematurely yellow or brown, lack of light may be one cause, but almost always in combination with other stresses: overheating, too much or too little water, lack of humidity, and possibly air pollution.

No flowers. When flowering plants appear healthy but form no buds, lack of light may be the cause. If growth is compact and well colored—"normal"—then too much nitrogen from fertilizer may be the cause. Some plants, the florist gloxinia in particular, will grow reasonably well and even form buds in weak light, but they will fail to open. Or, if the buds do open into flowers, the colors will be insipid. Greenhouse-forced flowering plants from florists often display this last symptom when they are placed as decorations in the relatively dark interior of a room.

Weak new growth. When you bring a full-grown plant into your home, or move an old one to another part of the house, and subsequent growth fails to attain normal size, lack of light is likely the cause. If the plant is new, make sure it is being grown at the proper temperatures and is receiving the right amount of moisture, humidity, and fertilizer. Look for signs of insects on new growth.

Weak stems. When plants with normally sturdy, self-supporting stems grow weak and spindly, lack of light is almost surely the cause, but overheating and overdosing with high-nitrogen fertilizer can also be the culprit, especially with a cool-weather plant being brought to bloom indoors such as the paperwhite narcissus.

All growth faces one way. Houseplants grow toward the light. The healthiest plant in the world, receiving optimum light, will still face mostly in the direction of the light source unless you give its pot a quarter turn in the same direction each time you apply water.

All growth stretches one way. If light is really poor, no amount of turning will keep the stems from reaching weakly toward the source of illumination.

Little or no growth. Insufficient light puts some plants in a state of semidormancy. Within reason this may have no harmful effects, providing the plant is moved to better light before it goes into terminal decline. Mature plants of calathea, maranta, dieffenbachia, schefflera, palm, dracaena, spathiphyllum, philodendron, pothos, clivia, Norfolk Island pine, and screw pine can be shifted to areas of dim light for decorative effect with no immediate decline in general health. However, at the first sign of any symptom I have described, move them back to stronger light.

For decorative effect, almost any plant can be moved anywhere in a room. The higher the plant's light requirements, the shorter the time it can endure a lack of

Water less than you would if the plant were receiving an ideal amount of light. This doesn't mean you should let the soil be bone dry between waterings, but do be careful not to water too much and too often or the soil will become soggy. Apply less fertilizer, perhaps a third the amount you would give a plant in ideal light. Keep the leaves clean by showering or wiping with a soft cotton cloth.

HOUSEPLANTS FOR A SEMISUNNY LOCATION

Semisunny indicates a situation that receives two to five hours of direct sunlight in the winter. Most windows, except those facing directly south or north, fit into this classification. In the spring and summer these plants do well in bright diffused light with little or no direct sun. They can be grown in a sunny location if protected by a curtain, or a screen of sun-loving plants.

A *cultivar of the bromeliad* Neoregelia carolinae *in the window of a Chicago, Illinois, grower illustrates how the light at any given moment in one small space can be at opposites. There are full, direct sun rays crossing the plant itself, yet look to either side, toward the walls flanking the window, and you will see low light, or shade in house gardening terms.*

light. It is all right to put a short, compact, flowering geranium in the middle of the dining table as a centerpiece for one meal, but then it needs to go back into the sun. By contrast, a bromeliad brought to flower in a sunny bright window can be enjoyed for several weeks in a low-light area without harm. In fact, flowers sometimes last longer when no direct sun shines on them. The amaryllis is a good example, but the minute the flowers fade, move it back to sun.

Obviously, the ideal thing for a light-starved plant is more light. However, if that is not possible, cater to its other needs. Provide ideal temperatures and humidity.

Acampe	*Bowiea*
Acanthus	*Brassavola*
Achimenes	*Browallia*
Aechmea	*Brunfelsia*
Aeonium	*Caladium*
Aerides	*Calathea*
Aeschynanthus	*Calceolaria*
Allophyton	*Callisia*
Alocasia	*Camellia*
Alpinia	*Carex*
Angraecum	*Caryota*
Aphelandra	*Cattleya*
Araucaria	*Ceropegia*
Ardisia	*Chamaedorea*
Asarina	*Chirita*
Ascocentrum	*Chlorophytum*
Asparagus	*Chrysalidocarpus*
Begonia	*Cibotium*
Beloperone	*Cissus*
Bletia	*Clerodendrum*
Boronia	*Clivia*

Clusia	*Fatshedera*	*Manettia*	*Pseuderanthemum*
Coccoloba	*Fatsia*	*Manihot*	*Pseudopanax*
Codonanthe	*Ficus*	*Maranta*	*Reinhardtia*
Coffea	*Fittonia*	*Mikania*	*Rhapis*
Coleus	*Fragaria*	*Mimosa*	*Rhipsalis*
Colocasia	*Fuchsia*	*Monstera*	*Rhoeo*
Columnea	*Gardenia*	*Muehlenbeckia*	*Rhoicissus*
Commelina	*Gasteria*	*Musa*	*Rivina*
Convallaria	*Geogenanthus*	*Nautilocalyx*	*Ruellia*
Cordyline	*Gesneria*	*Neofinetia*	*Saintpaulia*
Costus	*Gloxinera*	*Neomarica*	*Sansevieria*
Crassula	*Gloxinia*	*Neoregelia*	*Sarcococca*
Crossandra	*Guzmania*	*Nepeta*	*Sasa*
Cryptanthus	*Gynura*	*Nephrolepsis*	*Saxifraga*
Ctenanthe	*Habenaria*	*Nertera*	*Schefflera*
Curcuma	*Hatiora*	*Nidularium*	*Schismatoglottis*
Cycas	*Haworthia*	*Oncidium*	*Schizocentron*
Cyclamen	*Hedera*	*Ophiopogon*	*Schlumbergera*
Cycnoches	*Hedychium*	*Oplismenus*	*Scilla*
Cymbalaria	*Heliconia*	*Pandanus*	*Scindapsus*
Cymbidium	*Hippeastrum*	*Paphiopedilum*	*Scirpus*
Cyperus	*Hoffmannia*	*Parthenocissus*	*Selenicereus*
Dendrobium	*Homalomena*	*Pedilanthus*	*Senecio*
Dichorisandra	*Howea*	*Pellionia*	*Serissa*
Dieffenbachia	*Hoya*	*Peperomia*	*Serjania*
Dioon	*Huernia*	*Pereskia*	*Siderasis*
Dipladenia	*Hypocyrta*	*Petrea*	*Sinningia*
Dizygotheca	*Hypoestes*	*Petrocosmea*	*Smilax*
Dracaena	*Impatiens*	*Phaius*	*Smithiantha*
Dudleya	*Ipomoea*	*Philodendron*	*Sonerila*
Dyckia	*Jacobinia*	*Phoenix*	*Sophronitis*
Elaeagnus	*Justicia*	*Pilea*	*Sparmannia*
Ensete	*Kaempferia*	*Piper*	*Spathicarpa*
Epidendrum	*Koellikeria*	*Pistia*	*Spathiphyllum*
Epiphyllum	*Kohleria*	*Pitcairnia*	*Stenandrium*
Episcia	*Lapageria*	*Pittosporum*	*Streptocarpus*
Eranthemum	*Leea*	*Platycerium*	*Strobilanthes*
Eucharis	*Licuala*	*Plectranthus*	*Syngonium*
Euonymus	*Lycaste*	*Pleomele*	*Tillandsia*
Euphorbia	*Lygodium*	*Podocarpus*	*Tolmiea*
Eurya	*Malpighia*	*Polypodium*	*Tradescantia*
Exacum	*Mandevilla*	*Primula*	*Vriesia*

Woodwardia
Zamia
Zantedeschia

Zebrina
Zygocactus

HOUSEPLANTS FOR A SUNNY LOCATION

Sunny indicates a situation which receives at least five hours of direct sunlight in the winter. Most windows facing south fit into this classification, possibly those facing southeast or southwest as well.

Abutilon
Acacia
Acalypha
Acampe
Adromischus
Agapanthus
Agave
Allamanda
Aloe
Alternanthera
Amarcrinum
Amaryllis
Anacampseros
Ananas
Aporocactus
Aptenia
Astrophytum
Azalea
Bambusa
Bauhinia
Beaucarnea
Begonia
Beloperone
Billbergia
Bougainvillea
Bouvardia
Brassavola
Brunsvigia
Caladium

Calliandra
Callistemon
Calluna
Campanula
Capsicum
Carissa
Cephalocereus
Cereus
Cestrum
Chaenostoma
Chamaecereus
Chamaerops
Chorizema
Chrysanthemum
Citrus
Cobaea
Coccoloba
Codiaeum
Coleus
Conophytum
Cotyledon
Crassula
Crinum
Cuphea
Cyanotis
Cypella
Cyrtanthus
Cytisus
Dinteranthus

Dionaea
Echeveria
Echinocactus
Echinocereus
Echinopsis
Ensete
Erica
Ervatamia
Eucalyptus
Eucomis
Eugenia
Euphorbia
Fatshedera
Faucaria
Feijoa
Felicia
Fenestraria
Fortunella
Fragaria
Freesia
Gardenia
Gazania
Gerbera
Gloriosa
Glottiphyllum
Graptopetalum
Grevillea
Gymnocalycium
Gynura
Habranthus
Haemanthus
Hebe
Hedera
Heliconia
Hibiscus
Hippeastrum
Hoodia
Hoya
Hydrangea
Hydrosme
Hylocereus
Impatiens

Ipomoea
Iresine
Ixora
Jasminum
Jatropha
Kalanchoe
Kleinia
Lachenalia
Lampranthus
Lantana
Lapeirousia
Ledebouria
Leptospermum
Ligustrum
Lilium
Lithops
Lobivia
Lotus
Lycoris
Mahernia
Malpighia
Mammillaria
Mesembryanthemum
Mimulus
Moraea
Musa
Myrsine
Myrtus
Nerine
Nerium
Nicodemia
Nicotiana
Notocactus
Oliveranthus
Oplismenus
Opuntia
Oreopanax
Ornithogalum
Osmanthus
Oxalis
Pachyphytum
Pachyveria

Parthenocissus	Sedum	Asplenium	Monstera
Passiflora	Sempervivum	Athyrium	Nephrolepis
Pelargonium	Senecio	Aucuba	Pandanus
Pentas	Setcreasea	Begonia fl	Paphiopedilum fl
Petunia	Solanum	Bertolonia	Pellaea
Phormium	Sprekelia	Blechnum	Pellionia
Pittosporum	Stapelia	Caladium	Peperomia
Pleispilos	Stenotaphrum	Calathea	Phalaenopsis fl
Plumbago	Stephanotis	Ceropegia fl	Philodendron
Poinciana	Strelitizia	Chamaedorea	Phoenix
Polyscias	Streptosolen	Chamaeranthemum fl	Phyllitis
Portulacaria	Synadenium	Chlorophytum	Pilea
Pseudosasa	Tavaresia	Cissus	Pittosporum
Punica	Tetrapanax	Cordyline	Podocarpus
Pyracantha	Thevetia	Cyperus	Polypodium
Rebutia	Thunbergia	Cyrtomium	Polystichum
Rivina	Titanopsis	Darlingtonia fl	Pteris
Rochea	Trevesia	Davallia	Saintpaulia fl
Rosa	Trifolium	Dieffenbachia	Sansevieria
Ruta	Tropaeolum	Dracaena	Schefflera
Sansevieria	Tulbaghia	Episcia fl	Scindapsus
Santolina	Vallota	Hedera	Selaginella
Sasa	Veltheimia	Hemigraphis	Soleirolia
Saxifraga	Vitis	Howea	Spathiphyllum fl
Schefflera	Zantedeschia	Lapageria fl	Syngonium
Scilla	Zephyranthes	Lygodium	Woodwardia
Scutellaria		Maranta	Zamia
		Miltonia fl	

HOUSEPLANTS FOR A SEMISHADY LOCATION

Semishady indicates an area that receives bright light most of the day in winter, but little or no direct sun. In this situation, very few plants cultivated for flowers grow well, but those which do are followed by the abbreviation *fl*.

Achimenes fl	Aglaonema
Acorus	Amomum
Adiantum	Anthurium fl
Aechmea fl	Aspidistra

HOUSEPLANTS FOR A SHADY LOCATION

Shady indicates an area that may be dimly lighted even in the middle of a sunny day. The plants in this category tolerate low-light intensity but seldom thrive on it. To decorate with potted plants in such a situation, a rotation plan can be used: While one group of plants occupies the shady area, rejuvenate another in a semisunny place. Or, add supplementary electric light.

Aglaonema	Asparagus
Amomum	Aspidistra

Calathea	Pittosporum
Chamaedorea	Podocarpus
Chlorophytum	Polypodium
Cyperus	Polystichum
Dieffenbachia	Pteris
Hedera	Sansevieria
Maranta	Schefflera
Monstera	Scindapsus
Nephrolepis	Spathiphyllum
Ophiopogon	Syngonium
Philodendron	

A maxi light garden—which can be located anywhere from the basement, as here, to the attic and all between—has become standard equipment for serious gardeners. This one consists of two industrial or shop reflectors each fitted with two 40-watt bulbs in a fifty-fifty ratio of generic cool white and warm white. When burned fourteen to eighteen hours out of every twenty-four, and suspended directly overhead about eighteen inches, there is ideal light for gardening over a table or bench measuring four by four feet. How this precious space is used depends on the individual; some possibilities are propagation, bromeliads, gesneriads, begonias, orchids, scented geraniums, and 'Maid of Orleans' jasmine. Timers and automated watering can make such units more self-reliant.

BASIC FLUORESCENT-LIGHT GARDENS

The basic setup for a fluorescent-light garden two feet long and twelve to twenty-four inches wide requires two to four 20-watt tubes in one or more commercial or shop light reflectors suspended fifteen to eighteen inches above the table or shelf on which the plant containers will be placed. The next size larger would be to use 30-watt fluorescent bulbs, which are thirty-six inches long; I have used these in a bookshelf unit but this size may be inconvenient for replacements—go to the next size if you can, 40-watt bulbs, forty-eight inches long.

The classic fluorescent-light garden has always consisted of two 40-watt tubes in a reflector over a table or bench measuring two feet wide by four feet long. If four 40-watt tubes are used over this growing area, I call it a **maxi light garden**. In many ways this is equivalent to a **sunny** or **semisunny** sunlit garden, except the plants that can be accommodated within the configuration of the light garden have to be miniature by nature or sufficiently young and small—or short—to fit. The lights can be operated sixteen hours out of every twenty-four for general growth requirements. An automatic timer is a convenience and plants do better on a regimen of uniformly timed periods of light. In all cases, combining warm white and cool white fluorescent bulbs in a fifty-fifty ratio results in a balance of light rays suited to all types of plant growth; because the bulbs are generic, they cost less than those labeled "for agricultural purposes" and sold specifically for growing plants.

One other kind of electric light garden suits my admittedly conservative view of gardens that are both electrified and politically correct: Plants or flowers placed within the circle of brightest light cast on the table, desk, or floor by a lamp that is used for reading or general room illumination. A surprising amount of houseplanting can be done in this space. The spotlighting not only makes the flowers and leaves placed there look especially beautiful, it also helps provide the daily quota of light required to maintain plant life.

T E M P E R A T U R E S S U I T E D T O H O U S E P L A N T S

A temperature range of 60° to 75°F satisfies the majority of houseplants. The few kinds that need coolness, especially during the indoor heating season, are listed in the accompanying table. They can be grown on a frost-free sunporch, or in a seldom-used sunny bedroom. For special occasions, enjoy them anywhere in the house, but spare them the torture of long sessions in hot, dry air. Be aware that temperatures can vary considerably within one relatively small growing area. The only way to know precisely what goes on is to use a maximum-minimum thermometer (available from greenhouse growers supply houses), which will enable you to determine the highs and lows. Plants sitting on the floor may be considerably cooler than those hung from the ceiling or placed high on a bookshelf.

A *maximum-minimum thermometer like this one in the begonia house at Planting Fields Arboretum, a garden open to the public in Oyster Bay, New York, is a necessity in determining the extremes of cold and hot in a given growing space.*

H O U S E P L A N T S T H A T N E E D C O O L N E S S

These plants need 60° to 65°F during the daytime, with a drop into the 50s at night, throughout the heating season.

Acacia	Cypella
Acorus	Cytisus
Athyrium	Daphne
Aucuba	Darlingtonia
Azalea	Dionaea
Boronia	Erica
Calceolaria	Euonymus
Calluna	Fatsia
Camellia	Fragaria
Campanula	Freesia
Chrysanthemum	Fuchsia
Convallaria	Gerbera
Cyclamen	Gymnocalycium
Cymbalaria	Habenaria
Cymbidium	Hebe

Hedera	Odontoglossum
Lachenalia	Ornithogalum
Lantana	Osmanthus
Lapageria	Phyllitis
Ligularia	Physosiphon
Ligustrum	Primula
Lilium	Rebutia
Liriope	Senecio
Lycaste	Sophronitis
Miltonia	Trifolium
Moraea	Tulbaghia
Nerine	Veltheimia
Nertera	Viburnum
Notocactus	Zephryanthes

H O U S E P L A N T S F O R G I V I N G O F D R Y W I N T E R H E A T

In general, kinds originating in warm, dry, or desert regions are best suited to spending winter indoors where the air is mostly hot and dry. In some commercial buildings the rule by workday is hot and dry, by night and

The world continues to be filled with unknown plant treasures. This one is a myrmecophyte, so called for its synergism with the ants that live within the swollen bulb or caudex, hence its common name, ant plant, Hydnophytum formicarum. I was taken by this little-known relative of the gardenia while visiting Grigsby Cactus Gardens, Vista, California.

weekends cold and dry. No surprise, the plants in this list are familiar, for most have stood the test of time.

Aglaonema
Aloe
Begonias: hairy-leaved and wax, Begonia semperflorens
Cacti from dry regions, indicated by prominent spines
Cissus adenopoda
Crassula, including C. argentea, the jade plant
Dracaena
Epipremnum

Ficus elastica
Haworthia
Hydrophytum formicarum
Kalanchoe
Oxalis such as O. crassipes and O. regnellii
Peperomia
Philodendron, especially small-leaved trailers
Sansevieria
Spathiphyllum
Yucca

What are some effects temperature extremes have on plants? A plant that is either too cold or too hot may wilt visibly even though it has plenty of moisture at the roots. Growth can be killed at either extreme, especially below the freezing point or above 90°F. Gradually decreasing or increasing temperatures, over a period of days versus hours or minutes, are better tolerated than sudden changes. Some tropicals, the episcia is one, may better survive chilling if they are on the dry side when it occurs; conversely, extreme heat may be better tolerated by the majority of plants if their roots are adequately supplied with water at the time. Plants that came originally from parts of the world having either exceptionally high or low temperatures for a season may not flower as houseplants if the environment is always about the same.

HUMIDITY: A RELATIVE MATTER

The amount of moisture contained in the air is expressed in terms of relative humidity. Anything below twenty percent is considered "low," up to forty or fifty percent as "medium," and above fifty as "high" humidity, at least insofar as indoor plants are concerned. Although we lump the words "cold and damp" together as if in tandem they were inevitably unpleasant, the fact remains that when the air is suitably moistened, we—the human element—feel comfortable at lower temperatures than when the air is dry. For plants and people this constitutes

A hygrometer measures the moisture in the air, expressed as a degree of relative humidity. Misting the leaves of plants has a potentially beneficial effect, by removing dust and refreshing them, but this does not raise humidity more than momentarily. A frequent solution to low humidity is to group plants that are culturally compatible in a room where a humidifier and circulating fan can be used. This especially suits the needs of many begonias, gesneriads, orchids, aroids, bromeliads, ferns, and palms.

something of a catch-22: the drier the air, the higher we turn the thermostat, the more the heating system works, the more moisture is pulled from the atmosphere, the more uncomfortable we are. Temperatures around 68° to 72°F, combined with moderate humidity, suit most active humans and a vast number of houseplants. Cacti and other succulents native to arid places do well in low humidity, while plants from rain forests need high humidity. The amount of humidity can be measured by

the use of a hygrometer, which is often included with a household thermometer or barometer.

Humidity can be increased by adding more plants and by growing everything in unglazed clay or terra-cotta. Moisture evaporates—transpires—through the walls of these containers, thus serving constantly to moisturize the air in the immediate surround of the indoor garden. An earthy smell is also given off. Misting the leaves of houseplants is a 1970s' invention that benefits most leaves except the hirsute and serves as beneficial therapy for the indoor gardener, but does little to maintain higher humidity. I use a "rain bottle," a quart-size plastic bottle with a rose cap, intended for dampening down the ironing, to sprinkle all around my indoor garden. This helps keep leaves dust-free and rain-fresh and, unlike the breakdown-prone pistol-grip mister, the unit itself is foolproof. One of the first things I do each morning is to walk around my indoor garden watering, sprinkling, and removing any dead leaves or spent flowers.

Misting, sprinkling, and showering are all ways to refresh indoor plants, to keep leaf surfaces dust- and grime-free, rain-fresh, and naturally glossy. There are, however, numerous precautions. Don't make the mistake of placing houseplants directly outdoors in a rain. They need gradual conditioning to the open. Leafy types such as dracaena, palm, and large philodendrons are vulnerable to hard rains and strong winds. Also, unless the plants are in a waterproof surrounding indoors, one must be extremely careful so as not to inadvertently dampen wood, fabric, paper, or other surfaces. Despite the potential hassles, there is no denying that plants grown permanently indoors benefit from showering with tepid water at least twice yearly. It is important not to use too strong a stream or shower and to support each plant part from below as you are cleansing it from above. I do this for small ones at the kitchen sink. Larger specimens require moving to the bathroom tub and shower. This is always enjoyable for me despite the inevitable: At the end, the plants are all clean; the bathroom and I are disasters.

Humidity can be further increased by standing all pots on pebble trays kept supplied with water to a level that just misses the bottoms of the pots themselves. The word "pebble" is meant quite specifically—its size provides the optimal balance between water-covered surface and air spaces, resulting in the maximum amount of evaporation. Smaller or larger particles in a humidity tray will not perform as efficiently as pebbles of one-eighth- to one-fourth-inch caliper. In some growing situations it is workable to place one or more humidity trays on top of a forced-air or hot-water radiator that is itself turned off but remains warm as part of a larger system, such as that of a centrally heated apartment building. The more bottom heat there is, the more water is evaporated. During the coldest weather, some indoor gardeners like to keep a large vessel of water simmering on the kitchen stove. Certain herbs, potpourri, or essential oils may be added so that the steam given off moisturizes the air and also provides aromatherapy.

A convenient and expedient way of increasing humidity is to use a humidifier. Some residential heating systems already include one. However, more often than not the only humidifier in a home is a portable one used

There are plants that need such constant and high humidity, there is no way to grow them except in terrarium or Wardian case conditions. Plastic bubble bowls like this one holding a Begonia prismatocarpa *progeny for Vista, California, grower Mabel Corwin have become popular. Also useful are tiny greenhouses salvaged from food-to-go. Plants thus enclosed need bright light but not direct sun; a likely place for them is under two or more fluorescent bulbs.*

Some plants go into rapid decline when they are cut off from fresh air. Obconica primroses, available as a seasonal flowering plant in winter and spring, can't stand freezing or dry heat. In stale air they attract spider mites. Without sunlight they stop flowering. In fresh air and moderate temperatures this plant can go on blooming for several months.

as therapy for a head cold or other upper respiratory illnesses. There are cool vapor and steam vapor humidifiers, also regular electric and ultrasonic. Unless there is a need to provide heat along with the moisture—perhaps in a cold room—the cool vapor type is preferred for plants. It is of the utmost importance that the unit be cleaned thoroughly at the very least every seven days in order to prevent the build-up of potentially harmful bacteria that, if breathed, could cause human illness.

Air movement goes hand in hand with air moisture in the creation of an atmosphere that is nurturing to both plants and people. Humidifiers themselves have fanning devices that help move the air in their immediate vicinity. Small oscillating fans can be a big help in keeping plants healthy, since free circulation of fresh air helps suppress a variety of insects and diseases and the gentle shaking stems and leaves get as a result of air movement makes them stronger. Air movement also affects how much sunlight or heat a plant can tolerate without burning. At the other extreme, plants can sometimes be saved from freezing if the air around them can be kept moving until the temperature rises the few degrees that make the big difference between freezing and not freezing.

Humidifiers are used mostly during the heating season. Since air conditioners are designed to remove moisture from the air, it is pointless to operate a humidifier in the face of such competition. My indoor garden plants do best in spring and fall when the windows are kept open and no artificial heating or cooling is required.

The signs of too little humidity include overall lack-luster appearance, undersize leaves and blossoms (if any), browned leaf edges, and flowers that die prematurely. *Too much humidity* can lead to leaf diseases, blossom blights, and bothersome rots. Often the solution is as simple as spacing out the plants so that air can circulate more freely, to more promptly remove any dying or dead plant parts, and to use an electric fan.

HOW MUCH AND WHEN TO WATER

How much and how often to water is probably the biggest puzzle about gardening indoors. Beginners often ask for a precise schedule and amount, such as one cup of water every other day, but there are too many variables to make this possible, at least in most situations. "Enough, as needed," is the only answer that can be given with certainty. These steps help determine individual plant needs:

1) Feel the surface soil with your fingers. If the pot is large, say ten inches or more, take a pinch here and there. Presumably you will feel something between bone dry and soggy wet, which could include merely dry, on the dry side, damp, moist, or on the wet side.

2) An alternative method for determining existing soil conditions is to use a moisture meter. Relatively inexpensive models designed for home use are sold at garden centers and nurseries. While hardly any tool can be as sensitive or accurate as well-informed fingers, a potential advantage of the moisture meter is that its probe can indicate the amount of moisture several inches deep in a large container.

3) Except when resting or semidormant, virtually all houseplants do best in a range between slightly on the dry side to slightly on the wet side. Few plants thrive if left standing in water for more than a few hours. In other words, avoid extremes.

4) Outfit each pot with a waterproof saucer that is at least an inch deep. This is to facilitate thorough watering. If a plant has no saucer, there will inevitably be a tendency on the part of the gardener to water parsimoniously, in order to avoid runoff of the excess.

5) It is possible to develop a watering schedule based on the needs of each plant. This changes, however, depending on cloudy or sunny weather and on average temperatures. When heating units are working overtime during winter storms and plummeting temperatures outdoors, more water may be needed despite what may be protracted periods of overcast skies.

6) Plant watering needs are also based on the needs of the individual gardener. Some who practice plants as therapy may wish to organize everything so that almost daily watering is required. Others who love plants but have busy schedules or are often away from home can work out relationships between pots, plants, and growing mediums so that thorough watering on a weekly basis may be all that is needed.

In general, plants growing in unglazed containers need more water than those in plastic or ceramic. Water at room temperature or slightly warmer, tepid or lukewarm to the touch, is preferable. Many gardeners keep watering cans or plastic jugs filled so water is ready to use as needed, also to dissipate potentially harmful gases (from chemical treatment).

BOTTOM WATERING SAVES FERTILIZER

Some gardeners prefer to water potted plants from the top, others from the bottom. I've always done some of both, but have lately read that bottom-watered plants require less fertilizer, perhaps only half that needed when water and nutrients are applied from above. Since fertilizers are increasingly expensive, this could mean a considerable savings.

If you decide to go the route of bottom watering and fertilizing, mix the fertilizer at half the usual recommended strength, and apply every two weeks, or as instructed on the product label. Once a month apply plain water from the top until it drains freely from the bottom, in order to flush out any accumulations of mineral salts.

Bottom watering is especially effective for plants having fuzzy leaves that may be prone to spotting from cold water or rotting from being wet. These include the African violet, florist gloxinia, and episcia, all members of the gesneriad family. Bottom watering can be accomplished by pouring water into the plant's saucer, by the use of wicking such as one sees for miniature African violets, or by the use of capillary matting, the latter being popular among fluorescent-light gardeners who grow mega numbers of different plants in individual small pots. The special advantage of both wicking and matting is that more water needn't be added for several days, weeks, and sometimes not for months.

Whether water is applied from the top or by filling the saucer, it is important to pour off any that remains after the soil has soaked for an hour. Exceptions are semi-aquatic types such as cyperus or umbrella plant, scirpus or miniature sedge, watercress, and plain, old-fashioned Chinese evergreen or aglaonema, all of which do well in unglazed clay pots left standing in water. I have specified "unglazed clay" because this type of pot allows air to reach the roots and will produce better results than glazed ceramic or plastic used under these circumstances.

Water saved is water . . . Water left in the bottom of a salad spinner should not be poured down the sink but rather on a thirsty houseplant. After steaming vegetables, cool the water and use it to moisten your garden. When you are washing carrots, radishes, or other root vegetables under the faucet, do so over a pail or pan, so that the water can be saved and used for gardening. These measures may seem insignificant, but ultimately it will be seen that every drop counts.

Some signs of a plant consistently underwatered are overall stunting; little or no new growth; leaves pale or yellowish; few or no flowers; premature loss of leaves or flowers. ***Some signs of too much water*** are (also) premature loss of leaves or flowers, rank vegetative growth, few or no flowers, dead wilt from roots that have rotted for lack of oxygen.

POTTING MIX INGREDIENTS

Most of us who grow houseplants are aware, at least subconsciously, that their care constitutes beneficial therapy. Watering, misting, grooming, fertilizing, staking—all these activities are positive ways to relax, to enjoy quality time. They help to wind me up in the morning and to unwind me at night.

One of the most therapeutic aspects of growing plants is mixing potting soil. Psychiatric studies show that the farther removed we are from the earth, figuratively or literally, the greater is our need for living plants and all they represent. If you've ever smelled freshly plowed soil on a warm spring day, you know it is one of the most exhilarating of all scents. When you mix some potting soil for your plants, you can experience this same sensation.

Since it is possible to buy all kinds of different potting soils premixed for specific kinds of plants, you may wonder why I suggest doing it yourself. One reason is that working your hands in the varied textures of different ingredients is highly satisfying. The other is that by adding certain ingredients to packaged mixes you can get better growth responses.

For example, the typical packaged all-purpose potting soil, sometimes labeled for foliage plants, is too dense. I

Mixing potting soil can be beneficial therapy, especially when we recognize the different textures and particle sizes, and work with our hands until the mixture feels and smells right. Precise ingredients vary by region and supplier—and batch. Here California begonia grower Mabel Corwin is about to combine three parts commercial organic compost with one each of quarter-inch or smaller bark chips, perlite, and finely screened leaf mold.

usually mix two to three parts of this with one to two parts of coarse vermiculite, which is also available in packages where plants are sold. When I want to repot a flowering plant such as an African violet I start with a packaged soil labeled either for African violets or flowering houseplants. To two parts of this I add one part each of vermiculite and sphagnum peat moss. The vermiculite helps retain moisture but also allows air to reach the roots. Sphagnum peat moss provides organic matter which improves soil structure and moisture retention. A potting mix like this works well for most flowering houseplants—African violets, gloxinias, begonias, and gardenias, to name a few.

If I am going to repot a cactus or other succulent, such as kalanchoe, echeveria, or jade plant (*Crassula argentea*), I start with a packaged mix labeled for cactus. To four parts of this I add one part each of vermiculite and sphagnum peat moss. The reason I do this is that

packaged soil mixes for cacti dry out too quickly and become hard as cement.

If you have access to garden soil or well-rotted compost, you can use it in place of the packaged potting soil, ideally not before it has been put through a quarter-inch mesh screen and pasteurized in the oven at 180°F for thirty minutes to an hour. (The soil temperature needs to be maintained between 160° and 180°F for thirty minutes, to kill the more harmful organisms and weed seeds, but not so long that all beneficial life is destroyed.) Instead of vermiculite—or in addition to it—you can add well-rotted leaf mold, also screened and pasteurized; this is especially good for begonias, gesneriads, and philodendrons, in particular the bushy self-headers (versus the climbers) such as *Philodendron selloum* and *P. wendlandii.* There is really no substitute for genuine sphagnum peat moss; the dark powdery kinds add humus but do not have the bulk, the fibrous, spongy nature needed to aerate the soil in a pot.

SHOPPING FOR SOIL

Soil, in case you haven't noticed, is not dirt cheap, at least not at the rate of two dollars for four quarts (4.4 liters), which is what I paid recently at a plant shop in my neighborhood. At another, only a few blocks away, I found the same quantity of potting soil for half the price. The front of the two-dollar bag promised potting soil "scientifically improved and expertly blended; weed free and ready to use." The word "organic" also appeared. The dollar bag claimed to contain "all-organic potting soil; sterilized; expertly blended. Will not cake." The back of the two-dollar bag described its contents as a "scientific blend of compost, peat, perlite and humus, all mixed to a uniform consistency." For half the money I was offered a "scientifically balanced formula combining the proper amounts of quality soil, rich humus and organic additives."

Having read the labels, I next opened both bags, felt the soil with my fingers, and then examined it with a magnifying glass. As nearly as I could tell, they were exactly the same—one simply cost twice what the other did.

At the same time I also purchased a two-quart bag of soil labeled "African Violet Mix," for $1.19. It offered a "balance of peat, organic compost, bark and humus combined with porous rock and conditioners. Correct pH is assured." On examination I detected some "porous rock," probably perlite; otherwise the mix appeared to be exactly the same as those sold as "potting soil."

A bag marked "Cactus Mix," and also "guaranteed not to cake or pack," cost me two dollars for four quarts of a "scientifically prepared blend of sterile sand, vermiculite and firm soil as well as the right amount of natural growth elements." Label promises also included "sterilized, nonburning, expertly blended, odorless," the last being disappointing since I consider the smell of healthy soil highly desirable. Fortunately, when I opened the bag the pleasant aroma one expects from living soil was present. Examination of the mix itself showed more sand than the others but no vermiculite and not, in my opinion, enough humus for a potting mix described as "ideal for all cacti, as well as succulents and all bulbs."

Besides the obvious—that it pays to comparison shop—the conclusions I've drawn where convenience potting mixes are concerned are these:

1) Labels offer only a hint of actual content. "Peat," for example—is it the powdery, brown-black kind that is of little value, or the fibrous, spongy, reddish-brown sphagnum peat moss that is recommended for potting mixes and general soil improvement?

2) The words "expert" and "blend" have little meaning until you've proven them true in your own environment and with your own watering and fertilizing habits. The mixes I sampled seemed also to have been screened so finely that "blend" took on negative connotations, as if the ingredients had been put through some giant processor that reduced every particle to the size of a tiny grain of sand or speck of earth.

3) Most packaged potting soils are best used as one ingredient in mixtures "blended expertly" by your own hands, for the specific kinds of plants you are about to pot. This saves money, gives better results, and lets you enjoy more time in beneficial physical contact with the soil.

POTTING MIXES WITHOUT MIX-UPS

Soil- or loam-based and soilless are two ways to grow plants. Growers are successful with either approach and many of us use both. Overall, though, since soil-based potting mixtures are biologically active, they tend to produce foliage plants that can purify indoor air more efficiently than the same plants grown in a soilless medium that must be constantly fortified with applications of chemical fertilizers.

Traditional horticulture has always grown potted plants in a variety of loam-based potting soils. A typical all-purpose recipe appears below. If the mix needs extra humus for a leafy tropical from the rain forest, agolaonema for example, add one or more extra portions of well-rotted compost or leaf mold or sphagnum peat moss and call it a humus-rich, loam-based potting mix. If the mix needs extra drainage, perhaps for a cactus or other succulent, add an extra portion of sand or perlite and call it a well-drained, loam-based potting soil.

Loam-based Potting Soil

1 part garden loam or packaged all-purpose potting soil
1 part sphagnum peat moss
1 part perlite or clean, sharp sand

"Soilless" describes the growing mediums that are used in commercial horticulture. Because of their convenience, products such as Pro-Mix that were previously available only to professionals are now offered retail. There is also the soilless "peat-lite," referring to its content of sphagnum peat moss and the two horticultural "lites"—perlite and vermiculite. The concept of growing in a soilless medium came out of research done at Cornell University in Ithaca, New York, and has been increasing in acceptance over the past two or three decades.

If you grow soilless, your plants will be dependent on regular applications of an appropriately NPK- (nitrogen-phosphorus-potassium) balanced fertilizer of the petrochemical sort. If this disturbs your political consciousness, then grow with soil. Some alternative fertilizers—which work well with loam-based potting soils but not with soilless—are fish emulsion, liquid seaweed, bat manure or guano, cottonseed meal, blood meal, and bone meal. Manure tea can also be made by suspending a small mesh bag of well-rotted cow manure (which can be purchased dehydrated in bags) in a pail of water; steep as necessary, dilute and apply when the color of weak tea.

Cornell Peat-Lite Mix A

For one bushel of mix, good for seeds, rooting cuttings, or repotting plants:

  4 gallons #2 or #3 horticultural vermiculite
  4 gallons shredded sphagnum peat moss
  2 level tablespoons dolomitic limestone (do not use hydrated or "quick" lime)
  2 level tablespoons 20-percent superphosphate
  2 level tablespoons potassium nitrate or calcium nitrate

Add one pint warm water to the peat moss to moisten. Put all ingredients into a large plastic bag. Inflate by blowing into the end, then twist closed to keep inflated. Now shake, roll, and tumble the contents to mix well. Use at once or store in the bag.

Fertilizer added at mixing will last for three weeks of growth, then it will be necessary to fertilize regularly using a water-soluble fertilizer such as 20-20-20.

Cornell Epiphytic Mix

For one bushel of mix that may be used for aroids (aglaonema, dieffenbachia, scindapsus, philodendron), bromeliads, gesneriads (such as columnea, nematanthus, and aeschynanthus), cacti, orchids, and peperomia:

  ⅓ bushel sphagnum peat moss
  ⅓ bushel medium-grade horticultural perlite

  ⅓ bushel Douglas, red, or white fir bark (⅛- to ¼-inch size)
  ½ cup dolomitic limestone
  6 tablespoons 20-percent superphosphate
  3 tablespoons 10-10-10 fertilizer
  1 tablespoon potassium nitrate
  3 tablespoons granular wetting agent (any synthetic polymer designed to have the effect of making water wetter, more efficacious in its ability to moisten)

ORGANIZING A PLACE TO POT

Every garden needs a work center and this need is no different indoors than out. I do my serious gardening in the kitchen of my apartment. Soil-mix ingredients are stored in plastic dishpans on top of the cabinets; these are red and match the color scheme of the kitchen, which happens to be red and white. Pots and other necessities are stored in the cabinets. Stakes and ties are kept in the open, the stakes stuck in jardinieres or deep baskets among the plants, the ties, along with all kinds of other paraphernalia, tossed in various woven baskets that can be kept on the kitchen countertops or on shelves throughout the apartment in spaces left between the books. Fertilizers and insecticides are kept in an upper kitchen cabinet, safely out of reach of any very young visitors. Individual small plants can be potted or repotted within the confines of a plastic dishpan. If a bigger mess is anticipated, I spread several thicknesses of newspaper over the kitchen counter. Rarely, for a tree-size plant in a very large pot, I spread a plastic sheet such as a painter's drop cloth and do the work at the site.

TOOLS AND SUPPLIES FOR HOUSEPLANTING

Essential

Fertilizer
Gloves
Insecticidal soap
Pots and waterproof saucers
Potting soil
Pruners

Stakes, ties
Watering can

   Optional

Baskets for dressing up utilitarian pots
Fan to circulate air
Fluorescent light bulbs
Humidifier
Hygrometer for measuring the amount of relative humidity
Light meter
Maximum-minimum thermometer
Soil moisture meter
Soil pH meter

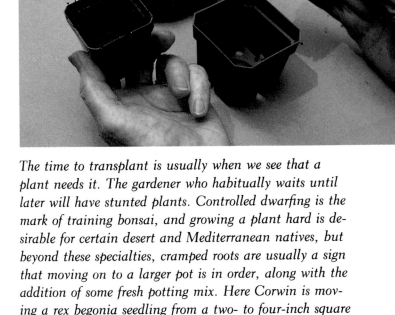

The time to transplant is usually when we see that a plant needs it. The gardener who habitually waits until later will have stunted plants. Controlled dwarfing is the mark of training bonsai, and growing a plant hard is desirable for certain desert and Mediterranean natives, but beyond these specialties, cramped roots are usually a sign that moving on to a larger pot is in order, along with the addition of some fresh potting mix. Here Corwin is moving a rex begonia seedling from a two- to four-inch square plastic growing pot.

REPOTTING

Repotting is a tried-and-proven means for rejuvenating an old plant, a spathiphyllum, for example, that over the years may have thinned out with some of the leaf clusters having become wobbly in the pot. Spring is perhaps the single best season of the year for this project. First you'll need to prepare some fresh potting mix. For spathiphyllum this could be equal parts packaged all-purpose potting soil, sphagnum peat moss, clean, sharp sand, and well-rotted compost or leaf mold.

Carefully remove the spathiphyllum from its pot and crumble away most of the old growing medium. Cut off and extricate any broken, discolored, or shriveled roots, along with any dead or weak top growth. Clean the old pot, or select a new one, and partly fill with the fresh planting mix. Position the spathiphyllum so that when you have finished adding soil the lowermost leaves emerge from along the stems at the surface. Firm the soil with your fingers; a chopstick can aid in getting soil between and snuggled against all the roots so there are no air pockets. Water well by setting the pot in a basin of water and allowing it to soak until beads of moisture appear on the soil surface.

To help the spathiphyllum recover quickly, enclose it in clear plastic—like that from the dry cleaners—for a few days, and place where no sun shines directly. When the leaves feel turgid and appear perky, gradually remove the plastic and position the plant where it is to grow.

Repotting may also be in order if the plants have been growing in the same soil for two years or more. Root pruning may or may not be part of the repotting process, but usually there is some benefit to the plant if part of the old root system is removed before it is set in a new (or cleaned) pot with fresh potting soil. If the roots coil around and around the rootball, maybe even out the drainage hole(s), this is a sign that some root pruning is needed as well as repotting. It is fairly standard practice to remove about a fourth to a third of the roots or, if top parts of the plant are pruned off, to remove a similar percentage or amount of the roots.

Amaryllis bulbs are potted with the upper shoulder and neck revealed and one to two inches of space between the bulb and the pot rim. Work with potting mix that is nicely moist. Use warm water to settle the bulb and roots. Water cautiously until top and root growth become active.

PRUNING HOUSEPLANTS

One advantage indoor gardeners have over outdoor types is that we can work comfortably in all seasons, in all kinds of weather, and at any time of day or night. Generally speaking, however, late winter and spring are the seasons of preference for major potting, repotting, and pruning of roots and tops. When it comes to pruning, whether below or above the soil, the usual procedure is to remove the obvious: the dead, the discolored, the excessive. Then, depending on the individual plant, one might remove a similar portion of the roots and the top, perhaps a third. Especially where woody plants are concerned, it may be preferable to do the root pruning and repotting, then to wait a couple of weeks to do the top pruning until signs of new growth are evident.

Besides the day-to-day or weekly grooming of indoor plants, there is also the situation where a plant has become so large that the top pushes against the ceiling and great masses of foliage block light from the windows. This problem is most acute for the gardener intimidated by the idea of cutting back. Fear of pruning can be overcome when one accepts that cutting back can actually promote vigorous new growth and at the same time help produce both a better-looking plant and garden. I never really got to enjoy pruning until after spending a season working alongside the professional gardeners at the Brooklyn Botanic Garden. Here are some guidelines:

1) Select a pair of pruners, also called clippers, that feels right to your hand. I prefer those having two blades that come together for the cut rather than the anvil configuration, which has one sharp blade that comes down on a flat cutting surface. Excellent clippers can be gotten for around ten dollars, although the better ones cost more. Serious gardeners often use the Felco brand, which can be taken apart for sharpening or repairing.

   Pruning shears or hand clippers are designed to cut fairly small growth, if woody, up to one half inch or so in diameter. Treat them with respect; they are not engineered to cut thick branches (use loppers for this task) or trunks (use a pruning saw). A quick way to ruin a good pair of shears is to appropriate them for use as a screwdriver, hammer, wire cutter, or crowbar.

   Never squeeze the handles of a pair of pruners until all your fingers are accounted for. If pruning is done hurriedly, in anger, or while stewing over some problem, both the plant and the gardener are at risk.

2) Carry pruning shears slung from your belt in the holster provided, or in a pocket of your gardening

happens and, after a few days, cut back healthy growth that is simply too big or generally out of bounds.

One indoor tree that responds especially well to pruning is the weeping fig, *Ficus benjamina*. Spring is an ideal time to clip off all dead or leafless twigs, and then to remove obviously weak branches. This thinning-out will allow more light and air to reach the leafy parts, and they too may benefit from being cut back as much as a quarter to a third.

Vines such as pothos and trailing philodendron often grow leafless from the base, and can be rejuvenated by starting new plants from the leafy tip parts. Cut back any leafless stems to four or five inches from the soil. Often this spurs new shoots from the base. Repotting may also

After I visited and photographed champion begonia grower Mabel Corwin, it was obvious that busy hands equal beautiful begonias. Grooming is an ongoing and never-ending activity that puts the house gardener on an intimate basis with each and every plant. When dried, yellow, or discolored leaves are removed, along with any spent flowers, the gardener sees if any special care or treatment is needed.

There is a precise cutting tool for every task indoors. Excepting the red-handled pruners, the ones here are especially suited to bonsai work. It is important that the tool feel right to your hands and that you carry it with you as in your garden.

apron. This encourages you to do a little pruning all along the way, rather than saving it up until the task may seem overwhelming.

3) When faced with a lot of overgrown plants that may not have been groomed or cut back for quite a spell, begin by arbitrarily removing every leaf and stem that is dead or obviously weak. Watch what

be needed if the plants have been in the same soil for two years or more.

Pinching is a less radical form of pruning that also helps produce plants with many branches, more flowers, and a compact, attractive habit. Coleus is nice to learn on because it grows easily and, when the growing tip is pinched out, two branches always grow out in its place. When the tip of each of these is pinched out, you soon have four branches, and, before long, a really nice plant. This kind of experience helps build confidence and is the very essence of what makes gardening therapeutic.

FERTILIZER FOR HOUSEPLANTS

In practice most of us use some chemical fertilizers even on plants in a soil-based mix, but the amount can be reduced or the need eliminated by including in the original recipe such natural slow-release ingredients as one or more parts well-rotted compost or leaf mold and a sprinkling of bone meal and blood meal. Acid-loving plants such as potted camellias, azaleas, gardenias, and Chinese hibiscus can be top-dressed in spring and again in summer with a sprinkling of cottonseed meal scratched into the soil surface and watered in. For those plants needing more alkalinity or "sweetness," scratch in some oyster shells (you can purchase these where poultry feed is sold).

Plants newly set in pots of fresh loam-based growing medium do not need fertilizer, at least in theory, until their roots begin to fill the pot. In practice most of us are in a hurry and always eager to help our plants grow better. Biologically rational gardeners opt for fish emulsion, liquid seaweed, manure tea, and bat guano. These work well for me with soil-based but not soilless mixes.

The miracles of chemical fertilizers have been acclaimed through much of this century. Despite my childhood reading of a magazine then called *Organic*

Gardening & Farming, the natural way espoused there took a few decades to sink in. Now I am torn. My old habits have produced beautiful results, but at what cost to the environment? When I buy plants in soilless mix, is it environmentally correct to give them the chemical fertilizers on which they are dependent, or should I transplant immediately to a soil-based mix and use organic fertilizers? I am presently collecting and testing old potting mix recipes that served well before gardeners—and plants—became chemically dependent. Here is one of them, for prize-winning African violets from *The African Violet* (M. Barrows, 1948). It came from an Iowa farmwoman and calls for three parts good black soil ("gumbo"), one part peat moss, one part compost (about half manure), one part rotted leaf mold, and two parts sand. To a bushel of this combination, add one six-inch potful of superphosphate and one gallon wood ashes.

An alternative to complete repotting as a means of rejuvenating a plant growing in the same container of soil for a year or more is to top-dress it with a biologically active fertilizer or top-dressing, such as *Restore for Foliage Plants* or *Houseplants Alive!* I have been particularly successful with mixing this kind of organic product with fresh potting soil at the rate suggested on the label and using it to replace the top inch or two of old soil.

HOUSEPLANT WASTE MANAGEMENT

All indoor gardens produce their share of solid waste—dead leaves, spent blossoms, used potting soil—that needs to be recycled through composting, not sent to a municipal landfill. When my consciousness was first raised I had no idea how to solve the problem in a city high-rise apartment. Initially I saved houseplant and kitchen vegetable matter waste in plastic bags that were carried at every opportunity to a friend's compost pile in the country. Now I have reorganized: I keep some plants

House gardens generate vegetable and other waste the same as those outdoors. I add old potting mix ingredients to my compost pile. Colorful petals are tossed onto the surface of various shallow baskets and bowls of potpourri for as long as they are pleasing to the eye and nose, then they too get composted.

2) Add garden waste (or vegetable waste from the kitchen) to the bag. Cut or chop up twigs or any fibrous or large growth; the smaller the pieces, the more quickly they can become compost. You may also crumble up used potting soil and add to any compost in the making.
3) Add enough warm water to the bagged garden waste to moisten everything. Fold over the top of the bag and place where the sun will shine directly on it for several hours daily.
4) About once a week, toss and turn the plastic bag to aerate and mix up the contents. Check to be sure it is warm and moist inside. If too dry, the composting process will be thwarted.
5) After several months the contents of the bag will have turned to well-rotted compost and will then be useful as an ingredient for mixing potting soil. Some container gardeners use only compost with superior results.

One of the pleasant sights in my indoor garden is a low bowl or basket in which scented or colorful flowers and leaves are tossed to dry before they've wilted. This has become an evolving sort of potpourri, and an alternative to composting blossoms, that is pleasing to the eye as well as the nose. Right now it includes petals from gone-by bouquets of roses, blue hydrangeas, lemon verbena, scented geranium leaves, and chrysanthemum petals. I never look in other people's medicine cabinets but I do have a sort of compulsion for smelling their potpourris. Most of the time the only smell is dusty and sort of repugnant. Unfortunately, a lot of commercial potpourri is bulked up with dyed wood shavings and artificially scented. If you happen to have a bowl of this stuff, add it to the compost and start over by saving scented leaves and flowers collected from your garden. Another means of processing garden waste is to use certain spent leaves as mulch around houseplants. I sometimes chop up dried rose or lemon geranium leaves for a fragrant, earthy mulch, rosemary or silver artemisia from the garden for gray. Pine needles cut into short pieces are attractive carpeting the surface soil even in a small pot.

in the windows, but most are arranged on the floor and on shelves four to six feet back, so that it is possible to walk along and have plants on either side, the same as along a garden path outdoors. Scattered among these plants I have baskets for collecting garden waste—yellowed leaves, wilted flowers. Periodically I collect everything in one black or dark green plastic garbage bag in which compost can be made without raising any objectionable smell. Here is the procedure:

1) Place the garbage bag in a large plastic dishpan. Punch a few holes for air all around the bottom of the bag.

HOUSEPLANTERS NEED GLOVES TOO

When it comes to wearing gloves, I always figure that indoor gardeners are not that much different from those who practice outdoors: We would prefer not to wear gloves. However, a fungus called *Sporotrichum scheneckii*, which is found in soil and on plants, in particular in the long-strand sphagnum moss used to keep tree roots moist during shipment and storage, has been implicated in a lymphatic disease in people and animals called sporotrichosis. Infection occurs when the spores of the fungus are introduced through an abrasion or scratch in the skin. A small, painless blister develops, as long as three weeks after infection, becomes inflamed, and slowly enlarges. Early diagnosis is important for successful treatment.

One way to avoid sporotrichosis is not to handle plants packed in sphagnum moss or to always wear rubber gloves when working with sphagnum moss. It also helps to wash your hands frequently and to treat lacerations and abrasions promptly. If a sore should develop, seek medical attention and advise your doctor as to the possibility of sporotrichosis.

Some particular pitfalls for the indoor gardener's hands and fingers are these:

1) Resist the impulse to use your thumb as a scrubber when cleaning pots and seed trays. Use a brush or a soap pad. (Soaking mineral-encrusted pots overnight in vinegar water works wonders, one cup vinegar to one gallon hot water.)
2) Potting mediums for orchids and other epiphytic plants can be highly abrasive. Wear adhesive bandages around fingertips most used, especially the thumbs.
3) Keep your nails trimmed short and buffed smooth at the edges. Long nails are more likely to be torn painfully. Once you become accustomed to very short nails, you will find your fingertips remarkably able to pick up even the tiniest of seedlings.

Gardeners categorically dislike wearing gloves, but sometimes sturdy ones are a necessity, or at least one or more well-placed strips of adhesive tape. We see in action the taped and no doubt green thumb of home orchid grower, advocate, and author Rebecca Tyson Northen, who has learned to protect her manicured nails from the sharp-textured materials used when potting orchids.

4) Begin a session of gardening by pulling your fingernails across a bar of soap. Afterward, a little nail brushing with soap and warm water, followed by gentle rubbing and massaging with a moisturizer, and your hands will feel good and be presentable.

SEASONAL MANAGEMENT

Outdoor gardens are moved onward inexorably by the changing seasons. Indoors the gardener is more in command. Here are some seasonal tips from my datebook:

Spring is for renewal. Repotting. Root pruning. Top pruning. Starting training projects; bonsai, espalier, tree-form standards, topiary. All kinds of propagation. More watering, more fertilizing. Consequently more staking and other grooming activities.

Top-dressing is a relatively mess-free, quick way to rejuvenate any large potted plant. Use your fingers, a chopstick, perhaps a kitchen fork or spoon, to loosen and remove the top two or three inches of old soil; replace with an enriched fresh mixture, such as equal parts peat moss, soil, and sand mixed with a tablespoon of timed-release fertilizer pellets (Osmocote 14-14-14, for example).

Or, instead of the pellets, you can use an additional portion of well-rotted compost or dehydrated cow manure, perhaps with a handful of steamed bone or dried blood meal.

Top-dress established geraniums, dwarf pomegranate, rosemary, and lavender with a sprinkling of oyster shells, also from the feed store. A tablespoon or so of chimney soot does wonders as a top-dressing for fuchsias, practically guaranteed to enhance flower color.

Summer moves the focus of many gardeners to the outdoors. Houseplants left inside must fend for themselves. Be sure to protect tropicals from air-conditioning drafts. Keep a watch for predatory insects and other potential foes that can get to houseplants placed outdoors, including too much hot sun, stormy winds, rain, and hail.

Fall is one of my favorite seasons for houseplants. It's the time to bring them in from outdoors (do this before the heating system has to be activated), to acquire new plants from specialist growers, and maybe to rearrange the furniture so that window light and plant needs are more in balance for the new season of house gardening. Clean the windows so that more sunlight penetrates room interiors; remove the screens if possible. If you are growing with fluorescents, replace the bulbs after one year of regular use. Plant bulbs; paperwhites will be first to bloom, in a few weeks. Also pot new bulbs of Dutch amaryllis. Make up pots of precooled Dutch bulbs or set the regular ones recommended for forcing in the vegetable crisper of the refrigerator for eight to twelve weeks (or until roots show through the drain holes).

Winter is a great time to enjoy gardening with your houseplants. After grooming, position each plant to show off its beauty and best provide its cultural needs. Read books and magazines. Study catalogs. Place orders. Write out the labels for what you have ordered. Plant seeds. Root cuttings. Make up potting mixes to have at the ready. Prepare for the potting, repotting, transplanting, dividing, layering, and the multitude of activities that become increasingly timely as the days grow longer and generally brighter, toward spring.

Protect everything from freezing temperatures and cold drafts. Boost humidity and air circulation. Water with extra caution—sometimes plants need more, sometimes less—it depends a great deal on the weather, the latitude, the existing relative humidity, and other factors. Avoid all extremes with regard to soil moisture at this season. Also, generally speaking, the drier the soil, the more cold a houseplant can tolerate, but only to a point. Remember, no extremes! Go easy with fertilizer, except in certain situations where there is lots of sun or reflected light from long periods of snow-covered landscape; also fluorescent-light gardens maintained on sixteen-hour days and moderate to warm temperatures will produce plants that need watering and fertilizing the same in winter as in summer.

The soil surface around large potted shrubs and trees (here a date palm) can be an ideal place for growing a shallow-rooted ground cover such as echeveria and for mulching with water-polished stones.

After several days of a warm spell, cut branches from outdoor spring-flowering shrubs such as forsythia, flowering quince, and pussy willow and set them in deep vases of warm water in a cool, airy, sunny place to force the flowers. This is how to have your first spring day several weeks ahead of the official date. Enjoy!

HOUSEPLANT NEEDS AT A GLANCE CHART

Name	Light	Temperature	Humidity	Uses
Achimenes	2-4	6-7	9-10	14-15
Acorus	2-4	5-6	10	20; 22
Aeonium	1-3	6-7	8; 11	22-23
African violet (*Saintpaulia ionantha*)	2-4	6-7	9	13-22
Agapanthus	1	6	9; 11	14
Agave	1-2	5-7	8; 11	23
Aglaonema	3-4	6-7	8-10	22-23
Aloe	1-4	5-7	8-11	22-23
Aluminum plant (*Pilea cadieri*)	2-4	6	9	22-23
Amaryllis (*Hippeastrum*)	1-2	6-7	8-11	14
Anemone	1-2	5-6	9; 11	14
Anthurium	2-4	6-7	9-10	14; 22
Aphelandra	2-3	6	9-10	14
Ardisia	1-3	5-6	9-10	14
Asparagus fern (*Asparagus*)	1-3	5-6	9; 11	15
Aspidistra	3-4	5-7	8-10	23
Avocado (*Persea*)	1-3	6	9; 11	12
Azalea (*Rhododendron*)	2-3	5	9; 11	14; 19
Baby's tears (*Soleirolia*)	2-4	6	9-10	20; 24
Bamboo (*Bambusa*)	1-4	5-7	9; 11	12
Basil (*Ocimum*)	1-2	6-7	9; 11	22; 23
Bay, sweet (*Laurus nobilis*)	1-3	5-6	9	12
Begonia, cane	2-3	6	9; 11	14
Begonia, Rex	2-3	6	10; 11	22-23
Begonia, Rieger	2-3	6	9; 11	14
Begonia, wax	1-3	6-7	8-11	13
Bird of paradise (*Strelitzia reginae*)	1-2	6-7	9-10	14
Bougainvillea	1-2	5-7	9-10	14; 19
Bridal veil, Tahitian (*Tradescantia multiflora*)	1-3	6-7	9; 11	15
Bromeliad	1-3	6-7	10	14
Browallia	2-3	6	9; 11	14
Brunfelsia	1-2	6	9; 11	12; 14
Cactus, desert	1-2	5-7	8; 11	14
Cactus, rain forest	2-3	5-7	9-10	14
Cactus, redbird (*Pedilanthus tithymaloides*)	1-2	5-7	8-9	14; 23

Name	Light	Temperature	Humidity	Uses
Caladium	1-3	7	9-10	23
Calamondin	1-2	5-7	9; 11	12; 14
Calathea	2-4	6-7	9-10	22; 23
Calceolaria	1-2	5	9; 11	14
Calla lily (*Zantedeschia*)	2-3	6-7	9; 11	14
Camellia	2-3	5	9; 11	14
Campanula	1-2	5	9; 11	14; 15
Cardamom (*Amomum cardamomum*)	1-3	6-7	9-10	21
Carissa	2-3	6-7	9-10	19; 22
Cercus	1-2	5-7	9; 11	14
Chenille plant (*Acalypha hispida*)	1-2	6	9; 11	14
Chrysanthemum	1-2	5-6	9; 11	14
Cineraria	1-2	5-6	9; 11	14
Cissus	2-4	5-7	8-10	15; 23
Citrus	1-2	5-7	9; 11	12; 14
Clerodendrum	1-2	6-7	9-10	14; 16
Clivia	2-3	5-7	9-10	14
Coffee (*Coffea arabica*)	2-3	6-7	9-10	12
Coleus	2-3	6-7	9; 11	22; 23
Columnea	2-3	6-7	9-10	14; 15
Copper leaf (*Acalypha wilkesiana 'Macafeana'*)	1-2	6	9; 11	12; 23
Crossandra	2-4	6-7	9-10	13; 20
Croton (*Codiacum*)	1-3	6-7	9; 11	12; 23
Crown of thorns (*Euphorbia milii 'Splendens'*)	1-3	5-7	8; 11	14
Ctenanthe	2-3	6-7	10	22-23
Cycad	2-3	5-6	9; 11	12; 19
Cyclamen	2-3	5-6	9; 11	14
Cyperus	3	5-7	9; 11	23
Cyrtanthus	1-2	5-7	9; 11	14
Dieffenbachia	2-3	6-7	9-10	12
Dizygotheca	2-3	6-7	9; 11	12
Dracaena	2-3	5-7	8-9	12
Echeveria	1-2	5-7	8-9	14; 23
Epiphyllum	2-3	5-7	9-10	14; 15
Episcia	2-3	7	10	14; 15
Eucharis	2-4	5-7	9-10	14
Euonymus, dwarf	2-3	5-6	9; 11	23
Euphorbia	1-3	5-7	8; 11	14; 17
Exacum	2-3	6	9-10	14; 23
Fatshedera	2-3	5-6	9; 11	12
Fern	2-4	5-7	9-10	15; 22
Ficus	1-3	6	9; 11	12
Fittonia	2-4	6-7	9-10	20; 24
Foxglove, Mexican (*Tetranema mexicanum*)	2-4	6-7	10	20; 22

HOUSEPLANT NEEDS AT A GLANCE CHART

Name	Light	Temperature	Humidity	Uses
Freesia	1-2	5-6	9; 11	14
Fuchsia	2-3	5-6	10; 11	14; 15
Gardenia	1-3	6	9; 11	14; 21
Gasteria	1-4	5-7	8	22; 23
Geranium, ivy	1-2	5-6	9; 11	13
Geranium, regal	1-2	5-6	9; 11	14
Geranium, scented	1-2	6-7	8; 11	21
Geranium, zonal	1-2	6	8; 11	13
Ginger (*Zingiber*)	2-3	6-7	9	21
Gloxinia, florist (*Sinningia speciosa*)	1-3	6-7	10; 11	14
Gloxinia, miniature (*Sinningia pusilla*)	2-4	6-7	10	13; 20
Gold dust plant (*Aucuba japonica*)	2-3	5-7	9; 11	12
Grevillea	1-2	6	9; 11	12
Haemanthus	1-2	5-7	9; 11	14
Hawaiian ti (*Cordyline*)	1-3	6-7	10; 11	12; 23
Haworthia	1-3	5-7	8	23
Hibiscus, Chinese (*Hibiscus rosa-sinensis*)	1-2	6-7	10; 11	12; 14
Hoffmannia	2-3	7	10	20; 22
Hoya	1-2	5-7	9; 11	14
Hydrangea	2-3	5-7	10; 11	14
Impatiens	1-3	5-6	10; 11	14
Iresine	1-2	6	8-9	22; 23
Ivy, English (*Hedera helix*)	1-4	5-7	9; 11	23; 24
Ivy, German (*Senecio mikanioides*)	2-3	5-6	9; 11	15; 23
Ivy, grape (*Cissus rhombifolia*)	2-4	5-7	9; 11	15
Ivy, red (*Hemigraphis colorata*)	1-2	5-6	9; 11	15
Ivy, Swedish (*Plectranthus australis*)	1-3	5-6	8-9	15
Ixora	1-2	6-7	10; 11	14
Jade plant (*Crassula argentea*)	1-4	6-7	8-9	19; 22
Jasmine (*Jasminum*)	1-2	6-7	9; 11	14; 21
Jerusalem cherry (*Solanum pseudocapsicum*)	1-2	6-7	9; 11	14
Jessamine, night (*Cestrum nocturnum*)	1-2	6	9; 11	14; 21
Joseph's coat (*Alternanthera bettzickiana*)	1-2	6-7	9; 11	22; 23
Kalanchoe	1-2	6-7	8-9	14
Kangaroo vine (*Cissus antarctica*)	2-4	5-7	9; 11	15
Kohleria	2-3	7	10	14; 22
Kumquat (*Citrofortunella*)	1-2	5-7	9; 11	19; 21
Lantana	1-2	5-6	9; 11	14; 15
Lavender, fernleaf (*Lavandula multifida*)	1-2	5-6	9; 11	21; 23
Lemon verbena (*Aloysia triphylla*)	1-2	5-6	9; 11	12; 21
Leopard plant (*Ligulavia tussilaginea 'Aureo-maculata'*)	2-3	5-6	9-10	22; 23
Lily-turf (*Liriope*)	2-4	5-6	9-10	22; 23

Name	Light	Temperature	Humidity	Uses
Lipstick vine (*Aeschynanthus*)	2-3	6-7	9-10	14-15
Lithops	1-2	6-7	8; 11	22; 23
Malpighia	2-3	6	9; 11	19; 22
Manettia	1-2	6	9; 11	15; 16
Maple, flowering (*Abutilon*)	1-2	6	9; 11	12
Mitriostigma	2-3	6-7	9-10	21; 22
Moses in cradle (*Rhoeo bermudensis*)	1-3	6	9	14; 15
Murraya	1-2	6-7	9; 11	12; 21
Myrtle (*Myrtus*)	2-3	5-6	9; 11	18; 22
Nautilocalyx	2-3	6-7	10	14; 22
Nematanthus	2-3	6-7	10	13; 22
Nephthytis	2-4	6-7	8-10	22; 23
Onion, pregnant (*Bowiea volubilis*)	1-3	6	8	15; 23
Orchid, cattleya	1-2	6	9-10	14; 23
Orchid, cymbidium	1-2	5	9-10	14; 23
Orchid, ladyslipper (*Paphiopedilum*)	2-3	5-6	9-10	14; 22
Orchid, phalaenopsis	2-3	6	9-10	14; 22
Oxalis	1-3	6	9; 11	13; 14
Palm	1-3	5-7	9; 11	12
Palm, ponytail (*Beaucamea recurvata*)	1-3	6-7	9; 11	12; 19
Parsley	1-3	5	9; 11	22; 23
Passiflora	1-2	6-7	9; 11	14; 16
Pellionia	2-4	6-7	9-10	20; 24
Pentas	1-2	6	9; 11	14; 23
Peperomia	2-4	6-7	8-10	22; 23
Pepper, Christmas (*Capsicum annuum*)	1-2	6-7	9; 11	14; 23
Philodendron	2-4	6-7	9-10	22; 23
Piggyback plant (*Tolmiea menziesii*)	2-4	6-7	9-10	15; 23
Pilea	2-4	6-7	9; 11	22; 23
Pine, Norfolk Island (*Araucaria heterophylla*)	1-3	5-6	9; 11	12
Pink polka dot (*Hypoestes sanguinolenta*)	1-2	6	9; 11	23
Pittosporum	2-3	5-6	9; 11	12; 21
Plemele	2-4	6-7	8-10	12
Podocarpus	2-3	5-6	9; 11	12
Poinsettia (*Euphorbia pulcherrima*)	1-3	6-7	9; 11	14; 23
Polyscias	1-3	6-7	9; 11	12; 19
Pomegranate, dwarf (*Punica granatum nana*)	1-2	6-7	9; 11	14; 19
Pothos (*Epeprimnum*)	2-4	6-7	9-10	15; 23
Prayer plant (*Maranta leuconeura kerchoveana*)	2-4	6-7	10	20; 22
Primrose (*Primula*)	1-3	5-6	9; 11	14
Purple passion (*Gynura aurantiaca*)	1-3	6	8-9	15; 23
Rhipsalis	2-3	5-7	9-10	15
Rivina	1-2	6-7	9; 11	14; 23

HOUSEPLANT NEEDS AT A GLANCE CHART

Name	Light	Temperature	Humidity	Uses
Rosary vine (*Ceropegia woodii*)	1-3	6-7	8-9	14; 15
Rosemary (*Rosmarinus officinalis*)	1-2	5-6	9; 11	19; 21
Rose, miniature (*Rosa rouletti*)	1-2	6	9; 11	22; 23
Ruellia	2-3	7	10	20; 22
Schefflera	1-3	6-7	9; 11	12
Scilla violacea	1-3	6-7	8-9	22; 23
Screw pine (*Pandanus*)	1-4	6-7	9; 11	12
Sedum, donkey-tail (*Sedum morganianum*)	1-3	5-7	9; 11	15
Selaginella	3-4	5-6	10	20; 24
Senecio	1-2	6	8-9	15
Serissa	2-3	6	9; 11	19; 22
Shrimp plant (*Justicia brandegeana*)	1-2	6	9; 11	14
Siderasis	2-4	6	9-10	22; 23
Smithiantha	2-3	6-7	9-10	14; 22
Sonerila	3-4	6-7	10	20; 22
Sparmannia	1-3	6	9; 11	12
Spathiphyllum	2-4	6-7	9; 11	14; 23
Spider plant (*Chlorophytum*)	2-4	6	9; 11	15
Stapelia	1-2	6	8-9	14; 23
Strawberry, alpine (*Fragaria vesca*)	1-2	5-6	9; 11	14; 23
Strawberry geranium (*Saxifraga stolonifera*)	2-4	5-6	9-10	20; 22
Streptocarpus	2-3	6-7	9; 11	13; 22
Streptosolen	1-2	6	9; 11	14; 23
Sweet olive (*Osmanthus fragrans*)	1-2	5-6	9; 11	21; 23
Synadenium	1-3	6-7	8-9	23
Thunbergia	1-2	6-7	9; 11	14; 16
Tibouchina	1-2	6	9; 11	12; 14
Trevesia	1-3	5-6	9; 11	12
Umbrella plant (*Cyperus alternifolius*)	1-4	5-6	9; 11	23
Vallota	1-2	6	9; 11	14; 23
Wandering Jew (*Tradescantia*)	1-2	6	9; 11	15; 24
Yucca	1-2	6-7	8; 11	12

KEY TO CHART NUMBERS
1 Sun
2 Half sun
3 Half shade
4 Shade (little or no direct sun)
5 Cool, 40° to 60°F at night in winter, to 70°F or so on a sunny day
6 55° to 65°F at night, to 75°F on a sunny day
7 60° to 75°F at night, to 80°F on a sunny day

8 Low relative humidity, to 20 precent
9 Medium relative humidity, to 40 percent
10 High relative humidity, 40 percent or higher
11 Needs fresh air circulation
12 Tree
13 Everblooming
14 Seasonal flowers
15 Hanging
16 Climbing

17 Suited to espalier training
18 Suited to topiary training
19 Suited to bonsai training
20 Suited to terrarium or bottle garden
21 For fragrant leaves or flowers
22 Suited to fluorescent-light culture
23 For sill, shelf, or table display
24 Suited as an indoor ground cover

When You Go Away

I leave my houseplants, at least a couple hundred, all the time. Since I often return to a lot of dead leaves, I have learned to look upon this as the plants' way of saying they have missed me. Since that is precisely the moment I need some plant therapy, it all works out. Here are some guidelines based on my experiences:

1) Before you leave, check for any signs of insects such as brown scale, mealybugs, or spider mites. Treat accordingly. Otherwise they may be out of control by the time you return.

2) If you have a lot of plants and can afford it, hire a professional. A friend who did this and returned to find her plants much healthier admitted, "I didn't know whether to be pleased or disappointed; not one plant said anything about missing me!"

3) Work out a buddy system with a gardening friend whose thumb is at least as green as yours. When you go away, he or she plant-sits, and vice versa.

4) If you have to leave your plants in the care of a person whose thumb shows no trace of green, write out plain instructions and go through the watering procedure together. If he or she walks out the door having forgotten gloves, umbrella, or, worse, the set of keys you've provided for reentry in your absence, back out of this one while you can.

5) Before you go away, repot any plants that have a habit of always needing to be watered. These are the ones that will go first in your absence.

6) Determine how much and how often you water each plant. A professional won't need this information, but it is vital to the inexperienced. Stick a label in each pot and be specific. For example, "1 cup water every Monday-Wednesday-Friday." Explain that in general no water need be added to the top of the pot if water is found standing in the saucer.

For a variety of reasons some gardeners don't like to have anyone coming into their home when they are not present. By taking a few steps, it is possible for most plants to do nicely on their own for a week or two, especially in cold weather when the thermostat can be lowered to 55°F. In addition, saturate the soil in each pot the day before you leave. If you expect to be away for an extended period, enclose each pot in a plastic bag and tie it at the top, snugly around the stem or base of the plant. Fill pebble humidity trays with water.

Light for plants in the gardener's absence is critical. Shades must be up or open, draperies pulled back, with curtains at most left in place for filtered sun. Plants left in darkened rooms for several days or more will lose many leaves and future flowers will be nipped in the bud. Light gardens plugged into an automatic timer can be reduced from long days of sixteen hours to short days of eight. This maintains the plants yet keeps them from needing water in your absence.

Living and Working with Houseplants

Body, mind, and soul, we have already determined that houseplants are good for us. In order to live and work surrounded by healthy plants, it is necessary to learn how to grow and display them so that they can be both healthy and decorative. Beautiful houseplants and beautiful interiors are not mutually exclusive, they are one and the same. Nothing is truly pleasing in an aesthetic sense unless everything about it is true. A sun-loving plant perfectly displayed in a dark corner is not aesthetically pleasing. A sun-loving plant perfectly displayed on a wood floor without a saucer to catch the water is not aesthetically acceptable. The whole idea of the new houseplant is honesty—embracing the plant as a necessary part of one's life and then setting about to make everything true—the environment, the visual impact, the relationship between plant and human.

Houseplants come in so many sizes and shapes and possess such varied needs as to light and temperature, it is possible to match one to almost any given spot where greenery or floral beauty might be appreciated. Presuming that the temperature is comfortable for you, and the light from windows or electricty is strong enough to read by, there is a plant to meet your every decorating need.

Kitchens and dining areas make ideal places for plants, especially a few favorite herbs such as parsley, basil, rose-mary, and thyme, some scented geraniums—finger-bowl lemon, old-fashioned rose, or apple-nutmeg—and a fragrant blossomer or two such as sweet olive (*Osmanthus fragrans*) and Sambac jasmine (*Jasminum sambac*). Sometimes a plant looks beautiful on the countertop: Dallas fern, syngonium, and pothos adapt well in reduced light. Or you might install a compact fluorescent grow-light unit with two 20-watt bulbs (one cool white, one warm white) under a cabinet for a countertop garden of miniature African violets or a terrarium.

If you don't have one, consider adding a bay window or greenhouse extension from the dining area. This can be made into a bower of hanging plants and trees, with vines trained on trellising and all kinds of bushy and shrubby flowering types displayed to best advantage.

Entry areas can be cold and drafty, and even on the dark side, yet there is no place where the sight of flora is more welcome. Fresh bouquets are a delight in warm weather and dried arrangements can be fun in winter. Dracaenas, especially the corn plant 'Massangeana', 'Janet Craig', and 'Warneckii'; ferns such as Boston, Dallas, rabbit's-foot davallia, and holly (*Cyrtomium falcatum*); sansevieria; aspidistra; and podocarpus can be relied upon for durable living greenery.

Living rooms and family rooms often afford a variety of lighting conditions, from direct sun to quite shaded.

*Take away the skylights, trellising crafted by Tony Bada-
lamenti, Mexican tile floors, wicker porch furniture, and
plants grown by Cleveland florist Don Vanderbrook and
what do you have? The oldest gasoline station in Chagrin
Falls, Ohio. Plant room makeovers give high return on
every dollar and drop of sweat invested.*

sumably. If there is no window, or light is dim, use small
foliage plants, rotating them as necessary to a recuperative
window garden. Cut flowers, fresh or dried, and a bowl
of fresh potpourri are always appreciated in a bathroom.

Once you get into the fun of room-to-room decorating
with plants, no room in the house will be safe. Laundry
and utility rooms often afford ideal conditions for growing
plants, starting seedlings, and rooting cuttings. Sun
porches that stay above freezing in winter can become
greenhouses, with pots of seasonal and fragrant flowers
in an emerald setting.

In the event you want a plant or bouquet in a dark
spot, add an electric spot or floodlight, keeping the bulb
at least three feet, better yet six, from the leaves or blossoms. It can be directly overhead, to the side, or from
below, depending on what looks best. A bulb called
"Wonderlite," from the Public Service Lamp Corpora-
tion, New York, New York, combines in one self-bal-
lasted, reflector flood the benefits of incandescent,
fluorescent, and mercury vapor. It was designed originally
for the jewelry industry, to give a true rendering of color,
and has turned out to be exceptionally well balanced for
plant growth. This must be used in a ceramic fixture; the
Wonderlite is also expensive, but it lasts several years and
can be effective both visually and horticulturally.

A few plants well chosen and outfitted with cachepots or
woven baskets are all that is needed to create a permanent
garden setting that will look even more appealing when
you add cut flowers, seasonal flowering potted plants,
and bowls of fresh fruit.

Bedrooms are a very popular place for plants, especially
a tree or two that casts leafy branches over the bed. It's
always nice to have a small plant or fragrant cut flower
on the headboard or nightstand.

Bathrooms with strong window light and increased
humidity can be ideal growing spaces for tropical foliage
and flowering plants. Bark-mounted orchids and bromeliads may be grown in the strongest light and given a
rain-forestlike shower as you are showering, daily pre-

DECORATIVE AND WORKING POTS

Most houseplants are grown in unglazed clay or utilitarian plastic pots. These are the working pots that assure
free drainage. As mentioned earlier, unglazed clay permits moisture to transpire through the walls and thus
increases moisture in the air immediately surrounding
plants, but also requires more frequent watering. Plants
in plastic pots require less watering.

Plastic pots may be square or round, while ordinary
clay ones are usually shaped like a flowerpot. Any pot

So many pots, so many plants. What to match with which? Earthenware pots are used all over the world for growing plants. Here the choice is Western, terra-cotta in the manner of classic Italian. Bonsai pots and trays and the ceramic pots used for traditional koten en gei—*the Japanese practice of growing in containers certain special plants—are similarly collectible and useful to the gardener with an Eastern view.*

that has the flowerpot shape may be tall, medium or low in its profile, which translates as follows:

Standard. This pot is as high as it is wide at the rim. Excellent for plants having a taproot, or an extensive root system.

Three quarter or azalea. This pot is three fourths as tall as it is wide at the rim. Recommended for azaleas, African violets, begonias, and any relatively shallow-rooted plant, also as a general purpose growing pot.

Bulb pan. This pot is half as tall as it is wide at the rim. It is recommended for growing bulbs, particularly forcing, and may also be put to use for any shallow-rooted plant; see previous paragraph.

A primary consideration for indoor containers is the surface on which they will be placed. Unless it is impervious to moisture, rotting and rusting are distinct possibilities. To keep this from happening, use saucers that are absolutely waterproof, ideally with some kind of ridging on the very bottom so that air can circulate underneath. There are also cork pads designed to be placed under pot saucers to absorb any moisture. The same considerations apply to pebble humidity trays. Without facilitation for air circulation, the basin sweats and over time this leads to rot or rust. If sills are a particular problem, an antirust treatment may be needed, or a replacement material impervious to water spills and condensation, a plastic laminate such as Formica, for example.

Cachepot and jardiniere. The French, as masters of style, have given us cachepot, one word that describes an ornamental container for holding a flowerpot. Either kash-PO or KASH-pot is correct. Jardiniere has a similar meaning but can also refer to a decorative stand for plants. "Cache" implies hidden treasure; "jardin" is French for garden.

A cachepot in the strictest sense is made of some kind of earthenware, clay, or ceramic that is glazed at least on the inside to make it waterproof. In practice, all kinds of decorative as well as primarily utilitarian containers can be pressed into service as cachepots: woven baskets of all kinds, pewter, copper, brass, and silver from the kitchen, cookie jars, ice buckets, or what-have-you from garage sales and flea markets.

If the cachepot is not waterproof, or if the inside might be scratched by the utilitarian pot it is about to receive, place a plastic saucer at least one inch deep in the bottom, then proceed.

When the right plant and the right cachepot get together, the visual effect adds up to more than the sum of its parts. Flowering plants such as African violets, cyclamen, amaryllis, azaleas, holiday cactus, and poinsettias often look best in a relatively plain container. Foliage types such as peace lily (*Spathiphyllum*), Boston and Dallas ferns, and Chinese evergreen aglaonema can give a pleasing effect in cachepots that are themselves decorated with flora or fauna.

In the end, nothing matters except that what you see gives you pleasure. Besides the mating of plant and cachepot, the room in which it will be displayed and enjoyed may influence the color and kind of container.

Take any beautiful potted plant like the giant green succulent aeonium and put it in almost any beautiful container, here everyday blue-and-white enamelware, that
can be found around the kitchen or dining room and you
will have an instant table centerpiece.

One rule is that the opening in the cachepot must be
slightly larger than the diameter of the pot in which the
plant is growing. Next, slip the plant inside to try for
size. A too-small plant will be swallowed up by a too-
large cachepot. Sometimes the cachepot will be too deep,
but otherwise just right; this can be corrected by placing
a block of wood or plastic foam or some other booster in
the bottom. It's best if the rim of the growing pot is at
least a half inch lower than that of the cachepot.

As a finishing touch, some kind of moss is often added
to carpet any exposed soil and to hide the growing pot
rim. This can be sheet moss gathered from your own
property, or a similar material purchased as florist sheet
moss. Spanish moss is another possibility. As a mulch I
sometimes add chopped dried scented geranium leaves
or lavender flowers and leaves.

Woven bsakets have become one of the hallmarks of
house gardening as we know it. They hide the working
pots and also give plants a natural-appearing base. The
only way this honestly works is to give each pot an ab-

solutely waterproof saucer, otherwise, unless you are uncommonly careful, the bottom of the basket will
eventually rot.

Large indoor trees like a Ficus benjamina *in the lobby of
a hotel in Birmingham, Alabama, need pots that are large
enough to hold ample soil and to be sufficiently heavy to
anchor them visually and for safety. It usually works best
if the plant is actually growing in a plastic tub, which
must be small enough to fit through the top of its decorative cover. Especially in public places, to discourage litter-
ing, the surface around such plants can be planted with a
variety of seasonal flowering and foliage plants.*

HANG UP A WALL GARDEN

Container plantings meant to be hung against a wall require a special wall basket or other container that is flat on the back, rounded or squared on the front. These have become widely available and can work wonders in turning a bare wall into a garden beauty spot, indoors or out. There are the utilitarian plastic half-rounds as well as the more horticultural wire, along with decorative clay, terra-cotta, and glazed ceramic.

If you choose a wire wall basket, line it with a substantial layer of presoaked (with water) and wrung-out long-strand sphagnum moss. Plain plastic pots suit some gardeners, while others may like to dress them up. J. Liddon Pennock, Jr., whose displays at the Philadelphia Flower Show are legendary, mixes two or three dark colors of flat quick-drying paint, then smudges them on with sponges until the pots are camouflaged into the surroundings.

Regardless of the kind of wall pot, add a cushion of moss around the lip or edge at planting time. Otherwise the plant stems will tend to bend too acutely or break when they rest on the rim.

Wall plantings that face the sun can take quite a beating when warm weather settles in. Portulaca makes an excellent choice outdoors, also trailing lantana, verbena, annual phlox, creeping zinnia, nolana, and phacelia. In a shady location, wall plantings help make the most of the light and may succeed where, only a few feet below, the ground is too dark to get any kind of satisfactory growth. Ferns can be the ticket here, as well as such begonias and gesneriads as achimenes and columnea.

Wall gardens, like all containers, especially those airborne, need lots of watering, which tends to leach out nutrients. I use timed-release pellets such as Osmocote 14-14-14 and also apply a liquid fertilizer from time to time such as 15-30-15 or 1-6-5 to bring out the flowers.

I enjoy combining several kinds of compatible plants in one wall garden. A favorite for earliest spring outdoors or in a sunny, cool growing space is to combine parsley, pansies or violas, primroses, lettuce, and even some bulbs such as hyacinth or a miniature cyclamen. Later some

of these may be extricated and replaced by a crop more suited to summer, small-leaved basil, for example, which revels in the heat.

A review of Chapter 4, in which some five hundred different kinds of houseplants are profiled, will yield a host of candidates for all kinds of house gardens. As soon as the notion is deserted that houseplants are made to line up in rows on a windowsill, the possibilities become exciting for trees, shrubs, vines, trained plants, seasonal and permanent flowering plants, and fragrant flowers and plants having scented leaves. Think in terms of what to place on the floor, what to raise a few inches, perhaps on an overturned clay flowerpot—one of the best plant pedestals ever employed by a gardener or decorator—or what to train on some kind of trellis.

PLANT DRESS UPS AND LIGHTING

Working from the utilitarian pot in which the plant is growing, we can now set about hiding anything that is not pleasing as we view the houseplant as part of a garden. Pot covers can be woven baskets, classic terra-cotta pots and window boxes, glazed ceramic cachepots, or almost anything that is gardenesque such as wood boxes. We can also add electric light for dramatic effect. The simplest of canister up-lights can emphasize the sculptural qualities of plants, often casting romantic and exotic-appearing shadows on the ceilings and walls at night. A 75-watt reflector flood or spotlight, placed at least three feet from the plant, can reveal its beauties at night.

Cut flowers. One way to turn a house garden of leafy foliage and mostly green plants into a flower show is to add some cut flowers. These needn't be "arranged"—the flower arrangement is a world unto its own, for another book—here I am talking about bunches of seasonal flowers that can be placed and emphasized with electric light. When a bouquet of something like roses or dahlias or chrysanthemums from the garden begins to fade, it can be withdrawn from the vase of water, bunched, tied, and hung to dry from a house tree, and thus enjoyed through

One of the most important lessons to learn about bringing the garden indoors is to lift plants to the heights where they look and can grow best. Boxes and pedestals can be purchased or built of plywood and painted. The treelike presence here is a bushy Philodendron selloum *whose trunk is a wood platform. Cycads stand on either side, positioned with an eye for garden design as well as the sun needs of the plants.*

yet another stage. I regularly bring home fresh-cut herbs from the country and hang them to dry from the branches of a weeping ficus that has lived many years in my living room. Bunches of sage, thyme, and rosemary look picturesque and provide a ready source to pick from for the kitchen.

SEASONAL FLOWERING PLANTS

Nothing has added so much to my experience of house gardening as the seasonal flowering pot plant that has become a staple of commercial horticulture. Usually these plants are offered at retail in anything from a four- to eight-inch growing pot. They are meant to be dealt with in much the same way as cut flowers—here today, gone tomorrow. I have chosen to write about the most popular seasonal pot plants here rather than in Chapter 4; some of these will grow again, others we enjoy for a time, then they go to the compost.

Amaryllis of the large-flowered Dutch type are definitely seasonal but since the bulbs from which they grow can be readily managed as permanent houseplants, I have placed them in Chapter 4 under *Hippeastrum*, their botanical genus name (see page 78).

Azaleas are sold potted as seasonal flowering plants nearly every day of the year. Miniatures are the most recent innovation in marketing these woody plants that may be evergreen or deciduous in habit. All azaleas belong to the genus *Rhododendron*, but all rhododendrons are not azaleas. The easy way to deal with them indoors is to think about the cool, airy spring weather that brings them to perfection outdoors. The more closely you can duplicate such conditions indoors, the longer the flowering season will last.

Of all gift plants, the azalea is among the more salvageable. The large-flowered singles and doubles were developed in Belgium from China's *Rhododendron simsii* and are cultivated mostly in greenhouses, or outdoors to Zone 8 (10° to 20°F minimum). These are commonly called Indian azaleas. The smaller flowered and single Kurume is an azalea of Japanese origin that can be brought to bloom in pots, but is also planted outdoors as far north as New York City and coastal Connecticut.

To keep an azalea as an indoor plant, remove the blossoms as soon as they fade. Cut back any wayward branches so that the bush has a pleasing shape and outline. If you wish to encourage a denser habit, prune back the entire bush by up to one third. As growth proceeds, pinch out the main tips once or twice, but not after midsummer or the new wood will not have time to ripen properly before the end of the season.

If an azalea is in a root- or potbound condition, prepare to transplant. To keep in the same container but foster renewed growth, follow this procedure:

1) Remove the azalea from the pot and set it aside in a shady, cool, moist spot. Clean the pot. If it is

Florist azaleas also come in miniature sizes that grow in two-inch pots and bloom twice or more yearly.

faithful you are with the watering can, and a lot of other variables. Too much sun pales or burns azalea leaves; not enough results in frail new shoots and rapid loss of older foliage.

It is vital for success with azaleas, in pots indoors or out, that the roots have moisture at all times. Standing in stagnant water won't do, but letting the roots become bone dry is the kiss of death to blossoms and soon results in massive leaf drop; plants habitually kept too dry also fall prey to devastating attacks of spider mites.

Since many potted azaleas are set in a soilless mix, it is necessary to apply fertilizer regularly. This tends to raise the pH; if too "sweet" or alkaline, pH 7.0 or higher, the azalea leaves will turn yellowish between the veins. Avoid this development by making regular applications of fertilizer specifically for acid-loving plants, or by dosing it with this old-fashioned remedy: one teaspoon cider vinegar mixed in one quart water, and applied to the soil monthly, or as indicated by the leaf color.

clay and has encrustations of mineral salts on the rim and exterior walls, soak in vinegar water (one cup to one gallon water) until the residue brushes off. Rinse.

2) Prepare some fresh potting mix, combining the standard half-and-half sphagnum peat moss and clean, sharp sand. Or you can use almost any packaged soilless medium or mix your own using, for example, about equal parts well-rotted oak leaf mold or pine needle mulch and sandy garden loam. Your goal is a humus-rich soil that absorbs and holds moisture, yet gives roots plenty of oxygen, and has a pH of 5.0 or thereabouts.

3) Take a big knife from the kitchen and slice an inch or two of the old matted roots and growing medium from all around the rootball.

4) Place a layer of pebbles or crushed clay pot pieces in the bottom of the container, add some fresh medium, then position the newly root-pruned azalea so that it stands at the same depth as before. Fill in with more soil all around, firming with your fingers or chopsticks. Water well.

5) Now do any pruning necessary to encourage the top part of the azalea. When roots are pruned it is accepted practice to remove a similar portion of a plant's top.

6) Set to grow in a half-sunny window garden. How much direct sun depends on the local climate, how

A mantle of green—Boston fern, scented geranium, Schefflera arboricola—is brightened by two pots of flowering chrysanthemum. It takes surprisingly few seasonal flowers—growing or cut—showcased in this way, massed by kind or color, to get a pleasing display.

If possible, place potted azaleas outdoors during warm weather, on a porch, or in a slathouse, where there is protection from harsh weather. If you live where September and October provide cool nights, with temperatures in the fifties, azleas like these will just naturally set buds and start blooming around the holidays. Commercial growers aiming for Christmas sales keep a schedule of 50°F at night from October 1 to November 1. Then the plants are moved to a warmer house—60° to 65°F maximum—for holiday blooms.

Chrysanthemum. The modern potted mum is nearly always available for a spot of color; in fact, if it has a fault, that's it—being too available. Despite this I like the plant that Miss Jean Brody called ". . . such a serviceable flower . . ." best in autumn, its presumably natural flowering season when selection is greatest and price favors the buyer. To prolong the life of such a mum, keep the soil evenly moist. Add more water before the leaves start to droop. Place in bright light; sun shining directly on the blossoms may age them prematurely unless there is plenty of fresh air circulation to prevent excess heat buildup.

When the last blooms begin to fade, cut the plant back to a couple of inches from the soil and set the pot in a cool but frost-free spot. Keep the soil barely damp (avoid extremes) and don't fertilize. When planting-out weather arrives in the spring, transplant the chrysanthemum outdoors. Potted mums come in basically two varieties, florist or greenhouse and hardy or garden. Florist mums usually have larger flowers and leaves and may not be winter-hardy in colder regions. Hardy or garden mums tend to have smaller leaves and flowers—but not necessarily—and they can be hardy into areas that have subzero temperatures.

Cineraria. The florist cineraria is something of an idealized daisy plant with a ruff of green leaves surrounding a bouquet of flowers in bright colors, more often than not in some shade of blue or a blue-and-white combination. Cinerarias need bright light and fresh air circulation when they are in bloom. They also need lots of water. Never leave one standing in water, but be sure the soil is never so dry the leaves go into a dead wilt. The florist cineraria as we know it is an annual, to be

Florist cineraria, often one of the bluest flowers in a winter or spring greenhouse, is a member of the daisy family that dislikes temperature extremes. Grow it in cool, sunny, airy, moist conditions and be prepared to treat constantly against green aphids on the growing shoots.

discarded after the flowers start to fade. For convenience the cineraria can be purchased in bloom but the price of even one is considerably more than a packet of seeds with the potential of producing many flowering plants in a variety of colors, combinations, and sizes. I can't think of a better project for a budding greenhouse gardener, or anyone who has a sunny, cool but frost-free winter garden, indoors or out.

Cinerarias are members of the daisy family and belong to the genus *Senecio*, which is highly varied, from the succulent string-of-pearls plant to large-leaved herbaceous perennials that make quite a show in outdoor borders. The cineraria we grow in pots, or in beds outdoors in mild winter climates, is a complex hybrid that has been developed to have a low crown of leaves that becomes almost entirely covered by a nosegay of daisies. They may be entirely white, pink, rose, or blue, but the colors banded with white are the most appealing to me. The blues seen in some cinerarias are hard to believe.

Cineraria seeds sprout quickly at about 70°F. Thereafter they do best on moderately warm days, 65° to 75°F, and cooler nights, to about 50°F. Transplant to individual pots as soon as the seedlings are large enough to handle. Cineraria seeds are small and relatively expensive for the better strains but they are quite dependable if sown on the surface of a moistened planting medium. Enclose in plastic or cover with glass until you see specks of green, then gradually expose to the open air and more direct sunlight. Green aphids almost always try to take up residence on cinerarias. Watch for them on the new growth. If detected, rinse off and down the sink using a fairly strong spray of water. If the aphids persist, try an insecticidal soap spray, but only in the cool of the day when no sun will shine on the leaves for several hours.

Cyclamen. Hardly any seasonal flowering plant is as lovely as a well-grown cyclamen. When I see a florist's window filled with them on a frosty evening they take my breath away. Often the first question asked is how to say the name. A lot of us say that when we purchase cyclamen they are "sike"-luh-men but after days or weeks in reduced light with too much heat and too much or too little water they become "sick"-luh-men.

I don't relish criticizing an industry, but there is no commercial pot plant more abused than the cyclamen. The ones regularly offered at my neighborhood supermarket appear to have been prepped in advance for immediate burial in a compost pile.

Therefore, my advice is to buy cyclamen only from a known source. If the plant has been stressed by chilling, overheating, drying, or overwatering, it will never fully recover.

To keep a healthy cyclamen going, it needs soil kept nicely moist through and through. Avoid both extremes of wet and dry. If the plant becomes dry enough to cause slight wilting of the leaves, the older ones will yellow and wither prematurely and any flower buds in the making will be killed.

Cyclamen persicum *is the florist cyclamen. Study this picture for the quality of dappled sun-shade light it needs. Note moisture droplets on the leaves, from an early morning watering on a sunny bright day. Add to this cool temperatures, 40° to 60°F, and fresh air circulation—no cold or hot drafts—and this houseplant will flower several weeks or months.*

Cyclamen needs bright light but protection from too much hot sun. If the plant receives ample circulation of fresh air, it can tolerate more direct sun.

Cyclamen does best in a moderate range of temperatures, 60° to 72°F. Besides fresh air circulation, it also helps if there is adequate humidity, which can be boosted by setting the pot on a pebble tray with enough water to keep the pebbles wet but never so much that the pot stands in water. Remove yellowed leaves and spent flowers by clipping as close to the base as possible.

A cyclamen that has all of the above-mentioned desirable conditions going for it will also benefit from very light applications of a fertilizer labeled as a blossom booster for houseplants such as African violets. By "very light," I mean applied precisely according to the directions on the container but at half strength.

A cyclamen plant that is overheated and underlighted will typically have new leaves with stems much longer and weaker than previously and there will be few if any flowers. Any cyclamen that is stressed is also much more likely to be attacked by an opportunisitic insect such as tiny spider mites or the cyclamen mite. Spraying with insecticidal soap will help, but to produce a healthy, long-in-bloom cyclamen, nothing takes the place of nurturing growing conditions.

Exacum is a fragrant charmer from the gentian family that has become a stock in trade for the seasonal flowering pot plant business. When one of the compact, base-branching plants is covered with bright green leaves and starry blue flowers, it is an almost idealized gift plant, as if conceived by an artist. Perhaps best, it adjusts well to average home and office conditions, at least for the duration of its initial bloom season. Thereafter the plant may be considered an annual (discard after bloom), biennial (cut back and get one more period of bloom), or perennial. If the plants are kept from year to year, they need to be sheared back in the fall for more compact growth. Seeds started in winter will bloom in a few months. I prefer to plant these small seeds—make that "tiny"—by scattering them on the surface of premoistened sterile milled sphagnum moss. The seedlings are transplanted when large enough to individual three-inch pots. Good garden loam mixed with well-rotted compost or other humus and perlite suits these plants well. Filtered light is welcome; hot, direct sun is a no-no.

Exacum affine is most often grown for its blue flowers centered by prominent yellow stamens. The species is native to the island of Socotra in the Indian Ocean. Cultivars are available with single or double (like miniature roses) flowers in various shades of blue to violet or lavender, also nearly white to pale greenish.

Hydrangea. No seasonal flowering plant thrills me more than a perfectly grown florist hydrangea, known botanically as *Hydrangea macrophylla*, and in England as *hortensia*. The whites are always white, regardless of

Exacum affine *is an annual, biennial, or short-lived tender perennial that is grown from seeds, occasionally from tip cuttings. The starry flowers vary from intense to sky blue to nearly white, and come also in doubles.*

the soil pH, but the colors vary from pale to dark pink in more alkaline conditions, to the purest of blues in acidic, with smoky pink-blues seen in between.

The most important thing to know about a potted hydrangea is that it needs lots of water in spring and summer. Even with ample moisture at the roots, the large leaves tend to wilt at midday in hot weather, suggesting the need for shade under such conditions.

During fall and winter the potted hydrangeas I have helped take care of are lined out in a sunny, airy, cool but frost-free home greenhouse. Soil is kept on the dry side and no fertilizer is applied. In late winter, as the length of the days and average temperatures increase, I begin to water more and to fertilize, at first with a balanced NPK such as 13-13-13 timed-release pellets or 20-20-20 diluted and applied as a liquid.

The large-leaved or florist hydrangea, Hydrangea macrophylla, *comes in various shades of pink through blue, depending on the acid-alkaline pH of the soil and the cultivar itself. In full leaf and bloom it is hard to overwater this luxuriant plant.*

Later in spring, as leaf growth becomes active, the whites and blues receive a 30-10-10 fertilizer and the soil from the pinks is top-dressed with powdered limestone or crushed oyster shells. Without being very scientific, or testing the soil pH, I get splendid results, to the point that the hydrangea has become one of my most appreciated flowers.

Prune back potted hydrangeas after they finish flowering, probably early to midsummer, to about one third their previous height. Repot at this time and water generously. Select early on which stalks are to bear the next season's flowers and nip in the bud any others that start to grow.

Kalanchoe. The species in general is discussed on pages 120–121. Here I will talk about the cultivars of *Kalanchoe blossfeldiana* which are now available as seasonal flowering plants nearly every week of the year. This is because professional growers are able to manipulate them to bloom on schedule by day-length control. At home under normal lighting conditions the seasonal cycle for kalanchoes is similar to that for amaryllis, which means they need to vegetate in spring and summer and rest in autumn in order to bloom in winter.

After the kalanchoe flowers have dried up, take scissors or sharp pointed pruning clippers and clip off all the spent growth. Set the plants to grow in a warm sunny spot. Water generously as soon as the surface soil approaches dryness and apply an all-purpose or foliage plant fertilizer.

Kalanchoe blossfeldiana *gives us the popular florist gift and seasonal pot plant, originally having flowers from bright to brick red, now also in cool to warm shades of yellow, orange, apricot, pink, and rose. Old plants can become sizable specimens if cut back and repotted. Individual tip cuttings root easily for Tom Thumb-size flowering miniatures.*

In a month or so, make tip cuttings, each at least two inches long. Strip away any leaves from the bottom inch of stem and insert this part in moist potting soil. Keep constantly warm (72° to 75°F), moist, and in bright, diffused sunlight. They will root quickly and can then be transplanted to individual three- or four-inch pots, or set three in a six-inch azalea pot.

Although kalanchoes of all kinds are easy to grow provided they have enough sunlight, warmth, and water during the seasons of active growth, best results occur when new plants are started annually. Commercial growers sow seeds, but these are extremely small; home gardeners are more likely to succeed with tip cuttings.

Watch out for bugs on kalanchoes, especially aphids on new growth shoots and mealybugs on the stems and leaf undersides of older parts. Insecticidal soap or neem sprays are an effective treatment, but apply only when the sun is not shining on the leaves.

I have had the best luck with kalanchoes when they spend the summer outdoors, with an abundance of sun, air, water, and fertilizer. If brought inside before danger of frost and placed in a cool (45° to 60°F) winter garden, with limited water and no fertilizer until flower buds are evident, they will shortly burst into bloom in winter after an increase in water and biweekly applications of 15-30-15 fertilizer.

Poinsettia is *Euphorbia pulcherrima*, from southern Mexico. It has succulent, tender new growth which matures to a woody, shrublike structure, and large, colorful bracts when the days are short in late fall and early winter. The commercial poinsettia is a sophistcated production. Chemical growth retardants are used to make the plants more compact, also to increase their shelf life and general durability. All things being equal, the home-grown product will be taller and more graceful—that's presuming you decide not to compost this year's holiday poinsettias.

The traditional summer treatment for Christmas poinsettia plants is to sink the pots to the rims outdoors when the spring weather is warm and settled, to cut the stems back to six inches at this time, and to bring them back inside before nights drop below 50°F. Use a trowel or garden spade to excavate the pots and most of the roots that have grown out through the drain holes. Minimize

the trauma by resetting each poinsettia, old pot and all, into a container at least one to two inches larger in diameter, or big enough to accommodate the roots that have grown on the outside. Fill in with moist potting soil and water well.

Poinsettias can be propagated from tip cuttings of half-ripened wood in late spring or early summer. Strip off the lower leaves and cut off up to two thirds of the remaining leaves, to reduce transpiration and wilting. Set the cuttings aside to dry overnight, so the milky sap that oozes from the cuts has congealed, then insert to root in moistened rooting medium. Keep constantly moist, warm, and in bright light. They will root and be ready to pot up in a couple of weeks.

Beginning in the fall, poinsettia plants need warm days and moderate nights, 60° to 75°F. Protect them from cold drafts as well as from blasts of hot air from the heating system. In order to bloom on schedule, poinsettias must be positioned so that no artificial light shines on them from sundown to sunup during fall and early winter— October, November, and early December. Novice growers often become confused and think it is necessary to place the poinsettia in a closet and leave it there continuously until the flowers appear. (This proves a disaster for all.)

If the room in which a poinsettia is growing cannot be kept completely dark during the normal long nights of this season, placing the plant in a closet is one possible solution. However, the plant must be moved daily in the morning to a sunny place, then returned to the closet before lights are turned on at night. Right away this begins to sound like a full-fledged part-time job.

It is also necessary during fall that the poinsettia be given adequate water and nutrients. Water well when the surface starts to dry out before the leaves wilt. Apply fertilizer at half strength every two weeks, or in very dilute amounts with every watering until Thanksgiving. Thereafter it is best not to fertilize. When fertilizing poinsettias toward flowering time, use a fertilizer containing nitrate nitrogen, not ammonia nitrogen, as an excess of the latter can cause burning of the bract and leaf edges.

Once the poinsettia is in full bract color it needs evenly moist soil, average house temperatures, protection from both hot and cold drafts, and light at least strong enough to read by. Poinsettias age prematurely if over- or underwatered, subjected to prolonged chilling (temperatures below 50°F), or placed in weak light.

The poinsettia can also be a useful houseplant just for foliage. I think the thriving young plants are beautiful. Unfortunately in my apartment garden they have been preferred stopping places for bands of whiteflies. Since poinsettias and other euphorbias have an allergic (phytotoxic) reaction to insecticidal soaps, I have given up keeping holiday poinsettias. I have never had an insect problem with the more succulent species of *Euphorbia* (see Chapter 4, page 125).

Primrose. The Clause Company in France has been breeding new cultivars of *Primula obconica*, the German primrose, with unusually large heads of flowers that are especially strong in the color ranges of blue and apricot, also a sort of crushed raspberry. These are being seen increasingly in the Paris cut-flower market. The German primrose has been traditionally treated as an annual grown indoors as a seasonal flowering pot plant. Under the right conditions, it is possible to keep these plants from year to year. Crumble away some of the old planting medium and repot in spring. In the process one usually discerns several crowns or leaf rosettes growing together, so division is possible (see page 57). It experiences best growth and bloom at cool to moderate temperatures (40° to 70°F) in a bright, airy, moist environment. They can also be brought to beautiful bloom in a cool to moderate maxi light garden (see page 9). If you wish to grow these from seeds, plant them in spring or early summer, for blooms the following late winter-spring. (These seeds need light to germinate; sow on the surface of the planting medium. Enclose in glass or plastic to maintain constant moistness. Seedlings appear in about three weeks.) One caution: "Poison" primrose is a common name for *Primula obconica* because the leaves can cause a painful rash when touched or rubbed against. I recommend you handle these primroses only with rubber-gloved hands.

Potted garden primroses are offered universally as seasonal flowering pot plants beginning soon after New Year's and all through the coming weeks or months until hot weather. They look beautiful briefly in the house and

last best in cool, moist, fresh air with semisun. The fairy primrose, *Primula malacoides*, lasts longer indoors, but must have constant moisture and air movement, otherwise spider mites will obliterate it. *Primula malacoides* can be kept blooming for several weeks or months, until summer heat relegates it to the compost pile.

FORCING BULBS AND BRANCHES

Hardly any indoor gardening activity is as exciting to me as forcing spring bulbs and flowering branches into winter bloom. In either case, the farthest away from natural bloom time you want a bulb or branch to flower, the longer it will take. For example, a forsythia branch cut after a few days of a winter warm spell in early January may take several weeks to bloom out indoors while it might take only a few days if brought indoors in March. A cool, moist time for bulbs to root and for branches to condition is also fundamental to their successful forcing later on at higher temperatures.

Some of my favorite branches for forcing indoors, besides forsythia, are witch hazel, flowering peach, flowering quince, flowering crab apple, and flowering dogwood. The best time to cut and start the forcing process is during a winter thaw or at least a relatively warm spell when day temperatures rise above freezing. If you are a city dweller and do not have a garden, a friend in the country may permit some branch cutting, especially if you have a reputation for being a sensitive (and sensible) pruner. Otherwise, purchase the branches from a florist or cut-flower vendor. At home, recut each branch, removing at least an inch of the old wood. It will help the branch soak up more water if you split the bottom inch of it once or twice with your pruning shears. Plunge the prepared branch immediately in a deep vase or bucket of tepid water.

Branches will force most luxuriantly if they are brought along in a cool, sunny, airy place, such as a spare bedroom where the temperatures are not as warm as in the main rooms of the house. It also helps if the branches are wrapped lightly with moistened burlap or several thicknesses of newspaper for the first five to seven days after they are cut and placed in water.

Bulbs for forcing are offered for sale at local garden centers and through catalogs beginning at the end of summer and extending through autumn. The species and cultivars suited to the forcing treatment are clearly indicated on the labels. Detailed instructions follow for crocuses, grape hyacinths, hyacinths, lilies-of-the-valley,

Branches from trees and shrubs that bloom early in the season outdoors can be cut during a winter thaw or warm spell, and brought to bloom indoors standing in deep vases of water. Eastern dogwood blooms in a window with flowering orchids—red Ascocenda, *blue-and-white* Vanda—*in an arrangement at Mädderlake, a New York City florist.*

narcissus, including daffodils as well, and tulips. Bulbs like these can usually be planted outdoors in a permanent location as soon as weather permits digging. Do not attempt forcing the same bulbs again, however, as the process takes a great deal out of them. They will recover outdoors after a season or two and bloom satisfactorily.

Crocus belongs to the iris family and grows from a small corm. There are species and hybrids, and kinds that bloom naturally in fall or earliest spring. I enjoy potting and forcing the spring-flowering species and mammoth or Dutch hybrid crocus. Plant the corms in autumn, an inch apart and an inch deep in loam-based potting soil. Water well, write out a label, and set away to root in a dark, cool place where below-freezing temperatures will not occur. The vegetable crisper of the refrigerator makes a suitable spot for as many pots as can be accommodated. Avoid places where freezing could occur or where rodents have access. After eight weeks, or when a thrifty root system makes its presence known through the pot drainage holes, forcing can begin. Bring the pots to a half-sunny but cool window or fluorescent-light garden, where temperatures range between 40° and 60°F. Expect flowers in two or three weeks.

Grape hyacinths belong to the genus *Muscari* of the lily family. They have beautifully formed teardrop-shaped bulbs about an inch in diameter, and the flowers may be in several shades of blue, from pale to dark, or white. Plant and force as described above for crocus.

Hyacinth. Dutch hyacinths are often seen blooming in hyacinth glasses filled with white roots and water. Bulbs specially prepared for indoor forcing—"pre-cooled"—are best for growing this way. Regular hyacinth bulbs can be forced for early bloom indoors by potting them in a soil or soilless mix and letting them root in a cool, dark place for eight to twelve weeks before bringing to light and warmth to force the flowers. The varieties sold as "Roman" are better for houseplanting than the very large Dutch hybrids of the outdoor garden.

According to the official bulb forcers' manual from the Netherlands Flower-Bulb Institute, success with forcing hyacinths hydroponically into early bloom indoors is dependent on choosing the right cultivar, a proper hyacinth glass or vase with shoulders to hold the bulb, and keeping the water level such that only the roots are in it, not the base of the bulb. Some of the best large-flowered "Dutch" hyacinths for growing in water are 'Amsterdam', 'Anna Marie', 'Eros', 'Pink Pearl', 'White Pearl', 'Blue Blazer', 'Blue Jacket', 'Ostara', and 'Carnegie'.

Store prepared hyacinth bulbs in an airy place where temperatures range from 48° to 55°F until ready to plant. Once positioned to root in a hyacinth glass filled with water, set in a dark place with a fairly constant temperature of 48°F. Add water as necessary, so that the roots never dry out even briefly.

After ten to thirteen weeks at 48°F, water-rooted hyacinths are ready to begin active forcing in a sunny, airy

Crocus species and cultivars force readily into out-of-season bloom from inexpensive corms. These were grown from a preplanted, all-you-add-is-water kit, for flowers in early January.

window garden having moderate temperatures, 55° to 65°F. For the first few days in this warm environment it is a good idea to cover the emerging leaves and flower buds with paper cones, to stretch growth sufficiently out of the bulb so that it can mature fully. As you roll each cone, leave a peephole at the tip, through which light can enter and toward which the hyacinth flower bud will reach, thereby pulling itself out of the bulb so that each floret will have room to develop. Forcing time varies from three to five weeks in December and January, to as little as one week in April. The same hyacinth bulbs cannot be forced again, but they can be set four to six inches deep in the outdoor garden as soon as the ground can be worked in spring.

The various recommended temperatures are ideals. The closer they are matched, the better the results will be. In practice, of course, gardeners manage to succeed at forcing hyacinths in a variety of conditions. Often we may think that a certain temperature range is not possible, yet with a thermometer in hand and a little ingenuity, exactly the right spot can be found. Sometimes an old refrigerator can be turned into a cooler for the all-important rooting period; it keeps rodents from eating the bulbs and the thermostat maintains constant coolness. Or an attic window may turn out to have the perfect environment for bulb forcing. Another possibility, if your window has a recess of at least eight inches, is to outfit it with shutters that can be closed from the inside, so that the space between them and the window glass is quite cool in fall and early winter. This can make a great place to grow bulbs and other plants needing a cool, airy atmosphere during the winter heating season that so often turns the interiors of rooms into dry, hot spots.

Lily-of-the-valley is *Convallaria majalis*, a fleshy-rooted member of the lily family from temperate Asia and Europe that is sometimes forced for its exquisite white or pink flowers and their fragrance. Buy prepared roots (pips) in the fall. Space one to two inches apart with the buds just above the surface in a loam-based potting soil. Keep evenly moist and cool, not over 70°F, in a dark place for about ten days, then gradually expose to light, finally moving them to a place with about two hours of

A pot of Dutch hyacinths about to burst into bloom can be purchased in winter for surprisingly little money. Watching them come out and catching the fragrance as you enter their space is a definite mood enhancer for the season of short days, long nights, and grumpy weather in general. The shiny-leaved plant in the background is Mitriostigma axillare, *the African gardenia, which has white and heavily scented single flowers.*

sun daily. They will bloom in about three weeks. Afterward, either plant outdoors in a shady place or compost. Be sure to order roots for forcing, otherwise the nursery might not ship your lilies-of-the-valley until spring.

Narcissus. Of all the bulbs that can be planted indoors, the paperwhite narcissus symbolizes for me all the hope and joy of the holiday season. By staggering the planting days for even a half-dozen bulbs it is possible to have fragrant blooms opening over a period of several weeks, even a couple of months. November 11 is about right for starting bulbs for Christmas blooms.

To casual observers, it might seem that all paperwhite narcissus are created equal. If that is your impression, look again, for breeders and growers have lately come up with at least ten new cultivars or species not requiring a period of winter cold to bloom well indoors. According to bulb specialist Brent Heath of Daffodil Mart (see Resources), "Several cultivars of *Narcissus tazetta—N. t. papyraceus* (paperwhite), *N. t. chinensis* (Chinese sacred lily), and *N. t.* 'Soleil d'Or'—have been cultivated and forced for winter color since before the coming of Christ." Now we can thank Israeli growers for a new array of relatively cold-tender narcissus that bring color and scent to fall and winter indoor gardeners everywhere, and to outdoor ones in the U.S. Sun Belt.

'Bethlehem' ('Nony' in Israel) is thought to be the progeny of crossing a paperwhite with the French 'Soleil d'Or'. Up to fifteen creamy white florets with pale yellow centers rise on stems eight to twelve inches tall, making this one of the shortest of the new wave. The fragrance,

Great emphasis is placed on the flowers and fragrance of paperwhites and other narcissus that grow readily in the house garden. Less obvious is the beauty of the foliage in all stages for at least six to eight weeks, and especially when it is backlighted by the sun's rays, as here.

described by Heath as "mild, sweet," is delicately reminiscent of 'Soleil d'Or' rather than the other parent, which some say is an advantage.

'Ziva' is the newcomer from Israel that is most widely available and easily mistaken as nothing more than an unusually vigorous and heavily scented form of the French paperwhite 'Grandiflora', which it is. 'Ziva' is also the quickest to bloom, two or three weeks after planting, with up to eighteen very white florets per sixteen-inch stem. If you want paperwhites in full bloom for Thanksgiving, this is the cultivar to plant.

'Galilee'—another selected clone of the French paperwhite, also developed by the Israelis—takes three to four weeks to bloom. Shorter than 'Ziva', to twelve inches, with up to fifteen white florets per stem, it gives off "moderate, musky fragrance, a bit strong for a small room."

Heath considers 'Israel', 'Omri' to Israeli growers, "the finest paperwhite yet"—probably a cross with a *Narcissus tazetta* hybrid, bred as a cut flower. One to three strong, fourteen- to sixteen-inch stems grow from each bulb. Up to twenty large florets—creamy yellow with paler centers—bloom three to five weeks after planting; the fragrance is mild, sweet, musky.

'Jerusalem', called 'Shelag' by the Israelis, is the largest of the selected paperwhites, with up to four strong stems, sixteen to eighteen inches tall, per bulb. The largest of all flowers are pure white and mildly sweet. Heath considers it one of the best to date; it blooms three to four weeks after planting. Staking is not usually required.

'Nazareth' ('Yael' in Israel) looks to have originated from crossing paperwhite with 'Soleil d'Or'. Stems, ten to fourteen inches, may need staking. Each bulb bears up to three stems and ten florets, cream and yellow with a mild, sweet perfume.

In addition, these narcissus are available for forcing in pots or garden planting in milder climates: Chinese sacred lily (*Narcissus chinensis*), favored for its delicate, nonassertive scent, takes three to four weeks to produce several stems, twelve to fourteen inches tall, each bearing five to ten white florets with orange centers. It does require staking, a task that has become an artful pleasure to many indoor gardeners who have discovered the ancillary fascination of various staking materials and earthly ties such as raffia and sisal. A double-flowered sport of *N. chinensis* called 'Constantinople' is in commerce but not yet up to speed in terms of availability.

'Cragford' forces readily without special cold treatment but can also be used outdoors in USDA plant hardiness

Zones 5 to 9. Eight to ten weeks after planting indoors, these produce stems twelve to fourteen inches tall bearing several white florets with orange centers with a mildly musky scent. Unless fast-forced at high temperatures, these stems will not need staking.

'Grand Soleil d'Or' is hardy outdoors (USDA Zones 7 to 9); when planted indoors it blooms in six to ten weeks. Stems, twelve to fourteen inches, bear ten to twenty orange on yellow florets with a light, refined scent—perhaps the finest from this class. Real success with this narcissus is rare; forcing to bloom in midwinter is more realistic than earlier.

Heath notes other cultivars that "force well with minimal cool in a 40°F greenhouse for six to eight weeks: the *tazetta* group includes 'Avalanche', 'Grand Primo', 'Polly's Pearl', 'Erlicheer', and *Narcissus canaliculatus*. Others that bloom after eight to ten weeks of coolness include: 'Hawera', 'Minnow', 'Little Gem', and 'Little Beauty', *N. bulbocodium conspicuus* and *obesus*, *jonquilla*, *henriquesii* and *fernandesii*, and hybrid bulbocodiums."

Does it make a difference if paperwhites and other narcissus are planted in pebbles or soil? Heath says, "Paperwhites may be forced on pebbles and water but better results and longer-lasting flowers occur when a potting soil is used." A recent trend in growing narcissus is to set bulbs in a soil-based medium and sow ryegrass seeds on the surface. A grass ground cover gives plantings a natural appearance, the same as daffodils in a meadow.

Paperwhites are available from early fall until year's end. If not planted immediately, store in a dark, dry place around 63°F. Failure with paperwhites usually comes from too much heat (above 70°F) and allowing the roots to dry out after active growth has begun. Never leave unplanted bulbs where the sun shines directly on them. Do not store narcissus bulbs of any kind in the refrigerator because they are poisonous and could be mistaken for onions.

Traditional answers for what to do with paperwhites once they finish have been to throw them out or, at best, to commit them to the compost. Our present preoccupation with reducing waste and conserving resources has left many gardeners reluctant to grow anything that is to be summarily destroyed after brief garden pleasure. Experimentation is currently going on to grow narcissus bulbs after bloom in such a way as to produce foliage of sufficient quantity and quality to build up buds so they can bloom again indoors. Or, alternatively, to set paperwhites in the outdoor garden even in areas as much as two zones colder in the hope of finding them hardier than expected.

As an apartment gardener, I bring narcissus center stage when they are beginning active growth, up close to chairs, placed on tables, or sitting on the floor along my garden walk. Later I use them as background greenery, often leaving on the dried flowers; at several paces it is not obvious they are over the hill. Since any indoor plant, active and leafy, contributes to the oxygen supply, I consider paperwhites worth growing, even if there is no apparent use for the bulbs after one extended season.

Narcissus that we think of as daffodils can also be brought to early bloom indoors, following an eight- to ten-week period of cool darkness for the formation of a vigorous root system. The plain 'King Alfred' and larger 'Unsurpassable' are the most popular of the big ones. There are also miniature versions such as 'Tete-a-Tete' and 'Jack Snipe'. Plant and treat these hardy types very much as tulips (see instructions following), except they do better if planted as early in the fall as possible. In other words, if you have a choice, pot up daffodils first, then the tulips.

Tulips. Pots of tulips in bud or bloom can be purchased for seasonal color beginning at Christmas and continuing until nearly summer. There are also on the market tulip bulbs that have been precooled and can be brought to bloom indoors as early as Christmas without any special treatment. The mail-order firm of Breck's (see Resources) pioneered in this area and now offers, in addition to tulips in many colors, precooled bulbs of crocus, hyacinth, lily-of-the-valley (actually pips, not bulbs), miniature blue *Iris reticulata*, grape hyacinth, and daffodils and other narcissus.

Spring flower shows often feature a challenge class in which each gardener who enters works with exactly the

There are tulip bulbs available that have been preplanted and prechilled so that when water is added at Thanksgiving and encouraging growing conditions are provided, they will bloom precisely for the Christmas holidays. Also in the picture a passiflora being trained on a bamboo cane tepee and a young Euphorbia lactea *(far right).*

same plant materials. I was once asked to prepare the growing instructions for such an event at the New York Flower Show, to be held that year the second week of March. All who participated received the same number of bulbs of 'Princess Irene' tulip, to be forced in a seven-inch clay bulb pan. This cultivar is a single, early, orange-and-purple tulip, twelve to fifteen inches tall, that needs nineteen weeks of cold, then twenty-two days with 63°F night temperatures to force bloom. Here is the game plan:

1) On receipt, until potting up, store the tulip bulbs at 63°F in an airy, dark, dry place.
2) Tulips grow best in a well-drained, sterilized planting medium having a pH of 6.0 to 7.0. Packaged soilless mediums such as Pro-Mix and Baccto Professional Planting Mix are sometimes used, as well as the usual all-purpose mix of equal parts soil, sand, and peat moss.
3) When potting tulip bulbs, place the flat side of the bulb facing the rim. This is done so that the lowermost big leaf will develop toward the outside of the pot.
4) Set the bulbs to root in the dark at 48°F. Be sure

they never lack for moisture. (Mice, chipmunks, and the like find tulip bulbs an irresistible delicacy, so in selecting a rooting place, try not to tempt them.) One of the most successful bulb forcers I have known, Zelma Clark, worked her magic in an old refrigerator she kept in the garage. Every fall and winter it was packed to the gills with nothing but pots of all kinds of different bulbs, each precisely labeled as to name, planting date, estimated date for forcing to begin, and finally the ETA—Estimated Time of Arrival in bloom.

5) When roots grow out of the bottom of the pot, decrease the temperature to 41°F.
6) When the shoots are about one inch tall, decrease the temperature to near freezing, 32° to 35°F, to retard shoot growth so that a high-quality plant can be produced when actual forcing at 63°F minimum night temperature begins about three weeks before blooms are wanted.

Based on a show date the second week of March, begin the rooting process from mid- to late October, with forcing beginning about three weeks before blooms are desired. This is some challenge, but at the very least you will have some beautiful tulips at home, even if they miss the show. These instructions apply in general to all non-precooled tulips. When flowering finishes, the bulbs can be transplanted to a sunny, well-drained site outdoors, or consigned to the compost.

REDECORATING AROUND HOUSEPLANTS

Eventually there comes a time when every indoor garden has to be renovated, the walls and plaster have to be repaired, windows and sills conditioned, floors overhauled. All living occupants take something of a beating. Here are some lessons freshly engraved on my memory from a complete fix-up of my apartment:

COMMON TROUBLES OF FORCED BULBS

The Symptoms	The Cause	What You Can Do
Foliage is stunted, yellowish	May be botrytis blight, basal rot, smoulder, or bulb mite	Discard plant and soil; inspect bulbs at planting time and discard any that show signs of disease (sponginess or dark specks that may be sclerotia, the resting form of a fungus)
New leaf growth and flower buds covered with white, gray, or green insects	Aphids	Spray weekly or as necessary with insecticidal soap or neem solutions
Buds dry up before opening	Bud blast	Next year, provide cooler temperatures; keep soil uniformly moist at all times; be sure bulbs have good root systems before forcing is begun

1) Accept this as a time to evaluate your plants and to get rid of any that no longer give you particular pleasure. This may sound coldhearted, but plants do grow out of bounds indoors, the same as outside, and selective culling can do wonders for the overall health and appearance of the garden.

2) Houseplants in general are more delicate than the same plants would be if grown outdoors where the breezes help them grow stronger. Be gentle in handling and moving those you wish to save. If possible, move them to another room while their usual space is being redecorated.

3) If plants cannot be moved, enshroud them in tents of clear plastic sheeting. You may need to add tall bamboo or other stakes so that the plastic does not crush the leaves and upper branches. If you are opposed to plastic, bed sheets can be used, but they require more support and greatly reduce light to the plant.

4) Be sure the soil is moistened through and through before enclosing in plastic or cloth. Check for any signs of insects, especially mealybugs and tiny spider mites; both have a way of getting quickly out of control when plants are in close quarters, without fresh air, and perhaps in reduced light.

5) Walls that are being refinished usually require sanding. Try to keep the dust away from plants, but if any leaves become coated, rinse clean as soon as possible. Seal all African violets and other hairy-leaved plants in plastic bags; it is impossible to remove plaster dust from their surfaces and they will suffocate.

chapter three

Which Plant and From Where?

I once participated in a radio talk show along with a couple of other indoor gardening specialists. The host, a consumer advocate, asked that we concentrate on advising listeners how to buy plants. One of my colleagues thought only in terms of proper decor and furnishings—matching plants and containers to Early American, Contemporary or High Tech, English Country, and so on. The other took a most unscientific approach, classifying foliage plants as "boy," flowering as "girl," and saying that "macho" persons must never grow "feminine" plants, or vice versa. This is all nonsense. Buy the plants you like, the best and most beautiful. What really counts is matching the needs of the plants—light, temperature, moisture, air quality—to the space you can provide. There is also the matter of budget.

When it comes to buying plants, one of the biggest mistakes is to sit at home poring over books and making lists, drawing up floor plans, and deciding exactly what kind and size of plant will go where. Go shopping first, determine what is available and the prices. Make lots of notes and take as many measurements as may be needed. Then go home, mull all of this over, and lay your plans based on realistic expectations. Plants that start off clean and healthy are most likely to succeed. I would much rather see the commonest variety grown well and dis-

played with respect than the rarest specimen languishing from neglect.

Trees, hanging baskets, and large plants in general, the popular foliage plants such as pothos and spathiphyllum, and seasonal flowering types such as miniature cyclamen, kalanchoes, florist gloxinias, Rieger begonias, and poinsettias are usually purchased locally. Nothing is as important about this transaction as knowing your source. I am categorically opposed to buying anything from a merchant who displays tropicals outdoors when temperatures are below 60°F. Before you buy a plant, pick it up, or at least get close enough to it in good light to see if there are bugs; to see if leaf edges and tips are brown and dead; and to see if lots of the leaves have had brown and dead areas trimmed off. It's nice to have a well-groomed plant, but signs of too much grooming suggest a plant that has been mistreated and may be in a decline that will be hard to reverse no matter how green your thumb.

As an inveterate plant shopper I have gotten perfectly wonderful and perfectly awful plants from florists, plant shops, garden centers, supermarkets, dime stores, flea markets, and garage sales. All things being equal, I would say your best chance for purchasing healthy houseplants on any given day is at a full-service garden center which

The vast plant world represented in a house garden, beginning top right and moving clockwise: Kentia palm is from Lord Howe Island in the South Pacific; calamondin orange from China; dieffenbachia from the American tropics; tree fern from Australia; florist gloxinia from Brazil; African violet from east Africa; calathea from the American tropics; alocasia from tropical Asia; bird's-nest fern from India to Queensland and Japan; and cyclamen from Greece and the Mediterranean islands to Syria.

also offers a wide range of growing supplies and equipment or from a professional florist whose plants are displayed in a greenhouse. A third place where houseplant treasures can be found is at one of the regular sales held as fund raisers by botanic gardens, arboreta, and civic garden centers. Some of my finest plants have come from the fall houseplant sale held annually at the Brooklyn Botanic Garden.

PLANTS BY MAIL

Like local sources, these run the gamut from superb to really bad, some even engaging in misleading and dishonest advertising. What you have to watch for and ignore are the screaming-headline, ridiculous-claim advertisements in the Sunday papers. Usually what you see on the printed page is a mature showpiece, the likes of which the exhibitors at the Philadelphia Flower Show would be proud to claim. What you get is a puny seedling or cutting—with roots if you're lucky. The by-mail sources listed in the back of this book (see Resources) represent the sublime; most of them have been in business for many years and all are first-rate professional plant people. If you can arrange to visit any of these growers in person, by all means do so.

HOW TO MULTIPLY HOUSEPLANTS

The day you begin to propagate plants is the day you enter into a new and engrossing world. Miracles will happen on a regular basis—sprouting seeds, rooting cuttings, bursting seedpods you have cross-pollinated, and first blooms on your own seedlings. The possibilities are endless, ranging from beginner (rooting a coleus cutting in a glass of water), to intermediate (making a mallet cutting of philodendron), to advanced (growing ferns from spores). All the numerous methods for plant multiplication can be subsumed into two groups—vegetative and seed. Vegetative, or asexual, propagation uses cuttings, stolons, offsets, divisions, air-layers, and grafts. Seed, or sexual, propagation utilizes seeds and spores.

VEGETATIVE PROPAGATION

By cuttings. A cutting can be a single leaf from an African violet, or a terminal shoot or "slip" taken from

Angel's-trumpet brugmansia serves as an example of a cutting made from half-ripened wood. Large leaf tips have been cut to reduce evaporation of moisture and concentrate the cutting's energy on root production. Note how the leaves have been cleanly cut from the lower, woodier part of the stem. Insert the cutting in clean rooting medium so that at least one, preferably two or three, nodes where leaves previously grew are buried.

a stem or branch of a begonia, fuchsia, geranium, or similar leafy plant. ("Slip" refers to the practice of slipping a cutting from another gardener's plant when he or she isn't looking. If I did this it would for sure turn out to be poison ivy; besides, I can't recall ever going empty-handed when I have asked a gardener for a "slip.") Cuttings in general are more likely to root and grow if they are mature but not completely hardened, middle-aged in other words. Professional gardeners often root cuttings in a sieved mixture of rich soil and sand. Beginners often root them in water. Cuttings can be rooted in a wide variety of mediums—coarse horticultural vermiculite, perlite, milled sphagnum moss, clean sharp sand, or almost any combination of these ingredients.

Cuttings root faster when given a close, humid atmosphere. This need not entail an elaborate setup. A single cutting may be covered with a drinking glass, an empty jar saved from instant coffee, or a transparent plas-

tic bag to create a greenhouse atmosphere. Similarly, for a tray filled with cuttings, invert a large plastic bag over the entire planting to heighten humidity and promote rapid rooting. If cuttings are short, set a pane of glass over the propagator. There are numerous seed starters and miniature greenhouses on the market which work well for propagation.

Plastic bread boxes with transparent covers make excellent containers for cuttings. Use a heated ice pick to force a few ventilation holes in the top. This simple propagator is large enough to accommodate a dozen or more leaf cuttings, or perhaps eight tip cuttings from Swedish ivy or coleus.

Another favored propagator is an eight- or ten-inch clay or plastic bulb pan (a shallow pot) with a three-inch clay pot placed in the center, its drainage hole closed with a cork. The pan is filled with a rooting medium and the small center pot with water. Moisture seeping through the clay walls of the center pot furnishes the steady dampness needed by cuttings.

Large transparent plastic boxes, about eight inches deep and twelve by sixteen inches in dimension, are sold as storage boxes for sweaters. They make wonderful propagators. I keep a box like this going all the time in my closet light garden. Whenever I obtain a new plant, I try to make a cutting or two as soon as possible and insert it in this propagator. If the parent should die, I aim always to have a rooted replacement. The idea also is to have on hand spare plants that can be given to friends who may express a special interest.

Glass-covered casseroles can also serve as leaf or seed starters. A shallow redwood box built especially for propagating, covered with a pane of glass, also makes a practical propagator, especially on a sun porch or under fluorescent lights.

Select a propagating container according to the size and number of cuttings to be propagated. If the container has drainage holes in it, cover them with pieces of broken clay pot, or unmilled sphagnum moss. Add the planting medium and set the container in a tray or sink filled with tepid water. When the planting medium shows beads of moisture on the surface, set it aside to drain. When working with propagators having no drainage holes, moisten the planting material before adding it to the container. If using sphagnum moss or sphagnum peat moss, it needs to be moist enough to form a loose ball when squeezed.

Light, ventilation, moisture, and temperature must be in harmony to promote successful plant propagation. A warm, humid atmosphere and moderate moisture induce faster rooting. The majority of houseplants root well at 70° to 75°F, but some tropicals such as croton and ficus prefer a range of 75° to 80°F. I find these temperatures are maintained in my fluorescent-light gardens, but they may also be found in such places as on kitchen counters, on top of the refrigerator, or on top of a radiator that is not turned on but which stays warm as part of a central heating system.

Cuttings root best in a bright but not sunny area. This means keeping them away from the direct sun rays but where light is bright. Again, the cool, constant light given off by the tubes in a fluorescent-light garden is ideal for cuttings. Slip the pane of glass or plastic covering away from the propagating case at least every day or two to keep the side walls and ceiling from filling with condensed moisture. Cuttings that root in two to three weeks, such as English ivy, philodendron, and begonia, seldom need additional water. Cuttings that take longer may need occasional watering.

The gardener who needs only one more African violet, begonia, or ivy (is there such a person?) may not want to bother with the preparation of propagators and special rooting mediums. If this is your situation, root the cutting in water. Stick the end in a glass or bottle of tap water and watch it root. The crucial part of this system lies in transplanting the water-rooted cutting to a pot of soil. Roots grown in water are thicker and more succulent than those produced in soil. When shifted to a soil-filled pot, this kind of cutting may take a while to reestablish in soil. (The transition can be eased by setting the water-rooted cutting in a two-inch pocket of vermiculite made within the pot of soil.) Another quick and easy way to root a single cutting is to insert it in a premoistened Jiffy 7 peat pellet. I find that cuttings inserted in these root with exceptional speed.

Several years ago during a visit to the research facilities of the United States Department of Agriculture in Beltsville, Maryland, I was shown how when the amount of carbon dioxide in the air of a greenhouse was increased, the plants increased their rate of growth. Until recently it did not occur to me that this finding could have any practical application at home. However, as I placed three cuttings of the jasmine known as *Jasminum tortuosum*, each inserted in a premoistened Jiffy 7 peat pot, in a plastic bag, it occurred to me that if I blew air inside and then quickly sealed the bag tightly to maintain the ballooned state, perhaps the cuttings would root more quickly. As happens in many such casual gardening experiments, no control was set up, meaning I did not have three identical cuttings to place inside a plastic bag that was not enhanced by human-produced carbon dioxide. Be that as it may, the three cuttings rooted with lightning speed. As a practical gardener I know that the rapid rooting could be simply that the cuttings were made at precisely the right moment when they were at the perfect growth stage between soft and hard wood and the moon was in exactly the right phase.

How to make a cutting. Take a knife or pruning shears and sever leafy cuttings, such as those from gardenias, geraniums, and Jerusalem cherries, one fourth inch below a node, or joint. The length of petiole (leaf stalk) left on can vary; a one-inch petiole is likely to produce better plants than a cutting with a longer stem. When little or no petiole is left on an African violet leaf, the likelihood of mutation is increased. Remove only enough of the lower leaves so that the stem can be set in the rooting medium. Dry out cuttings full of sap before planting them. With cacti, the drying period may extend to several days. Before planting geranium cuttings, let the cut surface callus overnight.

Make a hole in the rooting medium with a pencil or your finger, then insert leafy cuttings one third to one half their length in the medium and settle it firmly in place. Do not let leaves touch the soil because this may cause them to rot. Given optimum conditions of light, temperature, and moisture, it takes five to six months to produce a flowering plant from an African violet leaf

California grower Mabel Corwin demonstrates putting down a begonia leaf to root in clean, moist medium comprised of horticultural vermiculite, perlite, sphagnum peat moss, and charcoal chips. It is contained in the bottom of a clear plastic sweater storage box.

cutting. Stem cuttings of geraniums, gardenias, and Chinese hibiscus often start to bloom soon after they have established a thrifty new root system, in only a couple of months.

Rex and other rhizomatous begonia leaves can also be handled this same way, or they can be propagated from wedge-shaped pieces cut from a large leaf, each of which contains at least one prominent vein. When inserted in a moist rooting medium, each of these is capable of sending up one or more new plants. Gloxinia leaves with a half-inch or longer petiole can be rooted. After a time a new tuber will form at the base of the petiole. Eventually the old leaf dies, and a new plant grows from the young tuber.

A most interesting way to propagate gloxinias, streptocarpus, and rex begonias involves making small cuts through the veins on the back of a large, healthy leaf. Lay the leaf on a moist propagating medium in a covered propagator. Plantlets will form at each place where the veins were slit. When these are large enough to handle, remove with as many roots as possible, and transplant to individual pots. Cover the plantlets with glass or plastic until they are strong enough to withstand the open air.

Other plants which may be grown from leaf cuttings include sedums, kalanchoes, peperomias, and echeverias.

Leaf bud or mallet cuttings of philodendron, ivy, and rubber plant (*Ficus elastica*) are made by cutting the leaves with a node and about an inch of stem below and directly above. The leaf forms a handle, the node and stem the head, hence "mallet" cutting. Insert so that the node points up, and is slightly covered by the rooting medium.

Propagate sansevierias from one- to three-inch sections of leaves cut horizontally and inserted into a rooting medium. Such leaf cuttings usually reproduce new plants exactly like those from which they were taken. *Sansevieria trifasciata* 'Laurentii' is an exception. When this variegated plant is propagated by leaf sections, it reverts to the plain green of the species. To multiply the variegated form, divide an old plant at the base.

One way to propagate large alocasias, dieffenbachias, dracaenas, philodendrons, and Chinese evergreens is to cut the old main stems into four-inch pieces. Coat the cutting ends with horticultural dusting sulfur or powdered charcoal to help prevent rot, then lay them on the rooting medium in a propagator. New plants will develop from the eyes (undeveloped buds) on the cane.

Rooting stolons. Some plants increase by sending out stolons or runners, small plants which dangle from the parents. Examples include strawberry begonia (*Saxifraga stolonifera*), episcias, and the spider plant. Piggyback or pickaback (*Tolmiea menziesii*) bears new plants on the top of old leaves; foliar embryos also occur in some begonias and ferns, notably the mother fern, *Asplenium bulbiferum*. The walking iris (*Neomarica northiana*) sends out plantlets at the end of the long, irislike blade which has borne the flowers. Propagate any of these by removing the new plants and rooting them as cuttings. Roots develop quickly and the plants will be ready for potting in about four weeks. A slight variation is to place a small pot of rooting medium close enough to the parent so that the stolon can be anchored in its new home, severing it from the parent when roots have grown from its base.

Propagation by offsets. African violets, other gesneriads, fibrous-rooted begonias, bromeliads, and haworthias are only a few of the countless plants which grow offsets or suckers. These small plants appear at the base of the old stem. They may be cut off with a knife and rooted as other cuttings are. While African violets and haworthias may send out dozens of offsets, bromeliads usually send out only one or two, and these only after the parent has flowered.

Amaryllis, fisherman's net (*Bowiea volubilis*), and many other bulbous plants increase by sending out small bulbs as offsets from the side or base of the parent. Remove these when they are one to two years old or at repotting time in late winter or early spring and replant directly into separate pots. The sea onion (*Urginea maritima*) sends out dozens of bulblets which cluster on the mother bulb. They are easily removed and started in any rooting medium. In all cases, flowering-size is reached at two to three years.

Propagation by division. Any plant with more than one stem emerging from the soil can be divided. Clivia, cane-stemmed begonias, African violets, ferns, and sansevierias are among the easily divided kinds. There are two ways to divide a large plant: 1) Take a knife and cut directly through the roots and soil, removing the separate divisions; or 2) knock the plant from the pot and gently pry the divisions apart. The direct cut method does seem ruthless but the plant may not suffer as great a setback as it will if the roots are pried apart. With either method, repot the divisions in clean soil, apply water, and shade from direct sun until the leaves regain firmness.

Tuber, bulb, and rhizome divisions. Tuberous plants such as gloxinias, tuberous begonias, and caladiums can be divided by cutting their tubers into sections, each having at least one eye or growing point—like a "seed" potato in the kitchen garden. Coat the cut surfaces with powdered charcoal or horticultural dusting sulfur and set

Partridge breast, Aloe variegata, *is typical of a plant that can be propagated by removal of an offset with roots (as shown here) or by division of a mature clump.*

them in a propagator. Once rooted, in four to six weeks, they can be transplanted into individual pots of soil, for maturity in about the same length of growing season as for whole tubers.

A number of gesneriads such as achimenes, smithiantha, and kohleria grow from scaly rhizomes resembling very small pine cones. The individual scales can be separated from the rhizome and planted as small seeds on the surface of a clean, moist rooting medium. They will sprout within a month and come into flower four or five months later.

How to air-layer. When large rubber plants, dracaenas, crotons, or similar specimens lose bottom leaves and become leggy, it is time to rejuvenate them. This can be accomplished by air-layering. There are two easy ways to do this: either remove a strip of bark directly below a node, or cut a notch in the stem. Then wrap the peeled or cut portion of the stem with damp sphagnum moss and cover it with a piece of polyethylene plastic. Seal at the top and bottom with electrician's tape or twist ties. If the seal is complete, no additional watering will be needed until the moss is full of roots and the new plant is ready for potting. If the seal isn't tight, the moss will have to be moistened occasionally. When roots show through the moss, sever the new plant just below the root formation and pot it. The old plant may send out new growth too, after having its top cut away. The air-layering technique may also be used among the branches of a tree or shrub to root any number of new plants without in any way endangering the health of the parent.

Grafting. Although grafting is practiced mainly in the outdoor garden, the houseplanter may enjoy experimenting with this form of propagation. In grafting, a potted plant is chosen for the stock, or standard. A bud, or a twig having several buds, called the cion, is inserted into the growing wood of the standard. At present, most houseplant grafting is done with cacti. The Thanksgiving or Christmas cactus is often placed on an upright growing standard such as myrtillocactus, trichocereus, or pereskia. To prepare a standard, cut a V-shaped cleft in its center. Trim the cion of the holiday cactus to fit the standard. Pin the cion to the standard with long cactus needles or secure the graft by applying Krazy Glue. Water sparingly only when topsoil feels dry. If the graft is successful, the cion will show new growth within a few months.

Air-layering, seen here on a choice croton cultivar at Alberts & Merkel Brothers nursery, Boynton Beach, Florida, is a safe, sure way to multiply a choice woody plant without endangering its health. Moist sphagnum moss surrounds a cut in the stem; crimped aluminum foil holds it in place and helps maintain constant dampness until roots form.

Willow Extract for Difficult Cuttings

If you're having trouble getting your cuttings to root, try the willow extract treatment:

1) Select and cut shoots of a willow's current year's growth. It can be a pussy willow, weeping willow, or any other member of the genus *Salix*.
2) Strip away all leaves.
3) Cut the stems into one-inch lengths and place in a cup or mason jar. Cover with water.
4) Enclose or screw the lid in place. Let sit twenty-four hours on the kitchen counter but not in direct sun.
5) Remove and discard the willow pieces. Now stand your cuttings—from any houseplant or woody type from outdoors such as peach, spirea, or azalea— in the liquid that remains for about twenty-four hours. It may be necessary to add some plain water so that the cuttings do not go dry.
6) Now set the cuttings to root in your favorite medium, such as peat moss and sand or coarse vermiculite and peat or perlite. Stand back! Of course, it helps if the cuttings receive bright light, but not direct sun until roots start to grow. Plants having large or floppy leaves will root better if half or more of the foliage is cut off. Also remove any flower buds. Situate where there is fresh air circulation but protect from drafts of hot or cold air.

I have also heard that coleus cuttings placed in the same water with other cuttings will have the same effect as willow. In either case it is the chemical rhizocaline that stimulates the formation of roots.

Small pots filled with fresh potting soil and topped with a layer of milled sphagnum moss are used to start seeds at Longwood Gardens, Kennett Square, Pennsylvania. Individual plastic bag enclosures help maintain suitable conditions for each kind of seedling. As soon as seeds germinate, the bags are opened so that fresh air can foster sturdy growth.

PROPAGATING HOUSEPLANTS FROM SEEDS

Seeds are miraculous. Take, for example, the smithiantha. This plant bears seeds so small that almost two million of them placed together make only one ounce.

Yet one of these minute seeds will germinate ten days from sowing, and will come into full bloom within eight months. The magic of a seed's sprouting, and its transformation to a mature plant, require careful attention from the gardener. If the seeds are viable, you, as the sower, provide the conditions that will lead to their successful growth. Besides the enjoyment you will get from watching them develop, seeds will provide you with an inexpensive method of increasing houseplants, and often a way of obtaining rare plants not listed by dealers.

Seeds come from species, hybrids, or fixed strains. Species are plants so nearly alike that they all might have come from a single parent. Examples are *Saintpaulia grotei* (trailing African violet), *Sinningia pusilla* (miniature gloxinia), and *Pilea involucrata* (friendship plant). Seeds from true species reproduce replicas of the parent. Hybrids are obtained by the cross-pollination of unlike but related plants (this process is discussed later in this chapter). Fixed strains are hybrids which have been inbred through several generations until their outstanding characteristics become so stable they can be propagated from seeds just as true species. Several named varieties of impatiens and coleus come true to type from seeds.

How to Plant Houseplant Seeds

Houseplant seeds may be sown in any of the containers suggested earlier in this chapter for propagating cuttings. Use screened sphagnum moss, vermiculite, or a mixture of equal parts sand and peat moss for the top inch of medium. Bottom heat (between 70° and 75°F) aids the germination of seeds and growth of small seedlings. Small soil heating cables are available in several sizes to fit individual needs. Inexpensive models for seed flats are usually preset at 72°F. Larger ones, for greenhouse benches and outdoor hotbeds, may be thermostatically controlled.

Sow seeds sparingly and as evenly as you can. Seedlings that are bunched together will have poor air circulation. Such plants are more likely to succumb to the damping-off disease, a kind of rot that attacks the seedling at the point where it emerges from the medium. An easy way to deal with dust-size seeds is to add them to one-fourth teaspoon of sterilized sand placed in a clean salt shaker. Sprinkle the sand and seeds evenly over the planting area.

If the seeds are dustlike or powdery, they should not be covered, but sown on top of a moist medium. If they are larger, the rule of thumb is to cover them to the depth of their own thickness. When I am working with seeds the size of those of coleus, impatiens, and gloxinia, I press them into the planting medium surface with the palm of my hand. No further covering is necessary.

As you finish planting a pot or flat, set it to soak in a basin of tepid water. When beads of moisture show on the surface of the medium, set the container aside to drain. Then enclose in plastic or cover with glass to maintain constant moistness until the seeds sprout.

Label each sowing, stating the variety and date and any other information you may need. This is a handy reference when you want to determine how long it took certain plants to grow from seed to maturity.

Check seed sowings daily. Never allow the soil to dry out. If it shows signs of becoming dry, add water. The bases of containers with drainage holes can be submerged in a sink or tray of lukewarm water. Those without drainage can be moistened by misting the surface. Sometimes I use a tablespoon for the careful addition of water to such a planting. If the medium should become dripping wet and stay this way for several hours, leave the cover off until the surface appears just nicely moist.

When seedlings show, move the tray to brighter light. The first two leaves that sprout from most seeds are cotyledons, which nourish the stem tip and the foliage leaves that follow. Until the foliage leaves appear, do not allow hot sunshine to reach the seedlings for more than a brief time, an hour or so in the morning. You can determine the amount of light seedlings need by learning the light requirements of the mature plant. One ideal place for all seedlings is three to six inches directly beneath the tubes in a fluorescent-light garden.

As soon as the seedlings begin active growth, fertilize every two weeks with very diluted liquid fertilizer. If the container does not make a strength recommendation for seedlings, mix at one third to one half the rate suggested for houseplants.

When seedlings are started in an atmosphere of closeness and high humidity, it is necessary for them to go through a hardening-off period to accustom them to the open air. If a lid covers the container, leave it off at first for an hour or two each day. As the seedlings progress, leave the lid off all day or night, and finally entirely. If a plastic bag is used to cover a pot or small flat, it can be left open for short periods at first, then gradually lengthening the time until it is not needed. Throughout this period it is imperative that the growing medium never dry out severely.

Transplant seedlings before they begin to crowd each other. They can go into individual small pots, or space can be saved by transplanting several into a community pot or flat. As they grow, the largest ones should be transplanted into separate containers. Use your fingers and a sharp instrument like a nail file or pencil to separate and lift tiny seedlings. Reset them at approximately the same depth as they have been growing, and firm soil gently around the roots. Water thoroughly from below.

Until transplants are established, keep them in a bright, warm place, but out of direct sun. At the start they will benefit from a few days spent inside a propagator, where the air is moist and there are no drafts.

Some of the most interesting plants in my present collection have been grown from seeds obtained through the Brooklyn Botanic Garden's Signature Seeds program, in addition to a company called Banana Tree (see Resources). Here is a list of some that have given the most pleasure, both to me and my friend Hila Paldi, another New York City apartment gardener:

Bolusanthus speciosus. The African or Rhodesian wisteria is a subtropical tree that can grow to twenty feet, with nine-inch racemes of violet flowers. It is suited to bonsai training. A legume, the seeds of this plant will sprout more readily if they are first soaked several hours or overnight in water that is quite hot (but not boiling) at the beginning. Plant one half inch deep and maintain constant moistness from the moment the presoaked seeds are sown. Provide temperatures of 70° to 75°F. Seedlings appear in about two weeks.

Brachychiton discolor. The bottle tree from northern Australia, Queensland, and New South Wales belongs to the sterculia family and grows to a hundred feet in warm zones. It is suited to bonsai training. Its five-lobed leaves are vaguely maplelike, lightly red-haired, and form a dense crown. It makes a showy indoor tree that can be kept to manageable size by annual root and top pruning.

Brachychiton discolor, *a towering tree outdoors in its native northern Australia, grows readily from seeds to become a handsome indoor specimen. The plant pictured, in a blue ceramic bonsai pot, is a year old and was grown by New York City apartment gardener Hila Paldi.*

Cordyline australis (trade name *Dracaena indivisa*). While this member of the agave family can become a tree, we know it mostly in the juvenile stage, namely second-year seedlings used as the centerpieces for formal bedding arrangements outdoors, either in the ground or in containers, notably Victorian urns. Seedlings grow well indoors, forming a fountain of gracefully arching bronzy green leaves with a midrib of bright green.

Dorstenia contrajerva. This Caribbean tropical member of the mulberry family makes a facinating houseplant, eight to ten inches tall, with silver-marked, deeply lobed leaves and a curious periscopelike inflorescence—equivalent to an inside-out fig, another plant belonging to the same family. Seedlings reach flowering size in six months when provided with warmth, moisture, and placement in a bright to sunny window or fluorescent-light garden. When the white, calcareous seeds are ripe they are catapulted into the air with amazing force.

Eucalyptus citriodora (lemon-scented gum). As a juvenile this tropical tree from Queensland, Australia, offers considerable potential as a container plant. The pendent, lance-shaped leaves are golden green and strongly lemon-scented.

Ficus benghalensis (banyan, East Indian fig). In the tropics this very large tree spreads by accessory trunks, suggesting the possibility of handling it indoors as a rock-planted bonsai. The leathery leaves, broadly ovate to elliptic, can grow to eight inches long but will reduce considerably under bonsai treatment.

Ficus religiosa (sacred bo tree). In the sixth century B.C. Buddha is said to have received enlightenment under this tree, a large tropical indigenous to India and southeastern Asia. The smooth, thin, bluish-green leaves have ivory or pinkish veins in an appealing heart shape with a long taillike drip-tip.

Harpephyllum caffrum. The African plum is a thirty-foot tree from South Africa with glossy pinnate leaves, white flowers, and one-inch edible red fruits that are used in jellies. It has an appealing asymmetrical shape with irregular branching. Easily grown outdoors in warm zones, or indoors as potted specimen, it is a candidate for bonsai work.

Hibiscus taiwaniana. A rarely listed tropical hibiscus with vining habit. The flowers are white in the morning, changing by noon to pink or red. Easily grown in a sunny, warm, airy place with plenty of water and fertilizer.

Leea coccinea (West Indian holly). Not a true holly but a member of the grape family, this attractive evergreen shrub has glossy leaflets and may flower—an inflorescence of small red buds—when only a foot tall. Grows to eight feet in mild-climate gardens (zone 10)

and elsewhere makes an outstanding container plant in any sunny warm place.

Microsperma 'Golden Tassel'. With foliage similar to that of *Primula chinensis*, this plant is topped by two-inch bright golden yellow flowers with a center of pollen-tipped filaments. This is an exceptional flowering plant for growing under lights.

Murraya paniculata (orange jasmine or Chinese box). A small shrub with glossy green leaflets, it bears fragrant white flowers intermittently through the year, followed by red fruit. This is a popular hedge plant in the tropics and easily grown indoors. It can be trained as a bonsai or as a tree-form standard. Needs sunny warmth and plenty of water.

Passiflora caerulea (blue passionflower). This tendril-climbing perennial vine blossoms the first year from seeds. Its intricate blue-and-white flowers, two-and-one-half to three-and-one-half inches across, carry a light scent. It can be grown in pots or hanging baskets, indoors or out, but needs lots of sun, warmth, and fresh air.

Schinus molle. The Peruvian pepper tree is a fast-growing ornamental to thirty feet with graceful weeping branches, feathery pinnate leaves, and clusters of showy rose-red berries. The trunk takes on the gnarling of an aged olive tree. A subtropical, it is easily grown indoors.

Tabebuia spectabilis (trumpet tree). A small tree belonging to the bignonia family and native to Venezuela and Colombia, it bears leaves made up of five leaflets to four inches long. Tabebuias begin flowering at an early age, the blossoms orange-red and three inches long, and may be cultivated in the North as indoor-outdoor container plants. Sow the seeds one half inch deep and maintain constant moistness and temperatures around 70° to 75°F. Germination takes two to four weeks.

Tamarindus indica (tamarind). A tropical fruit tree that can grow to eighty feet high, it is known for the fruit's tart pulp which is used in chutney and numerous other dishes. It makes an ideal indoor tree, easily kept to an attractive size and shape with pruning. It has a branching habit, with feathery pinnate leaves that are pendant. Sow the seeds one inch deep and maintain constant warmth, 70° to 72°F. Sprouting occurs in two to four weeks.

Terminalia catappa (tropical or Indian almond). This

plant's obovate, one-foot-long leaves turn a rich red before they fall twice a year. Its spikes of greenish-white flowers are followed by greenish or reddish fruit up to two inches long that contain edible, oil-bearing seeds. This Malayan native reminds me of the fiddle-leaf fig (*Ficus lyrata*) but has proven a better plant for my apartment garden.

Thevetia peruviana (yellow oleander). With evergreen leaves reminiscent of those of oleander or willow, thevetia bears fragrant yellow flowers two inches across. It is from tropical America and easily grown from seed to bloom in two seasons.

Growing Ferns From Spores

In addition to being propagated by division, ferns are grown from the spores which are borne in masses of precise design, generally on the backs of their fronds. (Some grow on separate branches.) Professionals sometimes sow the spores in an agar solution such as that used for growing orchid seeds. I plant them successfully in sterilized potting soil. Spores are available from specialists, or you can harvest them from your own ferns. When the powdery spores are maturing, clip the whole frond and place it in a paper bag. As the spores ripen, they become brown and even more powdery.

As soon as possible after they ripen, sow the spores on top of a mixture of equal parts garden loam, sand, peat moss, and leaf mold. I run this through a sieve, sterilize it in the oven (see page 16), and place it in four-inch clay pots that have an inch of drainage material in them. After scattering the spores on top of the medium, place a pane of glass over the pot. I set the pot in a saucer of water, as it is vital that spore plantings be kept moist, and the plantings are placed in a bright but sunless window or near the end zones of a pair of 40-watt fluorescent lights burned fourteen to sixteen hours daily. When the ferns have grown large enough to be handled on the point of a knife or nail file, I transplant them into small pots of sandy leaf mold and keep them in the same location. Later, as they mature, I use the young ferns in planters, hanging baskets, and dish and bottle gardens.

HOMEMADE HOUSEPLANT HYBRIDS

One of the most exciting sources for new plants is from seeds you have cross-pollinated. At various times in my life I have fooled around with begonias, gloxinias, African violets, amaryllis, and, currently, with abutilon or flowering maple. What I have done is not very scientific, but it has produced some interesting results that, at least to me, are a great pleasure to watch unfold. I have been making random cross-pollinations among upright hybrids of abutilon and the more lax-stemmed *Abutilon × milleri*, thought to be a natural hybrid of A. *megapotamicum*. *Milleri* has apricot-orange bells borne from reddish calyces and it is a popular subject as an outdoor wall espalier in English gardens. One pollen parent I have used a great deal is the female-sterile 'Golden Chimes', which is large-flowered, showy, and in bloom practically every day of the year. My goal is to get the color and habit of *milleri* into the type and size flower of 'Golden Chimes'.

I encourage you to experiment in pollinating flowers and committing to the ongoing process of seeing the progeny bloom. Abutilons are easy to pollinate, ripen seeds in a matter of weeks, and can be brought to bloom in a few more months.

The actual act of cross-pollinating goes like this: Remove the pollen-bearing flower during a warm, sunny, dry time of day and brush it onto the stigma at the tip of the pistil in the center of the flower chosen to bear the seeds. When the stigma is ready for pollination it generally widens, breaking into parts as in an amaryllis; or it may show an opening as in a gloxinia; or a feathery tip as in a geranium. If the pollination has been successful, the flower usually wilts within a few hours. Soon a swelling occurs in the ovaries located at the base of the flower. If the pod continues to develop, allow it to remain on the plant until slight yellowing begins or the color becomes brown, or the capsule shows openings. Remove and place the pod in an open container to finish drying. The seeds can then be removed, cleaned of any chaff, and stored or planted at once. Professional plant breeders keep meticulous records, otherwise success would be achieved only randomly and possibly never replicated.

I have always been a pollen dabbler and seed collector,

Mabel Corwin demonstrates pollinating a female begonia flower (the pink one) with pollen from a male. Begonias produce both flower sexes on the same plant. (Hollies and kiwis, for example, produce male and female flowers on different plants.)

Here Mabel transplants begonia babies from the seed tray using a dentist's tweezers. The seedling leaves of all begonias look approximately the same, but the true leaves soon develop and take on their unique shapes and colors.

Mabel Corwin crossed a commercial hybrid 'Glamour Rose Picotee' Begonia semperflo-rens with an unidentified species obtained as seeds through the American Begonia Society and got this outstanding hybrid that has been formally registered as 'Christmas Candy'.

but since my move to Texas, there seem to be more opportunities. It pays to carry a supply of brown paper bags and plastic ones that zip or can be tied. Film canisters are also handy and a lead pencil or indelible pen for labeling. Sometimes one has no alternative but to gather seeds when they may be somewhat immature, or the capsule is wet from rain. In either event it is necessary that they be set out to dry within a few hours of their collection before rot sets in. Slightly green seeds sometimes draw enough sustinance from their encapsulation—the seed pod itself—to ripen into viability.

When collected seeds are dry, I clean them and store by kind in coin envelopes. As time permits, or the gardening spirit moves, some actually get sown. Others are shared with friends who garden. It makes for an interesting life in which one is always making new friends, both plants and people. Some of what I pick from other gardens and roadside ditches might be considered weeds but to me they hold some promise—for a pot on the terrace, a shelf on the wall, or maybe dwarfed for a fluorescent light garden in the house.

Houseplants Arranged by Families

I n this section more than five hundred different houseplants are arranged alphabetically according to plant families. For example, philodendrons are discussed with the Arum family. To find a plant whose family name you do not know, refer to the index. If you have only a plant's common name, the index will guide you to its botanical name and family. Unless noted otherwise, fertilize plants according to the general directions given on page 22.

My checkpoints for taxonomy—the botanical names for plants—have been *Hortus Third* (Macmillan Publishing Company, 1976), *Exotic Plant Manual* by Alfred Byrd Graf (Roehrs, East Rutherford, New Jersey 1974), *The American Horticultural Society Encyclopedia of Garden Plants* (Macmillan, 1989), and in particular these catalogs from houseplant specialists: Glasshouse Works Greenhouses, Kartuz Greenhouses, Lauray of Salisbury, and Logee's Greenhouses (see Resources for addresses).

ACANTHACEAE. *Acanthus Family.*

Tender perennials with simple, opposite leaves. They bear spikes of irregular, one- or two-lipped flowers. Genera of interest for houseplanting include *Acanthus, Aphelandra, Chamaeranthemum, Crossandra, Eranthemum,* *Fittonia, Hemigraphis, Hypoestes, Justicia, Pachystachys, Pseuderanthemum, Ruellia, Stenandrium, Strobilanthes,* and *Thunbergia.*

Acanthus mollis (bear's breech), three to four feet high, from southern Europe, has handsome, large, toothed foliage. Bears showy spikes of white, rose, or lilac flowers. An indoor/outdoor plant, its leaves are a motif in classical architectural ornamentation. Needs semisunny situation, 50° to 70°F in winter, and fresh, moist air. Give evenly moist, loam-based potting soil. Propagate by seeds in spring; divide in spring or fall.

Aphelandra is the zebra plant, known for its distinctively cream-variegated glossy green leaves on nearly black stems. Growing strongly upright, two to three feet, it is topped from late summer through fall with a colorful, long-lasting, yellow bract from which ephemeral white flowers appear. The best specimens are those started from tip cuttings in late winter to early summer. Since the largest leaves wilt badly at first, it helps if you scissor off one half to two thirds of their length before setting them to root. Turgid new leaves in two to three weeks indicate the roots are growing; transfer to individual six-inch pots. Stressed aphelandra invites spider mites and mealybugs.

Beloperone is a name once used for the popular shrimp plant. See *Justicia.*

Chamaeranthemum gaudichaudii is a small Brazilian creeper with silver-centered dark green leaves that are small and oval. *Chamaeranthemum igneum* from Peru has more pointed leaves, brownish green with a soft suedelike appearance, and veining in shades of red and yellow. *Chamaeranthemum venosum* from Brazil differs in having small, hard leaves netted with silver. All bear small but showy clusters of bracted flowers and are ideal for terrariums. Needs semishady or light garden, average house temperatures, moderate to high humidity (no drafts). Give it humus-rich, loam-based potting soil kept evenly moist. Propagate from late winter to summer by tip cuttings in moist rooting medium and high humidity.

Crossandra infundibuliformis (formerly *C. undulifolia*), a native of India growing one to three feet high, really gets up, grows, and blooms when the spring season finally turns consistently sunny, warm, and humid. This makes a beautiful specimen in terra-cotta pots outdoors in summer. Tubular blossoms, expanded at the top, are borne on fairly long, thick, four-sided spikes and are heavily bracted in green. The color is salmon-orange and a well-grown plant can be nearly everblooming; in winter, it's an excellent candidate for a warm maxi light garden. Propagate from midwinter to early summer by sowing fresh seeds, or by taking tip cuttings, and keeping in constant warmth (70° to 80°F) and high humidity.

Eranthemum nervosum, one to four feet high, from India has small, ovate, rough leaves above which appear bracts of one-inch gentian blue flowers in midwinter. A wonderful Texas gardener, Mrs. Morris Clint, sent me my first eranthemum when I was a child in Oklahoma. Later, her daughter Marcia C. Wilson became a correspondent in the pursuit of unusual species of *Hippeastrum*. They both had an unerring eye for plant beauty that transcended the ordinary. Eranthemum care is the same as for *Crossandra*.

Fittonia verschaffeltii, the nerve plant from Peru, is a semiupright (to eight inches) or trailing plant with pink-veined leaves. The variety *argyroneura* has white-veined leaves; *F. v.* var. *pearcei* has papery, thin, olive-green leaves with carmine veins. There is also a miniature, *F. v.* var. *argyroneura* 'Minima', having white-veined green

Chamaeranthemum igneum.

leaves about an inch long. All are excellent choices for terrariums, or as ground cover around an indoor tree in a large container. They need bright diffused sun or a light garden and average house temperatures with moist air. Provide humus-rich loam-based potting soil kept evenly moist. Tip cuttings will root in warmth and high humidity.

Hemigraphis colorata (red or flame ivy) is a creeper from Java with smooth, glossy leaves that are reddish purple in semisun, silver in shade. It bears pleasant clusters of white flowers. Its culture is as for *Fittonia*, but it is too large for a terrarium. Often used in outdoor bedding-plant schemes in warm weather.

Hypoestes sanguinolenta (freckle face or polka dot plant), one to two feet high, from Madagascar, has pointed, oval, dark green leaves spattered with pink to rose to pure white markings. Recent breeding work has produced a generation of low, base-branching hypoestes that make nearly ideal ground covers for a variety of indoor gardening situations. As a rule, the stronger the light, whether from sun or fluorescent tubes, the more prominent the leaf color differences. Grow in a sunny bright or maxi light garden, with average house temperatures and fresh, moist air. Give it a loam-based, humus-rich potting soil kept evenly moist. Easily propagated from seeds or cuttings. Second-season plants can be rejuvenated in spring by cutting back to an inch from the soil and repotting.

Justicia brandegeana (shrimp plant), listed until recently as belonging to *Beloperone*, is wiry stemmed, to one and a half feet, and needs frequent pruning to prevent scraggliness. The brick red, overlapping and drooping bracts that surround the flowers resemble its namesake. The true flowers, small and white, are not very noticeable. The cultivar 'Yellow Queen' has chartreuse bracts. The best specimens I have seen were managed as indoor/outdoor plants in pots, boxes, and hanging baskets. Grow in a sunny or maxi light garden with average house temperatures and fresh, moist air. Give it a loam-based, humus-rich soil kept evenly moist spring and summer, and on the dry side during fall and winter. Propagate by cuttings anytime.

Justicia carnea (Brazilian plume or king's crown), from Brazil, is listed in earlier books as *Jacobinia carnea*. It grows three to four feet, has large, dark green, quilted leaves topped with a huge, bracted head of clear pink, arched, two-lipped blossoms. It blooms spring and summer and is best started annually from tip cuttings in winter or early spring.

Pachystachys lutea (lollipop plant) has large golden bracts held like candles in a candelabra, with ephemeral true white flowers. Start from cuttings each winter or spring for summer flowers. This is an excellent container plant for indoor/outdoor existence. Care as for *Justicia*.

Pseuderanthemum alatum (chocolate plant), one foot high, from Mexico, has coppery brown leaves blotched with silver-gray near the main rib. *Pseuderanthemum atropurpureum tricolor*, a small shrub from Polynesia, is more beautifully variegated. It has heavier-textured, almost leathery leaves of metallic purple irregularly splashed with green, rose, and white. Excellent for terrarium culture when small enough. Otherwise, treat as for *Crossandra* (see page 67).

Ruellia amoena, one to two feet, from South America, is noted for its bright red, pouched blossoms borne in sprays from the leaf axils. It has green, papery leaves narrowed at both ends. *Ruellia makoyana*, a low, spreading plant from Brazil, is valued chiefly for its foliage, small satiny, olive-green leaves with purple-red shadings and silvery veins. Its flowers are funnel-shaped, a rosy carmine. Care the same as for *Crossandra* (see page 67).

Stenandrium lindenii, six to twelve inches, from Peru, is a trailing plant with broadly oval, dark green, velvety leaves. These have a feathering of creamy white along the veins, and purplish undersides. The flowers are yellow, held on three-inch spikes arising from the axils. Excellent for terrariums, otherwise care the same as for *Crossandra* (see page 67).

Pachystachys lutea *(yellow)*, Acalypha hispida *(red)*.

Strobilanthes dyeranus (Persian shield) is a showy foliage plant that originally came from Myanmar. The leaves, up to eight inches long, combine silver, phosphorescent rose, and purple on an upright, branching shrub to two feet tall. Pale blue-violet flowers to one and one half inches across occasionally appear in late summer, but it is for the leaves that this plant is cultivated.

Persian shield needs constant warmth and moisture in half shade to half sun. It looks especially beautiful outdoors in warm, frost-free weather in the company of dusty miller and any pink flower, such as impatiens, petunia, dwarf hardy aster, or chrysanthemum.

Bright light brings out the leaf color. Protect from strong midday sun outdoors in summer. Winter over indoors in any exposure affording warmth and some direct sun, or cut back as necessary and place in a light garden. Needs tropical warmth, 60° to 80°F, and fresh, moist air; protect from cold or hot drafts. During spring and summer keep it evenly moist; no extremes of wet or dry. Give Persian shield humus-rich, loam-based soil, preferably made up of well-rotted compost, leaf mold, and sphagnum peat moss mixed with some clean, sharp sand. Best foliage color develops when plants are outdoors in bright diffused light, with moderate to high humidity. Shower leaves daily when outdoors. Indoors set pot on pebble humidity tray and mist once or twice daily. Apply fish emulsion or liquid seaweed every two weeks spring through summer.

Start fresh from tip cuttings, four to five inches long, in the late winter to early spring (young plants have the most colorful leaves). Keep constantly warm and moist; enclose the planting in glass or plastic until emerging new leaves signal that rooting has occurred. To rejuvenate an old Persian shield, repot in late winter or spring. Crumble away a third of the soil and roots and cut back the branches by one third to one half. Return to the same pot or one a size larger. Fill in with fresh soil, water well, and keep in a warm, shaded place for five to seven days, then move to stronger light with some direct sun.

Thunbergia alata (black-eyed Susan vine), a four- to six-foot vine from tropical Africa, has apricot or white flowers with purple centers. It is a tender perennial usually cultivated as an annual from seeds sown in a warm, sunny place or light garden in winter or spring. After a period of heavy bloom, cut back nearly to soil level. This promotes new growth and more flowers. This cutting back combined with regular fertilizing and yearly repotting can be used to keep *T. alata* as a perennial indoors, ideally summered outside. It can be trained as a hanging basket, around a twelve- to fifteen-inch wreath form, or on a three- to four-foot tepee of bamboo stakes. *Thunbergia grandiflora* (blue-sky vine), ten to fifteen feet, from India, is a shrubby vine with showy blue flowers. Nice for a large sun porch, it needs to be trimmed back as necessary after flowering. For care, see *Strobilanthes* above.

AGAVACEAE. *Agave Family.*

About twenty genera from dry regions in the warmer parts of both hemispheres. Members are rhizomatous, perennial herbs, long-lived, rosette-forming or woody, branched and treelike. Their leaves are usually narrow, sometimes marginally toothed, often densely spaced in a basal rosette or at a branch tip. Members of this family have appeared variously in the past as being from both the lily and amaryllis families. Of interest here are the genera *Agave, Beaucarnea, Cordyline, Dracaena, Pleomele, Polianthes, Sansevieria,* and *Yucca.*

Agave desmettiana, formerly A. *miradorensis* (dwarf century plant), from Mexico, has broad, gray-green leaves arranged in a symmetrical rosette, to two feet across. *Agave americana* 'Marginata', variegated century plant, also comes from Mexico, combines blue-green and yellow in its long leaves, and is grown potted while young (and small enough to accommodate). There are many other agaves, but their armament and huge size frequently prevent use indoors. They are often confused with aloes (members of the lily family). The spine-tipped leaves of agaves are tough and fibrous, with hard, sharp teeth, while those of the aloes are soft, fleshy, almost pulpy. I can worship the beauty of a well-grown agave, but I am always aware of the harmful potential of its dagger-pointed leaves. Give your agaves a sunny place and average house temperatures with warm, fresh air. They need well-drained, loam-based potting soil kept

Agave americana *'Marginata' surrounded by cacti.*

evenly moist in spring and summer, on the dry side during fall and winter.

Beaucarnea recurvata, to thirty feet, from Mexico, has a swollen base that inspires the common name elephant foot plant and in which it can store a year's supply of water. Topping the bulbous base is a rosette of thin, exceedingly long, tough leaves that form a graceful fountain effect as they fall all around, the reason for its other popular name, ponytail. Books say it produces panicles of whitish flowers, small and lightly fragrant, but I have never seen them. My specimen lives five feet back from a half-sunny window, on top of an old sewing machine. This beaucarnea began as a one-year-old seedling, a gift to my daughter Jeannene, now twenty-eight, when she was in grammar school. Someday I expect to pass it back to her, the very sort of sculptural plant that will look at home in Colorado, where she lives. In a long corridor at the Brooklyn Museum there is a row of beaucarneas in matching planters, each standing at least six feet

tall, that seem to have adapted well to the bright diffused light and a situation where the air is alternately drafty or stale, chilly or overheated. Beaucarnea is tough and adaptable. It can't take freezing, burning, or standing indefinitely in water; otherwise, this succulent that can vary from bonsai-tree-size to shoulder high or more, gets all the stars I can give for a great and durable houseplant. Ideally beaucarnea needs half to full sun, fresh air that circulates freely, and a loam-based potting soil that is kept between evenly moist to on the dry side. It requires no pruning but tips that die back can be trimmed at the discretion of the gardener. Propagate by sowing seeds to depth of their own thickness in spring in moist potting soil.

Cordyline terminalis, from India, and its many cultivars, including the popular Hawaiian ti, are potentially showy and durable foliage plants. They mature with a crown of palmlike leaves atop a trunk or cane which may grow to ten feet or more outdoors in warm climates, but considerably less when the roots are restricted by a pot.

It is important to long-range health (no prematurely dead leaf tips) and freedom from spider mites that Hawaiian ti and other such leafy sorts have plenty of root room in fresh soil and a constant supply of moisture. *Cordyline australis* and *C. indivisa* are grassy, rosette-forming plants grown from seeds and known in the nursery trade as dracaena; they are the familiar central fountain element in Victorian urn plantings, and make tough houseplants for a sunny spot having fresh air circulation. Care as for *Agave* (see page 69), but add more humus to the soil and water a little more often.

Dracaena (corn plant) is a genus that has given us decorative foliage plants with sword-shaped leaves, often vertically striped in a lighter shade of green, even silver, white, or cream. A recent introduction is miniature *D. deremensis* 'Janet Craig Compacta', a genetically dwarfed form of one of the most popular foliage plants in cultivation. While the regular 'Janet Craig' will grow quickly to several feet, right up to the ceiling in a few years, 'Compacta' has been described as "maddeningly slow-growing." The gardener who has plenty of sunlight and space probably won't find this little plant of much interest, but for me it is an enduring spot of encouraging green on a side table that is at least ten feet back from my living room windows.

'Janet Craig Compacta' forms a rosette of medium to dark green leaves that measures about eight inches across and in a year's time may grow only a few inches taller. One of my books says it can be two to three feet tall, but I have never seen one more than half this height.

More recently introduced is *Dracaena deremensis* 'Warneckii Compacta', which has the same white lines through silvery green and dark green leaves as the standard 'Warneckii', yet it too might be said to be maddeningly slow-growing. Since this variety has variegated foliage, it looks nice sitting next to the plain green 'Janet Craig Compacta'.

Either of these compact dracaenas is the perfect size to grow in a five-inch pot. Use a loam-based potting soil and water so that the roots always have some moisture. Avoid extremes. Dead tips on older leaves are a sign that the soil is becoming too dry between waterings.

Although no amount of fertilizing will make 'Compacta' dracaenas grow rapidly or revert to their original larger forms, light applications of foliage plant fertilizer will give the leaves a lively sheen and boost new growth. Since these are small plants, they can be easily showered in the sink every week or two to keep them rain-fresh. Insects aren't likely ever to take up residence on either of these tough and, to me at least, beautiful foliage plants that thrive in the same temperatures and lighting conditions we enjoy indoors. They can be propagated by rooting two-inch portions of older, leafless stems, or from three- to four-inch tip cuttings inserted in moist rooting medium and kept evenly moist in bright light.

Dracaena fragrans, from Ethiopia, Guinea, and Sierra Leone, was the species best known to Victorian homes, a large-growing plant with soft, leathery leaves of shining green. Its cultivars show extremely colorful variegation, being banded, striped, or margined in yellow or cream. The species sends up terminal racemes of small, creamy white, fragrant flowers on occasion.

Dracaena goldieana, from upper Guinea, is broad-leaved but grows in rosette form. The foliage is cross-banded with pale green or white, and this is considered the jewel in the crown of dracaena foliages. It will appreciate extra warmth and humidity in bright diffused sunlight. Excellent companion for bromeliads, orchids, and gesneriads.

Dracaena marginata, from Madagascar, has long, narrow, dark green leaves banded marginally in red, set rosette fashion along slender, twisting canes. Its cultivar 'Tricolor' combines white, pink, and at least two shades of green in thin, distinct bandings up and down the narrow leaves. These plants are typically sold as rooted cuttings, from eighteen inches to several feet tall.

Dracaena surculosa (formerly *D. godseffiana*), from Guinea and Zaire, and its cultivars/varieties display an entirely different growth habit from most dracaenas. These are small plants, at least in their parts, inclined to be shrubby, with wiry stems, bearing leaves in pairs or tiers of three, irregularly marked with yellow or white. They often appear in dish gardens but when potted individually, one plant can increase in size over a period

Dracaena marginata *'Tricolor'*.

of a decade to the point of filling an eighteen-inch tub and rising four to six feet high.

Pleomele (song of India) is closely allied with dracaena; *Hortus Third* lists it as *Dracaena reflexa* but I am entering it here under *Pleomele* since that is the name used in trade. The plain green *P. reflexa*, from Malaysia, and its yellow- or cream-striped cultivar 'Variegata', from southern India and Sri Lanka, make outstanding large indoor foliage plants that may be trained as bushes or tree-form standards. Pleomele will adapt to mostly bright light, but also grows well in up to a half day of direct sun. Any branches pruned or broken accidentally will readily root if stuck in moist soil. An older pleomele can be revitalized by repotting and removal of the oldest, woodiest branches near the base. This will encourage new shoots from the ground and vigorous growth in general. I have been using two large pleomeles as a room divider in my living room for some years. They serve as living curtains, affording privacy from the apartment building opposite without shutting out the outdoors.

Polianthes tuberosa (tuberose), reaching a height of three and a half feet in bloom, bears its leaves in a one-and-a-half-foot-tall basal rosette, arising from the fleshy rhizomes. This very fragrant summer- and fall-flowering plant with single or double blossoms is not known in the wild. It is not grown as a houseplant but rather adapts well to pot culture for indoor/outdoor life. Potted specimens brought into bloom outdoors in summer will last several weeks when brought indoors to bright light, average house temperatures, and good air circulation. Outdoors they require full sun and a humus-rich, loam-based potting soil. Water them abundantly in spring and summer; keep dry and cool during fall and winter, during which time the pots can be turned on their sides in a basement or other frost-free place.

Sansevieria consists of about sixty species and untold numbers of varieties and cultivars of stiff, erect perennial herbs from the arid parts of Africa and southern Asia. *Sansevieria cylindrica*, to five feet, from South Africa, has round, tapered, dark green leaves and pink flowers. *Sansevieria trifasciata* (snake plant, mother-in-law's tongue), from India and tropical Africa, and its many varieties are grown for their stiff, usually spearlike, often variegated leaves. They may be divided into two classes—

Sansevieria cylindrica.

the bird's-nest types which form low (to eight inches), neat, compact rosettes of foliage, and the tall kinds (to five feet), whose leaves stand erect from the soil surface. The leaves may be plain green or crossbanded with lighter or darker shades, or banded or margined with near white or bright yellow. Occasionally sansevierias send up tall, showy, arching sprays crowded with small, greenish white, fragrant flowers that drip with honey. These are among the most collectible of houseplants, enduring and tolerant of almost all conditions except freezing, burning, and drowning. Three or four different sansevierias thoughtfully potted and groomed can make a beautiful and lasting tablescape or shelf scene, indoors or out.

Ideally, the sansevierias need half to full sun and a loam-based potting soil kept between evenly moist and on the dry side. They can be propagated by division, from late winter to early summer, or from two-inch leaf wedges, the latter ineffectual for variegated sorts having a contrasting band of color along the leaf edges, since plantlets that arise from this type cutting will revert to their plainer-leaved relatives.

Yucca includes about forty species found in the warmer regions of North America. Some from drier regions are outfitted with dagger-pointed leaves and these are definitely not user-friendly as houseplants. However, Y. *aloifolia* 'Marginata', Y. *elephantipes* and its cultivar 'Variegata', and Y. *gloriosa* and its cultivar 'Variegata' all make satisfactory houseplants. They require sun, average house temperatures, and good air circulation. Give them well-drained, loam-based potting soil kept evenly moist in spring and summer, on the dry side fall and winter.

AIZOACEAE. *Fig-Marigold Family.*

Subtropical tender succulents with single, daisylike flowers. Genera include *Aptenia, Argyroderma, Cheiridopsis, Conophytum, Delosperma, Dinteranthus, Erepsia, Faucaria, Fenestraria, Gibbaeum, Glottiphyllum, Hymenocyclus, Lampranthus, Lithops, Mesembryanthemum, Nananthus, Ophthalmophyllum, Pleiospilos, Rhombophyllum, Titanopsis,* and *Trichodiadema.*

Dinteranthus wilmotianus *var.* impunctatus.

Aptenia cordifolia, a creeper or trailer from South Africa, has small, mealy, light green, heart-shaped leaves and tiny purple flowers in spring and summer. When allowed to cascade from a hanging basket, it will reach a length of one to two feet in a season. This is one of the several popular ground covers called ice plant. Needs sun, warmth, fresh air, a loam-based, well-drained soil, and more moisture in warm weather. Propagate by stem cuttings in late winter and spring.

Dinteranthus is a genus of small succulents from the Cape and Southwest Africa known as split rocks, for the cleft in the stemless succulent leaves. D. *wilmotianus* var. *impunctatus* is very small, 2 cm. in diameter, pink-tinged gray. In summer there are glowing daisylike flowers arising from the center. There are numerous species, some spotted or dotted grayish brown, but all having similar shapes and flowers. They are readily confused with *Lithops.* Care as for *Lithops* (see page 74).

Faucaria tigrina (tiger jaws), from South Africa, has a low rosette (three inches) of pairs of fleshy, triangular leaves having teethlike structures along the edges, hence its common name. The gray-green leaves are heavily spotted with white. Tiger jaws bears flat, large, daisylike yellow flowers in autumn. *Faucaria tuberculosa* (knobby tiger jaws) has similar leaves that are dark green and warty.

Both need sunny, warm, fresh air and soil made up of one part peat, one part loam, and two parts sand; or six parts sand, three parts loam, two parts leaf mold, and one part crushed brick. Water well, then not again until nearly dry. Propagate by seeds in spring or fall or by cuttings of young basal offsets in late spring. Allow cuttings to air dry a few hours or overnight, then set to root in barely moist sand.

Fenestraria aurantiaca (yellow flowers) and *F. rhopalophylla* (white flowers) are miniature succulents one to two inches tall from South Africa. They form clusters of toelike leaves, hence their common name baby toes. The translucent area at the top of each succulent body is called a window. Care as for *Faucaria*.

Lampranthus emarginatus (ice plant), one foot high, from South Africa, has very narrow leaves attractively set off in summer with many purple, daisylike flowers. *Lampranthus multiradiatus*, also from South Africa, is more trailing in habit, to two feet, when allowed to cascade

Fenestraria aurantiaca.

from a basket or shelf; it bears two-inch pink flowers. It needs sunny, warm, airy conditions and a loam-based, well-drained soil kept evenly moist in summer, on the dry side in other seasons. Propagate by seeds or cuttings in spring or fall. Often used outdoors in warm weather as a bedding or container plant in full sun.

Lithops is a large genus of small South African plants which consist of a pair of close-set, fleshy leaves separated by a cleft. The common names "stone face" and "living stone" come from their uncanny resemblance to a small, split rock. In autumn they produce yellow, white, or orange blossoms larger than the leaves. After flowering the plants become dormant, looking quite dead until they break open to show two new leaves. It is a fatal mistake to think that lots of water and fertilizer will boost these plants into growth. Like lampranthus, lithops needs sunny, warm, airy conditions. Give it a soil made up of six parts sand, four parts loam, and one part finely crushed brick. Keep evenly moist May to November and dry the balance of the year. Propagate by seeds sown in moderate humidity at 55° to 60°F in spring.

Trichodiadema bulbosum, from Port Elizabeth, South Africa, has bulbous roots exposed above the soil; the leaves have white bristle tips. The flowers, appearing in summer, are a lovely crimson; this plant, well-grown and displayed in a bonsai pot will make you very happy. Save a place for it that gets lots of sun, or directly beneath the tubes in a maxi light garden; it needs warm, fresh air. Give it a well-drained, loam-based potting soil kept evenly moist in summer and on the dry side at other times. Be careful never to leave this one standing in water. Propagate in spring or summer by cuttings of mature to half-ripened stems set in barely moist sand.

ALSTROEMERIACEAE. *Alstroemeria Family*.

Four genera of monocotyledons native to tropical and subtropical America, formerly considered members of the amaryllis family, differing in their leafy stems and not strictly umbellate inflorescence. The genera *Alstroemeria* and *Bomarea* are of possible interest as houseplants.

Alstroemeria aurantiaca, to three feet, from Chile, gives us many of the cultivars that produce the popular cut flowers. *Alstroemeria caryophyllaea*, to one and a half feet, from Brazil, has umbels of rose-pink-tipped white flowers that give generously of carnation fragrance. Individually these are up to two inches in diameter, formed of six segments, the ones at the two o'clock and ten o'clock positions typically butterfly zoned in a more intricate design than the other four. *Alstroemeria psittacina*, to three feet, from Brazil, has dark red flowers that are green-tipped and brown-spotted. These plants may be grown outdoors in frost-free weather; the roots are sometimes planted in the ground in colder climates, to USDA zones 8 and 7, often against a south-facing wall, and mulched deeply for winter protection. The *aurantiaca* hybrids in particular are notable for flowering when soil and air temperatures are quite cool, around 55° F. They need sunny, cool temperatures in fall and winter, and good air circulation with a high level of humidity. Give them humus-rich, loam-based potting soil kept evenly moist in cool to moderate temperatures and during the active growing season, and on the dry side the remainder of the year. Alstroemerias grow readily from seeds and reach flowering size in about three years. The plants need half to full sun when they are growing. When grown in pots they can be dried off in summer and kept active from fall to spring in a sunny, airy, cool indoor garden, with flowering possible for several weeks or months through winter and early spring.

Bomarea contains over a hundred different twining, tuberous-rooted herbs, native mostly to the highlands of tropical America. They are cultivated for bell-shaped flowers, pale yellow suffused with pink in *B. andimarcana*; these appear in summer and fall on the new stems produced that season. Maintain nearly dry while dormant in winter. Their treatment is also much the same as for *Gloriosa* (see pages 147–148).

AMARANTHACEAE. *Amaranth Family.*

Tender annuals and perennials often possessing highly colored foliage or showy flower heads. Two perennials are of interest here, *Alternanthera* and *Iresine*, both for their colorful leaves used in warm-weather bedding-out or in containers. Indoors they need a sunny place, average house temperatures, and fresh air. Propagate from cuttings in winter and spring for planting out when the weather is warm and settled.

Alternanthera bettzickiana is sometimes called miniature Joseph's coat for its twisted narrow leaves that are irregularly marked with colors ranging from creamy yellow to salmon red. (Joseph's coat is also the common name of a large outdoor garden relative of alternanthera, *Amaranthus tricolor*.) *Alternanthera versicolor*, three inches, from Brazil, is a compact plant with almost round leaves, crisped and corrugated, of dark green or coppery red with purplish veining and pink-and-white edging. These and their numerous varieties and cultivars were necessities for Victorian bedding-out; they may be used to similar effect as container plants, especially when placed in the company of gray- or silver-leaved plants or at floor or ground level so their arrangement and contrasting colors are viewed from above.

Iresine herbstii (chicken gizzard plant), to one foot, from Brazil, and its cultivars such as 'Aureo-reticulata' have rounded leaves noticeably notched or dimpled at the tip. *Iresine lindenii*, one foot, from Ecuador, and its cultivars such as 'Formosa' have pointed leaves. Foliage

Iresine herbstii.

of all iresines is highly colored, predominantly dark crimson-red, the reason for another common name, bloodleaf. Yellow and green areas in the leaves, especially along the veins, make these foliage plants attractive and understandably popular in bedding-out schemes.

AMARYLLIDACEAE. *Amaryllis Family.*

Mostly tropical bulbous plants that differ only slightly from members of the lily family. Amaryllid flowers have six segments, and are usually borne in umbels above the foliage. The principal genera of interest for houseplanting are *Agapanthus, Clivia, Crinum, Cyrtanthus, Eucharis, Habranthus, Haemanthus, Hippeastrum, Nerine, Scadoxus, Sprekelia, Tulbaghia,* and *Vallota.* Some books list *Agave* in this family but I have placed it with Agavaceae (see page 69).

Agapanthus africanus, one and a half to two feet high, from the Cape of Good Hope, is known as blue African lily. The white A. *orientalis albus,* two to three feet, from South Africa, is known as lily-of-the-Nile; it is also available with blue flowers. These are large, tuberous-rooted, summer-flowering plants best handled in roomy tubs and rarely disturbed. Agapanthus needs a loam-based, humus-rich soil. Keep dormant in winter, giving it only enough water to keep the strap-shaped leaves from collapsing. Keep cool but frost-free during this period. Beginning in spring, give full sun, warmth, lots of water, and begin applications of liquid manure tea every two weeks until late spring; all of this works together to bring on flowering at the beginning of summer.

Other agapanthus include *Agapanthus orientalis* 'Dwarf White', with flower stems only about eighteen inches tall; 'Peter Pan', a graceful miniature with foliage to eight inches long and blue flowers on two-foot stalks; and A. *globosus* 'Flore Plena', a small plant with fully double, dark blue blossoms. Any of these smaller agapanthus are better suited as a houseplant than the larger sorts favored for the indoor/outdoor life.

Propagate by division in early spring. Repot only after the mature plant has been in the same container several years; otherwise, top-dress at the beginning of the growing season in late winter–early spring with an inch or two of fresh potting mix that has been enriched with an extra portion of dehydrated cow manure or well-rotted compost.

× *Amarcrinum* is an intergeneric hybrid between *Amaryllis belladonna* and *Crinum moorei. Amarcrinum howardii* (called *Crinodonna corsii* in Italy) has fragrant pink flowers held in clusters atop three-foot stems in autumn. 'Delkin's Find' is similar though smaller, with more perfectly formed flowers. 'Dorothy Hannibal', also pink, may bloom any season. Care as for *Clivia.*

Clivia miniata, one to two feet, from Natal, South Africa, is a tender, evergreen, bulbous plant with thick, fleshy roots. It is noted for its clusters of yellow to scarlet trumpet-shaped blossoms. Clivias should never be allowed to dry out completely. Water sufficiently to keep the large strap-shaped leaves in good condition. Successful flowering depends on implementing a consistent regimen; it needs warmth and moisture in the spring and summer and a fall and winter that are cool and on the dry side; avoid nasty extremes such as below freezing temperatures or bone-dry soil. If mealybugs become entrenched in clivia, almost-daily soakings of all affected parts with insecticidal soap or neem solutions will be needed until the plant is certifiably clean.

To my mind the clivia (in case you were wondering how I pronounce the word, the plant was named for Lady Clive, the wife of Robert Clive, Baron of Plassey, the British administrator and military leader who brought India into the British Empire; it is also pronounced to rhyme with "Olivia") is a starring-role houseplant. For many years I had a collection of clivias that fairly filled the entire main window in my living room garden. The foliage looked great and it always made me feel good after an hour or so had been spent carrying each plant to the sink or tub for showering and grooming. They did not bloom satisfactorily, however, despite my best intentions; in the end mealybugs invaded while I was away on a photography expedition and caused such devastation that on my return I immediately sacked the whole mess. I will be back with clivias, though, but probably not until

Clivia miniata.

my garden can come down to earth outdoors in warm weather and where there can also be a season that is definitely cool but frost-free. There are also the more unusual species *Clivia nobilis* and *C.* × *cyrtanthiflora*, both having more tubular and graceful flowers in muted pastels than the common clivias, and treasured by collectors and pollen dabblers. All clivias can be propagated by removing offsets at repotting time in late winter or spring; take great care to preserve as many roots as possible. Fresh seeds are another possibility; plant as soon as possible after they are ripe, one half to one inch deep in moist potting soil. Keep constantly warm and moist. When the seedlings are an inch or two tall, transplant to individual five-inch clay pots. Do not move to a larger size until after the first flowering, which should be in three to five years. Clivias do well in a turfy potting soil, one which includes well-rotted compost and leaf mold as well as the usual garden loam, sphagnum peat moss, and sharp sand.

Crinum kirkii, two to four feet, from Zanzibar, has white blossoms with a red center stripe in summer. *Crinum moorei*, two feet, from South Africa, has large pink to rosy red flowers in late summer or fall. 'Ellen

Bosanquet', two to four feet, a well-known hybrid crinum, has dark wine red blossoms in autumn. *Crinum* × *powellii* 'Album', three feet, is a choice cultivar with pure white flowers.

Crinums are evergreen plants arising from very large bulbs which need to be potted half in and half out of rich soil. Although inclined to grow too large for use in house gardens, crinums can be grown in tubs which are held in semidormancy in a cool place during the winter, then brought into full growth outdoors at the beginning of warm weather. They need an abundance of water in spring and summer, much less in fall and winter. Their bold simplicity lends a commanding presence among other plants. I once grew one from seed (picked up from a sidewalk in Nassau) to repeated flowerings (beginning after three or four years) in a semisunny house garden. They can also be readily started from offsets. Watch out for mealybugs, however, as they are potentially lethal. Care as for *Clivia*.

Cyrtanthus flanaganii, nine inches, from South Africa, has fragrant, yellow, slender trumpet flowers. *Cyrtanthus mackenii*, twelve inches, from Natal, has fragrant, pure white flowers. *Cyrtanthus sanguineus*, twelve inches, from South Africa, has orange-red flowers. The cyrtanthuses are relatively unknown. Their flowers are more tubular than lilylike, and the foliage is like that of a miniature hippeastrum. Care is the same as for *Hippeastrum* (see page 78), except the plants, being so much smaller on average, are more readily manageable by the house gardener. Propagation is by removal of the offsets at repotting time in late winter or spring, or from seeds sown as soon as ripe in shallow drills made in moist potting soil. Seedlings reach flowering size in three years. The Brooklyn Botanic Garden has a collection of cyrtanthus, the best and most floriferous of which are displayed annually among other winter-flowering plants in the warm temperate part of the Steinhardt Conservatory.

Eucharis grandiflora, one to two feet, from the Andes of Colombia, is a bulbous plant of great beauty, bearing umbels of showy white, fragrant, narcissuslike flowers in late winter, spring, or early summer. With mindful attention to watering, and to the diminishing of it after flowering, eucharis may be brought into bloom several times a year. It needs bright diffused light, average house temperatures, and reasonably moist, fresh air. Use a humus-rich, loam-based potting soil. Water freely during spring and summer, less in fall and winter. Set six bulbs in a ten-inch pot and do not disturb until they become crowded, usually after three or four years. Otherwise, remove some surface soil and replace with a fresh mixture every spring. The lovely miniature *E. fosterii* (glossy leaves to eight inches tall with lightly lemon-scented, pendulous, white flowers) thrives in filtered south light. It has flowered regularly for me in the spring. The only problem is that *fosterii* is rarely available. My supplier is no longer in business but I have hope that some grower will eventually propagate this species so that it can be enjoyed more widely. Since the effect of both these eucharis is similar to that of various spathiphyllums, which are commonly grown houseplants, I often suggest eucharis as something to grow that is a little different and a bit of a challenge.

Habranthus brachyandrus, twelve inches, from Brazil, has lavender-pink blossoms with a crimson throat. *Habranthus robustus*, nine inches, from Argentina, has larger, purplish pink flowers, while *H. texanus*, twelve inches, from Texas, which has recently become available, has dark yellow flowers stained reddish gold outside. By allowing habranthus bulbs to go completely dry occasionally, then soaking them, they can be made to flower several times a year, hence their common name rain lily. It needs sun, winter temperatures of about 70°F, and good air circulation. Give it a humus-rich, loam-based potting soil. Propagate by offsets at repotting time, late winter into spring, but only when the pot has become overly crowded. The active growth that leads to flowering is encouraged by being generous with water, light, fertilizer, and warm temperatures. When this regimen is changed to lean for several weeks or months, meaning much drier, no fertilizer, and cooler temperatures, flowering occurs soon after this fast is broken.

Haemanthus albiflos, one foot, from South Africa, bears up to a hundred or more white flowers in each closely packed umbel during summer or fall. Its stiff, haired foliage is gray-green. *Haemanthus coccineus* is the summer-flowering blood lily, which blooms first (tiny red flowers with prominent yellow stamens, surrounded by showy, fleshy, red or pink bracts), then sends up foliage. It is likely that most of the plants you've known as haemanthus have been shipped off to another genus in the amaryllis family, *Scadoxus* (see page 81).

I am presently helping to grow a very healthy *Haemanthus albiflos* that began four or five years ago as an offset with a few roots taken from a large plant. Its home is a sunny, warm greenhouse that is not air conditioned in the summer, only some fans and vents are kept open, so the haemanthus gets quite baked but receives enough water and fertilizer to keep the leaves in fine form. In early fall, as temperatures moderate and the days grow shorter, the blooms come out in profusion. For general care and propagation as houseplants, treat the same as for *Scadoxus* (see page 81).

Hippeastrum vittatum, two feet, from Peru, is the plant from which many of today's popular amaryllis originated. Hybrids of Dutch, American, or South African strains are available. The flowers of all tend to be lily-shaped, and are composed of three outer and three inner segments which are nearly equal in size and equidistant from each other, though often not identically marked. They are borne atop stout scapes (leafless stalks), usually in two to five clusters. In color the flowers may be pure white or of pink or red tones, including salmon, wine red and violet-rose. They may have throats of lighter or darker tones, or they may be banded, striped, or bordered in contrasting color. Many times a single bulb will send up as many as three scapes, resulting in a magnificent, long-lasting display.

The large-flowered hybrids are best known. Collectors go for the smaller sorts which tend also to be more evergreen in habit. *Hippeastrum evansiae* from Bolivia is typical of these, with salmon orange flowers having light chartreuse centers. While yellow is elusive in the large hybrids, it is seen among the smaller species, some of which also have green and burgundy leaves. The late Marcia C. Wilson of Texas shared many seedlings with me, which I have continued to cultivate in my various

Hippeastrum *'Sumac Pinini' with* Hedera helix *wreath.*

1) Unusually tall growth, also referred to as "stretched" or "etoliated," can be the result of excessive temperatures, water, and fertilizer high in nitrogen such as 30-10-10 or fish emulsion, possibly in combination with insufficient sunlight.

2) Amaryllis bulbs that bloom weakly without evidence of roots or new leaves may have been too cold and too wet at a critical stage, or they may be diseased. Unless rare or valuable, compost these without further ado.

3) The amaryllis we grow in pots are usually members of the genus *Hippeastrum*. Most have been produced through generations of breeding work; some are more complex than others. After their first season of bloom, the mass-marketed hybrids often take a year or more to regain strength and establish a natural flowering time. The species and smaller amaryllis, which may tend to be evergreen rather than deciduous, can be brought to bloom twice or more yearly by boosting growth for a couple of months (Mrs. Hardgrove's system), then holding on the dry and cool side but continuing in the same light for several weeks, followed by a return to the original conditions of abundance.

4) The production of multibloom stalks, each having many flowers, is the result of a strong bulb. This means having clean stock, free of the fire disease or any other virus, not to mention the potentially disastrous narcissus bulb fly and mealybug.

light and window gardens and hope eventually to breed. Steve Lowe, a horticulturist at the zoo in San Antonio, has become the new caretaker of the Wilson collection of amaryllids. I have a pale yellow and bright pink but seem to have lost the 'Sumac Pinini'.

Amaryllis have numbered among my lifelong favorite plants. A Mrs. Hardgrove of Wewoka, Oklahoma, got me started when I was a child. She grew her amaryllis in a jerry-rigged greenhouse and had a system for producing blooms three and four times a year from each bulb. She did this by pouring on all the good stuff— light, warmth, water, fertilizer—until at least eight strong leaves had formed, then drying off the bulbs for a couple of months. Soon after resuming the water and fertilizer, flowering occurred. Here are some of the finer points of their culture I have since learned:

Strong bulbs develop when the plants receive direct sun for a half day or more, are potted in a mix that includes soil and sand as well as humus, and are watered thoroughly then not again until on the dry side. Printed instructions given out with amaryllis bulbs usually say to pot them so that the neck and shoulder or upper third of the bulb is above the soil surface. This produces a pleasing effect and seems to work for container culture; the same kinds of bulbs are planted permanently in the ground of outdoor gardens in the Deep South, with the necks three or four inches deep. Amaryllis do not in general benefit from having their roots disturbed, so it

Hippeastrum *hybrids in a Netherlands greenhouse.*

often pays to top-dress a mature planting with an enriched soil mix in early spring instead of completely repotting it. Propagate by removing at the time of potting or repotting any offset bulbs that have formed from the base of the parent; pot these separately in five-inch pots. They will bloom in two or three years. Amaryllis can also be grown from seeds, which need to be planted as soon as they are ripe, sideways in drills made in moist potting soil. Maintain constant warmth (72° to 75°F) and moisture to help the seeds sprout instead of rot.

I find that amaryllis thrive on sunlight and fresh air but, like an athlete, they grow stronger when stressed a bit. Bulbs planted in a peat-based medium tend to weaken even as they are sending out huge leaves.

There is a fine point here, however, about how stress is applied. When a regular amaryllis bulb is ready to dry off in the fall, it is best to do this gradually, first withholding fertilizer, then water. Do not ever remove the leaves green, but rather let them die down naturally so

as to store in the bulb all the energy they have collected. This season of ripening off is critical for success.

To initiate drying off, bring amaryllis indoors before night temperatures drop below 50°F. Stop fertilizing and gradually reduce the amount of water until the oldest, outermost leaves are beginning to yellow and shrivel. At this point you must decide whether to dry off the amaryllis completely, or merely to keep it on the dry side during its normal period of rest. If we could study the family tree of any given amaryllis, it would likely yield conflicting needs since one parent could be evergreen by nature while the other could come from a drier climate where it loses all or most of its leaves during an annual period of drought.

Maintain this regimen, keeping the plants at moderate temperatures (50° to 65°F). Flowering occurs shortly after a rest of from eight to twelve weeks, when the "fast" is broken, by increasing temperatures, watering more, placing in sun, and beginning light applications of fertilizer.

A newly popular way to market amaryllis is to offer one large pot filled with three bulbs. These tips should bring them back to bloom, year after year:

- After flowering finishes, and at the beginning of a new growing season, use your fingers or a kitchen fork to remove about an inch of soil from all around the surface. Replace it with a mixture of fresh garden loam, steamed bone meal, and well-rotted compost.
- Water them with liquid manure every two weeks, diluted to the color of weak tea.
- Follow the regimen outlined above for culture.

Nerine bowdenii, one and a half feet, has pink flowers, while *N. curvifolia*, one to one and a half feet, has brilliant scarlet flowers. Its variety *fothergillii* has two-and-a-half-inch crimson or salmon red flowers. *Nerine sarniensis*, two feet, the Guernsey lily, has salmon or orange-scarlet flowers. Nerines, all from South Africa, are some of the most elegant of flowering bulbs. It is possible to get bloom from them from late summer into winter. A prominent feature of the blossoms is the manner in which the stamens (usually straight) protrude past the recurving petals.

Nerines need sunny conditions, coolness, temperatures not exceeding 65°F in the winter, and fresh, moist air. Use a humus-rich, loam-based potting soil. Pot any time from August to November, allowing half of the bulb to extend above the soil. Plant one to a four- or five-inch pot, three to a six- or seven-inch pot. Do not apply water until a flower bud or foliage is visible, then keep evenly moist and make biweekly applications of houseplant fertilizer until May. Stop fertilizing and keep on the dry side through summer. In August remove some of the old topsoil and replace with a fresh mixture of loam, dehydrated manure, and sand. Propagate by removing offsets at repotting time, necessary every three or four years.

Scadoxus multiflorus, the blood lily, an amaryllid from tropical Africa, is an all-time first-rate performer for indoor gardens. Known commercially as *Haemanthus multiflorus* and botanically as *Scadoxus multiflorus*, it grows actively in spring and summer, producing its reddish orange puffball or fireworks flowers in early summer as the new leaves are emerging. The plants need warmth, moisture, fertilizing, and half to full sun until they are dried off in autumn.

Stop watering and fertilizing the blood lily as soon as the leaves start to yellow, something they do on their own in response to dwindling day length and cooler temperatures. Leave the foliage to ripen and die down; do not cut it off green or the bulb will be weakened.

Store a resting blood lily in the pot at moderate temperatures, around 60° to 70°F, in a closet or cupboard. Add only enough water to keep the bulb from shriveling. In late winter or early spring bring to a warm window garden and water well. You may carefully remove an inch or so of the old soil from the surface and replace with a fresh mix; avoid disturbing the root system once it is established. A six- to eight-inch bulb pan or azalea pot is ample for a specimen-size bulb.

The name "blood lily" refers to the blood-red spotting that appears on the bulb's upper parts as well as the leafstalk; it becomes more pronounced at the onset of flowering. I have grown blood lily in a pot for many years. It is perhaps one of the most satisfactory flowering houseplants and deserves to be better known. It is more easily reflowered than the average large-flowered amaryllis and is unusual enough to thrill even the experienced gardener.

The only drawback to blood lily—the same as for amaryllis, clivia, and agapanthus—is that mealybug can become established at the base of the leaves and down inside between the onionlike layers of the bulb. If not entirely eradicated by removal with cotton swabs dipped in rubbing alcohol—or in extreme cases by cleaning and soaking the bulb for a half hour in a fifty-fifty mix of alcohol and water—the insects will decimate the resting bulb.

Sprekelia formosissima (sometimes called *Amaryllis formosissima*), two feet, from Mexico and Guatemala, bears handsome crimson flowers that resemble those of a cattleya, leading to one of its common names, orchid-lily. It's also known as the Jacobean lily and St. James's lily. Blooms may appear from March to June, usually preceding the attractive, small, linear leaves which grow eight to twelve inches long. It needs sun, average house temperatures from February to September and 50° to 60° F September through February, and good air circulation with moderate to high humidity. Use a loam-based potting soil. Bulbs are available for potting in late winter or spring. Cover two thirds of the bulb and keep evenly moist from the time growth appears (as early as February) until September. Keep dry and withhold fertilizer September through February; the resting potted bulb can be kept in a light or dark place where the air circulates freely and temperatures are moderate, around 60°F. Propagation, top-dressing, repotting: see *Nerine* (page 81).

Tulbaghia fragrans (pink agapanthus), from Transvaal, sends up slender stems crowned by an umbel of lavender-pink, fragrant flowers, above a fan of strap leaves about fifteen inches tall. *Tulbaghia violacea* (society garlic), from South Africa, has narrow, garlic-scented leaves, and umbels of showy, lilac, star-shaped flowers atop eighteen-to twenty-four-inch stems; it is also available in a form having variegated foliage. They need sunny to semisunny situations, average house temperatures, and good air circulation. Give them loam-based potting soil kept evenly moist to on the dry side. Propagate by removing offsets or by division at repotting time in late winter to spring.

Vallota speciosa (Scarborough lily), two to three feet, from South Africa, has showy crimson flowers in late summer and autumn. There is also a white form. The flowers are borne in clusters of five to ten above straplike evergreen leaves one and one fourth inches wide and one and one half to two feet long. The lower leaves have a purple cast which makes them especially attractive on a sun porch or in a cool room with other plants in winter. Maintain cool temperatures (40° to 65°F) and keep on the dry side September through March, then maintain at 55° to 70°F until warm weather comes. They need good air circulation all year round. Apply fertilizer beginning in spring and into early summer, then stop and hold on the dry side until September. Water generously while in bloom, keep in moderate temperatures, and out of hot sun that could prematurely fade the exquisite blossoms. Propagate by removing offsets at repotting time,

necessary every three or four years, and best done in June or July. If vallota fails to do well, and other conditions seem in order, check to be sure the soil has a pH near 6.0.

APOCYNACEAE. *Dogbane Family.*

Tender perennials with milky juice and smooth-edged leaves. Flowers are regular (the parts of equal size, regularly and symmetrically arranged), either solitary or in clusters. The genera of particular interest here are *Adenium, Allamanda, Carissa, Ervatamia, Mandevilla* (also called *Dipladenia*), *Nerium, Pachypodium, Plumeria, Trachelospermum,* and *Vinca. Adenium, Ervatamia,* and *Pachypodium* will be covered here. All the others are in Chapter 8 excepting *Carissa,* Chapter 5.

Adenium obesum, from tropical East Africa, has thickened stems that can grow into a spreading bush four to five feet high and as wide. The glossy dark green leaves are obovate and deciduous, tending to cluster at the tips of the branches. It is ideal for indoor/outdoor gardening and basically needs lots of sun, with warmth, water and fresh air spring and summer, cooler but not freezing temperatures and soil on the dry side in fall and winter. The flowers, reminiscent of the related *Plumeria,* are large and showy. For all finer points of care and propagation, see *Plumeria* (page 228).

Ervatamia coronaria, six to eight feet, from the Old World tropics, has many common names, including crape jasmine, fleur d'amour, butterfly gardenia, East Indian rosebay, Adam's apple, and Nero's crown. In addition, it is sometimes classified as *Tabernaemontana divaricata.* By any name, ervatamia is a delightful evergreen shrub which may be cultivated in a twelve- to fifteen-inch pot or tub, and kept pruned back as necessary in February or March. In the summer it bears clusters of one-and-one-half- to two-inch waxy, white, funnel-shaped, fragrant flowers. There is also the double-flowered 'Flore Plena' that grows on a compact plant and is recommended for container gardening indoors/outdoors. It needs sunny brightness, no temperatures colder than 55°F, and fresh, moist air. Give it humus-rich, loam-

longest days of the year when it needs full sun and fresh air, preferably outdoors. Drench the soil with water and not again until the surface is quite dry. Fertilize lightly during this period with fish emulsion.

During cold weather, keep pachypodium in a sunny window with temperatures varying from moderate to warm, ideally not below 60°F. Water less during this period, but take care that the soil doesn't dry to the point of shriveling the fleshy trunk. Apply no fertilizer during this semidormancy.

A frequent problem with pachypodium is the loss of older leaves for no apparent reason and new growth that is blackened from the tips inward. The usual causes are

Pachypodium lamerei.

Adenium obesum.

based potting mix and keep evenly moist spring and summer, somewhat drier during fall and winter. Root cuttings of half-ripened stems in spring; high humidity and warmth will promote rooting.

Pachypodium lamerei (Madagascar palm) has a thick, fleshy trunk with long sharp spines and a tuft of long slender leaves at the top, extending at right angles from the trunk, to three or four feet tall or more. Somewhat surprisingly this exotic-looking plant is botanically allied with the commonplace oleander and vinca. It hails from arid tropical regions and grows actively during the hottest,

inadequate light and moisture. Succulents like this can survive long periods of inadequate light, a situation in which less water is better than more, but eventually they go into decline. Increasing the amount of sun, fresh air, and water during the spring and summer months is the only way to reverse such a decline.

ARACEAE. *Arum or Calla Family.*

Mostly tropical plants with bitter, sometimes poisonous juice, and smooth-edged leaves which are often lobed attractively. The tiny flowers are clustered on a fingerlike spadix which protrudes out of, or is shielded by, a leaf- or funnel-shaped spathe. While the true flowers are not individually showy, the spathe in many genera is large, colorful, and long-lasting. Genera of particular interest for houseplanting are *Acorus, Aglaonema, Alocasia, Amorphophallus, Anthurium, Caladium, Colocasia, Dieffenbachia, Epipremnum, Homalomena, Monstera, Philodendron, Pistia, Rhektophyllum, Scindapsus, Spathiphyllum, Syngonium, Xanthosoma,* and *Zantedeschia.*

Acorus gramineus pusillus, two to three inches, from Japan, has tufts of irislike leaves; *A. g. variegatus,* six to nine inches, also from Japan, is similar, but attractively marked with creamy white. Both known as miniature sweet flag, they are small, slow-growing, grassy perennials, great for terrariums, and dish and water gardens, for foliage effect as the flowers are of no consequence (except to the plants). They need a semisunny to semishady situation, average house temperatures—on the cool side in winter—and fresh, moist air. Give them a humus-rich, loam-based potting soil and keep wet, only slightly less so during winter coolness. Divide the clumps in spring or fall.

Aglaonema is the genus name for the Chinese evergreen, one of the single most enduring foliage plants for indoor gardens, so durable in low light as to be taken for granted and often neglected. New cultivars are constantly coming on the market, usually bushy and combining some shade of green with silver, pewter, cream, or white; there are also some having rosy pink stems.

Aglaonema *(center, rear),* Syngonium *(left and right),* Asplenium nidus *(center, front),* Hedera helix *ivy.*

Aglaonema commutatum, one foot, from Sri Lanka and the Philippines, has silver markings on dark green leaves. *Aglaonema modestum,* to two feet, from Guangdong, has durable, waxy green leaves that are oblong, moderately narrow, tapering to a thin tip, and closely set along thin canes. *Aglaonema pictum,* one and one half feet, from Malaya, has dark green leaves mottled with metallic gray and white, and A. *pseudobracteatum,* one to two feet, from Malaysia, has brightly variegated leaves splashed with creamy white to yellow and cream-colored stems. *Aglaonema roebelinii,* two feet or more, from Borneo and Malaya, makes a wonderful houseplant, similar in appearance to a dieffenbachia. This aglaonema is often called schismatoglottis. Its leaves are almost entirely silver except for the dark green edges and midrib area. *Aglaonema simplex,* one and one half feet or more, from Java, is similar to A. *modestum,* and A. *treubii,* one and one half feet, from the Celebes, has narrow, lance-shaped leaves of light green with cream to chartreuse variegation.

A frequent problem with aglaonema is that the silver or other color variegation fades, an indication that stronger light is needed. Another problem is that growers crowd three or more rooted cuttings in one pot. The interior leaves, somewhat jammed together, are starved for light and air; they soon die. If you want to grow really nice specimens, pot them separately so there is room for all the leaves to develop symmetrically. A solution for aglaonemas that are truly light-starved is to put them on a rotation plan. Keep some of the plants near a half-sunny to bright window while the others are doing duty in the proverbial dark corner. After a few months, switch them around. They need loam-based, humus-rich soil kept evenly moist.

Where I live in the city, an appalling amount of grime settles on houseplant leaves like these in a matter of weeks, so it pays to shower aglaonemas at least once a month, using tepid or barely warm water. Plants that have been in the same pots for several years can also get a new lease on life and brighter color variegation by transplanting them to fresh soil, a mix of equal portions soil, sand, peat moss, and well-rotted leaf mold or compost.

Although it is not desirable to jam several rooted cuttings of aglaonema in one pot, if you plant one in a good-size container, in time it will send up several offshoots. This natural progression from one plant to a clump will produce the best effect over the long haul.

Alocasia hails from tropical Asia and Indonesia and grows from rootstocks that are almost tuberlike, with heart- or arrow-shaped leaves often displaying noticeable vein patterns rising on long stalks. These handsome aroids can be grown outdoors when the weather is warm and humid, but need protection from strong winds. Late winter or spring is the time to repot, using a mixture of two parts coarse sphagnum peat moss to one each of potting soil and clean, sharp sand or perlite. Another suitable medium is humus-rich, loam-based potting soil. Fish emulsion makes an appropriate fertilizer from spring to fall, during which time the plants need generous watering. In winter, when days are shorter and average temperatures cooler, keep the soil a little on the dry side and do not fertilize. Misting the leaves on sunny days is beneficial.

Alocasia cuprea, one foot, from Borneo, has heavy, waxy, prominently veined leaves, dark metallic green above, maroon-purple beneath. *Alocasia lowii* (fancy taro), with bluish green metallic patinaed leaves that have pale silver margins and veins, is a highly recommended houseplant. *Alocasia watsoniana*, to five feet or more, from Sumatra, is a magnificent plant with huge, corrugated, leathery, blue-green leaves veined and edged in silver-white, with purple on the reverses.

Alocasia is closely allied to *Colocasia antiquorum*, the ubiquitous elephant's-ear or taro. Alocasias need high levels of light, partial shade to diffused sun, combined with air that is constantly humid and warm, never below 62°F. Such conditions are not found in most homes but it is entirely possible that you have a special plant room where conditions can be maintained similar to those in the tropical rain forest.

I tried several alocasias in my apartment and while they did not die overnight, decline seemed inevitable. However, at one time there was a woman in New York City who grew thriving alocasias in a terrarium the size of a walk-in closet which she had constructed out of one-by-two lumber and sheet plastic in front of a large sunny window, with a radiator underneath. There was a small fan inside to keep the air moving and a humidifier to keep the air saturated with moisture. Also accommodated in this walk-in Wardian case were numerous orchids, bromeliads, gesneriads, and tropical ferns. It was a heavenly spot and an idea worth copying or adapting in an endless variety of situations.

Amorphophallus rivieri, to four feet, from southeastern Asia, has a trunklike petiole (brownish green, dark-purple-spotted) which supports one much divided leaf blade that grows up to four feet across. This dies down during fall and winter when the tuber, up to twelve inches in diameter, is resting. Given abundant warmth, water, and light once the active growing season (spring to summer) begins, a blackish-red inflorescence appears, to three feet tall, with a sixteen-inch spathe and a twenty-one-inch spadix, and with it a not very pleasant odor, the stench of which is meant to attract pollinating insects. Care as for *Caladium* (see page 87). This plant can be grown in outdoor gardens to USDA zone 7 if situated next to a south-facing wall and mulched deeply for winter. It is a fascinating houseplant since it makes such an extraordinarily large show of foliage in summer and disappears completely in fall and winter.

Anthurium as a genus can be divided roughly into two groups—species that produce showy, flowerlike spathes and those grown for foliage. In the first group, *Anthurium andraeanum*, from Colombia, as well as its many varieties and cultivars, has patent-leatherlike spathes in white, pink, coral, and red. These flowers look as though they have been varnished or highly waxed, and last for several weeks.

Anthurium scherzeranum, from Costa Rica and Guatemala, is the source of many smaller growing and flowering hybrids that are well suited to indoor gardens. Typically marketed as "flamingo flowers," these aroids need an atmosphere that is constantly warm, humid, and bright, but without hot sun shining directly on the leaves at midday in order to bloom. "Warm" in this case means winter lows of 60° to 65°F, to at least 20 degrees warmer in other seasons and at other times of day. Combine this with at least 80 percent relative humidity and we are talking about an environment that would feel close to a steam bath to most of us.

If you do not have a plant room or other growing space that can be turned into a microcosm of a tropical American rain forest, try treating anthuriums as if they were African violets or phalaenopsis orchids—place them in or near an east or bright window, one that is protected from the sun's midday rays. A maxi light garden is one likely spot for making these plants comfortable.

Flamingo flower anthuriums are naturally low-growing and clump-forming. They are also relatively small, which adds to their potential as popular flowering houseplants. One or more can be readily adapted to a larger terrarium, with walls of glass or plastic producing the desired constant warmth and high humidity.

Although anthuriums vary between air and earth, epiphytic and terrestrial, the flamingo-flower hybrids being sold in four- to six-inch plastic pots are grown mostly in a soilless mix based on peat moss or in a medium that can be blended at home from equal parts each of coarse sphagnum peat moss and well-rotted leaf mold. Allow this to feel almost dry at the surface, then water gener-

ously. Do not leave anthuriums standing in water and do not let them become dry enough to wilt.

Anthuriums in the second group, the velvet-leaved foliage types, include A. *clarinervium*, from Mexico, A. *crystallinum*, from Colombia and Peru, and A. *warocqueanum*, from Colombia. *Anthurium pictamayo* (begonia-leaf anthurium), and A. *pentaphyllum*, both palmately lobed with fingerlike segments, are examples of the anthuriums grown for their oddly cut foliage. Others are cultivated for highly attractive leaves which are neither velvety nor cut. These include A. *cordifolium*, a waxy bluish green, from the West Indies; A. *recusatum*, dark green and wavy-edged with prominent pale veins, from eastern Cuba; and A. *veitchii*, quilted, rich metallic green, from Colombia.

Anthuriums differ widely in their habits, and may be vining, self-heading, treelike, or shrubby. They may cling to trees, grow on rocks, or be content to have their roots in a pot of humus-rich, loam-based potting soil.

Shower the leaves of indoor anthuriums at least once a week with lukewarm water. Be sure to direct a strong stream to the leaf undersides, which is where tiny spider

Anthurium species at Planting Fields, Oyster Bay, New York.

mites could take up residence. Propagation is by removal of offsets at repotting time, usually late winter or spring, or from seeds planted as soon as ripe in a fifty-fifty mix of coarse sphagnum peat moss and clean, sharp sand; keep constantly moist, warm, and in high humidity.

Caladium is a genus that gives us beautiful leaves from many different cultivars, usually for colorful foliage effect in spring and summer. *Caladium humboldtii*, from Para in Brazil, eight to twelve inches, is relatively miniature, with green and snow white arrowhead leaves; in a warm maxi light garden this species can be cultivated in any season, as can the dwarf forms of today's commercial fancyleaf caladiums. They need sunny to semishady, average house temperatures and fresh, moist air during spring and summer. Give them humus-rich, loam-based potting soil, and keep amply supplied with water during their growing season. Withhold water and fertilizer gradually beginning in autumn until all the foliage dies down. Store the tubers where temperatures do not fall below 55°F. Clumps of tubers may be divided at potting time, early spring.

Colocasia esculenta (elephant's-ear), from Hawaii and Fiji, produces predominantly green, heart-shaped leaves that may reach three feet or more in length, "elephant's-ears." *Colocasia* 'Kapo' (miniature taro), to twelve inches, has small shield-shaped leaves and darker veins emphasizing pink-blushed centers. They are exciting indoors or out, wherever there is space for the leaves to unfurl. Spring and summer are the active times; provide extended winter dormancy. Care as for *Caladium*.

Dieffenbachia can be found wherever plants are sold. Like most of the aroids we grow as houseplants, they are noteworthy for bold leaves that are sometimes so colorful they stand out as if they were exotic blossoms. 'Arvida', for example, sends out new leaves that are predominantly white with a narrow margin of green. As these age they darken to mostly green. It is the habit of some dieffenbachias to remain small, under two feet, almost indefinitely. Others will grow at the rate of one to three feet a year until they reach the ceiling.

Dieffenbachia does well indoors in or near a bright window. Protection is needed from hot, direct sun at midday but insufficient light is a primary cause of gradual decline. Overwatering can also be a problem. If the canes thin out, with ever-increasing distances between the new leaves, this is one sign of too much water. Another is new leaves that are increasingly smaller and a drop of water can be seen at the tip of each. The solution is to water less, but avoid extremes on either end.

Dieffenbachia comes from tropical rain forests and does best in warm temperatures, 60° to 85°F, and moderate to high humidity. In practice these plants adapt well to most houses and offices. It does help to mist or shower the leaves well, both tops and undersides, at least once a week to keep them clean and to discourage spider mites. The most persistent problem I've experienced with dieffenbachia is that mealybugs get on the leaf undersides and crawl down into the sheath where the leaf attaches to the main stem. The only way to get rid of them at this stage is to spray purposefully down into every sheath using insecticidal soap, a neem solution, or a dilution of half denatured alcohol and half water. Repeat once a week until the plant is clean.

To help maintain vigor and give the leaves a natural sheen, apply fish emulsion fertilizer every two weeks in spring and summer, once a month or not at all during fall and winter. Dieffenbachia is very sensitive to excess fertilizer, however, especially the petrochemical type, so take care not to overdo. If your plant is not growing as quickly as you'd like, the solution may be to repot to a larger container, adding fresh potting soil, and possibly to relocate it to a brighter place. Dieffenbachia thrives in a loam-based, humus-rich soil kept evenly moist. Repot yearly or when the roots have filled the soil, usually in late winter or spring. Tip cuttings root easily, also lengths of old, leafless stem cut into logs three to six inches long and laid on the surface of moist potting soil; new plants will grow up from each eye along the stem where a leaf once grew. Very large dieffenbachias are sometimes air-layered in order to produce a short, strong new plant with leaves nearly all the way to the soil.

Epipremnum aureum is the nearly omnipresent pothos of commercial and private horticulture, also known as devil's ivy. At an earlier time it was known as *Scindapsus aureus*, but this genus has been reserved for another aroid. 'Marble Queen' is the most popular, with leaves that may be more white than green. 'Orange Moon', 'Silver Moon', and 'Yellow Moon' are newer varieties with coloration varying from apricot to creamy yellow to pewter. Most epipremnums sold as houseplants are in their juvenile stage. Mature plants need stronger light and considerable space. Care for them as for *Philodendron* (see below). I grow pothos trained around twenty-four inch wire wreath forms that were pushed together from the sides so as to create a more oval shape, then anchored upright in the pothos pots, which happen to be twelve-inch terra-cotta ones. These stand on forty-two-inch high pedestals (that I made out of plywood and painted) placed behind and out from each end of my living room sofa. Over the years I wound yards and yards of new pothos vines around the wire forms and when they were as leafy as possible, I pruned yards of excess growth away. Pothos thrives in bright diffused light, average house temperatures, and fresh, moist air. Give it a loam-based, humus-rich potting soil kept evenly moist; avoid extremes of wet and dry. Pothos is remarkably free of bugs and bothers. Propagate from tip cuttings. Remove the lowermost couple of leaves, then insert the bare stem in moist rooting medium. Keep constantly moist, warm, and in bright light. Rooting occurs in two to four weeks. It will help if the cuttings are enclosed for the first week in glass or plastic.

Homalomena, sometimes called *Schismatoglottis*, includes more than a hundred different Asian and American tropicals. There is a Bangkok species with two-inch heart-shaped leaves with silvery flecking in low rosettes that is recommended for terrariums and miniature tray-scapes. There are also newly offered cultivars such as 'Queen of Hearts' and 'King of Spades' that form a mass of foliage somewhat bigger than a bushel and are tolerant of low light levels in houseplantings, to around one hundred footcandles. Semisunny to semishady is the range preferred, average house temperatures, fresh, moist air, no cold drafts. Give it humus-rich, loam-based potting soil and keep evenly moist, saturating the entire soil and root mass each time you water. Propagate by division

or removal of offsets in late winter–early spring. Miniatures and young plants are recommended for fluorescent-light gardens.

Hydrosme is a genus name often found in literature along with discussions of commercial offerings such as voodoo lily, sacred lily of India, and devil's-tongue. Here I have chosen to limit the discussion to one that has grown well for me as a houseplant; see *Amorphophallus* (page 85).

Philodendron and *Monstera*. Two plant names that were unheard of in the year 1900, philodendron and monstera, have become household words in this century. Until recently these genera have been mostly taken for granted and promoted entirely as durable indoor foliage plants. This notion of them represents only a beginning. Any gardener who has ever seen a philodendron bloom wants immediately to know how this can be encouraged. Both true philodendron and the related monstera are tropicals that respond to a definite seasonal cycle comprised of "lean" conditions in fall and winter, "fat" in spring and summer. Give these plants cool but frost-free temperatures in fall and winter, keep the growing medium on the dry side, and do not fertilize. In spring and summer, boost temperatures to constantly warm—65° to 85°F—and water freely. Apply fertilizer regularly, alternating between a foliage type such as 23-21-17 and a flower booster such as 15-30-15. Also situate the plant in the brightest light possible, but protect from direct rays

Miniature Philodendron *cultivar with red petioles.*

Silver-blue trailing Philodendron *cultivar.*

or sun hot enough to burn the leaves, and provide high humidity, 60 percent or more.

There are self-heading or bushy-growing philodendrons that have palmate or split leaves. One often seen at local garden centers is *Philodendron selloum*. It is a tough plant that often survives in very low light. However, to grow full, short, and strong, some direct sun is needed, along with all the other good things that we associate with a warm greenhouse or a rain forest.

One of the plants often marketed as splitleaf philodendron is in fact the fast-growing juvenile stage of *Monstera deliciosa*. In its youth this plant typically has small, roundish leaves that are entire, which is to say they are neither split nor perforated. In the rain forests of southern Mexico where this so-called splitleaf philodendron originates, it would start from seeds or perhaps a chance broken-off part that acts as a cutting. Initially this new plant trails along the ground, then starts up a tree trunk, climbing by means of aerial roots. The more light and air the juvenile receives, the larger the leaves become. As it climbs, the larger leaves encounter more wind and rain resistance and so they adapt by developing the splits and occasional perforations for which the plant is known. Finally, when the maturing plant tops out in full blazing sunlight the spaces between the leaves will greatly reduce, until that part of the plant is more bush than vine.

Under the right growing conditions a mature *Monstera deliciosa* will flower and bear edible fruit, which has been known to occur in captivity, but probably not that often on a strictly house-grown specimen.

Vining philodendrons can be propagated from tip and stem cuttings at almost any time when warmth, moisture, and bright light can be provided. Remove the lowermost leaves and insert the bare lower part of the stem in moist rooting medium. Self-heading or bush philodendrons can be propagated by removing offsets, usually in late winter or spring.

Pistia stratiotes is the pantropical "water lettuce" that can be an invasive weed in regions where it does not freeze out in the winter. To me this plant bears no resemblance to other aroids, yet it does have flowers enclosed in a leaflike spathe. Its rosettes of pale green leaves are noticeably longitudinally veined. These float in water with long feathery root systems. It needs sun to semishade or a fluorescent-light garden, average house temperatures, and high humidity.

Rhektophyllum mirabile, from Nigeria, Cameroon, and Zaire, has arrowhead leaves, dark green with silvery cream veins that form the outline of a fern frond. They're held in a basal clump rising to two feet. Care as for *Syngonium* (see page 91).

Scindapsus pictus 'Argyraeus' (velvet pothos), from the Malay Archipelago, Indonesia, has a heart-shaped leaf nearly three inches long by two inches wide, satiny on the upper surface, olive green with brushings of silver. The leaf undersides are pale green. A new leaf appears along the trailing or vining stem approximately every three or four inches. This plant was given to me originally by a friend who has since left for another realm. What began as a small rooted cutting has grown into at least a half dozen twelve-inch wreaths, which have found homes with other gardeners. The vines can also be trained around and around the surface of a fairly broad but not necessarily deep pot, so that the velvety leaves form a smooth mound of foliage. If the light is bright enough for you to read by, it is bright enough for velvet pothos. Bright diffused light will encourage its silvery brushings. Give it average house temperatures, fresh, moist air, and

a humus-rich, loam-based potting soil kept evenly moist; avoid extremes of wet and dry. Fertilize to encourage more rapid growth when plant has adequate warmth and light.

Spathiphyllum cannifolium, one and one half to two feet, from Guyana and Venezuela, is a choice plant with pale green foliage and large, fragrant white flowers. *Spathiphyllum clevelandii*, one and one half to two feet, is the forerunner of millions of tissue-cultured spathiphyllums that enter the marketplace regularly; *S. wallisii*, from Colombia and Venezuela, is similar but smaller. *Spathiphyllum floribundum*, one foot, from Colombia, has velvety green leaves and white spathes which are smaller than those described. The production and current availability of a super breed of spathiphyllums has been made possible by the science of tissue culturing. It is characteristic of these spathiphyllums to produce many beautiful leaves and flowers all at once, and to be able to maintain this appearance for a relatively extended time in average house conditions. I saw some in a New Orleans hotel lobby that looked too good to be true; my disbelieving fingers checked and the plants were real.

I was also impressed when the Pot Plant Research Center at Aalsmeer, the international flower market in the Netherlands, discovered through research that, all things being equal, a spathiphyllum does better with less light rather than more. This is good news for indoor gardeners. Too much hot, direct sun may not only burn disfiguring holes in the leaves, but the plant can actually be inhibited from flowering by too much light. If your spathiphyllum has plenty of water at the roots and is still wilting in the sunlight, the message is probably that less would be more. Spathiphyllums that are habitually allowed to become so dry they go into a dead wilt soon go into decline. Conversely, they do not like to be left standing in water for an indefinite time. That is usually when a spathiphyllum kicks the bucket, or rather that rot sets in and takes the roots permanently out of service.

Spathiphyllums look best if they are regularly showered in tepid water, leaving the leaves naturally shiny and dust-free. Remove discolored or dried leaves by grasping them at their base and pulling downward so as not to uproot the plant. If many of the leaves have dead tips, this is a sign that there is too much light, not enough water, maybe too much fertilizer, possibly not enough light—one or more stresses. Groom by clipping off the dead tips; try to diagnose the stress and minimize it. Old flower-bearing stems may be removed by clipping them below the average height of the foliage so that no stubs are left showing.

I used to recommend repotting spathiphyllums every year or two in order to maintain vigor. To be honest, there is one sitting only a few paces from where I am writing that looks as beautiful as ever, after at least ten

Spathiphyllum *cultivar*.

years in the same pot and the same soil. It is medium-size S. *clevelandii* and has a leaf span of thirty-six inches. It is in a ten-inch clay pot which stands atop a forty-two-inch pedestal set to the side of a sunny bright window, getting direct sun only a couple of hours late in the day. This old plant gets watered nearly every day when I am home and a half-strength or less fertilizing every week or two unless the weather has been generally cold and wet. I have used petrochemicals and bioorganic fertilizers—no pesticides, though, of any kind, ever.

Spathiphyllums do well in a loam-based, humus-rich potting soil kept evenly moist and in moderately moist to humid air that circulates freely. Propagate by the removal of offsets or by division of large, multistemmed plants at repotting time, usually late winter or spring.

Syngonium has until recently been known mostly as nephthytis, arrowhead vine, or trileaf wonder. The original plain green plant was not true *Nephthytis*, another genus in the aroid family, and it was usually left to fend for itself in the shadier windows or parts of the garden in warm weather. I first saw it blooming in the Garden of the Groves in the Bahamas, where the parent plant had climbed a steep embankment that was darkly shaded, finally reaching full, baking tropical sunlight on top of a rock. It was resplendent with larger-than-life leaves and numerous calla-lilylike blossoms, the likes of which aren't likely to occur indoors.

Beginning especially with the introduction of 'White Butterfly' in 1978, this family of foliage plants has undergone a complete transformation through the selection of naturally suckering plants with the most attractively colored leaves, and by tissue culturing the best of these. This has resulted in an explosion of new material on the market and a much greater consumer awareness.

One thing I've learned in growing syngoniums is that when mealybugs appear, they can be hard to control using the usual soap sprays since there are so many creases in the plant's growth that afford protection. However, if a bug-infested syngonium is cut back to bare stems an inch or so from the pot, repotted with some fresh soil, and put in encouraging growing conditions, it will soon grow once again into a mound of clean new foliage.

There are thirty distinct cultivars of *Syngonium po-dophyllum* alone, according to the *Florida Foliage News-letter*. Watch for the likes of these at your local garden emporium: 'White Butterfly', 'Pink Allusion', 'Maya Red', 'Chocolate', and 'Flutterby'. They make great desk and floor plants that can be enjoyed indefinitely at home and at work.

The *Florida Foliage Newsletter* also recommends the use of 19-6-12 slow-release fertilizer applied every three months at the rate of slightly less than half a teaspoon per four-inch pot. Presumably this applies to syngoniums being grown in a soilless medium such as Pro-Mix. They will also thrive in a loam-based, humus-rich potting soil kept evenly moist. Ideal light is half shady to half sunny.

No matter how much a young syngonium plant may form suckers and thus become bushy in form, it will start to climb eventually. Light levels consistently below 150 footcandles are an inducement to vining new growth— the plant senses it is time to seek out the sun.

The best way to discourage a syngonium from vining is to cut the shoots back to one or two leaves from the soil. Do not save and root all the tip cuttings thus removed unless you are planning on going into the foliage plant business. They will make excellent compost.

Syngonium *cultivar (left and right)*, Senecio cruentus *cultivar (center)*, Pellaea rotundifolia *(front)*.

Syngoniums having variegated foliage almost invari-ably fade from the more youthful and pronounced co-lorations to green or at least a dulled-down version of the original. Plants that receive adequate sunlight, are main-tained slightly on the dry side (but not so extreme as to cause wilting), and aren't overfertilized with nitrogen will display the brightest leaf coloring.

Syngonium podophyllum albo-variegatum is a varie-gated form of syngonium that sometimes has new leaves that are entirely creamy or rosy white. With this one your goal will be to keep it from sending up all-green shoots. These reversions need to be promptly removed from the base, otherwise they will overshadow and ultimately over-come the variegated form.

Xanthosoma lindenii 'Magnificum' from Colombia is a horticultural form having prominently silvery-white-veined arrowhead leaves that are dark green; at a glance this aroid is easily mistaken for a green-and-white calad-ium, to which it is related. A chief difference is that this xanthosoma is evergreen; it does best in constant warmth, high humidity, and bright diffused sunlight. *Xanthosoma violaceum* (blue taro), two to three feet, from Puerto Rico and Jamaica, has brownish purple leaf stalks and sagittate leaves that are dark green with a purple margin. The leaves have an overall bluish "bloom" on the upper sur-face, and purple veins on the underside of the leaf. This species is semiaquatic; it needs to stand in water most of the time. Winter warmth is very important. Other-wise, including propagation, treat as for *Alocasia* (see page 85).

Zantedeschia aethiopica, two to four feet, from South Africa, is the florist's (and photographer's) white calla lily. Its best flowering season is in the winter and spring. Abundant sunlight, water, fertilizer, and warmth (65° to 70°F on average) encourage luxurious leaf growth and large flowers. 'Childsiana' is a dwarf, floriferous cultivar. *Zantedeschia elliottiana*, two to three feet, also from South Africa, is a lovely calla with dark yellow spathes and foliage spotted with translucent silver. It blooms in summer. *Zantedeschia rehmannii*, two feet, from Natal, has rosy pink spathes in summer, and long, slender, lance-shaped leaves.

Xanthosoma lindenii.

The rhizomes of *Zantedeschia aethiopica* are planted in late summer or early autumn; those of the summer-flowering species are potted in late winter or spring. These plants need a sunny, airy, moist and constantly warm atmosphere while in active growth. Use a humus-rich, loam-based potting mix and, once root and leaf growth has been activated, leave the pots standing in saucers of water, a practice that should be maintained until the end of the flowering season. Nothing else you do when a calla lily is in active growth is quite as important as providing a constant supply of water. Dry off at the end of the season; when the leaves have died down, remove them and set the pots away to rest in a dry, frost-free, dark place for a season of rest, usually four or five months. When potting, cover the rhizomes with about two inches of soil; a twelve-inch pot is sufficient for three to six callas. Propagate by removing offsets at potting time, or by sowing seeds in winter or spring in warmth (70° to 80°F) and moisture. Manure tea is a tonic for calla lilies in active growth.

Note: Flowering calla lily plants brought into the house as seasonal decorations may succumb to spider mites after a couple of weeks owing to the stress of reduced light and air. When returned to the outdoors or a sunny, airy plant room, they can be cleaned and revived by spraying weekly with insecticidal soap, keeping the pots standing in saucers of water, and fertilizing every seven to ten days with fertilizer mixed at half strength.

Zantedeschia elliottiana *in front of* Hedera helix '*Goldheart*' *topiary.*

ARALIACEAE. *Ginseng Family*.

Members of this family that are cultivated indoors for their foliage represent tropical as well as temperate parts of the world. Leaves may be simple or compound, and the flowers, apparently insignificant except to the plants themselves, are greenish white, held in clusters, racemes, or panicles. Genera of interest for houseplanting include *Brassaia*, *Dizygotheca*, × *Fatshedera*, *Fatsia*, *Hedera*, *Polyscias*, *Schefflera*, *Trevesia*, and *Tupidanthus*.

Brassaia actinophylla (umbrella plant) is the plant widely known as *Schefflera actinophylla*. By either name it comes from Australia and Java, and is a rapid-growing plant with large, palmately compound leaves. *Brassaia arboricola* (Hawaiian elf) is a relatively recent arrival that has proved durable as a houseplant. It can be shrublike or trained as a tree-form standard. There are varieities having bright yellow or cream variegation in the otherwise dark green leaves. Both types of schefflera, large and small, can be grown following the detailed regimen set out for *Polyscias* (see page 95), a related genus. Always bear in mind that any plant called schefflera or brassaia needs as much light as it can be given. Some of the most beautiful I have seen were growing outdoors in full sun in the tropics. Perhaps surprisingly, I have also seen specimens of both the large and the Hawaiian elf looking healthy and well adapted to northern house gardens.

Dizygotheca elegantissima, from the New Hebrides, has palmately compound, leathery leaves of dark greenish brown with lighter veins, the leaf stalks mottled with white. It is known as false aralia and has probably led to some false arrests because of its resemblance to the leaf of *Cannabis sativa*. *Dizygotheca veitchii*, from New Caledonia, has leaves of similar shape, coppery green above, reddish beneath, and with light red veins. Both of these plants are slender, graceful shrubs which tend to grow with a single, bark-covered trunk. Care is the same as for *Polyscias* (see page 95).

× *Fatshedera lizei* (tree ivy) is a bigeneric hybrid between *Fatsia japonica* and *Hedera helix* (English ivy), both belonging to the same family. The original fatshedera is an erect, weak-stemmed shrub, with glossy dark green leaves very much like those of its ivy parent. A horticultural form, *F. lizei* 'Variegata', has creamy white markings along its leaf edges. It is attractive but more difficult to grow than the all-green variety. It requires sun to semishade, average house temperatures (though on the cool side in winter), and fresh, moist air. Give it a humus-rich, loam-based potting soil kept evenly moist. Propagate from cuttings in late winter or spring.

Fatsia japonica, to fifteen feet, from Japan, is an evergreen shrub with lobed leaves much like those of the castor-bean plant. The foliage of *F. japonica* is glossy dark green, while that of the cultivar 'Variegata' displays an irregular edging of cream-white. Either may be called rice-paper plant, a name more properly applied to *Tetrapanax*. Fatsias are best used as specimen plants indoors to provide a highly decorative, exotic, tropical accent. Pot them in fairly large containers, and shift, as they require it, to larger pots until you reach the ultimate size you can handle. Do not keep them too warm, or where the air is stale, as either of these conditions may lead to spider mites. For best care and propagation, study the details for the related genus, *Polyscias* (see page 95).

Hedera canariensis (Algerian ivy), a trailer from the Azores, Canary Islands, and Morocco, has large, leathery leaves to eight inches across that are plain, glossy green or creamy variegated. *Hedera helix*, also a trailer, from Asia, Europe, and North Africa, is available in seemingly countless varieties, many of them delightfully (or frustratingly) unstable, tending to revert to, presumably, their former selves. The named varieties include those presenting large leaves, small leaves, five-lobed leaves, three-lobed leaves, ruffled or marginally curled edges, and numerous kinds with white or yellow variegation. They comprise one of the largest groups of foliage plants from which the indoor gardener may choose. The true *H. helix*, English ivy, is often seen as ground cover in public gardens and parks, but is a bit coarse for cultivating in house gardens.

Today's varieties of *Hedera helix* seem to grow like weeds when they are provided with an abundance of sun, fresh, moist air that circulates freely, a moist, nutrient-enhanced growing medium, and moderate temperatures,

60° to 75°F. They go to pieces—or the spider mites move in for the kill—when stressed by rapid loss of light, water, or nutrients, or when subjected to uncustomarily hot, dry air. My best advice is to try for conditions that will encourage the ivy, not the mites. I have found that ivies, especially those enjoying an indoor/outdoor existence, grow inherently stronger, with glossier, thicker foliage, when they are potted in a humus-rich, loam-based soil. It must be well drained and, when it is, allowing some water to remain in the saucer after watering is acceptable. I have enjoyed small ivy plants in more than imperfect lighting situations and admire their ability to adapt, survive, and even work at cleaning the air under what might seem impossible circumstances. In recent years, however, hardly any potted ivy in my reach has been safe from recruitment for plant training projects (see Chapter 5). Propagate from tip cuttings of half-ripened wood at any season. Remove the lowermost leaves from the bottom inch or two of stem and insert this part in moist rooting medium. Keep constantly moist, in moderate temperatures, and bright light. *H. helix* ivies send out roots along the stem wherever a moist surface is available, so this natural habit can be taken advantage of if you have a moss-stuffed topiary form. They also make wonderful hanging basket plants and I like to set pots of them on the soil surface of large container trees, so that they spill gracefully over the sides.

Polyscias fruticosa, native to Polynesia and tropical Asia, has inedible leaves that look like those of curly parsley, hence its common name, parsley aralia. If you can grow it well then you can grow all the relatives—varieties of English ivy or *Hedera helix, Dizygotheca, Brassaia, Trevesia, Tupidanthus* and, for that matter, all manner of other species of *Polyscias*. It is to me a great plant, the sort of thing that reaches out and grabs you as you are shopping for plants—or maybe you weren't actually shopping. Just walking by. Anyhow, a real specimen of parsley aralia, showing a trunk with some age and character, crowned by a leafy mantle—and we're talking money, possibly hundreds of dollars—is suddenly, inexplicably on its way home with you.

Speaking in general terms, parsley aralia should adapt and become a thriving plant in or near almost any window that receives direct sunlight for part of the day. Maintain the growing medium in a range between evenly moist to slightly on the dry side at the surface. When I hear that a gardener has purchased a potted plant costing hundreds of dollars it always flashes through my mind that they may water too little too often. The idea is to water the soil so that it is moistened through and through. If isolated root pockets remain dry, the corresponding branches may die even though they are surrounded by healthy growth. Conversely, a large plant that has been overwatered can also be a problem; its roots may die as a result of drowning for lack of oxygen. Don't leave one standing in a saucer of water for more than a few hours. Instead, borrow the bulb baster from the kitchen and use it to draw off the excess water that remains in the saucer after the soil has had an hour or so to absorb all it needs.

Another problem inherent in large indoor plants is that after a few weeks they become dusty. This is not to imply the gardener is not a good housekeeper, but it is a fact of life. A feather duster can help keep parsley aralia leaves dust-free, but nothing takes the place of a refreshing shower of lukewarm water in the shower or tub, or outdoors, weather permitting.

During the spring and summer months, parsley aralia will benefit from being fertilized every two weeks. You may use the organics such as fish emulsion or liquid seaweed, or any fertilizer labeled specifically for foliage plants. The more direct sun polyscias receives, the more water and fertilizer that can be assimilated. Average house temperatures suit the polyscias, along with plenty of good air circulation. Young parsley aralias are often potted in bonsai trays or bowls and are known as ming aralias.

At repotting time, in late winter or spring, or when roots have filled the pot, give polyscias a loam-based, humus-rich potting soil. At the same time, remove up to a third of the old roots and a similar portion of the plant top parts, especially any leafless or dead branches. Healthy tip cuttings can be rooted by inserting an inch or two of the stems in a fifty-fifty, moistened mix of sphagnum peat moss and sand, ideally in late winter or spring.

Two more things you should know before bringing home a parsley aralia. This plant gives off a peculiar odor; it doesn't bother me but your nose will have to be your judge. The other watchword is that brown scale insects frequently inhabit polyscias—be ever on the alert. P.S. If you need to grow small, there is *Polyscias fruticosa* 'Bonsai', a miniature aralia perfectly suited to life as a bonsai or in a terrarium.

Schefflera is a genus in the ginseng family, but the popular schefflera of commerce is to be found under the genus named *Brassaia*.

Trevesia palmata, from northern India to southwestern China, is an evergreen that can become a small tree, to seven or eight feet tall as a houseplant. The palmately lobed leaves, to twelve inches across or more, are uniquely cut so that there is a sort of webbing of foliage tissue around the central portion of each leaf. The cultivar 'Micholitzii' (snowflake plant) has silvery white variegation. This is a most unusual foliage houseplant that would become more popular if it were not so difficult to propagate, the only reliable method being air-layering. Otherwise, treat it the same as *Polyscias* (see page 95).

Tupidanthus calyptratus, four to twelve feet, from India to Cambodia, grows as a bush in cultivation but is by nature a high-growing woody vine. The ones I have seen potted look like young specimens of ordinary schefflera (*Brassaia*). Care and propagation as for *Polyscias*

Tupidanthus calyptratus.

(see page 95). Tupidanthus seems to be less susceptible to spider mite than common schefflera, or perhaps it is just more adaptable to a variety of conditions.

Trevesia palmata.

ASCLEPIADACEAE. *Milkweed Family.*

Mostly tropical herbs, shrubs, vines, and cactuslike succulents bearing regular flowers and containing a milky juice. Genera considered here: *Ceropegia*, *Dischidia*, *Hoya*, *Stapelia*, and *Stephanotis*.

Ceropegia barkleyi, from Cape Province, is very similar to *C. woodii* (see page 97), except its leaves are more pointed. *Ceropegia caffrorum*, from eastern South Africa, has plain green arrowhead leaves set on long wiry stems while *C. debilis*, from Nyasaland, has plain green, very slender leaves scarcely one eighth inch wide. *Ceropegia sandersonii*, from Natal, has succulent stems, set at distant intervals with plain green leaves; *C. stapeliiformis*, from Cape Province, has stout succulent stems, one half to one inch in diameter, with stapelialike flowers about three inches long in summer. *Ceropegia woodii* (string of hearts, rosary vine) from Natal, has small, silver-mottled, heart-shaped leaves on long wiry stems; small bulbs develop along these. The purplish flowers are about one-and-one-half-inches long, and bottlelike—round at the bottom, slender in the middle and capped by several hairy spokes, leading to another common name, umbrella vine. All of the *Ceropegia* species mentioned above are trailers or twiners having thread- or cordlike stems and

Ceropegia fusca.

subtly colored flowers shaped on the order of those described for *C. woodii*.

Ceropegia fusca, from the Canary Islands, is a decided departure from the vines of the genus. *Fusca* grows rigidly upright, to three or four feet, in jointed but smooth stems that rise together in the pot like a bundle of gray-green bamboo stakes. I first saw this plant at Grigsby Cactus Gardens, Vista, California, and have every intention of growing it at the first opportunity.

When I wrote of this genus in the original *World Book of House Plants* (1963), I said, "The ceropegias compose a strange genus. Only *C. barkleyi* and *C. woodii* are truly attractive. The others are interesting because they are bizarre or grotesque." I have mellowed. No plant is "strange" to me. All plants are truly "attractive," although I prefer to keep certain ones, such as poison ivy, at least a little beyond arm's length.

Ceropegias need lots of sun, average to warm house temperatures, and good air circulation. Give them loam-based potting soil kept between evenly moist and on the dry side. They can take more water in spring and summer than during the cooler seasons. Propagate from late winter to summer by removing and potting the small bulbs that have formed on mature stems, or by making cuttings of half-ripened growth.

Dischidia albida (propeller vine) has propeller-shaped pairs of gray-green leaves on soft swollen stems that may be pendant or climbing. *Dischidia milnei* has stiff, slender stems and masses of coin-shaped leaves; a recommended houseplant. There are numerous other dischidias. They are closely allied with and require similar care and propagation as the *Hoya*.

Hoya bella, from India, is a dwarf, nearly upright plant with pink- or purple-centered flowers. It was among the first I became acquainted with and is still a favorite with me for window and light gardens and also for hanging or shelving outdoors in summer. *Hoya carnosa*, the popular wax plant, from Queensland and southern China, has very fragrant, pinkish white flowers, each set in the center with a red, star-shaped crown. *Hoya carnosa* 'Variegata' has leaves broadly bordered in white and pink-tinged and 'Silver Leaf' has silver and pink markings on

Hoya carnosa 'Variegata'.

decided differences between a "fat" or active growing season and a "lean" or half-resting season in order to bloom. Culture includes a sunny to semisunny situation, average house temperatures, fresh, moist air. Plant in a humus-rich, loam-based potting soil and do not repot until after the first flowering. In spring and summer, with adequate light and warmth available, water freely, just don't leave standing in water. In fall and winter, with cooler temperatures, between 50° and 70°F, and less light, keep on the dry side and do not fertilize. This has a beneficial effect on the hoya's root system. Flowering tends to occur at the beginning of the "fat" season, spring and early summer, but may continue for several months. These are plants worth growing well!

Old-fashioned hoya vines were often trained to frame half-sunny to merely bright windows. In Europe, shaping them into a wreath twelve to fifteen inches in diameter is traditional. Prune only to remove stems that have died; be careful of removing the living parts that contain the bloom spurs. Hoyas propagate readily from cuttings of half-ripened stems, also leaf mallet cuttings, from late winter to summer.

Stapelia gigantea, from Zululand to Zambia, to one foot, has blooms up to eighteen inches across, pale yellow with irregular crimson lines crossbanding the petals. They have a smell resembling that of a dead horse; if you grow this plant and it actually blooms in your house, there

Stapelia nobilis.

long green leaves and bears maroon flowers. Some smaller *Hoya* species especially suited to growing as houseplants include *H. pubera*, *H. serpens*, *H. engleriana*, *H. lineraris*, *H. lacunosa*, and *H. pauciflora*.

Although hoyas are well known as houseplants, the major factor in their care seems to be little understood. As a consequence, too few amateur growers have the satisfaction of seeing the plants bloom. The most important detail is this: Do not remove the stem or "spur" from which flowers have been borne; next season's flowers will appear in the same place.

Hoyas are extremely adaptable, but they also need the

will be trouble unless you were already living alone. *Stapelia nobilis*, from Transvaal, has tufted pale green leaves and enormous flowers, to 15 cm. across. The smaller, less smelly *S. variegata*, from South Africa, grows four to six inches tall, and bears chartreuse and maroon-brown flowers about three inches across. These succulent plants need full sun, fresh air, and average house temperatures. Set them in a well-drained, loam-based potting soil kept evenly moist to on the dry side in spring and summer. Spring is the time to divide and repot or make cuttings. Flowering occurs in summer. Keep on the dry side and withhold fertilizer in fall and winter.

Stephanotis floribunda, the Madagascar jasmine, is better known as the bride's flower. It is a wiry twiner with opposite, oblong, leathery leaves that are glossy dark green. It bears clusters of tubular flowers, most abundant in summer, that are waxy white and intoxicatingly fragrant. As a houseplant, I prefer to train stephanotis as a living wreath, fifteen to eighteen inches in diameter (see pages 193–194). The vines grow rapidly in spring and summer and respond to generous watering and fertilizing. Never drop your guard with regard to mealybugs and stephanotis; if found, treat at once—cotton swabs dipped in denatured alcohol will do nicely—or say good-bye to your bride's flower. Flowering occurs in response to a season of baking in the sun followed by a time of coolness (50° to 70°F) and relative dryness. Soon after this "fast" is broken in the spring, with more light, more water, more warmth, flowering occurs and may continue on sun-drenched vines for several months, ending finally with the development of large pods filled with parachute-equipped seeds, thus revealing the family tie to the milkweeds. Stephanotis does well in a loam-based, humus-rich soil and can be propagated from cuttings of half-ripened wood from late winter to spring.

BALSAMINACEAE. *Balsam Family*.

Watery-stemmed, warm-climate herbs with simple leaves and showy, spurred flowers. One genus is of interest here, *Impatiens*.

Impatiens 'African Queen'.

Impatiens wallerana, to three feet, native from Tanzania to Mozambique, has small, reddish leaves and burgundy-colored stems veined with red. Countless hybrids exist in almost every color of the rainbow. Any of these may be called "patient Lucy," and "impatience" has been heard in the presence of those whose impatiens were stubbornly refusing to perform satisfactorily. A series of miniature cultivars named for the five largest Hawaiian Islands has been introduced through The New York Botanical Garden and Kartuz Greenhouses (see Resources). They are 'Hawaii' (a white and rose-purple bicolor), 'Kauai' (dark rose-purple), 'Maui' (coral red), 'Molokai' (a pink-and-rose bicolor), and 'Ohau' (salmon pink). Kartuz advises frequent pinching to keep these plants small and covered with flowers.

Impatiens 'African Queen' (one-inch orange-red and yellow flowers produced all year on dark brown succulent stems) and 'African King' (large, one-and-one-fourth-inch cornucopia-shaped flowers of dark crimson constantly produced in many-flowered clusters among showy dark quilted leaves) have been recently brought into cultivation. *Impatiens auricoma* (synonym *I. comorense*) has light green tapered leaves on succulent stems. Everblooming, it bears bright butter yellow balsam-shaped flowers with red striping in the throat.

Impatiens platypetala aurantiaca, to two feet, from the Celebes, has green leaves and two-inch flowers of subdued salmon orange. Each has a scarlet eye, the center of which is set with an emerald green ovary. *Impatiens repens* (trailing impatiens), from India and Sri Lanka, has succulent creeping red stems set with tiny leaves and one-and-one-half-inch yellow balsam-shaped flowers. Suggested for hanging baskets, shelving, and as a ground cover around large container plants.

Outdoors in the summer, or in any frost-free season, in a spot where there is some shade, impatiens are peerless providers of season-long flowering. Many strains are started from seeds sown midwinter (in a sunny, airy greenhouse or early in a maxi light garden), and brought to flowering size by warm weather. The fancy-leaved, large-flowered New Guinea hybrids are more likely propagated from tip cuttings; these need full sun in order to bring out the leaf colors and to promote flowering.

Impatiens in general are a problem if brought inside after they have come into full growth outdoors. For some reason spider mites inevitably take over when the impatiens is stressed—dry, stale air and reduced light being the duo that seems to do in outdoor-grown impatiens. They are surprisingly easy to manage in home greenhouses or any sort of sun room where water can be splashed around and the air can be kept circulating freely with fans and vents. Considering that the impatiens was only a folk plant until after World War II, passed from gardener to gardener in the form of cuttings, it has come a long way, becoming one of the largest selling of all commercial plants. What we have lately learned is that, all things being equal, more sunlight is needed rather than less to promote heavy flowering. The plants do well in a humus-rich, loam-based potting soil kept evenly moist and in fresh air that can circulate freely.

BEGONIACEAE. *Begonia Family*.

Mostly succulent herbs from tropical parts of the world; each flower is of one sex only. The male flowers have two petals (excepting many-petaled doubles developed in cultivation), the females two to five, with a three-angled ovary (seed capsule). Typically the leaves are lopsided. Besides *Begonia*, two rarely cultivated genera are included in the family, *Hillebrandia* and *Symbegonia*.

The various kinds of begonias are as different as any members of the same genus could be. There are miniature, terrarium-size begonias, and giants which can top six feet; begonias with innumerable small round leaves, and those with star-shaped or lobed leaves a foot or more across; varieties which grow like dwarf bushes covered with clusters of colorful blooms, those which dangle heavy bouquets from the tips of their stems, kinds which send up tall stems with airy showers of flowers on top, and types which hide their flowers under some of the most brilliant foliage in the plant world.

Because of the many variations, begonias don't seem to fall neatly into clear-cut classifications. I sort them out according to types of roots—fibrous, rhizomatous, and tuberous—and each of these in turn seems to subdivide into several smaller groups.

Wax begonias. Among the fibrous-rooted begonias, the best known are the *semperflorens* (everblooming) or wax begonias, with many compact branches covered with nearly round, waxy green or reddish leaves and bearing flowers all over at intervals throughout the year. The commercial bedding plant begonias are grown annually from seeds sown in early winter for thrifty seedlings that have gone all to bloom by selling time for the new gardening season outdoors. When one knows the possibilities in this large class of begonias, the bedding plant type is hardly worth having as a houseplant, except possibly to start the seeds for an outdoor planting. Josephine Shanks in Houston has a pale pink *semperflorens*-type species with bronzy foliage that reaches two feet tall and self-sows in a volunteering sort of way that looks wonderful in a cottage garden or mixed flower border. A begonia that has self-sown into an outdoor garden will not have the soldier-sameness of the commercial bedding plant but rather is inclined instead to natural variation.

A current trend in begonia breeding is to cross two different *semperflorens* lines in order to get a new plant that is showy and has hybrid vigor and a taller, more graceful habit than can be found in ordinary wax begonias. Mabel Corwin, a grower in southern California, has pioneered in this type of breeding. Her cultivar 'Christmas Candy'—gotten by crossing a named commercial *Begonia semperflorens* and an unidentified *semperflorens*-type species obtained through the Seed Fund of the American Begonia Society—has large, almost angel-wing-begonia-size leaves that are crisp bright green with the finest of red lines along the edges, and generous clusters of warm, bright red flowers that are thrust outward from the plant in a way that dramatizes their beauty. There are also *semperflorens* having semidouble blossoms called "thimble" or "crested," and double, "rosebud" or "camellia," with green, bronzy, or mahogany-red foliage. Because these begonias are succulent, their soil needs to dry a bit at the surface before it is moistened. For fullest flowering, provide several hours of sun daily in the winter, and all but the hottest in summer. They do well in any maxi light garden. These everyday working begonias need a humus-rich, loam-based soil kept evenly moist to on the dry side, average house temperatures, and good air circulation. They benefit from applications of fertilizer at half strength every two weeks in spring and summer, about half this amount or frequency in the fall and winter.

The calla-lily begonia is a form of *Begonia semperflorens* having white-variegated leaves; some leaves as they emerge are entirely white, edged in pink, and furled so as to resemble a real, albeit very small, calla lily. The "magic" involved in succeeding with this uncommon form of a very common plant is to treat it more as a succulent. In other words, grow "hard," or on the dry side, but nothing too extreme, wet or dry. Plants having colorfully variegated foliage generally need more sunlight than the matching monocolor counterpart.

It also pays to go easy on fertilizers having a high nitrogen content when growing colorful leaves. Where the calla-lily begonia is concerned, for instance, you may wish to fertilize alternately with a balanced formula such as 20-20-20, to build a strong plant generally, and a low- or no-nitrogen formula, such as 0-6-5 or 1-6-5, to bring out maximum leaf coloration.

It is hard to let bedding begonias go to the first killing frost. These shallow-rooted plants transplant readily if taken up with a modicum of soil, and can be enjoyed indoors for several weeks. When they start paling and stretching, the best treatment, drastic though it sounds, is to cut the plant back to an inch or so from the soil. Clean out all the weaker and dead parts that remain. Now the very heart of the plant is exposed to light and air and before long there will be new basal shoots that can be expected to start blooming in a month or so.

Tip cuttings of bedding begonia will root, but they tend to branch poorly. Cuttings of branched basal shoots work better, although where most *Begonia semperflorens* are concerned, starting fresh from quality seeds is the way to have lots of thrifty, flower-covered seedlings for a new gardening season.

Cane-stems, also fibrous-rooted, are popularly known as angel-wing begonias because the lopsided leaves are shaped like, and hang like, wings. They have sturdy stems with swollen, widely spaced joints. While quite small they may begin to drip heavy clusters of large flowers. These plants resent constant moisture in the soil and will quickly drop their lower leaves in response to either extreme of wet or dry. Pinching out the growing tips occasionally will keep them more compact and attractive, and after the main flowering season, often in spring or early summer, it is good policy to repot and remove to

Begonia *'Tiny Gem', a miniature cane-stem.*

Begonia *'Cathedral'*, *a rhizomatous begonia.*

the base about a third of the oldest canes. These plants vary from miniatures under six inches to specimens six feet tall and as wide—or more. Propagate them from late winter to summer from tip or stem cuttings of half-ripened wood.

Hairy-leaved begonias, which are mostly fibrous-rooted, wear a coat of bristly or velvety hair on their leaves and outside the flower petals. They trail beautifully from hanging baskets or shelf plantings, and among their lot are a great number of unclassifiable "odd" and rare types. Propagate from tip or stem cuttings of half-ripened wood.

Rhizomatous begonias have a fleshy rhizome that is a thick, scarred, ground-level stem which creeps over the soil (not through it) and sends down shallow roots. From the top of the rhizome, leaf and flower stems grow up out of the eyes. The blooms generally appear high above the foliage in late winter and spring, the small individual white or pale pink flowers forming a cloud over the plant foliage. *Begonia masoniana* (iron-cross begonia), with pale green leaves marked with a distinctive chocolate brown cross, is an example of a rhizomatous begonia that is easily mistaken for a rex, which it closely resembles. Propagate from late winter to summer from rhizome or leaf cuttings.

Rex begonias are mostly rhizomatous, but they are known and grown as a separate class because their main attraction is their foliage of gorgeous colors and patterns. As a rule, they require more warmth and humidity than most other begonias and not much sun, but rather bright diffused light. Spring and summer are the active times for the rexes; they are kept cooler and drier in late fall and winter. A warm maxi light garden kept to long days of sixteen to eighteen hours will maintain rexes in active growth at any season. Propagate from rhizome or leaf cuttings from late winter to summer.

Tuberous begonias. The larger-flowered begonias offered in cellophane or plastic wraps at the supermarket are likely to be Riegers, a recent development that in appearance is somewhere between a bedding begonia and

Begonia rex *cultivar.*

a large-flowered tuberous type. The Riegers do well at moderate temperatures, 50° to 60°F at night, up to 75°F by day. Don't leave the pots standing in water, but also be careful not to let the soil dry out enough to cause even slight wilting, otherwise the flower buds will dry up.

Rieger begonia (center), Adiantum *maidenhair fern, and* Hedera helix *ivy.*

Riegers will go on blooming indefinitely in bright light or with an hour or two of dappled sunlight, as through a lace curtain. About once a week, or as often as needed, go over each plant and remove any fading flowers or petals that may have fallen on the leaves. This makes the plants look better and helps avoid leaf blight. There'll be more blooms if the plants are given very dilute applications of fertilizer with every third or fourth watering. If the fertilizer you use calls for a teaspoon to two quarts of water, use only a quarter teaspoon.

Finally, when a Rieger goes out of bloom, and sooner or later they all do, compost what is left and start over with a youthful plant. I suppose a plant that it obviously dead is easier to part with than one that is still fairly green. I am sure there are gardeners who have perpetuated Riegers from cuttings or by pruning back the parent plant, but this is usually more trouble than it is worth.

Summer-flowering tuberous begonias are started from seeds in early winter—a maxi light garden is ideal—or from purchased tubers in late winter and early spring. They need to be placed outdoors in dappled sunlight to nearly full shade as soon as the weather is warm and settled. The larger, more obviously showy male flowers tend to predominate in summer during the longest days while the female ones will be more apparent in autumn, at which time no further fertilizing is needed and they can be gradually dried off. Keep over winter in moderate temperatures (50° to 60°F), nearly dry, and in a dark place. I am particularly interested in the species *Begonia martiana* (from Mexico; two feet tall; fragrant two-inch pink flowers; the hollyhock begonia) and *B. sutherlandii* (from Natal; one to two feet; pale green leaves on arching reddish stems; coppery or salmon red flowers all summer), and recommend them for outdoor containers in warm weather.

One of the first begonias I fell in love with as a child was the Christmas begonia 'Lady Mac', with pink flowers trailing down the stem one after another. A more recent cultivar is 'Marjorie Gibbs' and both are of the Melior type, originated from tuberous species that normally bloom in winter when days are short. (The summer-flowering tuberous types bloom mostly when the days are longest.) Unfortunately the commercial growers have dropped the Meliors in favor of the Riegers, perfectly lovely seasonal flowering plants but somehow not holding half the romance of the old Christmas begonias. Thankfully the latter are still in cultivation and may be obtained from specialist growers such as Logee's (see Resources). Start Christmas begonias from leaf cuttings in late winter or spring. They need bright light but protection from hot, direct sun during warm weather. Provide good air circulation at all times. Set in a humus-rich, loam-based potting soil and keep evenly moist.

Begonias with Fragrant Flowers

Fragrance is something rarely associated with the begonia, yet there are many different ones with flowers that have a light lemony or floral scent, especially on a sunny morning as the air becomes warm enough to volatilize the essential oils.

BEGONIA SPECIES WITH FRAGRANT BLOOMS

B. *aptera*	B. *lubbersii*
B. *attentuata*	B. *luxurians*
B. *baumannii*	B. *malabarica*
B. *convallariodora*	B. *martiana*
B. *decora*	B. *mazae*
B. *deliciosa*	B. *nitida*
B. *dipetala*	B. *odorata*
B. *echinosepala*	B. *picta*
B. *gemmipara*	B. *pilifera*
B. *grandis*	B. *roxburghii*
B. *handelii*	B. *solananthera*
B. *heracleifolia*	B. *valida*
B. *herbacea*	B. *veitchii*
B. *hydrocotylifolia*	B. *venosa*

BEGONIA HYBRIDS WITH FRAGRANT BLOOMS

B. 'Bessie Buxton'	B. 'Cininc'
B. 'Bright Eyes'	B. 'Curly Fire Flush'

B. 'Decorus'	B. 'Maphil'
B. 'Ella Keyes'	B. 'Martha Floro'
B. 'Eunice Gray'	B. 'Orange Rubra'
B. 'Fire Flush'	B. 'Perfectiflora'
B. 'Gloire de Seaux'	B. 'Pink Parade'
B. 'Grace'	B. 'Rogue'
B. 'Ionic'	B. 'Shasta'
B. 'Irene Nuss'	B. 'Tamo'
B. 'It'	B. 'Tea Rose'
B. 'Kristie'	B. 'Undine'
B. 'Lenore Olivier'	B. 'Washington Street'

BROMELIACEAE. *Bromeliad or Pineapple Family.*

Mostly epiphytic plants from the American tropics with rosettes of stiff leaves. The foliage is almost always interesting, the flowers showy. Genera of particular interest for houseplanting include *Aechmea, Ananas, Billbergia, Cryptanthus, Dyckia, Guzmania, Neoregelia, Nidularium, Tillandsia,* and *Vriesea.*

Since most of us become acquainted with a bromeliad when it is mature and flowering, here is a simple scenario for how to produce another round of growth and bloom:

1) Keep in mind that the glorious leaf colors of many bromeliads, especially that of aechmeas and neoregelias, are pronounced in bright light. Spring is the time to put them in the sunshine. Be sure to do it gradually. Bromeliads sunscorch easily and a burned leaf destroys the symmetry of the plant. Well grown in full sunlight, the colors glow, but be cautious about too much at midday in summer. Plants that have soaked up their quota of sun rays during warm weather can get along on less in the fall and winter.

2) A key to success with bromeliads is to keep the potting medium very light and fast-draining, such as a mix of redwood chips, redwood mulch, perlite, turkey grit, and horticultural charcoal. This is a loose mix which will spill if the pot is knocked over,

so I prefer the heavier clay pots to plastic in this situation. The mix is efficient-draining and effective for almost any epiphytic houseplant.

3) Avoid allowing bromeliads to go unwatered for any length of time. This will prevent salt buildup and leaf tip burn. Also, whenever possible, use rainwater to prevent lime marks on the leaves. Fertilize every two weeks in spring and summer, monthly at other seasons, using a liquid fertilizer such as 23-21-17. If you use fish emulsion or liquid seaweed, apply the solution to the potting medium, but do not leave it standing in the cups or vases formed by the leaves since this kind of fertilizer will quickly turn foul when left standing.

Aechmea fasciata, one and one half feet, from Brazil, has a cultivar, 'Purpurea', that has purple to maroon bands with silver markings on the leaves. In late summer a flower spike bearing pink bracts and blue flowers appears. The bracts age to purple and rose, and may last five months. 'Foster's Favorite' has glossy, wine red leaves and pendent spikes of dark blue flowers in winter, followed by blue berries. *Aechmea orlandiana* 'Ensign' is a showy cultivar developed from a Brazilian species with leaves prominently banded gray-green, white, and rosy pink. There are dozens of cultivars listed, making this genus fair game for collectors.

The leaf rosettes of aechmeas are vaselike in their ability to hold water; understandably they're also known as the living vase plant. In tropical gardens it is not uncommon to see orchid or hibiscus flowers placed within these living vases to provide color to plants not in bloom. Since these flowers do not require water in order to stay fresh for short periods of time, and since neither has a long stem which can penetrate to the base of the rosette, this does no harm. However, many amateur growers have taken up this practice, often using cut flowers which use up water and, worse, have long, stiff stems which can damage the heart of the plant, where its own flower spike develops. If you have an aechmea, don't risk injury to the plant by trying to gild the lily, or rather the aechmea. Have patience and your plant will send up its own mag-

Aechmea orlandiana 'Ensign'.

nificent spike of long-lasting, highly colored blossoms. For care and seasonal management, see the general discussion at the beginning of this section, page 104.

Ananas comosus, from Baia (Bahia) and Mata Grosso in Brazil, the pineapple of commerce and as such the most famous bromeliad, can also make a rewarding houseplant. It takes about eighteen months from the time the top is set to root until fruiting becomes a possibility.

1) Slice the top from a very ripe fruit. Preserve all of the leaf rosette's base where it grows out of the fruit. Scrape away any soft fruit that still adheres to the base; air-dry for twenty-four hours.

2) Prepare a six-inch pot of sandy, humusy growing medium such as equal parts packaged, all-purpose potting soil, sharp sand, sphagnum peat moss, and well-rotted leaf mold. Moisten well.

3) Make an indentation about two inches deep with your fingers in the center of the pot of growing medium. Set the pineapple top in place. Firm all around with your fingers.

4) Enclose in a plastic bag and set to root in a warm (about 70° to 75°F), bright spot, but not in direct

sun. A maxi light garden is ideal. Remove the plastic weekly and add a little water if the medium seems dry.

5) When the top firms up and shows signs of growing, gradually remove the plastic over a week's time, until it is no longer needed. Also gradually move the pineapple to a window that receives direct sun part of the day; if you have a maxi light garden, this is an excellent place to continue growing.

6) Water so as to keep the medium evenly moist, letting the surface go slightly dry. Never leave a pineapple pot standing in water more than an hour or two.

7) When the pineapple is several months old, begin fertilizing every two weeks with 20-20-20 or 23-21-17 or apply timed-release 14-14-14 pellets or something similar that will last for three or four months.

8) When the pineapple is approximately eighteen months old, switch to a blossom-booster fertilizer such as 15-30-15.

9) If the pineapple plant shows no signs of fruiting by the time it is two years old, try this: Enclose the pot, plant and all, in a plastic bag with a very ripe Jonathan or Cortland apple. Seal and tie. Place in a warm room, out of direct sun, or in a light garden. After seventy-two hours, remove the bag and apple and discard. Set the pineapple back in its usual growing space. Ethylene gas, a natural ripening agent given off by all apples to some degree, but especially by the two named, helps trigger flowering and thence fruiting in the pineapple. You can apply this forcing technique to any mature bromeliad to boost budding. After blooming and fruiting, the pineapple plant will send up offsets that can be removed and potted separately when they are large enough to handle, the same as for other bromeliads.

Billbergia amoena, from southern Brazil, has rose-colored bracts and blue-edged, green flowers on a plant twelve to eighteen inches tall. *Billbergia iridifolia concolor*, from Espirito Santo, Brazil, has pale pink bracts and yellow flowers, while *B. venezueleana* has rose bracts, white sepals, and chartreuse petals. *Billbergia nutans*, from Brazil, Uruguay, and Argentina, called queen's tears for its nodding inflorescence of rosy bracts and violet-edged green flowers, and silvery bronze leaves, is among the most enduring of all bromeliads cultivated as houseplants. It was one of the first species brought into cultivation and written up favorably in the popular gardening press. The care of these is as for other rain-forest bromeliads, detailed on page 104. They are highly rated houseplants.

Cryptanthus—meaning hidden flower—is the genus name for these generally low-growing, ground-hugging rosettes of colorfully marked leaves. Their lovely common name is earth star. One of the most beautiful is *C. bromelioides tricolor*, whose bright green leaves are vivid rose at the base and on the margins, edged and striped ivory-white. Another colorful favorite is *C. zonatus zebrinus*, from Brazil, with bronzy purple leaves cross-banded brown. Recent arrivals favored for their compact habit and vivid tricoloring are 'It' and 'Ti', the latter being a mirror image of 'It', with all the colors in alternate positions. Many new cultivars are available; this is a highly collectible genus. Care as for other bromeliads; see page 104. The cryptanthus are generally small enough for a terrarium or bowl garden; they do especially well four to six inches beneath the tubes in a maxi light garden.

Dyckia brevifolia, from southern Brazil, has starlike rosettes twelve to eighteen inches in diameter of stiff, succulent, glossy green leaves that are silver-lined beneath. It has an off-center inflorescence, a long stalk bearing bright orange flowers. *Dyckia fosterana*, from Parana in Brazil, has a dense rosette of silvery purple leaves, prominently silver-spined, and bears orange flowers on a spike. This genus is xerophytic terrestrial, meaning it comes from drier regions than the rain-forest bromeliads. Mulford Foster, for whom the species was named, told me near the end of his life and with great glee that after he located the original colony of what was to be named *D. fosterana*, other plant explorers asked him to pinpoint the exact spot so that they could retrace his steps. Foster deliberately misled them. Dyckia culture

Cryptanthus *species and cultivars.*

is approximately the same as for other bromeliads, see page 104, but lots of sun is a necessity while high humidity is not.

Guzmania, from the Andean rain forests, especially the species G. *lingulata* and its cultivars 'Major' (scarlet star, originally collected in Ecuador) and 'Minor' (orange star) have become popular for the flowering pot plant market. They have smooth-edged, flexible leaves in a twelve-inch rosette and an obviously showy, long-lasting flower bract. These do well in window and light gardens. Provide bromeliad care, discussed at the beginning of this section.

Neoregelia carolinae 'Tricolor', from Brazil, is one of the showiest plants in this grouping. Its twelve- to eighteen-inch rosettes of bright green leaves, precisely striped with lengthwise bands of ivory, become suffused with phosphorescent rose-pink in spring, or at the onset of maturation and flowering. This bright coloring remains into autumn or for several months. Neoregelias in general are mostly erect bromeliads, many with colorful foliage, often spiny-edged, and bear their blossoms low within the leaf rosettes. Neoregelia spectabilis has a twelve- to eighteen-inch rosette of olive green leaves that are tipped with glowing red, thus inspiring the common name fingernail plant. Follow bromeliad care (see page 104).

Vriesea carinata (lobster claws) from southeastern Brazil, has pale green leaves in a twelve- to eighteen-inch upright rosette and a flattened spike with dark yellow bracts that are glowing crimson at the base. Vriesea splendens 'Major' (flaming sword), from Guyana, has slender blue-green leaves crossbanded dark purple, and a flattened fiery red bract from which are borne the yellow flowers. These and other vrieseas are among the showiest of the bromeliads; for care, see page 104.

CACTACEAE. *Cactus Family.*

Succulents from the American tropics with fleshy, thickened stems, usually spiny, and colorful, decorative flowers. It can be said that all cacti are succulents; all succulents, however, are not members of the Cactaceae. This is a vast family; genera included here are *Aporocactus, Astrophytum, Cephalocereus, Chamaecereus, Cleistocactus, Echinocactus, Echinocereus, Echinopsis, Epiphyllum, Gymnocalycium, Hatiora, Hylocereus, Lobivia, Mammillaria, Notocactus, Opuntia, Pereskia, Rebutia, Rhipsalidopsis, Rhipsalis, Schlumbergera, Selenicereus,* and *Zygocactus.*

Aporocactus flagelliformis (rattail cactus), from Mexico, has slender trailing stems with ten to twelve ribs, and showy, bright red flowers. It is ideal in a hanging basket or as a shelf plant. Give it a sunny situation, average house temperatures, fresh air, and a well-drained, loam-based potting soil kept evenly moist in spring and summer, on the dry side the balance of the year. Propagate by removing offsets, or by rooting cuttings in damp sand. Flowering occurs in spring, following a lean time of cool (40° to 50°F) but frost-free temperatures, little water, and no fertilizer.

Astrophytum asterias (sand dollar, sea-urchin cactus), from northern Mexico, forms a low, spineless dome divided into eight segments that are distinctively marked. It has large red-throated yellow flowers. *Astrophytum myriostigma* (bishop's cap), two inches, from central Mexico, is spineless, star-shaped, divided into five segments, and covered with soft white scales. Golden yellow flowers with many petals arise from the center in summer. Care as for *Aporocactus* (see page 107).

Cephalocereus senilis (old-man cactus), from Mexico, has a covering of long, snowy white, hairlike spines. Grows rigidly upright to the height of a small tree in the right situation and bears night-blooming flowers that are rose-colored and showy. Care as for *Aporocactus* (see page 107).

Chamaecereus sylvestri (miniature peanut cactus), from Argentina, has clusters of short, six- to ten-inch cylindrical branches and orange-scarlet flowers. The entire plant is covered with soft white spines. Care as for *Aporocactus* (see page 107).

Cleistocactus baumannii (scarlet bugler), from Argentina and Paraguay, is an old-time favorite that can grow its erect stems to five or six feet tall, with bright red, tubular blossoms in summer; *C. strausii* (silver torch cactus), from Bolivia, also red-flowered, is distinguished by long silvery hairs on an erect stem to six feet tall. Care as for *Aporocactus* (see page 107).

Echinocactus is the genus name for a large group of very spiny plants, popular as specimens in their juvenile stages, and especially attractive when they form clumps. They are easily raised from seeds planted in late winter or spring on the surface of moist, sandy potting soil, making balls of spines when young, aging to a broadly cylindrical shape, and maturing to huge size, literally the size of a forty-gallon barrel. The bell-shaped flowers are mostly yellow and showy, in the spring or summer. These may be called barrel cacti, but related genera (*Notocac-*

tus, Rebutia and *Lobivia*) are known by the same popular name. Care as for *Aporocactus* (see page 107).

Echinocereus blossoms are large and brightly colored, in red, purple, pink, yellow, and white, and appear during the summer. They are easy to care for, small and capable of bearing large flowers at an early age in spring or summer. They are among the easiest of all cacti to bring into flower. Popular names include hedgehog cactus and rainbow cactus. Care as for *Aporocactus* (see page 107).

Echinopsis multiplex (Easter lily cactus), from southern Brazil, has large white, pink-tinged blossoms in spring and summer. The genus comprises small globular or cylindrical plants noted for their wealth of large, outstandingly beautiful, trumpet-shaped blossoms. The pink or white flowers unfurl toward dusk, remaining open through most of the following day. They are among the easiest of cacti to grow, and have a reputation for being free-flowering. Care as for *Aporocactus* (see page 107).

Epiphyllum oxypetalum is one of several cacti that are known as night-blooming cereus. Big, leafy branches thrust up, out, and every which way on strong stems; a height and width of three to six feet are not uncommon. The flower buds grow from the notches—areoles—in the leaves where most desert cacti send out thorns. In this species, mature buds unfurl at dusk or in early evening, changing in a matter of minutes from something that looks vaguely like a just-hatched turkey to a dinner-plate-size, fragrant beauty that is nothing short of dazzling. At this point most gardeners want everyone to share the excitement and an impromptu party is declared.

Besides *Epiphyllum oxypetalum* there is a whole group of epiphyllums known as orchid cacti, many of which are not as rangy as *oxypetalum*. Individual orchid cactus flowers are typically five inches across and ten is not unusual. The colors are indescribably beautiful; to say they are like a glorious sunset suggests their palette. Spring through early summer is bloom time.

Culture for the epiphyllums, both *oxypetalum* and the orchid-cactus types, is the same. They need room to grow, at least a space three feet wide and as high in a half-sunny window or near one that receives full sun.

Ideally they should spend the summer outdoors in a lath house or hanging from the branch of a shade tree. Some sun part of the time is the rule, but not hot and direct during midday.

Since the epiphyllums are rain-forest cacti, humidity is important, fifty percent or more. Mist the leaves once or twice daily. Adventitious, or air, roots that form along the stems absorb moisture from the atmosphere; if it is too dry, their purpose is thwarted. The Epiphyllum Society (see Resources) recommends a growing medium of two parts well-rotted leaf mold to one each of garden loam, well-rotted manure, and coarse gravel. Fertilize regularly in spring and summer, but not at all in fall and winter.

During warm, sunny weather, with daytime temperatures generally above 70°F, water epiphyllums enough to keep the medium between moist and on the dry side.

Epiphyllum *cultivar*.

Water less in rainy, cloudy, cool weather and especially when temperatures stay mostly below 70°F. They can survive brief periods of bone-dryness but the leaves may shrink or even die back from the tips. It is important in fall and winter to keep them on the cool (50° to 70°F) and dry side, but in moist air.

Epiphyllums are fun to multiply from six-inch cuttings of mature "leaves" (actually they are flattened branches). After taking a cutting, set it aside on a table or shelf in open air, but not in direct sun, for several days. This is to allow a callus to form over the cut tissue. Then plant with the base of the leaf an inch or two deep in regular epiphyllum potting soil. If necessary, stake the cutting upright. Keep barely moist for three or four weeks, then gradually apply more water. Rooted epiphyllum cuttings will do well for one to two years in five-inch pots. Older epiphyllums can be left for three years at a time in the same eight- to twelve-inch pots or hanging baskets. They bloom best when slightly potbound.

Gymnocalycium gives us the chin cacti. Easily grown, these small globular plants, two to four or five inches in diameter, have large and beautiful long-lasting flowers, usually white or pink, rarely yellow, in spring or summer. They receive their common name from the protuberant growth beneath each areole which suggests a double chin. Care as for *Aporocactus* (see page 107).

Hatiora epiphylloides 'Bradei' is a branching miniature resembling a tiny holiday or Christmas cactus. *Hatiora salicornioides* is a rain-forest species from southeastern Brazil that has bottle-shaped branchlets. Yellow-and-salmon flowers, quite small, in fall or winter are followed by red-tipped translucent fruit. Hatiora looks like no other cactus unless you've seen the allied *Rhipsalis*. It is a superb houseplant, in window or fluorescent light, usually displayed hanging or on a shelf. Care as for *Epiphyllum* (page 108).

Hylocereus undatus, from Brazil, is semitrailing and probably the largest-flowered of the cacti known as night-blooming cereus. Care as for *Epiphyllum* (page 108).

Lobivia aurea, to four inches, from Argentina, with large yellow flowers, and *L. binghamiana*, to three inches, from southeastern Peru, with purple-red flowers, are merely a hint of what this genus of small cacti with large flowers has to offer. There are many species and varieties, outstanding for house gardens or for the indoor/outdoor life. They bloom in spring or summer. Care as for *Aporocactus* (page 107).

Mammillaria is an extremely large genus, comprising hundreds of species. Mammillarias blossom from a hairy or woolly areole between the older nodular growths at the top of the plant. Among the favorites in this group are species called old lady cactus, golden stars, feather cactus, powder puff, lady finger, thimble, and rose pincushion. Most are clustering types, soon filling a small pot or tray with unusual beauty only a few inches tall. Care as for *Aporocactus* (page 107).

Notocactus is a genus of cacti prized for their easy culture and free-blooming habits in spring or summer. They are small plants with brightly colored spines and large, showy flowers, predominantly yellow. Lemon ball (*N. submammulosus*) is a very free-blooming species that will mature in three years. Golden ball (*N. leninghausii*) has golden spines. Care as for *Aporocactus* (page 107).

Opuntia represents one of the best known genera of cacti. Some, the platyopuntias, are known as prickly-ears or pad cacti, the first from their fruit, the second from the shape of their disklike branches. Others, the cylindropuntias, known as cholla (pronounced "choya"), have

Mammillaria prolifera.

branches which are almost perfectly cylindrical, joined together in link fashion. Of the two groups, the pad cacti are preferred for indoors, as the chollas have vicious spines.

Bunny-ears, a pad type (*Opuntia microdasys*), has spineless pads covered with bright golden tufts of soft glochids (minute barbed bristles). Beaver-tail (*O. basilaris*) is another spineless one. They can grow to two or three feet, but under one foot is more likely for houseplant specimens. The pads of others may be variegated with white and pink, or thickly hairy, or of odd shapes. They do not flower freely in cultivation. Care as for *Aporocactus* (page 107).

Pereskia aculeata (lemon vine), from tropical America, is a leafy shrub or vine with woody stems set with thorns. In late summer or fall the branches are laden with greenish white flowers, sometimes yellow or apricot-burnt orange, which yield a delightful fragrance like that of citrus blossoms. It can be grown in hanging container or provided with a trellis and trained upright. Care as for *Aporocactus* (page 107). Don't be afraid to prune the branches back to possibly more convenient size for indoors after flowering.

Rebutia species make valuable houseplants. They bear in spring or summer a circle of large blooms, usually red or orange, near the lower part of their tiny barrel-shaped stems, hence their name crown cactus. Rebutias form clumps, with the small plants also encircling the parents in crown fashion. Care as for *Aporocactus* (page 107).

Rhipsalidopsis gaertneri, from southern Brazil, is the popular Easter cactus, named for its habit of producing vivid red blossoms in the spring. This bushy epiphyte needs care similar to that given *Schlumbergera* or *Zygocactus* (see page 111). There is also the lovely pink-flowered *R. rosea*, dwarf Easter cactus, that makes a first-rate houseplant.

Rhipsalis is a genus of leafless epiphytes from the moist, warm tropical forests, found from Florida to Argentina; one species is said to have escaped to Africa. The common name mistletoe cactus is evocative of the overall appearance of the numerous species, which typically have half-inch flowers, white, pink, or pale yellow,

Pereskia aculeata.

Schlumbergera bridgesii *cultivar*.

at the branch tips in spring, followed by round, pearly, or opalescent fruits, also reminiscent of mistletoe fruits. It takes a certain sophistication to appreciate these cacti. I think of them as ideal companions for epiphytes in general, including orchids, bromeliads, gesneriads, and many ferns, palms, and cycads. A small rhipsalis plant can be hung from the branch of almost any indoor tree. Watering on a drench-and-dry cycle, with no lingering at either extreme, is recommended. Daily misting is beneficial, especially in fall and winter. Light can be sunny to merely bright, with fresh, moist air. Cuttings set in moist growing medium root easily in warmth, bright light, and high humidity.

Schlumbergera and *Zygocactus* are botanical names one hears in the presence of the holiday cacti, both the Thanksgiving and Christmas. (*Rhipsalidopsis* is the Easter cactus.) All have rain-forest origins and have proved to

be among the most rewarding and enduring of popular houseplants. Too much chilling combined with too much water, most likely to occur in winter, is the greatest threat. A heavy loss of leaves (they are actually flattened branches) in winter can be caused by too much or not enough water, or from freezing.

Spring is the ideal season for repotting Thanksgiving and Christmas cacti, early summer or when flowering has finished for Easter cactus. Remove the plant from its pot and crumble away most of the soil. Cut out any roots or branches that are not alive and well. Replant at the same level as before in a mix of approximately equal parts soil, sand, peat moss, and well-rotted leaf mold (or compost). Keep on the dry side until the roots take hold, usually ten days to two weeks. Do not apply fertilizer until considerable new growth has occurred, usually by midsummer. Young holiday cacti may need a size or two larger pot nearly every spring. Mature plants, in eight-inch or larger containers, can go two or three years without repotting.

Holiday cacti thrive in or near a sunny window. If you have a half-shady to fully sunny place for plants outdoors in warm weather, this plant will greatly benefit from being in the fresh air and abundant light. Be careful at first, however, otherwise the leafy branchlets will sunburn.

What makes these cacti go all to bloom at holiday time has to do with strong growth made in warm weather, which is then ripened and made ready to bloom by a reduction of the summer weather profile: less heat and less light provided by the time of year, and less moisture and less fertilizer provided by the gardener. When night temperatures fall to 55°F or below, flower buds are set. It is crucial at this point not to make any abrupt changes in the plant's care or placement; simply hold steady and the buds will soon be bursting into glorious flowers. The Easter type apparently needs a longer gestation period and flowers in response to increasing day length while those of Thanksgiving and Christmas get the urge to bloom as day length dwindles.

I once surveyed my newspaper readers and found that there are many holiday cactus specimens still being cultivated after fifty years and more. Sometimes the plant has reached the status of a family heirloom. The oldest reported cactus was in the hands of an Illinois woman who wrote, "I am in my early sixties and have a Christmas cactus that belonged originally to my grandmother. According to my father, it is 120 years old. It grows in a clay pot, has not been transplanted and is not fed supplemental food. In the summer I place the cactus under trees in the garden and bring it in the house in early October. The base is about three inches across, the leaves stand two feet tall and I water once a week. It blooms profusely." An Indiana correspondent said her Christmas cactus was " . . . well over a hundred years old," inherited from a brother. "It is in a 30-inch butchering kettle and measures 16 and one-half feet around, at one point more than 5 feet across. There are about a thousand blooms each year. I feed it plant food in October and again after flowering. In warm sunny weather I apply

about one gallon of water every ten days to two weeks. The plant stands in a window where a street light shines on it each night and is too large to be moved outdoors, or even turned for that matter."

What often surprises me is that these venerable specimens are as likely as not growing from what appears to be unadultered "dirt," which is what I call soil that has been abused. It no longer has "tilth"—meaning it lacks air, humus, and the dynamic bacterial activity that renders soil as a living thing able to efficiently support plant life. Their epiphytic origins permit these cacti to survive, even thrive, despite poor quality soil.

Selenicereus is a genus of vinelike, climbing cacti that are among those known as night-blooming cereus. *Selenicereus macdonaldiae* is an exceptionally beautiful one with gold-and-white blossoms often a foot across and equally long. Princess of the night, *S. pteranthus*, is another with very large, white, fragrant blossoms. Queen of the night, *S. grandiflorus*, has blossoms which are white inside with salmon-colored outer parts, smelling of vanilla. Care as for *Epiphyllum* (page 108).

Zygocactus is no longer recognized. See *Schlumbergera* (page 111).

CAMPANULACEAE. *Bellflower Family.*

Herbs from temperate as well as tropical parts of the world, with alternate leaves and regular flowers, often bell-shaped, and usually lavender, blue, pink, or white. One genus is of interest to the indoor gardener.

Campanula elatines, from southeastern Europe and the Adriatic region, is a variable species, the cultivated forms of which are known as Adria bellflowers. The variety *alba plena* has double white flowers; *flore plena*, double blue. *Campanula fragilis*, from Italy, is a delicate trailer with small, intense blue flowers, and C. *isophylla alba* (white) and C. *i. mayii* (blue), also from Italy, are much loved for their starry masses of flowers in summer. All of these campanulas make excellent hanging plants. They have bright green leaves set on tender stems. While several kinds are known as star of Bethlehem, this name more properly belongs to *Ornithogalum*. They prefer a sunny to semisunny situation, fresh, moist air, and cool temperatures, not over 70°F in winter. Give them humus-rich, loam-based potting soil kept evenly moist in spring and summer, on the dry side in fall and winter, at which time the plant can be trimmed back and kept more or less on hold until it's time to cut it back to two or three inches and repot in spring. Be sure to turn as many of the cut-off branches into cuttings as possible. Strip off the lowermost leaves and insert each stem one to two inches deep in moist potting soil.

CELASTRACEAE. *Bittersweet Family.*

Evergreen and deciduous vines, trees, and shrubs widely cultivated in American gardens. One genus is of interest for houseplanting.

Euonymus japonicus, from Japan, comes in several variegated varieties suited to indoor growing, and varying in size from semitrailers under twelve inches to rather rigidly upright stems forming bushes to three or four feet tall. Variegations in these small-leaved plants include green with gold centers, white borders or marginal coloration, but even the all-green varieties are decorative for their glossiness and pleasing conformation. Euonymus may be pruned into almost any desired shape and may even be appropriate for bonsai training (Chapter 5). Give it a semisunny to semishady situation, not over 70°F in winter, fresh, moist air, and humus-rich, loam-based potting soil kept evenly moist. Root cuttings of half-ripened wood (see page 54) in fall or winter in a light garden. Pruning can be done at the time you wish to take cuttings or as needed in spring or early summer.

COMMELINACEAE. *Spiderwort Family.*

This family contains the several familiar plants known as wandering Jew. These and others in the group are cultivated mostly for showy leaves which alternate along succulent, watery stems. The flowers usually have three sepals and three petals, and may be regular or irregular. Genera of interest for houseplanting include *Campelia,*

Campelia zanonia.

Cyanotis, Dichorisandra, Geogenanthus, Palisota, Rhoeo, Setcreasea, Siderasis, Tradescantia, and *Zebrina.*

Campelia zanonia, from the West Indies and Mexico to Brazil, to six feet, gives a bamboolike appearance; 'Mexican Flag' has white-striped, red-margined leaves and makes a showy houseplant. 'Scream' is said to be less spectacular but more tolerant of house garden conditions. Care as for *Geogenanthus* (page 114). Propagate by division in late winter or spring, or from stem cuttings of half-ripened growth.

Cyanotis kewensis (teddy-bear plant), from Malabar, has velvety brown hair on both leaves and stems; *C. somaliensis* (pussy ears), from Somaliland, triangular green leaves covered with white hair. *Cyanotis veldthoutiana* (white gossamer), from South Africa, is the most colorful, having dark green leaves with purplish reverses and purple stems, all covered with a thick coat of fluffy white wool. All three are small creepers. Give a sunny to semisunny situation, not over 70°F in winter, fresh air, and a well-drained, loam-based potting soil kept evenly moist in spring and summer, on the dry side fall and winter. Propagate by cuttings any time.

Dichorisandra thyrsiflora (blue ginger), from Brazil, grows upright to three feet with spirally arranged silvery green leaves and terminal clusters of cobalt blue flowers. Care as for *Geogenanthus*. This is a must if you collect blue-flowered houseplants.

Geogenanthus undatus (seersucker plant), from Peru, is a low-growing foliage plant with puckered leaves. They are broad and oval, dark green with the metallic sheen characteristic of the family, and are banded with silvery gray. The reverses are dark purple-red, as are the stems. This is one of the most rewarding of plants in this family because it develops suckers freely, and will soon fill a pot with its colorful and unusual foliage. Give a semisunny to semishady situation, average house temperatures, fresh, moist air, and a humus-rich, loam-based potting soil kept evenly moist. Propagate by detaching the suckers at repotting time, late winter–spring.

Palisota pynaertii 'Elizabethae' sports greenish yellow or ochre midveining and feathering in wide, dark green, short-stemmed leaves to eighteen inches long by six inches wide; cones of white flowers in spring or summer are succeeded by purple berries. Care as for *Rhoeo*.

Rhoeo bermudensis (synonym *R. spathacea nana*; *R. discolor*), to one foot or more, from Mexico, has an upright rosette of lance-shaped leaves, dark olive green above, iridescent purple beneath. Above each leaf base two large bracts hold a number of small white flowers. Also known as Moses in the cradle. *Rhoeo bermudensis* 'Variegata' has creamy yellow vertical stripes in the upper surface of the leaves. Needs a sunny to semisunny situation, average house temperatures, fresh air, and a humus-rich, loam-based potting soil kept evenly moist. Propagate by removing offsets at any time, or transplant the seedlings which spring up around the parent.

Setcreasea pallida 'Purple Heart', from Mexico, is an erect, to sixteen inches, fleshy-stemmed, white-hairy plant that has a strong purple leaf color. The tripetaled flowers are violet-purple. Care as for *Tradescantia* (below).

Siderasis fuscata, from Brazil, would not be taken for a member of the spiderwort family at first glance, as it has long, densely hairy leaves in clustering rosettes. Closer inspection, however, reveals the kinship through the contrasting band of silver discernible in the leaves, the barely visible taffetalike sheen, and the dark purple leaf reverses. The flowers are produced close to the base of the plant, sometimes hidden beneath the arching leaves, typically tripetaled, reddish violet-blue, and each lasting but a day. This plant gets on well in a semisunny to semishady garden, or under lights, in average house temperatures, with good air circulation. Give it a humus-rich, loam-based potting soil kept evenly moist to slightly dry at the surface. Propagate by removing offsets at repotting time, late winter–spring, or when expedient.

Tradescantia albiflora albovittata, from Central America, has large blue-green leaves striped generously with white, *T. a. laekenensis*, or 'Rainbow', has iridescent lavender and white stripes on green, and *T. blossfeldiana*, from South America, has the coloration of *Rhoeo bermudeusis*, but trails rampantly and bears loose clusters of lavender flowers. *Tradescantia multiflora* (Tahitian bridal veil), from Jamaica, is a small trailer with narrow dark green leaves and white flowers. *Tradescantia navicularis*, from Peru, a small plant with boat-shaped, brownish green leaves, seems to have an affinity for desert conditions, and is often listed with cacti and other succulents. Any of these tradescantias may be called inch plant or wandering Jew. (See also *Zebrina*.) Likes a sunny to semishady situation, temperatures not over 75°F in winter, and good air circulation. Give it a humus-rich, loam-based potting soil kept evenly moist except during the winter. Then let the surface go slightly dry before watering. Propagate by cuttings at any time.

Zebrina pendula, from Mexico, and its many varieties are the wandering Jew plants which have long been favorites for indoors. They are characterized by trailing, fleshy, almost watery stems, which will root at each node if in contact with damp soil. Strong light intensifies the foliage coloration, which includes green, red, purple, yellow, pink, and silver, the bands of contrasting colors running the length of the leaves, and with the reverses often highly colored. For care and propagation, see *Tradescantia*.

COMPOSITAE. *Composite Family*.

The world's largest plant family includes trees, shrubs, vines, and herbs. The foliage varies widely, but the flower heads are similar. They may consist of petallike ray flowers, as in a daisy, of tubular, tiny disk flowers, as in the center of a daisy, or of both, hence "composite." Genera of interest here: *Centratherum, Chrysanthemum* and *Argyranthemum, Euryops, Felicia, Gynura, Ligularia, Piqueria, Senecio,* and *Wedelia*.

Centratherum intermedium (Manaos beauty, Brazilian button flower, Martinique bachelor's-button), to two feet, from Brazil, the West Indies, and naturalized in Florida, has pineapple-scented leaves and bluish lavender flowers resembling those of a miniature Canadian thistle. This plant will bloom nearly constantly in a sunny window or light garden. It also self-sows in outdoor gardens as far north as USDA zone 7 but not in a weedy way. Needs a sunny to semisunny situation, average house temperatures, fresh, moist air, and a loam-based potting soil kept evenly moist. Propagate from seeds or cuttings in warmth, high humidity, and bright light in any season.

Chrysanthemum as a florist potted flowering plant is discussed on pages 222–223. The Boston daisy, *C. frutescens*, with white or yellow flowers, figures in the indoor/outdoor scheme and has also been given a new botanical name: *Argyranthemum frutescens chrysaster*. It can be wintered over and even flowered in a cool, sunny, airy, moist greenhouse or sun-heated pit, but this plant is not up to spending long periods of time in a warm dwelling.

Euryops pectinatus (gray-leaved euryops) and *E. spathaceus* (wax-leaf euryops, with shiny green leaves) are

Siderasis fuscata.

newly popular yellow daisy-flowered tender perennials from South Africa that are everblooming for outdoor container gardens in warm weather. They have taken the Sun Belt by storm and behave as permanent perennials in frost-free regions. The stems become woody, forming bushes three to four feet tall and as wide. They need loam-based potting soil kept evenly moist and generous fertilizing with 20-20-20 and 15-30-15 during warm weather. Cut back by half or more in late winter and early spring. Tip cuttings of half-ripened wood root readily in spring or summer. Euryops can be wintered over

Euryops pectinatus.

in almost any cool, frost-free spot indoors, kept on the dry side and not fertilized. Watch out for aphids, however, and spray with insecticidal soap or neem solution as necessary.

Felicia amelloides is the kingfisher or blue daisy. It is also available in a form having variegated leaves, white and silvery green. This is not for a warm, dry apartment, but if you can give it a sunny, moist, airy, cool but frost-free situation, it will bloom in winter. Propagate by seeds or cuttings in spring.

Gynura aurantiaca (purple passion), two feet, from Java, is a stout, branching plant with leaves and stems completely overlaid with short, close-set, vivid purple hairs. In spring or summer it may bear yellow daisylike flowers. Give it a sunny situation, average house temperatures, good air circulation, and a well-drained, loam-based soil kept evenly moist. Propagate by cuttings anytime. Begin pruning when the plant is small to eliminate spindly, single-stalked development which will occur with unattended gynuras.

Ligularia tussilaginea 'Argentea' (with creamy or white leaf margins) and *L. t.* 'Aureo-maculata' (leathery, smooth leaves blotched with yellow; leopard plant), both from Japan, make choice specimen foliage plants to eighteen inches tall and as wide that look beautiful in just the right terra-cotta or glazed ceramic bonsai pot. It is best not to let the yellow daisy flowers develop; after they finish the entire plant will go into decline. They like a semisunny to semishady situation, temperatures not over 72°F in winter, fresh, moist air, and a humus-rich, loam-based potting soil kept evenly moist. Propagate by removing offsets at repotting time, late winter–spring.

Piqueria trinervia (stevia), from Mexico, Central America, and Haiti, is an erect, perennial herbaceous plant, two to three feet tall, topped by a large number of white daisy flowers in winter. It is grown traditionally by florists for its sweet scent and as a cut flower. Propagate from cuttings or divisions at repotting time in late winter–spring, much the same as for garden and florist chrysanthemums (see page 222). Give it a sunny situation, cool temperatures in fall and winter (as in a sun-heated pit greenhouse or sun porch), and fresh, moist air. It needs a loam-based potting soil kept evenly moist; let the surface get dry in fall in order to harden up the new growth that will flower.

Senecio is a genus containing plants of widely varying habit. *Senecio cruentus*, one to two feet, from the Canary Islands, is the cineraria of florists; see page 39. *Senecio confusus* (orangeglow vine), from Mexico, is a vine with toothed, pointed oval leaves and clusters of orange-red daisy flowers borne over a long season. This species belongs in the indoor/outdoor crowd. *Senecio mikanioides* (parlor or German ivy), from South Africa, has thin, bright green, ivylike leaves on thin stems. It is an excellent houseplant for semisunny to semishady situations with moderately cool winter temperatures (not over 70°F) and fresh, moist air. Give it a humus-rich, loam-based soil kept evenly moist. Propagate by cutting in late winter–spring.

Finally there are the succulent senecios: *Senecio scaposus*, from South Africa, forms short, basal rosettes of long, slender leaves covered with white felt. *Senecio gregorii* is called peppermint stick because its leafless, jointed stems are sometimes striped lengthwise with green, cream, and pink. *Senecio stapeliiformis* has thick, many-angled stems and may be called candy stick. *Senecio rowleyanus* var. *variegatus* is a variegated form of a species from Southern Namibia, with creeping stems set with beadlike leaves marbled green and white, hence "string of pearls." The stems root where they come in contact with moist soil. They need a sunny to semisunny situation, average house temperatures, good air circulation, and a well-drained, loam-based potting soil. Water well, then not again until dry. Propagate by cuttings in spring or summer.

Wedelia trilobata, from south Florida and tropical America, is a creeping and rooting plant, growing to six feet or longer, with yellow to orange-yellow flowers. It has become a popular and even naturalized ground cover in USDA zones 10 and 11. The cultivar 'Outenreath Gold' is splashed and slashed with gold variegation. It is recommended for hanging baskets and to spill over the sides of other containers outdoors in warm, frost-free weather; give it lots of sun. Care as for *Senecio confusus*.

Senecio rowleyanus *var.* variegatus.

CONVOLVULACEAE. *Morning-Glory Family.*

Vines, shrubs, and trees, mostly from the tropics, with alternate leaves and trumpet- or funnel-shaped flowers that are twisted in the bud stage. Genera of interest to the houseplanter include *Ipomoea* and *Evolvulus*. A search of the catalogs will lead to other candidates from this family. Those that vine adapt readily to trellis or wreath training.

Evolvulus glomeratus (Blue Daze of commerce) is a dwarf or miniature bush morning glory, twelve to eighteen inches tall and as broad, from tropical America that has white-hairy leaves on lax stems set with fresh blue flowers every morning. I have gotten it to thrive and bloom in a sunny window but in the maxi light garden there are more flowers over a longer season. Likes a sunny

Ipomoea *'Heavenly Blue' with* Cissus adenopoda.

to semisunny situation, average house temperatures, fresh air, and a humus-rich, loam-based potting soil kept evenly moist. Root tip cuttings of half-ripened wood (see page 54) any time. Rejuvenate at the beginning of spring by cutting back sharply, so that new shoots can come from the roots.

Ipomoea, the morning glory of summer gardens, adapts readily to sunny house gardens, and looks especially well when trained wreath style; see Chapter 5 for details. Plant two or three seeds in a six- to eight-inch pot filled with loam-based potting soil. Keep constantly warm and moist in a sunny window or maxi light garden. Provide support soon after the seeds sprout, for they grow quickly and will soon be reaching out for something about which to twine. *Ipomoea batatas*, from the East Indies, is the sweet potato of commerce, and the vine often cultivated in window gardens. Since many of the potatoes in commerce have been treated to prevent sprouting, it is nec-essary to start with a tuber which shows sprouts. Plant upright or horizontally, depending on the container. Any planting medium which will hold moisture may be used, or just clear water with the lower half of the tuber submerged. Change the water weekly. Chips of charcoal in the bottom will help keep the water fresh. Best growth occurs in warm, sunny conditions, or about six inches beneath the tubes in a light garden.

CORNACEAE. *Dogwood Family.*

Hardy shrubs or trees, noteworthy for their showy flowers, fruit and, in some species, colorful bark. I often cut and bring inside for winter decorations the red- (*Cornus sericea*) and yellow-twig (*C. s.* 'Flaviramea') dogwoods, which produce an abundance of straight or gracefully curving branches from the ground. *Aucuba* is the genus of primary interest for growing indoors.

Aucuba japonica (gold dust plant), the Japanese laurel, to three or four feet tall and nearly as broad, has large, leathery leaves, usually yellow-splotched and spotted. It is hardy outdoors to USDA zone 7 and air-pollution tolerant. Bold in appearance, it is a durable foliage houseplant except in hot, dry situations. Shower frequently to keep the broad leaves naturally shiny and dust-free. Needs semisun to semishade, temperatures not over 72°F in winter, fresh, moist air, and humus-rich, loam-based potting soil kept evenly moist. Make tip cuttings in spring or summer; cut the larger leaves back by half to prevent wilting in the early stages of rooting.

CRASSULACEAE. *Stonecrop Family.*

Succulent plants with fleshy, pliable stems and leaves, and small, perfect flowers held in showy clusters. Genera valued for houseplanting are *Adromischus, Aeonium, Crassula, Echeveria, Kalanchoe, Pachyveria,* and *Sedum.*

Adromischus festivus (plover eggs), a clustering succulent to two inches tall from South Africa, has cylindrical leaves that are silvery green with maroon marbling and flattened toward the tip. *Adromischus maculatus* (calico hearts), to three or four inches, from South Africa, forms a low rosette of thick, flat, almost round leaves that are convex on both sides. Indented at the tip, they are gray-green with red-brown flecking. Give it a sunny situation, average house temperatures, fresh air, and a well-drained, loam-based potting soil. Keep it evenly moist in spring and summer, on the dry side in fall and winter. Take stem or leaf cuttings in late winter–summer.

Aeonium is the genus name for a succulent that looks for all the world like a giant green rose. Only in recent times has aeonium been considered a genus separate and distinct from *Sempervivum*. One noticeable difference is that sempervivums tend to hug the ground, each rosette in time surrounding itself with smaller ones. By contrast, aeoniums grow upright, eventually displaying rosettes of thick leaves at the tips of woody branches. The species name of the most widely cultivated species, A. *arboreum*, means "of treelike habit."

Another difference, and an important one to know as a gardener, is that the sempervivums are evergreen perennials from the Old World, generally able to tolerate temperatures to 0°F, while the aeoniums, which hail mostly from the Canary Islands, cannot withstand freezing. What the aeoniums can tolerate, however, is varying amounts of light, the same as jade plants. Mine grow as compactly and well-colored a few inches beneath the tubes in a light garden as those I have seen outdoors in California on decks where they received full sun and sometimes salt spray.

Besides *Aeonium arboreum*, which forms rosettes of green leaves, there is its variety 'Atropurpureum', with dark purple leaves that glow pale green at the base; A. *canariense*, the velvet rose, which forms rosettes of bright green leaves to the diameter of a bushel basket; A. *domesticum* 'Variegatum', a much smaller variety with green-and-white leaves; and A. *tabuliforme*, or saucer plant, from Tenerife which forms very flat rosettes of closely overlapped leaves to a foot across.

Whether indoors all year or kept outdoors as container plants in warm weather, grow the aeoniums in a potting mix made of one part each garden loam or soil and sphagnum peat moss (or well-rotted compost) to two parts clean, sharp sand. During warm, sunny weather in spring and summer, maintain the soil between evenly moist and slightly on the dry side. Fertilize lightly and regularly.

During the fall and winter when days are shorter and temperatures generally cooler, keep aeoniums on the dry side. Do not fertilize. Never leave the pot standing in water.

When cool, dry conditions are followed by warmth and moisture, aeoniums send up cone-shaped clusters of daisylike flowers, usually yellow but sometimes white, pink, or red. Propagate from cuttings, or by sowing seeds, between late winter and midsummer.

Crassula argentea (jade plant), from South Africa, is typical of one distinct type of crassula. It has visible, branching stems which form shrub- or treelike plants. There are various forms, varying in size and leaf color. They make wonderful collectibles for any sunny house garden or an indoor/outdoor life.

The other type crassula is typified by *Crassula hem-*

Crassula argentea 'Sunset'.

Most are free-flowering, producing bright, long-lasting spikes of tubular blossoms at various times of the year depending on the species. There are countless different echeverias. *Echeveria affinis*, from Mexico, has leaves that are almost black if given enough sun; *E. elegans*, from Hidalgo, has leaves of waxy pale blue with white, translucent margins and coral-pink flowers on pink stems; *E. 'Pulv-Oliver'*, a hybrid, has red-tipped plushlike leaves. Care as for *Crassula* (page 119).

Kalanchoe blossfeldiana, originally from Madagascar, is the primary source of the seasonal flowering kalanchoe of commerce, discussed on pages 42–43. The genus is worth exploring, expecially if you have a house garden that is sunny and warm, or if an indoor/outdoor existence is possible. *Kalanchoe beharensis* has large lobed leaves completely covered with a heavy felting of brown hair; *K. pinnata* (air plant, magic-leaf), from India, forms baby

Echeveria.

isphaerica, from Namibia, which consists of small, low plants with the stems all but hidden under closely packed rosettes of leaves. There are hundreds of crassulas, most of them making splendid houseplants, and many well known by their popular names such as propeller plant (*C. cultrata*), silver beads (*C. deltoidea*), scarlet paint-brush (*C. falcata*), buttons-on-a-string (*C. perfossa*), rat-tlesnake (*C. teres*), and miniature pine tree (*C. tetragona*). They need a sunny to semisunny situation, average house temperatures, and fresh air. Give them a well-drained, loam-based soil kept evenly moist in spring and summer, and on the dry side fall and winter. Make leaf or stem cuttings in spring and summer.

Echeveria are frost-tender rosette-forming plants noted for their beautifully colored and textured leaves. They display a variety of forms, some being tiny ground covers, while others form rosettes at the ends of heavy stems.

Kalanchoe farinacea.

Kalanchoe *species with plantlet on leaf tip.*

plants along its scalloped leaf edges, especially when a mature leaf is laid on moist soil; *K. tomentosa* (panda plant) has small leaves covered with white felt, the tips toothed and marked with brown; and *K. tubiflora* is called palm plant from the fancied resemblance of its curved stems to a palm tree. Like *K. pinnata*, this kalanchoe also forms plantlets along its leaf edges. A relatively recent acquaintance of mine, *K. farinacea*, has gray leaves and showy red flowers; it blooms in summer while most kalanchoes seem to bloom in winter, presumably in response to day length. I became acquainted with *K. farinacea* at Grigsby Cactus Gardens (see Resources).

× *Pachyveria* is a made-up genus name for crosses between two members of the Crassulaceae, echeveria and pachyphytum. Numerous pachyverias exist, and they are so attractive and useful as houseplants that mention is made here of them. They are succulents with plump,

richly colored leaves in thick rosettes. Care as for *Crassula* (page 119).

Sedum morganianum (burro's-tail), from Mexico, is a much favored plant for growing in hanging baskets or situated so that stems up to three feet long bearing waxy, pale, blue-green leaves may cascade from a shelf or tree branch. *Sedum multiceps*, from Algeria, looks like a miniature Joshua tree and *S. stahlii* (coral beads), from Mexico, has fat, egg-shaped leaves of reddish color (poor soil enhances this coloration). Other sedums may be shrubby, to a foot or more in height, or they may be mat-forming. Care and propagate as for *Crassula* (page 119).

CUPRESSACEAE. *Cypress Family.*

Conifers including *Chamaecyparis*, *Cupressus*, *Juniperus*, and *Thuja*. *Cupressus* is of interest here.

Cupressus cashmeriana, from Kashmir and Tibet, a tree to sixty feet, has an ascending columnar habit and pendulous blue-green branchlets. It is a recommended houseplant and considered hardy outdoors in USDA zones 9 to 11. It needs a sunny to semisunny situation, average house temperatures, fresh, moist air, and a loam-based potting soil kept evenly moist. Any excessive growth can be pruned off in late winter or spring. Propagate from cuttings in summer using an automatic intermittent misting device if available.

CYCADACEAE. *Cycas Family.*

Primitive palmlike, evergreen shrubs or trees. The frondlike leaves, in rosettes, are so stiff to the touch that they are sometimes mistaken for plastic. The genera here, *Cycas*, *Dioon*, and *Zamia*, are of interest for pots. All of these plants have persistent and broad evergreen leaves that need showering with tepid water at least once a month to keep them dust-free and naturally shiny.

Cycas revoluta, the sago palm, grows to ten feet tall, its individual fronds measuring to five feet. It is extremely slow-growing. A bushel-size specimen is relatively costly, but it will stay house-size indefinitely. It needs sun to semishade, average house temperatures, preferably moderate (55° to 70°F) in winter, and fresh, moist air. Place outdoors in frost-free weather if possible. give it a humus-rich, loam-based potting soil kept evenly moist. Propagate by removing and rooting basal growth buds in spring.

Dioon edule (chestnut dioon), to six feet, from Mexico and Central America, has leaves three to six feet long, with young pinnae toothed at the tip, entire in mature plants. It needs less sun in the house than *Cycas*, otherwise its care is the same. *Dioon* is sometimes classed as belonging to the Zamiaceae or Zamia family, considered cycads in the broadest sense, but having sufficient differences to be placed in a separate family.

Zamia pumila, synonym *Z. furfuracea* (Florida arrowroot, Sago cycas, comptie, coontic, Seminole-bread), from Florida, the West Indies, and Mexico has a trunk to six inches high, sometimes entirely in the ground, and leaves two to four feet long. It is planted in gardens outdoors in USDA zones 10 to 11. As a houseplant, give it the care outlined above for *Cycas*. The genus *Zamia* is sometimes classified as belonging to the Zamiaceae, or Zamia family, considered cycads in the broad sense but narrowly as distinct and separate.

Cycas *with* Epiphyllum *at Montreal Botanical Garden.*

CYPERACEAE. *Sedge Family.*

Superficially similar to, but not the same as, true grasses. Sedges have triangular, solid stems and small, inconspicuous green flowers. Of special interest here are the genera *Carex*, *Cyperus*, and *Scirpus*. However, almost any sedge growing wild can be potted and enjoyed for a time indoors.

Carex elegantissima, from Japan, is, as its name suggests, an elegant, water-loving plant which resembles tufts of tall-growing grass, with white stripes along the margins. It is of limited use except in terrariums with other plants which need wet soil, semisunny to semishady lighting, and moderate temperatures, 55° to 70°F in winter.

Cyperus alternifolius, to four feet, from Madagascar, is the well-known umbrella plant (but not to be confused with schefflera, see *Brassaia*, page 94). The dwarf form, *C. a. gracilis*, to two feet, is of special interest for houseplanting. *Cyperus diffusus*, from Mauritius, suckers

Cyperus papyrus.

flowers. *Elaeagnus* is the genus of interest as a houseplant.

Elaeagnus pungens, from China and Japan, is known in its cultivar 'Aurea' as an evergreen shrub with oval, wavy-edged leaves bordered with yellow, the undersides silvery. The fragrant white flowers flare above a cylindrical tube and are borne in clusters arising from the leaf axils. It needs semisun to semishade, temperatures on the cool side (45° to 60°F) in winter, and fresh, moist air; place outdoors in frost-free weather if possible. Give it a humus-rich, loam-based potting soil kept evenly moist. Propagate by cuttings in spring; keep warm, moist, and in high humidity.

ERICACEAE. *Heath Family.*

Mostly evergreen shrubs from the north temperate zone, widely cultivated outdoors in American gardens. Only the rhododendrons known in commerce as azaleas have become popular as houseplants, mostly for their use as seasonal flowering pot plants (see pages 37–44). They have recently become available as flowering miniature and dwarf plants and are suited to training a variety of ways, such as bonsai or tree-form standard (see Chapter 5). The related genus *Vireya* is discussed on page 229.

Growers force azaleas to bloom at Christmas, on through the winter to spring and Easter. Coolness (50° to 60°F) will help the flowers stay on longer, and the foliage to remain greener. Mist the plants daily with room-temperature water. In mild climates, greenhouse-forced azaleas may be planted outdoors in spring in a semishaded place where there is humusy soil enriched by quantities of sand (for drainage) and peat moss (to hold moisture and provide air for the roots). There they will resume their natural perennial habit. In cold climates, transplant to a pot one size larger, using moist sphagnum peat moss, and place outdoors in summer in a cool, partially shaded growing area. Keep moist and fertilize regularly, supplementing occasionally with an iron chelate or other acidifier. Bring indoors in autumn, place in a bright, cool spot (about 50°F), and keep the soil barely moist until December or January. Then move to

freely, has fairly broad leaves, is a rapid grower and will fill a pot within a season. *Cyperus elegans*, from tropical Africa, is similar, but has narrower leaves. *Cyperus papyrus*, from Egypt, is the Egyptian paper plant. If you find yourself the owner of this species, pot it in a large tub and give it room to grow—the stems often exceed eight feet. They need bright diffused sunlight to semishade, average house temperatures, preferably on the cool side (45° to 60°F) in winter, and fresh, moist air. Give them humus-rich, loam-based potting soil, standing in water while in active growth, wet at other times. Propagate by division in late winter–early summer.

Scirpus cernuus (miniature bulrush), four to six inches, from the East Indies, produces tufts of translucent green thread leaves tipped with straw-white bracts. Give it a semisunny to semishady situation, average house temperatures, and a constant supply of moist air. Pot in a humus-rich, loam-based soil; leave scirpus standing in water. Propagate by division in late winter–early summer.

ELAEAGNACEAE. *Oleaster Family.*

Generally hardy trees and shrubs with smooth-edged leaves, golden or silver underneath, and inconspicuous

a sunny, moist, cool place, and begin to apply more water and occasional feedings. Homegrown azaleas can be spectacular as they burst all into bloom. After a plant has been nurtured and trained several seasons, there will be much more of a show.

EUPHORBIACEAE. *Spurge Family.*

Trees, shrubs, herbs, and cactuslike succulents with alternate leaves, milky juice (generally somewhat poisonous), and true flowers that are inconspicuous compared to the surrounding colorful bracts. There are over 3,000 species in this genus; a great many are fair game for houseplanting.

Acalypha hispida (chenille plant), from western Pacific regions, is prized for its long, fluffy, bright red (pinkish white in cultivar 'Alba') flower spikes which dangle gracefully from the leaf axils. *Acalypha repens* is a small trailer with wispy button flowers that elongate into what the

Acalypha hispida 'Alba'.

Glasshouse Works Greenhouses (see Resources) catalog describes as ". . . resembling roseate chenille pendant woolyworms fat on steroids." Depending on your imagination that might not sound like what you want hanging over the table in your sun room but in real life this is a beautiful and unusual plant, ideal in the indoor/outdoor scheme. *Acalypha wilkesiana*, a monoecious shrub from the Pacific Islands, growing to fifteen feet, is the source for fifteen different named varieties (all listed by Glasshouse Works), each chosen for distinctive foliage color variegation. 'Macafeana' (copper leaf) has silky red leaves marbled bronze; 'Mooreana Black Magic' (maroon beefsteak plant) has wide, uniformly furled, blackish purple leaves (aging to a rusty tone), congested on upright stems; and a third, 'Petticoat', has ruffled coppery ochre leaves margined with parchment scallops—it is large and showy. Give them a sunny to semisunny situation, average house temperatures, fresh, moist air, and a humus-rich, loam-based potting soil kept evenly moist. Propagate by cuttings taken in the fall.

Codiaeum is the genus name for the plants universally known as croton. *Codiaeum variegatum pictum*, from Sri Lanka, Malaya, southern India, and the Sunda Islands, has given rise to almost countless hybrids. There are oak-leaf shapes and broad elliptical ones. Colors range from the palest yellow through pinks, reds, oranges, and browns, to every possible shade of green. There are spots, blotches, marginal colorings, and veins often showing contrasting colors. *Codiaeum variegatum* 'Interruptum', from Polynesia, is red and yellow, with the midrib appearing to extend beyond the leaf blade. Another, possibly a sport of this, has two distinct leaf blades connected by the main rib. *Codiaeum variegatum* 'Spirale', from Malaysia, has green leaves brightly splashed with yellow and red, and twisted like a corkscrew. Many crotons have young growth of one color that matures to quite another. Very seldom will two leaves on any plant be exactly alike.

I recently enjoyed photographing the croton cultivars in the collection of Jean Merkel at Alberts and Merkel Brothers Nursery, Boynton Beach, Florida. After a life of searching the world for the most extraordinary of tropical plants, Jean has some very special crotons. These are multiplied by means of air layers placed at various points along thrifty branches.

Crotons probably do best as outdoor plants, at least if they can have one or two seasons outdoors. They are also adaptable; if all needs are met except one, for example only bright light, no direct sun, otherwise nicely moist soil and occasional applications of fertilizer, the plant will be able to achieve an acceptable level of growth and appearance. Crotons stressed for light or water are vulnerable to spider mites and mealybugs. The ideal is sunny to semisunny, average house temperatures, fresh, moist air, and humus-rich, loam-based potting soil kept evenly moist. Propagate from cuttings in warmth (70° to 80°F), humidity, and bright diffused light.

Euphorbia lactea (candelabra plant), from India and Sri Lanka, can become treelike, with candelabra branches. A height of four feet and eighteen inches across is more likely from a twelve-inch pot. Other names are hatrack cactus and, in Vietnam, dragon-bones. The small leaves that appear along with new branch growth in euphorbias of this type (and there are many) are called ephemeral. Even if the plant has adequate water with no extremes of wet or dry, the leaves will not persist for long. Whether or not you hand-pick the dried up ones depends on your gardening style and standards for grooming. Personally I like to keep dead leaves picked up from my house garden. It's my way of staying in touch with each plant. Where *E. lactea* and its purple form are concerned, as with other euphorbias of this spiny type, they make great houseplants but it is not wise to attempt working with them until you have on long, strong gloves. Another of the spiny species, *Euphorbia paseudoburuana*, from Africa, produces a showy terminal cluster of greenish yellow flowers in summer. Ideally, these euphorbias need semisun to semishade, fresh air circulation, and a loam-based potting soil kept between evenly moist and on the dry side. Propagate from stem cuttings of half-ripened growth, each at least three or four inches long. Allow the cutting to dry overnight, then plant at least one inch deep in sandy rooting medium. Keep warm and in bright light or some sun to encourage roots to form.

Euphorbia pulcherrima, from southern Mexico, is the Christmas poinsettia. It is a seasonal flowering potted plant whose needs and care are discussed on pages 43–44.

Euphorbia milii 'Splendens' (crown of thorns), from Madagascar, is another species cultivated as a houseplant. It has stout stems thickly set with gray spines, small leaves that are sparse and short-lived, and one-half- to one-inch floral bracts ranging from yellow to salmon pink, rosy red, and scarlet. There are many cultivars, ranging from dwarfs—under twelve inches—to substantial plants several feet tall. 'Splendens' itself is sometimes trained to an upright wreath form; there is a large specimen at the Como Park Greenhouses, St. Paul, Minnesota, trained as a large heart shape on a wire form.

Euphorbia tirucalli (pencil cactus, milkbush), from tropical and South Africa, a spineless tree to thirty feet, has smooth green branches about the thickness and length of a pencil. Like other members of the family, the branches are filled with milky sap. Toward the tips there are very small ephemeral leaves that shrivel and disappear soon after they emerge. This plant will grow well in sun or shade, hot or cold, wet or dry. Just don't burn, freeze, or drown it.

Jatropha multifida (coral plant), a native from Texas to Brazil, is a fairly recent introduction as a houseplant.

Euphorbia pseudoburuana.

It is an attractive shrub with almost-round, palmate leaves which are finely cut and lobed. Showy clusters of coral red flowers can be nearly everblooming. It needs a sunny to semisunny situation, average house temperatures, fresh air, and a well-drained, loam-based potting soil kept evenly moist in spring and summer, on the dry side in fall and winter. Sow seeds (they are rapid germinators), or make cuttings of hard young branches (let dry slightly before setting in the rooting medium).

Pedilanthus tithymaloides (devil's-backbone, redbird cactus), from Central America, grows mostly upright with zigzagging stems. After the plant has been chilled in winter, small, birdlike, scarlet blossoms appear in the spring. The lance-shaped leaves are light green with suffusions and splashes of rosy red, white, and dark green. Give it a sunny to semishady situation, average house temperatures except quite cool (but above freezing) in winter, and fresh air. Pot it in well-drained, loam-based soil and keep evenly moist in spring and summer, on the dry side during fall and winter. Make cuttings in the spring.

Synadenium grantii (African milkbush), eight to twelve feet tall, from Africa, is a succulent shrub with

Jatropha multifida.

the milky sap typical of this family. The cultivar 'Rubra' has fleshy, wine red leaves to three inches long set on thick, fleshy stems which become shrubby with age. This showy, unusual foliage plant likes a dry, sunny situation, indoors or out. Pot in a well-drained, loam-based soil and keep evenly moist spring and summer, on the dry side in fall and winter. Make cuttings in the spring; seal the cut ends in a flame to prevent excessive loss of sap.

GENTIANACEAE. *Gentian Family.*

Herbs from cool parts of the world, except *Exacum*, from Socotra in the Indian Ocean. They have opposite leaves and much-admired flowers, frequently blue. Exacum is the only genus of this family used in houseplanting and is covered as a seasonal flowering pot plant on page 41.

GERANIACEAE. *Geranium Family.*

Herbs, sometimes woody-stemmed, sometimes succulent, with simple leaves and umbels of showy flowers. Two genera, *Erodium* and *Pelargonium*, are of interest for houseplanting.

Erodium chamaedryoides in 'Album' (white flowers), 'Roseum' (light pink with darker pink veining), and 'Roseum Double' or *E. c.* 'Flore Plena' (tiny multipetaled flowers like minuscule roses) are ground-hugging alpine geraniums that adapt well to pot culture, especially on an indoor/outdoor scheme, and bloom in the spring. They need a sunny, airy, cool (they are hardy to 25°F), moist situation in winter; excellent candidates for a sun-heated pit or cool greenhouse. Erodiums can be grown through the summer in part shade outdoors, in a place where the air can circulate freely. Pot in a loam-based soil and keep evenly moist. Be sure not to let them dry out severely at any time. Propagate by removing offsets while repotting in late winter or earliest spring.

Pelargonium × domesticum represents a complex grouping of hybrids characterized by all-green leaves crisply crinkled by veins and spring flowers that are extraordinarily large, plentiful, and beautiful, often dis-

Pelargonium × domesticum *'Dolly'*.

with a horseshoe-shaped zone of brownish green; they are also known as zonal geraniums. They bear heavy clusters of large single to double flowers in shades of red, salmon, pink, lavender, and white. Hundreds of cultivars are available.

Pelargonium peltatum is the ivy-leaf geranium, with long, trailing stems angled at the joints, and glossy ivylike leaves. These give a beautiful display of bloom in summer and in southern and coastal California they are a popular ground cover on sunny banks. 'Sunset' (also sold as 'L'Elegante') is a noteworthy and old cultivar whose ivy-shaped leaves are variegated with pink and white when the soil is kept on the dry side and there is plenty of warm sunlight; it bears light lavender flowers. 'Sybil Holmes' has clusters of pink flowers, the individual blossoms looking uncannily like unfurling rosebuds. 'Rouletta' has dark red-edged white flowers. There are also cascade geraniums, intermediate in habit and appearance between bed-

Pelargonium × hortorum *'Rose Lady'*.

tinctively blotched on the upper petals with a contrasting color; these are the Martha Washington, show, or regal geraniums. Several dozen cultivars are available. The small-flowered types in this grouping, purple-and-white 'Madame Layal', for example, are called pansy geraniums and are more likely to succeed as houseplants. After spring flowering, cut the plant back by one half or more and set the pot outdoors in partial to full sun for the summer. Bring it back indoors in fall before frost; reduce the watering and keep cool and on the dry side. Start weak but regular weekly applications of a balanced fertilizer toward the end of winter, or as the flower buds first appear. Night temperatures of 50° to 55°F are required in order to set buds on *domesticum* geraniums.

Pelargonium × hortorum is another grouping of complex hybrids that represents the house or bedding geranium. These are mainly upright, thick-stemmed, branching plants with scalloped. roundish leaves marked

Pelargonium peltatum *'Rococo'*.

ding and ivy-leaf varieties, and alpine or Swiss balcony geraniums noted for single flowers borne in great abundance.

Pelargoniums That Make Scents

Besides the more usual rose, lemon, and apple, there are scented geraniums that smell of apricot, coconut, ginger, lime, nutmeg, orange, and strawberry. Breeders are also working to give us scenteds that have beautiful flowers for a more extended period than is the usual habit of this class.

As houseplants, scented geraniums need as much direct sun as possible and temperatures ranging from 50°F to as high as 75°F with good air movement. If the plants grow rangy, cut them back by as much as a third. Encourage bushiness by pinching out the growth tips from time to time.

Scented geraniums do well in almost any well-drained, all-purpose potting soil. Fertilize lightly from midwinter to late summer, not at all in the fall and early winter. During the shorter days and cooler average temperatures these plants benefit from a short rest.

Look for scented geraniums at your local garden center. They are often sold along with potted herbs. The more unusual species and flowering hybrids come from geranium specialists such as Shady Hill Gardens and Logee's (see Resources).

My idea of a heavenly sunny bay window garden, or of a sunny outdoor terrace, is to have a collection of as many different scented geraniums as possible, all in clay pots. Apple and nutmeg make wonderful hanging plants and most of the others make attractive bushes, or tree-form standards. The small-leaved finger bowl lemon geraniums (*Pelargonium crispum* 'Prince Rupert' and 'Prince Rupert Variegated', also called 'French Lace') can be trained in a year to a nice tree eighteen inches tall, and the more vigorous rose geranium (*Pelargonium graveolens*) can become a tree four feet tall with a head the size of a bushel in twelve to eighteen months.

A delightful bonus from scented geraniums is that when the leaves dry up, they can be picked and used in

Assorted scented geraniums (Pelargonium species, varieties, cultivars) in spring bloom.

making potpourri. One called 'Mabel Grey' is outstanding for this purpose; its leaves give off a potent lemon scent long after they have dried.

If you long for scented geraniums but have no sunny window, they can be grown in a maxi light garden. Pinch out tips on a regular basis in order to keep the plants of a size and shape that works well in this configuration of growing space.

Geranium Growing Tips

Light. Full sun in winter, directly in a window facing east, south, or west. Outdoors in summer, shade at midday is acceptable, even desirable for the ivy-leafs. The miniatures, dwarfs, Goblins (strain of miniatures), and Deacons (strain of compact floribundas), as well as the scenteds, all having a naturally compact habit may be grown successfully in a maxi light garden.

Temperature. Human comfort spells geranium comfort, 70° to 80°F days, dropping by as much as 20 degrees at night. Ivy-leafs and regals (*Pelargonium × domesticum*) are fussier, especially about too much heat; in fall and winter they need 50°F nights, and up to 70°F or so on sunny days.

Humidity. Here is where geraniums move to the head of the class as flowering houseplants since they don't need lots of moisture in the air. They also don't need to be misted; in fact it is better not to as droplets of water can lodge in flower buds or new leaf buds and cause rot. As necessary, shower the leaves in tepid water to keep them rain-fresh.

Soil. Give them two parts garden loam (or packaged all-purpose potting soil), clean, sharp sand (or perlite), and sphagnum peat moss (or well-rotted compost). Repot at least once a year.

Moisture. In warmth, keep evenly moist to slightly on the dry side. If constantly below 60°F, keep on the dry side. Avoid extremes.

Fertilizer. To promote blooms, use 5-10-5, 15-30-15, or any product labeled as a blossom booster. Hold the fertilizer in fall and early winter, to give the plants a rest.

Lack of Bloom Is Caused By . . .

1) Insufficient direct sunlight.
2) Temperatures that are consistently too warm.
3) Temperatures that are too cold.
4) Too much nitrogen. Use a fertilizer having little or no nitrogen but plenty of phosphorus and potash, such as 1-6-5 or 0-6-5.
5) Depleted soil. Plant needs to be cut back drastically and repotted in fresh soil to boost vigorous new growth and bud shoots.
6) Regals won't bloom on schedule from late winter to early summer if they are too warm in fall and winter (consistently higher than 60°F).

Some Favorite Scented Geraniums

Name	Scent
'Apple' *Pelargonium odoratissimum*	Apple
'Atomic Snowflake'	Spicy rose
'Attar of Roses'	Full-bodied rose
'Coconut' *Pelargonium parviflorum*	Coconut
'Dean's Delight'	Pine
'Little Gem'	Rose
'Mabel Grey'	Lemon verbena
'Old Scarlet Unique'	Pungent
'Orange' *Pelargonium citriodorum*	Citrus blossom
'Spring Park'	Strawberry-lemon

Geranium Leaves Turn Yellow From . . .

1) Lack of fresh air circulation.
2) Lack of light.
3) Letting the soil become bone-dry between waterings.

4) Allowing the plant to stand in water.

5) Spider mites, which cause the leaves to pucker and cup downward. In time there will be yellow speckles and nearly invisible grayish webs. Treat by dipping the plant in lukewarm water to which you've added a few drops of liquid dishwashing detergent, such as Ivory Liquid, every five days. It will also help if you are careful not to let the soil become severely dry, if you boost fresh air circulation, and shower plants with water often enough to keep them dust-free.

6) Root rot. If a geranium plant remains wilted despite plenty of soil moisture, the root rot disease known as geranium black leg or black rot may be present. This is often accompanied by leaves having yellow or brown spots and splotches and darkened and shriveled leaf stems that disintegrate into blackish brown rot at the soil line. This is mostly the result of overwatering or poorly drained soil, which can be aggravated by watering and fertilizing too freely before a geranium is well-rooted, or at any time when light and temperatures are below optimum. It is often possible to salvage cuttings from the upper parts of the stems that have not yet been infected.

7) Jet lag. Although you may be lucky enough to have a geranium specialist in driving distance, most of us have to enlarge our collections by ordering from catalogs. Almost inevitably geraniums that are packaged for shipment, no matter how expertly, suffer a kind of jet lag—the result of having no light and little air. The grower will likely include instructions, but in any event, unpack immediately on arrival, moisten any that are dry, and remove any leaves that are obviously discolored. Growers usually ship rooted cuttings in Jiffy 7 pellets or thumb pots. These are ready to move to four-inch pots, preferably unglazed clay as it allows more air to reach the roots than will plastic or ceramic.

8) Old age. It is also perfectly natural for every geranium leaf eventually to mature, turn yellow, and die. The sooner you remove such a leaf, the better, so that light, air, and nutrients can be channeled to developing shoots. The same is true of flower clusters; if you have the time and are so inclined, the life of each can be prolonged if you carefully remove individual blossoms as they fade, otherwise they may cause other buds in the same head (called a "truss" in geraniums) to rot.

Geraniums may have other plagues and problems visited upon its house.

1) Holes eaten from leaves, especially plants outdoors, are often the work of a very small green worm resembling a cabbage worm. If you are persistent, handpicking is an effective control measure.

2) Edema causes watery blisters to form on upper and lower geranium leaf surfaces, in particular the ivy types; eventually these blisters burst, leaving behind corky, dried spots. This is caused by an imbalance between air temperature and soil moisture, specifically too cold and too wet at the same time. During cool, cloudy weather, water less and try for better air circulation.

3) Botrytis blight causes geranium leaves and clusters of flowers to rot. While encouraged by warmth, high humidity, lack of air circulation, and too much shade, the direct way to deal with this malady—even to avoid it entirely—is to keep your geraniums clean at all times—no dead flowers or yellow leaves permitted!

4) Whiteflies don't usually attack geraniums but where the regals are concerned, they seem inseparable, as are some of the scenteds, in particular the apple and nutmeg types. One sure treatment is to spray every week with insecticidal soap and water. But you must work silently and quickly so as not to alert the whiteflies, otherwise they will fly away to a safe spot until you go away with your sprayer.

Propagating Geraniums

Propagate geraniums from cuttings to produce new plants exactly like the parent. Growth that is too young

Pelargonium × hortorum 'Appleblossom Rosebud'.

or soft may not root, nor will the oldest, woodiest parts. What you want is a piece of stem that will break cleanly in two, the same as a fresh snap bean, and about four to six inches long. Remove the lower leaves from the stem as well as the papery green or brown stipules which occur along the stem wherever leaves grow; these appear insignificant but if not removed before planting they almost invariably cause the cutting to rot.

Set the cutting to root with at least one node where leaves once grew buried in the medium—which can be clean, sharp sand, a fifty-fifty mix of sand and peat moss, or a premoistened Jiffy 7 peat pot.

Geraniums root quickly in temperatures ranging from 60° to 75°F, with bright light and all but the hottest sun. Keep the medium nicely moist at all times, neither wet nor dry. Promptly remove any leaves or stems that wither or show signs of rotting. Do not enclose geranium cut-

tings in plastic or cover with glass as the lack of fresh air will encourage rotting, not rooting.

Some manuals say to leave geranium cuttings to dry a few hours or overnight before planting. This may be valid in a humid environment but in most growing conditions it is better to plant at once or within a few hours. One point all agree on is that using a rooting hormone powder is not necessary and may even be detrimental to geraniums.

The other way to multiply geraniums is from seeds, which are tan or brown, about the size of a small grain of rice, and as easy to sprout as just about anything. I recently found a packet of hybrid geranium seeds that was four years old. Much to my surprise, a germination test of twenty seeds yielded seventeen seedlings two months later large enough to transplant to individual three-inch pots. Since it takes five to six months of growing to reach blooming size, judge planting time accordingly. Start geranium seeds in the same clean or sterile medium you might use for tomatoes or marigolds. Distribute the seeds as evenly as possible, a half to one inch apart in a large shallow pot or flat. Cover with a scant layer of vermiculite, then set in a basin of water to soak until beads of moisture show on the surface. Remove, drain, then enclose in plastic or cover with a sheet of glass or newspaper and set to sprout where temperatures average 72°F. As soon as seedlings show, remove the cover and set to grow in a sunny place or three inches beneath the tubes in a maxi light garden. Be sure never to let the sowing dry out, not even once, or the seedlings will be killed.

When geranium seedlings start to crowd in the community pot, transplant to individual pots. If growth seems spindly, more sun or light is needed. You can offset this by pinching to encourage branching, also by keeping temperatures on the cool side. They can be planted outdoors when there is no danger of frost.

Cutting Back and Pruning

One of the most persistent questions about geraniums is what to do with them at the end of the outdoor season.

The way to be both safe and sure is to cut back old plants arbitrarily to five inches and set in pots or shallow flats of soil in a cool, frost-free, bright place until spring. Keep barely moist.

In order to have geraniums that are in a constant state of bloom as well as rejuvenation, practice this pinching technique: When any given stem is as tall as you'd like, or you wish to encourage branching or new basal shoots, pinch out its growing tip but not the flower bud forming alongside. By this mindful pruning you allow the terminal bloom cluster to mature and give pleasure while the removal of the growing tip has set into motion the desired activity below. By the time the top blooms fade, new growth may be already budding.

A quick way to get a compact bush out of a tall, scraggly geranium having leaves at the top of mostly bare branches is to cut everything back to five inches. Then make tip cuttings of all suitable parts and stick these to root right in the same pot.

Like any everblooming plant—African violet, wax begonia, *Oxalis regnellii*—geraniums benefit from almost daily grooming, or at least once a week. On the other hand, they can be neglected for weeks or months and still give a welcome appearance.

Gesneriaceae. *Gesneriad Family.*

Handsome, often velvety leaved plants from the tropics with wheel-shaped, tubular or bell-shaped flowers. The leaves may be hairy or glossy. Some of the genera of special interest for houseplanting are *Achimenes*, *Aeschynanthus*, *Chrysothemis*, *Columnea*, *Episcia*, *Gesneria*, *Kohleria*, *Nematanthus*, *Saintpaulia*, *Sinningia*, *Smithiantha*, and *Streptocarpus*.

Achimenes, also called nut orchid and hot-water plant, grows from a scaly rhizome and is primarily active in spring and summer. The shape and size of the rhizome vary but are generally between that of a pistachio nut and a willow catkin, each rhizome comprised of many tightly packed fleshy wedges. Plant six scaly rhizomes one inch deep in an eight-inch hanging basket in late winter or early spring and by autumn of the same year a tenfold

Achimenes '*Pink Charm*'.

increase will not be unusual. More than a hundred years ago, the achimenes was already popular, long before the African violet or saintpaulia was cultivated. Because it grows in warm weather and goes dormant in cold, the achimenes traveled well with the early settlers and is something of a folk plant. There are intergeneric hybrids between *Achimenes* and *Smithiantha* called × *Achimenantha*; according to Kartuz Greenhouses (see Resources) these are sturdy, exceptionally floriferous, have a longer blooming season and are more tolerant of a variety of growing conditions than either of the parents.

For success with achimenes, always keep in mind their need for constant warmth, except in winter when moderate temperatures sustain the dormant rhizomes. I think of them as summer bulbs, to be started indoors a couple of months before the weather outside is warm and settled. They are superb flowering plants for all kinds of containers outdoors, especially hanging baskets or spilling over the sides of window boxes or large planters of any kind. Achimenes have lagged in becoming popular in the crowded Northeast owing to their sensitivity to air pollution. Elsewhere, however, they deserve to be much more widely cultivated. In recent years breeders have shown renewed interest in the genus. As a result there are new colors and some having hose-in-hose or double flowers. Achimenes need shade to semishade, warm temperatures, and fresh, moist air. Set the scaly rhizomes one inch deep in a humus-rich, loam-based soil. Water freely and maintain evenly moist in the spring and summer; dry off and store barely damp in a dark place having moderate temperatures (50° to 60°F) in fall and winter. Propagate by dividing the scaly rhizomes at planting time in the spring, or by sowing seeds in the winter in a warm maxi light garden.

Aeschynanthus (lipstick vine) is one gesneriad that gained recognition during the houseplant craze of the 1970s. It became popular enough to generate an impressive number of questions in my column, almost inevitably having to do with nonbloom, bud drop, or mealybugs discovered in the reddish brown, waxy calyx that holds the flower. Michael Kartuz, an accomplished grower of plants in general and all gesneriads in particular, says, "Bud drop is caused by insufficient humidity at a critical time or letting the growing medium be too dry or too wet. Keep these plants evenly moist and provide at least fifty percent humidity. Soil moisture extremes also result in wilted leaves that rapidly yellow, shrivel up, and drop; the bare stems left behind usually die back from the tips."

If you have a healty lipstick vine that doesn't set buds at all, Kartuz advises more light, including some direct sun. This gesneriad needs more sun than its relative the African violet in order to flower well.

Most lipstick vines bloom in the summer or early fall. They tolerate a wide range in temperature and don't seem to require anything special in order to set buds. The winter-flowering species *Aeschynanthus ellipticus* and *A. obconicus* are likely to bloom better if night temperatures are ten degrees or so cooler than daytime through the fall and winter.

After a lipstick blooms, Kartuz says to cut back any stems that seem too long or out of proportion to the overall plant. Also remove any stems that have lost a number of leaves; cut these back to the base. Use a light, porous growing medium, like that used for African violets. Kartuz uses a soilless mix of 2 quarts sphagnum peat moss, 1 quart each of vermiculite and perlite, and 2 tablespoons ground limestone. Mix this together well,

being sure to wear rubber gloves and a face mask so as not to breathe in tiny particles of dust that will become airborne. Kartuz fertilizes a little with every watering, using a formulation for flowering plants, 15-30-15 for example. Keep aeschynanthus evenly moist; avoid extremes or the plant will drop leaves all over the place.

With regard to mealybugs on lipstick plant, there are two possible courses of treatment, the first if you have time and patience, the second if you are in a hurry:

1) Rub out every trace of mealybug with cotton swabs dipped in denatured alcohol. Go over your work with a magnifying glass. Repeat at weekly intervals until the plant is absolutely clean.
2) Dip the plant in a large pail or basin containing insecticidal soap or neem solution and water. Repeat this treatment weekly until there are no more bugs.

Propagate aeschynanthus from tip or stem cuttings, leaf mallet cuttings, or by sowing seeds. These activities can be done at any season in a warm maxi light garden, otherwise the period from late winter through spring is best.

The older aeschynanthus such as *lobbianus*, the typical lipstick vine, have been superseded by showier species and cultivars. At a recent show conducted at the annual meeting of the American Gloxinia and Gesneriad Society I was delighted with 'Coral Flame', which Kartuz describes in his catalog as having "clusters of flaring coral-red flowers. Closely set round, waxy leaves. Trailing, compact."

Also the species *Aeschynanthus hildebrandii*, which blooms young and grows readily from tip cuttings, is one of the most attractive flowering houseplants I have encountered in many years. Kartuz says of it: "Clusters of very showy bright red tubular flowers at the tip of every branch. Everblooming. Very dwarf, compact. Best aeschynanthus for growing in a light garden."

Other aeschynanthus favored by Kartuz include: easy-growing, nearly everblooming 'Greensleeves' with red flowers striped purple and yellow from green-striped calyxes in clusters, small elliptical leaves, and a trailing habit; 'Holiday Bells', bearing yellow- and purple-striped red flowers from translucent coral-rose bell-shaped calyxes in winter and summer; and 'Mandalay', a recent entry in the field that is semiupright and makes a nearly everblooming potted specimen. Its clusters of flowers are large, burnt orange, and very showy. The tapered leaves are marbled with purple in the manner of the once popular *Aeschynanthus marmoratus*.

Alsobia dianthiflora (formerly *Episcia dianthiflora*) is a trailing, stoloniferous plant having small, downy, green leaves arranged in rosettes. The flowers are white and deeply fringed, in the manner of a dianthus blossom. Give it a semisunny to semishady situation, average house temperatures, fresh, moist air and a humus-rich, loam-based potting soil kept evenly moist. Root stolon cuttings in warmth and high humidity at any time.

Chrysothemis pulchella 'Amazon', under twelve inches, is a tuberous plant, with tapered, dark copper leaves held on short upright stems. It produces clusters of red-marked yellow flowers from long-lasting orange calyces. Care as for *Sinningia* (page 139).

Columnea is rich in plants such as the fall blooming, yellow-marked, orange-red flowered *C. arguta* from the mountain forests of Panama that can be enjoyed indoors or out in warmth, bright light, and fairly high humidity. Kartuz notes ". . . considering the outstanding performance of these plants, it is hard to understand why they have not become widely popular for summer shade gardens in the Snow Belt, or outdoors all year in frost-free areas." Columneas do well alongside orchids and rainforest cacti such as schlumbergera, rhipsalis, and epiphyllum.

Although many different columneas are in cultivation, I have chosen six from the Kartuz collection that are everblooming:

'Aladdin's Lamp' produces the largest, showiest, dark red flowers of any hybrid to date, with small, purple-black leaves.

'Mary Ann' is noted for its slender coral-red flowers in great abundance, borne on a semitrailing plant that is both dwarf and compact. Kartuz says it is the easiest to grow and flower of the genus.

'Orange Sherbet' is a vigorous trailing plant that produces quantities of large flaming orange flowers all year. If you like the color orange in flowers, this plant will cause excitement.

'Top Brass' has extra-large yellow flowers produced on a plant having a semitrailing habit and small, dark bronze-green leaves.

'Volcano' trails vigorously and produces large bright red-orange flowers with yellow throats, set among dark purple-bronze leaves.

Columnea linearis 'Purple Robe' is an exception among columneas for it grows upright, forming a compact bush of narrow, glossy, dark green leaves and an abundance of slender rose-pink flowers from showy purple calyces. It is an obvious choice for a maxi light garden.

Because of their partly epiphytic habit, columneas need a growing medium that allows the roots to have air but retains enough moisture to prevent severe drying. I get excellent results using a mixture of equal parts soil, sand, sphagnum peat moss, well-rotted leaf mold, and chopped live sphagnum moss, adding a handful of horticultural charcoal chips to each quart of mix and a dusting of dolomite limestone. Daily watering may be required in hot weather. The idea is to maintain a drench-and-dry regimen, trying not to linger at either extreme of wet or dry. Alternate feedings of 30-10-10 and 15-30-15 will produce excellent results. Columneas can be multiplied by taking cuttings and placing them to root in moistened growing mix at any time. Provide moderate

Columnea arguta.

to warm temperatures, moderate to high humidity, and bright light. Columneas will grow all year in semisun to semishade or in a maxi light garden. If average temperatures cool, however, to a range of 50° to 68°F, maintain by watering less and withholding fertilizer.

Episcia is a genus of luxuriant foliage plants six to eighteen inches tall and as wide that also bloom on occasion. They need high humidity, bright diffused light, and warmth (average house temperatures with no cold or dry drafts or sudden drops in temperature to below 60°F). Pot them in a humus-rich, loam-based soil and keep evenly moist. A maxi light garden is to their liking and some of the more colorful cultivars, such as the elusive 'Pink Brocade' (also called 'Cleopatra'), with bright pink leaves, shaded creamy white and pale green along the center, are ideal for terrariums. Specialist growers list many new cultivars, yet on any given day not one of them would ever have been heard of at your local garden center.

Episcias may be readily propagated by rooting the stolons. Under terrarium culture, all stolons may be pinched out as soon as they can be discerned from flower buds, thus forcing a single-stemmed plant having unusually large leaves. In window light or outdoors in settled warm weather episcias are ideal for hanging baskets, to display along shelving with the many stolons cascading, or standing on a pedestal. I don't mean in any way to discourage the growing of episcias; quite the contrary. They are worth the initial trouble it may take to obtain the plants and thereafter they are readily grown under home conditions. The episcia's only problem is that it isn't tough enough to withstand the rough-and-tumble world of commercial horticulture. This could also be a blessing in disguise; an unusually beautiful plant that for whatever reason is somewhat difficult to obtain will always have its devotees.

Gesneria cuneifolia, four to six inches tall and as wide, has glossy, dark green leaves and tubular red flowers. 'Lemon Drop' bears yellow flowers nonstop. These and other dwarf evergreen plants in the genus are everblooming and of exceptional promise for fluorescent light gardens and terrariums. Give them a semisunny to shady

Episcia *'Pink Brocade'*.

Gesneria cuneifolia *'Quebradillas'*.

position, average house temperatures, moist air, and a humus-rich, loam-based potting soil kept evenly moist. Propagate by sowing seeds or by division at repotting time (late winter and spring for window culture, at any season in a warm maxi light garden).

Kohleria eriantha 'Longwood' is one of the showier of the gesneriads. It grows from a scaly rhizome and is thought to have originated at Longwood Gardens, the garden showplace open to the public in Kennett Square, Pennsylvania. Numerous other kohlerias have been treasured by indoor gardeners for several generations, although they have never gotten to be nearly as popular as certain other gesneriads. Old books refer to these plants variously as isoloma and tydaea. Today's botanical name honors Michael Kohler, a nineteenth-century Swiss teacher of natural history.

The scaly rhizome of the kohleria is about the size of your little finger. The genus is terrestrial in habit and is native from Mexico to the northern part of South America. The 'Longwood' kohleria is everblooming when afforded a half-sunny bright window or a place in a maxi light garden. Grow with minimum night temperatures ranging from 60° to 65°F. Kohlerias make great porch plants in warm weather, or in any outdoor room that affords protection from wind, rain, and the hottest sun— a slathouse, gazebo, or summerhouse. Kohlerias root easily from tip cuttings, a procedure that may also result in uncommonly short plants bearing an unusually large number of flowers. The big bonus comes in the formation of numerous scaly rhizomes in the soil, and sometimes even along the maturing stems. The usual procedure is to carry kohlerias through the winter in barely moist but not completely dry soil and to repot in spring, using only the scaly rhizomes and discarding the rest, except possibly for promising tip cuttings.

Since the African Violet Society of America was founded in 1946 and the American Gloxinia Society (which has become the American Gloxinia and Gesneriad Society) in 1951, taxonomists, botanists, and horticulturists have spent an inordinate amount of time on this family. The botanical names have been in a constant state of flux. Popular names are often descriptive but they

Kohleria eriantha 'Longwood'.

are even more elusive. When gesneriads first became popular after World War II, the goldfish plant, then called *Hypocyrta nummularia*, was introduced. This became *Alloplectus nummularia* in *Hortus Third*, published 1976. It has small hairy leaves set along trailing stems, with vermilion-red and yellow pouched flowers in season, and is somewhat epiphytic.

Meanwhile, back in the Brazilian rain forests, a botanist discovered a similar plant having pouch flowers and named it *Hypocyrta strigillosa*. Since it was showy and easy to grow, commercial interests thought the sell might go better with a familiar-sounding name—like goldfish plant. P.S. *Hortus Third* gave this one a new name too, *Nematanthus strigillosus*.

We see that for a brief moment in plant history there were two species of something called hypocyrta that were both known by some growers as goldfish plant. The original *nummularia* has all but dropped out of sight and *strigillosus* has been eclipsed by, forgive me, a veritable school of new hybrid nematanthus, known variously as goldfish or guppy plants.

Lately there have been on the market goldfish plants labeled *Nematanthus speciosus*, a name that *Hortus* says has ". . . no botanical standing." Since the word "*speciosus*" means "showy" or "handsome," it is often applied rather capriciously to a newly cultivated plant, almost always by a gardener, horticulturist, or marketer, not by a botanist whose specialty is taxonomy. This may come as a surprise, but taxonomic botanists do not exist to change plant names and confuse us. In fact, the modus operandi of the taxonomic botanist is to look for similarities among plants and to practice under the motto, "Love it, don't label it." By contrast, the gardener/horticulturist/marketer looks for every difference and distinction—sometimes no matter how slight—between plants and is quick to give each of these a name, a label, so that everyone knows exactly what is being advertised or cultivated.

Botany aside, the only nematanthus I can find listed currently in a catalog as goldfish plant is the cultivar 'Black Gold', which has yellowish orange, pouch-shaped flowers on a compact, trailing plant with small purple-black, glossy leaves. It is easy to grow and a true beauty for a sunny, bright window or light garden.

Care and propagation of nematanthus is the same as that for *Columnea* (page 134).

Saintpaulia ionantha, from east Africa, was brought back to Europe by Baron Walter von Saint Paul around 1890. Among the many plants which botanical explorers have endured hardship to collect and introduce, none could give the discoverer more pride and satisfaction than the saintpaulia. If the Baron could see today's thousands of glamorous African violet cultivars, he would feel that his work was a great success.

The popularity of African violets in America began in 1936 with the introduction of the first named varieties. It spread fast, like a harmless but infectious disease. Today a plant lover has only to see a well-grown specimen, with a lush rosette of velvety leaves nearly hidden under a blanket of colorful flowers, to catch the contagion. Warning: It is not possible to bring one plant into bloom without wanting more.

Historical perspective suggests that the modern African violet burst on the scene during a time of world tensions, wars, and tremendous personal losses. Grief in some cases could best be managed by nurturing a new interest in growing and propagating African violets. The cynic might see nothing here, but I see that millions of people have practiced plants as therapy in response to war, particularly the recovery years following World War II, and all wars/years since. The African violet continues to profit in all this, well-deservedly I might add, for its perennial effectiveness in promulgating hope.

Nobody can count accurately the number of named cultivars of African violets. Hundreds of new hybrids are introduced regularly, some very similar to others—only

Nematanthus *'Tambourine'*.

the names are different. If you want a few plants to bloom in or near a window, you might stay with well-known kinds which have been proved sturdiest and most free-flowering. If you're building a collection, you'll shop through catalogs and swap with other collectors until you have plants in several sizes—miniature, standard, and extra large—with all types of foliage and flowers. The leaves may be nearly smooth or soft-velvety, corrugated with indented veins, fringed, or waved on the edge, round or pointed, flat or cupped, solid green or variegated with creamy white.

African violet flowers may be single, semidouble, or double and in varying shades of blue, pink, lavender, wine, purple, and white. The bicolors have two shades of the same color; multicolors have more than two colors per flower. And there are novelties like star-shaped flowers, or petals bordered with another color (chimeras), or contrastingly streaked and splashed flowers.

It's easy to understand why African violets are popular, for these plants will flower not just during one annual season but off and on all year long. They take up little space, and they keep healthy and contented without a great deal of fuss. But don't let the popular name mislead you. They are not violets, and they do not grow like the "Russian" or "English" violets as we know them. Rather, take "African" as a clue to their care, and try to give them growing conditions similar to their tropical homelands. Since a plant that is not cultivated has no one to groom it or to shield water-sensitive leaves from the rain, I've always imagined that the saintpaulia in situ must be glorious in season, when the natural conditions all come together in support of its needs, and that at other times, on any given day, the plant might look pretty ratty by comparison to one on the show table at a meeting of specialist African violet growers.

African violets need a semisunny position in winter and shade from the hottest sun in other seasons. Insufficient light is a frequent cause of failure to flower. African violets thrive under fluorescent-light culture (see page 9). They like average house temperatures, ideally 68° to 75°F in winter, with fresh, moist air. Give them a humus-rich, loam-based potting soil kept evenly moist. Another

cause of failure is allowing the violet plant to become too dry between waterings. This results in the formation of plantlets ("suckers") where flower buds would otherwise emerge. Fertilize regularly using a product labeled specifically for African violets. The growers who win show ribbons tend to fertilize a little with every watering. Always use water of room temperature or slightly warmer on violets; if the water is too cold, unsightly markings will appear in the foliage. Water alternately from the top and bottom, so that nutrient salts cannot form a crust on the soil. Bottom watering means setting the pot in water and allowing it to soak until beads of moisture show at the surface. Growers who have large numbers of African violets favor the wick watering system, which may use a wick to each pot or a common mat on which many pots stand.

When potting up an African violet, place the plant so the crown is slightly elevated, with the soil sloping ever so slightly down around it, to prevent crown rot. Over-potting also invites rot; keep pot sizes as small as feasible. African violets need repotting at least once yearly, sometimes twice or more. They bloom best when the roots have room to expand, but not as well if the pot is either too small or too large.

African violets are often healthiest and flower best when they have only one crown of leaves. Remove any additional crowns that start to develop immediately upon discovery if they are not needed for propagation, otherwise wait until large enough to remove and root as divisions. Keep the leaves clean with a soft-bristled brush or, and this is better, turn the pot upside down (hold the soil in place with your fingers or a piece of foil) and gently swish the leaves through lukewarm water containing a little mild household detergent. Set the plant aside to drain and dry before returning to its growing quarters.

The most common problem with African violets—failure to flower—is usually caused by insufficient fluorescent or window light, temperatures too high, humidity too low, too many crowns on a plant, chilling the plant with icy water, or a combination of these factors. It's true also that some cultivars flower more easily and profusely than others. Specialist growers' catalogs offer clues to current cultivars which have the most stamina.

African violets may be propagated by seeds, leaf cuttings, or division. For leaf cuttings, select a mature but not old leaf, cut it with an inch of stem, using a knife or razor blade, and insert in a moist rooting medium up to the leaf blade. For division, use a knife to cut down between the crowns, severing them below the soil surface. More suggestions for African violet propagation techniques are on pages 53–57.

Sinningia speciosa, a botanical name used for florist gloxinia, represents a fascinating group of tuberous-rooted gesneriads that are native to Brazil. What a triumph it is to plant a thick, dry, brown, and barren-looking tuber and watch it produce a luxuriant plant with layers of large, oval, velvety leaves topped with a crowning glory of immense, flaring, tubular flowers in rich patterns and glowing colors. Before the large-flowered hybrids had become a gardening household word, there were slipper gloxinias, with smaller flowers facing out instead of up. Fortunately these have been kept in cultivation by amateurs and the slipper configuration has lately reinfatuated breeders. One example is the Diego Series, which produces a medium-size plant that can be finished in a four-

Sinningia speciosa *Buell Hybrid*.

to five-inch pot and bears as many as thirty to forty open blossoms at once in red, rose-pink, or violet.

Some of the finest slipper-flowered gloxinias ever produced are those bred by Albert Buell of Eastford, Connecticut (see Resources). These come in a full color range in plants having compact habit—but definitely larger than the Diego Series.

A fresh gloxinia tuber feels firm and lively; it is neither dry and shriveled nor soft with rot. If it is a large tuber, plant in a six- to eight-inch pot, preferably a shallow bulb pan. Add enough humus-rich, loam-based potting soil to fill the pot halfway; set in the tuber, cupped side up, and cover it completely with soil. The finished soil level will be about a half inch below the pot rim, and will cover the top of the tuber with about a half inch of soil.

Moisten the soil and pot thoroughly by setting it in water nearly to the rim. When the top of the soil is shiny and moist, remove the pot and let it drain. Then, put in a warm spot (60°F minimum) where there is bright diffused light and protection from any drafts. Bottom heat (70° to 80°F) will speed rooting. Water only enough to keep the soil slightly moist until leaves begin to show.

Now, move the plant to its permanent growing quarters—a warm window where some sun will reach it but where there's shade against very hot rays, or, perhaps, under the tubes in a maxi light garden. In either case, if the indoor air is dry (and in winter it usually is), increase the humidity by setting the pots on, not in, a layer of gravel in a humidity tray (see page 12) at least as large as the plant's mature leaf-spread.

Step up the watering schedule so that whenever you touch the soil, it always feels nicely moist—but never so much that the roots drown from soggy wetness. Water of room temperature or slightly warmer is best and won't make white marks on the leaves. Fertilize as for *Saintpaulia* (above). If the stems begin to grow long, if the plant gets spindly, if the leaves curl under on the edges, you'll know that the light is too dim, the air too dry, and your gloxinia probably won't flower freely; the buds, if formed, may drop. Sometimes it helps to enclose the plant in a tent of clear plastic, at least until flowering gets started.

When the last bud has opened and the last flower has faded, cut off the old stems and leaves and look for signs of new growth from the tuber. If you see new leaves, continue watering and fertilizing, and repeat the complete process as long as new sprouts are produced after flowering. If there is no new growth, water the plant a little less each time, until the soil is nearly dry. Store the tuber in the pot in moderate temperatures (50° to 60°F) and dim light. Check the resting tubers frequently, and water often enough to keep them plump. When small new leaves appear, repot in fresh soil and start over.

The basic florist gloxinia and the larger slipper types are best grown as summer porch plants, which can be started indoors a month or two before the arrival of warm planting-out weather (the sort needed by tomatoes and eggplants). Around Labor Day these need to be gradually dried off and stored to rest for the winter. Perhaps surprisingly so, this is also the ideal time to start these exciting plants from seeds. The seedlings will need to grow in a warm window or, ideally, a maxi light garden. By spring they'll be blooming. Here's the procedure:

1) Gloxinia seeds are tiny spheres that can easily get away from you; avoid sneezing while handling. Don't open the packet until you are ready to hold it over the prepared planting bed, which can be any sterile product labeled specifically for seed-starting and rooting cuttings. I have had good luck using pure horticultural vermiculite.

2) Sprinkle the seeds over the premoistened surface. Do not cover with planting medium, rather gently press them in place with your fingertips.

3) Enclose the planting in a clear plastic bag. Set in bright light, not direct sun, where temperatures range between 70° to 80°F.

4) As soon as you see the tiny seedling leaves, gradually open the bag to harden them to the open air. Be sure the planting medium remains constantly moist; one drying can kill seedlings.

5) As the true leaves start to grow, begin very dilute feedings. At this stage I use a little fish emulsion with every watering and find this produces thrifty seedlings in record time.

6) Before the seedlings start to crowd, dig each out with the point of a pencil and transfer to its individual four-inch pot. Use humus-rich, loam-based potting soil.

Through the winter gloxinia seedlings will grow best in a maxi light garden where long days of sixteen hours out of every twenty-four can be maintained. Minimum night temperatures of 65°F, warming to 72° to 80°F by day are ideal. Add 40 percent or more humidity and a small fan to keep the air moving, and you are all set to have your own gloxinia babies coming into bloom by spring. What's more, by the end of the first flowering season, each will have formed a tuber in the soil that can be kept for next season. Heirloom tubers have been reported, passed from one generation of gardeners in the family to the next for a half century.

Miniature gloxinias such as *Sinningia pusilla* are among the most enchanting of plants that can be grown indoors. They are frequently grown in recycled plastic containers that once contained cream for coffee, or in one-inch clay or plastic pots. Constant high humidity is required, so they need to be placed inside a terrarium (see pages 209–214). *Sinningia pusilla* has brown-veined green leaves hardly the size of your little fingernail, in a basal rosette the diameter of a silver dollar. The slipper-shaped flowers are pale lavender, about an inch long. There are many other miniature gloxinias, some species of *Sinningia*, others hybrids. There are whites and then a whole range of pinks, vivid scarlets, reds, rose-violets, and purples. They grow well in average house temperatures and tend to bloom intermittently all year. Growers who specialize in gesneriads are the major source for these tiny treasures (see Resources).

Streptocarpella saxorum (formerly *Streptocarpus saxorum*), from Tanzania, has small, oval, fuzzy leaves in whorls on succulent stems. From the base of these grow the wiry stems which bear white-throated, lavender-blue flowers. In the right situation this plant can become a near bushel-size display almost indefinitely, usually hanging, that is like a blue cloud. Cultivars include 'Ballerina' (small light green leaves, self-branching, orchid-rose flowers all year), 'Blue Horizon' (many large pale blue flowers carried well above tiny dark green succulent leaves), 'Boysenberry Delight' (violet-rose flowers, compact, self-branching), 'Butterfly' (largest flowers to date, dark blue on a compact dwarf plant), 'Concord Midnight' (dark violet-blue), 'Sassy' (dark violet-blue), and 'Sparkle' (rosy purple, self-branching, compact). Streptocarpellas need a sunny to semishady situation, average house temperatures, fresh, moist air, and a humus-rich, loam-based potting soil kept evenly moist. This gesneriad is sometimes cultivated along with cacti and other succulents, in which case the leaves and stems will be reduced overall and paler in color, the result of being grown hard. Propagate by tip cuttings set to root in a moist medium at any season; keep constantly moist, warm, and in bright light.

Streptocarpus grandis, from Zululand, Natal, is a most unusual plant which has only one leaf in its lifetime. From a dust-size seed, only twelve to eighteen months are required to attain a leaf up to three feet long, two feet wide, and eighteen inches tall. Near its base, along the midrib, small blue flowers appear on clustered stalks up to eighteen inches high. *Streptocarpus* × *hybridus* suggests the popular name Cape primrose, with its large, showy flowers appearing almost as constantly as in the better cultivars of saintpaulia. Some names for today's showiest Cape primroses are 'Arline' (shocking pink, striped throat), 'Black Panther' (dark violet, almost black flowers), 'Blue Mars' (light blue frilly flowers with dark violet-blue throat), 'Captain Blood' (very large ruffled true red, striped throat), 'Double Trouble' (mid-blue double flowers with dark blue lines radiating from the center), 'Elfrieda' (large salmon pink), 'Isobel White' (very large ruffled white flowers with yellow throat), 'Jeannette' (clusters of bright pink flowers veined and netted red on lower lobes), 'Raspberry Froth' (multiple clusters of dark pink flowers with darker rose-pink markings radiating from throat to lower lobes), 'Rosebud Tetra' (polyploid sport of 'Rosebud' with shorter, broader leaves; flowers dark rose-pink with extra petals clustered in center), 'Royalty' (giant ruffled flowers of velvety royal purple, striped throat), 'Strawberry Crush' (vivid, red-veined, coral-salmon flowers), and 'Velveteen' (very large dark violet-blue flowers, white-striped throat). *Streptocarpus rexii*, from South Africa, is a small, blue-flowered plant that

Streptocarpus *'Holiday'*.

is still cultivated by collectors; it has been much used in breeding for the × *hybridus* group. The culture and propagation for these streptocarpus is essentially the same as that for *Saintpaulia* (page 137). They are exceptionally fine plants for a maxi light garden.

GRAMINEAE. *Grass Family*.

Mostly slender plants with round, hollow stems and slender, pointed, parallel-veined leaves arising from swollen joints. They are cultivated as cereals and fodder, for sugar and molasses, for starches, beverages, and many industrial uses, for pastures and lawns, and for garden ornament. It is the genera in the last category which are of interest to the indoor gardener: *Arundinaria*, *Bambusa*, *Oplismenus*, and *Stenotaphrum*.

Arundinaria falcata (sickle bamboo), to fifteen feet, from the Himalayas, has hollow canes to one half inch thick that mature to a warm yellow-green; they are set with blue-green leaves one to six inches long. Care as for *Bambusa nana*.

Bambusa nana, three to ten feet, from China and Japan, is the smallest bamboo commonly cultivated as a potted plant. Small, light green leaves with bluish undersides are sparsely set on dense-growing, thin, hollow canes. Give it a sunny to semisunny situation, average house temperatures, fresh, moist air, and a humus-rich, loam-based potting soil kept evenly moist. Divide large clumps in spring.

Oplismenus hirtellus variegatus, a creeper from the West Indies, has thin, papery leaves striped with white and pink. It is called basket grass and may be used as a regular potted plant, perhaps with the growth cascading from a shelf. Care as for *Bambusa nana*.

Stenotaphrum secundatum variegatum, from the tropical parts of America, creeps rapidly (plantlife is fraught with oxymorons) by stolons, and sends up straight, slim, round-tipped leaves of creamy white on green. In its plain-leaved form, this is the popular St. Augustinegrass of the South. Care as for *Bambusa nana*.

IRIDACEAE. *Iris Family*.

Herbs with flattened fans of sword-shaped or grassy leaves and showy flowers. Three genera are of interest here: *Freesia*, *Gladiolus*, and *Neomarica*. A fourth, *Crocus*, is covered in the section on forcing (page 45).

Freesia represents a genus of South African plants that has been extensively hybridized for the flaring, tubular flowers that occur in a one-sided cluster at right angles to the stem and to the tall (to twenty inches high), erect leaves. Mostly yellow or white in the less developed selections, the flowers of hybrids appear in pastels and some

fairly vivid blue-purples and orange-scarlets. Some but not all freesias give off a fragrance that is surely among the most loved in all the world of flower perfumes. Corms for winter and spring blooms are planted from August to November, in a loam-based potting soil one inch deep and two inches apart. Keep the plantings in a sunny, cool (40° to 50°F after planting; up to 60°F in active growth) position getting fresh, moist air. Keep evenly moist while in active growth—fall to early spring—and dry at other times. Store the resting corms in a dry, dark place in summer, where temperatures are around 60° to 70°F. Sow seeds in spring; remove offsets at repotting time.

Gladiolus tristis, two to three feet tall, from South Africa, grows from corms planted in pots filled with a humus-rich, loam-based potting soil from September to

Gladiolus tristis.

October. Set in full sun with average house temperatures and exposure to fresh, moist air. When up and growing, fertilize every two weeks with 20-20-20. Provide support. Thin, tall leaves extend up among the yellow-white flowers at the top of the plant; these are more fragrant than freesia, appearing around March to April. They are also so much more graceful than the ordinary tall, hybrid gladiolus, it is a little hard to believe they belong to the same genus. Dry off (stop watering and fertilizing) G. *tristis* by June and keep the corms resting in a warm dark place until time to replant in early fall. This is the time to remove offsets.

Both known as the apostle plant, *Neomarica gracilis*, (white with blue flowers), native from Brazil to Mexico, and N. *northiana* (white with violet, brown, and yellow flowers), from Brazil, have the habit of developing twelve leaves in a fan. The flowers, small and irislike, are short-lived and appear on a leaflike scape, following the production of each set of leaves. When flowering has finished on N. *northiana*, baby plants develop from the same place which produced blossoms. When these are large enough, the scape bends over so that the new plants may take root in soil, hence its other common name, walking-iris. *Marica* was the former name for this genus. Both species need a sunny to semishady position, average house temperatures, preferably not over 72°F in winter, fresh, moist air, and a humus-rich, loam-based potting soil kept evenly moist. When foliar embryos are large enough, pin down to small pots of soil; sever the scape when the new plant has formed its own roots. Propagate also by division at repotting time in spring.

LABIATAE. *Mint Family*.

Tender and hardy herbs, some tropical shrubs, mostly with square stems, opposite, aromatic leaves, and irregular flowers. Several genera are of interest as herbs (see page 202), including *Lavandula*, *Marrubium*, *Mentha*, *Nepeta*, *Ocimum*, *Origanum*, *Rosmarinus*, and *Thymus*. Genera of special interest here are *Coleus* (recently reclassified as *Solenostemon*), *Plectranthus*, and *Scutellaria*.

Coleus blumei, one to three feet, introduced in England in 1853 from Java, and its hybrids are erect plants with highly colored leaves, most of them displaying two or more colors in more or less regular patterns. 'Pineapple Beauty', which first appeared in an 1877 catalog, is still available and classic for training as a tree-form standard. 'Red Mars', known also as 'Purple Duckfoot', is a non-blooming species that forms compact globes of reddish purple leaves on a base-branching plant that makes a showy ground cover around large container trees. *Coleus rehneltianus*, from Sri Lanka, is the parent of most of the prostrate or creeping forms. All are primarily foliage plants which will grow more luxuriantly if the flower buds are picked off as soon as they are noticed. There are, however, coleus grown especially for their annual season of flowering (C. *thyrsoideus*, with its vivid blue

Coleus *in C. Z. Guest's greenhouse.*

flowers held in long spikelike racemes). Certain species are so succulent they are at home in the dry garden of cacti and other succulents (*C. amboinicus* or Spanish thyme; *C. pentherii*, potpourri mint, has hairy, sharply fragrant leaves on cascading stems). One of the largest collections of named species and cultivars of this genus of foliage plants, which have been called "fashionable weeds," is maintained outside of London at Wisley, where plant trials are conducted by the Royal Horticultural Society. In case of boiler breakdown or other accident, this collection is duplicated by the Grounds Department of Reading University in England.

Coleus need a sunny to semisunny situation, average house temperatures, fresh, moist air, and a humus-rich, loam-based potting soil kept evenly moist. Grow from seeds or cuttings in winter for planting out in warm weather. Favorite plants from outdoors can be potted and brought in before frost, or cuttings made and carried over in a window or light garden for the following year. Mealybugs are a great liability when they infest a coleus plant; only the most thorough and consistent spraying with insecticidal soap or neem will afford control.

Plectranthus australis (Swedish ivy), from Australia and various Pacific islands, has waxy green, scalloped leaves held on trailing stems and spikes of white flowers. *Plectranthus behrii* grows upright with slightly hairy green leaves that are rose-pink beneath. It displays showy spikes of pink flowers in autumn. *Plectranthus coleiodes* is a small upright-growing plant having aromatic, white-margined, green leaves, while *P. fosteri* 'Marginatus' has deep veins through leaves variegated chartreuse and green. *Plectranthus oertendahlii*, from Natal, has silver-veined leaves, purple-margined and purple beneath, and spikes of pale pink flowers; *P. prostrata* is a creeper having tiny, succulent, gray-green, aromatic leaves—a great choice for the shelf or hanging basket; *P. purpuratus*, from Natal, is smaller than the other species. It has velvety, fleshy leaves with purple beneath, and lavender flowers. Care as for *Coleus* (above); propagate from cuttings.

Scutellaria costaricana.

Plectranthus fosteri 'Marginatus'.

Scutellaria costaricana (scarlet skullcap), one and a half to three feet, from Costa Rica, has deeply quilted dark green leaves and orange-scarlet flowers in a one-sided raceme from a purple calyx. This is a knockout when it blooms. *Scutellaria javanica* has slender angled spikes of tubular violet flowers. Give them a sunny to semisunny situation, average house temperatures on the warm side, ample fresh, moist air, and a humus-rich, loam-based potting soil kept evenly moist. Does well from cuttings started late winter–spring in a warm, humid, bright place.

LEEACEAE. *Leea Family.*

One genus of woody plant native to Old World tropics, from New Guinea across the Malay Archipelago, India, northern Madagascar, and central Africa. Included until recently with Vitaceae, but removed and treated as distinct because there are no tendrils.

Leea amabilis, six feet, from Borneo, has bronzy velvet, slightly toothed oval leaflets which are reddish when young. The leaflets have red midribs and white veins. The palmate leaves of *L. coccinea*, six to eight feet, from Burma, are glossy, toothed, and wavy-edged, with new growth tending to be copper-tinged. Flowers are held in flat-topped clusters, red in bud, opening pink. Leeas are beautiful small shrubs or trees, often flowering in spring or summer when quite small, and always attractive because of their interesting foliage. Needs a sunny to semisunny position, average house temperatures, fresh, moist air, and a loam-based potting soil kept evenly moist. Propagate by sowing seeds or rooting cuttings in late winter or spring.

LEGUMINOSAE. *Pea Family.*

The legumes are characterized by butterflylike flowers, as in the sweet pea. Of the five hundred or so genera, several are of interest as houseplants. *Poinciana* and *Tamarindus* seedlings, for example, grow easily in a fluorescent-light garden and adapt to bonsai training (see Chapter 5). *Acacia* and *Calliandra* are of particular interest.

Acacia armata, *A. baileyana*, and *A. farnesiana* are

Calliandra haematocephala *var.* alba.

shrubs or trees, four to ten feet, much loved for their sprays of puffy yellow, fragrant flowers from February to April. They will grow only in a winter atmosphere that is sunny or semisunny, airy, moist, and cool—35° to 40°F at night. Pot in a loam-based soil and keep evenly moist, except on the dry side in autumn and early winter. Prune after flowering. Sow seeds or make cuttings in the spring.

Calliandra haematocephala, *C. surinamensis*, and *C. tweedii* are suggested for pot culture in an indoor/outdoor scheme. They become tub-size trees, six to ten feet, with locustlike leaves and red powderpuff flowers. They are principally winter-flowering, except *tweedii* tends to be everblooming. The foliage is attractive in all seasons. They need a sunny situation, moderate temperatures to 70°F in winter, fresh, moist air, and a loam-based potting soil kept evenly moist. Prune back after flowering. Make air-layers or cuttings in spring.

LILIACEAE. *Lily Family.*

Herbs, vines, and treelike plants, often bulbous, with leafy veins mostly running parallel. The regular flowers are six-parted and have a superior ovary (that is, it occurs inside the flower). Genera of special interest for houseplanting include *Aloe, Asparagus, Aspidistra, Bowiea, Chlorophytum, Convallaria, Eucomis, Gasteria, Glo-*

riosa, *Haworthia*, *Lachenalia*, *Lapageria*, *Ledebouria*, *Lilium*, *Liriope*, *Ophiopogon*, *Rohdea*, *Scilla*, and *Veltheimia*.

Aloe vera, a perennially popular houseplant, is actually a misnomer for *Aloe barbadensis*, also known as Barbados aloe, Curaçao aloe, medicinal aloe, and unguentine cactus. It is originally from the Mediterranean region. The genus *Aloe* contains more than two hundred distinct species, all native to the arid, warmer regions of the Old World, primarily Africa. They can be perennial herbs, shrubs, or trees, but as young plants, hardly any aloe could fail to do well in a pot. Some adapt perfectly as miniatures, for pots hardly bigger than a thumb, while others will grow quickly to the girth and height of a bushel basket.

As houseplants aloes need all the direct sun they can get, yet they adapt remarkably to reduced light levels. The smaller rosette-forming aloes do beautifully in a light garden, with the leaf tips about six inches directly beneath the tubes.

Aloes are generally pest-free. However, mealybugs and brown scale sometimes appear, especially down in the heart of the plant where new leaves are in the making. If discovered, apply alcohol with a cotton swab; be sure the alcohol reaches all crevices. Repeat as necessary until clear.

Aloes grown in very sunny windows, or placed outdoors in warm weather in a half day or more of sun, will bloom, often in fall or winter when the warm colors—yellow, orange, red—are most welcome. Aloes can be grown in almost any container, but they probably look and grow best in ordinary unglazed clay pots. Use a well-drained mix such as equal parts soil, sand, peat moss, and well-rotted compost or leaf mold. Water freely in warm, sunny weather, but do not leave the pots standing in water. When temperatures are cool, mostly 70°F or less, keep aloes on the dry side, watering lightly perhaps once a week. Apply fish emulsion at half strength every two weeks in spring and summer. Don't fertilize in fall and winter.

Aloes send up many offsets from the roots. These can be removed at repotting time, which can be whenever

the plant has offsets and you have need for more aloes, maybe to share with a friend. Aloes are fun to collect. Besides in friends' gardens, look for them wherever plants are sold. Young ones often can be found along with small cacti and other succulents sold for making dish gardens. Catalog specialists (see Resources) have many rare species as well as some recently developed hybrids.

Asparagus asparagoides 'Myrtifolius', a small climber from the Cape of Good Hope, is the baby smilax used by florists in wedding and other decorations. *Asparagus densiflorus* 'Myers' (foxtail asparagus) has erect stems densely set with dark green cladophylls (needles), resembling long plumes; *A. d.* 'Sprengeri' (asparagus fern) has flexuous stems, drooping and loosely branched, to three feet. It bears white flowers in spring and summer, followed by green berries that ripen to bright red in fall and winter. *Asparagus setaceus* is the lace fern, commonly known as *A. plumosus*, from South Africa. It is climbing and needs thin trellising—bamboo, wire, or string—for upward mobility. Give these plants a sunny to semisunny situation, average house temperatures but not much over 72°F in winter, fresh, moist air, and a loam-based potting soil kept evenly moist. Sow seeds or divide clumps in spring.

Asparagus densiflorus 'Myers'.

Aspidistra elatior, eighteen to twenty-four inches tall, from China, has been a staple foliage houseplant for several generations, better known as the cast-iron plant, named for its durability in the face of adverse conditions. In addition to the species, with its plain, shiny, blackish green leaves which often measure two feet in length, there is a variegated type, *A. e.* 'Variegata', with leaves alternating green and white stripes in varying widths. *Aspidistra elatior* 'Milky Way' has creamy yellow spots in the dark green leaves. These plants need semisunny to semishady conditions, average house temperatures not over 75°F in winter, fresh, moist air, and a humus-rich, loam-based potting soil kept evenly moist. Propagate by dividing roots at repotting time, late winter–spring.

Bowiea volubilis (climbing onion), from South Africa, is a novelty houseplant. It is a large, light green bulb which sends up almost leafless, branched stems which twine if support is furnished, or they can be permitted to grow over the sides of the pot. The flowers, in spring or summer, are small and greenish white. Give it a sunny to semishady situation, average house temperatures not over 75°F in winter, and good air circulation. Pot it in well-drained, loam-based soil and keep it evenly moist in spring and summer, quite dry in fall and early winter. Propagate by removing offsets in spring and summer.

Chlorophytum bichetii, from Thailand, is a miniature, tuft-forming, grassy plant with white-margined and striped leaves. Its cultivar 'Longwood Emerald' is plain green and makes a nice houseplant ground cover or planted individually in a very small bonsai pot, *mame* style (miniature bonsai). *Chlorophytum comosum mandaianum* (white-striped leaves), *C. c.* 'Picturatum' (yellow-striped leaves), and *C. c.* 'Vittatum' (white-striped leaves) are all South African plants with informal rosettes of daylilylike foliage, twelve to eighteen inches tall and as wide. All send up tall, slender racemes of small white flowers at almost any season which are followed by new plants borne in the air; they share the common names of airplane plant and spider plant. As soon as the weight of the new plants is great enough, the stem bends over and, if it comes in contact with moist soil, promptly roots and takes off; after a few weeks the stolon may be cut

from the parent. These plants need semisun to shade, average house temperatures, good air circulation, and a humus-rich, loam-based potting soil kept evenly moist. Propagate by removing aerial plantlets or by division at any time.

Convallaria majalis (lily-of-the-valley) from temperate Asia and Europe, is sometimes forced for its exquisite white or pink flowers and their fragrance (see page 46).

Eucomis autumnalis (*E. undulata* of commerce; pineapple lily) is a bulb that sends up strap-leaf rosettes twelve to eighteen inches tall of bright green leaves in summer from which arise the spikes of green flowers in late summer that are topped by tufted, leafy bracts. *Eucomis vandermerwei* is a dwarf bulb with ornate, short, maroon-spotted fleshy, nearly evergreen leaves having fluted margins. The "pineapple" yellowish green inflorescence is six inches tall. *Eucomis zambesciaca* has been recently made available through seeds distributed by the Royal Horticultural Society; it has green leaves and white flowers held on a two-foot stalk. Give them a sunny to semisunny situation, moderate temperatures in winter, fresh air, and a humus-rich, loam-based potting soil. Keep evenly moist in spring and summer; in fall and winter maintain the more evergreen types on the dry side and dry off—stop watering and fertilizing until the leaves die down—the deciduous species such as *E. autumnalis.*

Gasteria (ox-tongue plant) species have stiff, tongue-shaped leaves, often smooth but sometimes warted. They range from one- to two-inch miniatures up to one foot tall or more and are perfectly suited to pot culture for, tolerating some neglect, they will reward the thoughtful grower with numerous offsets and freely borne spikes of green-tipped pink or red tubular flowers in winter and spring. All of them come from South Africa. They need a semisunny to semishady position, average house temperatures, and good air circulation. Pot in loam-based soil and keep evenly moist in spring and summer, on the dry side during fall and winter. Remove offsets for propagation purposes in spring and summer.

Gloriosa rothschildiana, from Uganda, the climbing or glory lily, climbs four to six feet by means of tendrils which are long extensions of the leaf tips. The flowers, of true lily form, with sharply reflexed petals, arise from the leaf axils as the plant grows. Most species have blossoms crimson at the outer parts, golden toward the base, but some are entirely yellow. A few have crisped petals, a trait which adds to their beauty. Plant the cigar-shaped tubers four inches deep in humus-rich, loam-based potting soil in winter or spring. Provide strings or wires for the plants to climb on, as their heavy, branching stems require firm support. *Gloriosa rothschildiana* blooms in spring and summer, but by resting the tubers after flowering for two or three months, it may be brought into bloom at any time. Other species flower in late summer and fall. Give a sunny to semisunny position, average house temperatures, and fresh, moist air. Keep evenly moist during the growing season, nearly dry at other times. Propagate by tuber division at repotting time in spring, or by sowing seeds in winter or spring, for flowers in two to four years.

Haworthia contains nearly a hundred species of succulents native to South Africa, and their rosettes of thick leaves, from two to eight inches, exhibit a wide variety of forms. One of the best known is *H. fasciata*, called zebra haworthia for its dark green leaves crossbanded with rows of white "warts." *Haworthia attenuata* (wart plant) has these raised white dots set thickly all over its leaves. The windowed haworthias such as *H. truncata* from South Africa are completely different from those with firm leaves. Their rosettes are comprised of soft leaves which have translucent edges or tips, thus permitting light to penetrate to the main part of the plant even when it is mostly underground during the droughts of its native habitat. *Haworthia viscosa* represents a third type, which forms a stiff, triangular column nearly eight inches tall. All three types need a sunny to semisunny situation, average house temperatures, and good air circulation. Pot in loam-based soil and keep evenly moist spring and summer, on the dry side in fall and winter. Divide or remove offsets at repotting time in late winter or spring.

Lachenalia (Cape cowslip) is a South African genus of small, bulbous, spring-flowering plants, with spikes of bloom similar in form to those of hyacinths but brightly and variously colored. Give it a sunny position fall

Haworthia truncata.

through spring; keep in darkness during its summer dormancy. It likes cool temperatures, not over 70°F, in fall and winter. Fresh air circulation is important. Pot in loam-based soil and keep evenly moist fall through spring, dry in summer. Propagate by removing offsets at potting time in early fall.

Lapageria rosea (Chilean bellflower), an evergreen woody vine from Chile, has glossy, long-pointed leaves and rose-colored bellflowers to three inches long and two inches wide; the variety *albiflora* has white blossoms. This plant is not for the warmer parts of America. However, it can be among the most beautiful of vines if the container can be put outdoors in semisun to semishade in summer, and brought in to a cool (45° to 60°F), sunny, airy greenhouse in winter. Pot up in a humus-rich, loam-based soil and keep evenly moist. Propagate from seeds, cuttings, or layers in late winter or spring.

Ledebouria socialis (synonym *Scilla violacea*), to eight inches, from South Africa, has fleshy, slender, olive green leaves spotted with silver and lined with maroon beneath. It bears spikes of blue-tinted white flowers with reflexed petals on delicate stems in winter. Easy and adaptable, it's an excellent beginner plant. Give it sun to semishade, average house temperatures, and fresh air. Pot up in a loam-based soil and keep evenly moist, except slightly less so in summer and early fall. Propagate by removing offsets at repotting time in autumn.

Lilium longiflorum eximium, the Easter lily, is sometimes a transient houseplant. Be sure to give it plenty of water in a fairly bright place, but without too much direct sun. A cool location will prolong the blossoms. After flowering has finished, and the stalk begins to look yellow, reduce the amount of water given until the plant goes completely dry and the top can be removed with a slight, twisting pull. Set the pot in a cool, dark place until the weather permits setting the bulb (unpotted) in the outdoor perennial bed where there will be some shade from midday sun, covering it with six to eight inches of sandy, humusy soil. Here it may flower again, either the same season or another year. Once forced for pot-flowering, lily bulbs are of no further use as houseplants.

Liriope is a genus of grassy plants that make interesting pot specimens. There are some greatly miniaturized forms seen especially in Japanese container gardens and often collected by bonsai growers. Care as for *Ophiopogon*.

Ophiopogon is a genus of grassy plants that sometimes bear ornamental bright blue berries. The foliage is ev-

Ledebouria socialis.

ergreen, and may be plain or variegated. The flowers are usually white, nodding, and held on foot-long stems. Often called lily-turf. Most ophiopogons grow from short, thick, rhizomes, with underground fibrous roots which may act as stolons, or thicken into tubers. *Ophiopogon arabicum* is distinguished by having almost black leaves and berries, with lavender flowers. They like semisun to semishade, temperatures on the cool side in winter, not over 72°F, fresh, moist air, and a humus-rich, loam-based potting soil kept evenly moist. Propagate by division at almost any time.

Rohdea japonica (sacred lily of China), to about twelve inches, from Japan, has broad leaves arising from a clustering basal rosette and aroidlike white flowers in spring or summer that are followed by red berries. *Rohdea japonica marginata* (sacred Manchu lily) has black-green leaves that are white-bordered. Hundreds of different forms are recognized in Japan, often grown for exhibition in bonsai pots, a practice known as *koten engei*, or classic plant culture. Needs a semisunny to semishady position, average house temperatures (best not over 72°F in winter), and fresh, moist air. Pot up in a loam-based soil and keep evenly moist spring and summer, on the dry side in fall and winter. May be divided at repotting time in spring.

Scilla peruviana, to eight inches, from Algeria, is a bulbous plant that produces in spring–early summer a domed cluster of starry lilac-blue flowers with blue stamens and yellow pollen held above soft, bright green leaves in a basal rosette. It likes sun, average house temperatures, fresh air, and a loam-based potting soil kept evenly moist fall through spring, dry during the summer rest that follows flowering. During summer dormancy the potted bulb can be kept in any convenient place where it will not be inadvertently watered before time to start the new growth cycle.

Veltheimia viridifolia represents this genus of handsome bulbous plants from South Africa, having shiny green leaves one foot long and tubular, green-tipped pink flowers borne in late winter or spring in dense racemes atop tall stalks above the basal foliage rosette. Care as for *Lachenalia* (see page 148).

LOGANIACEAE. *Logania Family.*

This large family includes two popular ornamental shrubs, *Buddleia* and *Gelsemium*, both of which may figure in the indoor/outdoor scheme. The buddleia of interest here was formerly called *Nicodemia* and makes an excellent houseplant shrub.

Buddleia indica, formerly *Nicodemia diversifolia,* two to three feet, from Madagascar, has bluish green leaves shaped like those of the English oak, hence its common name indoor oak. It provides an interesting color contrast in a collection of green plants and is sometimes trained as a bonsai. Give it a semisunny to semishady position, average house temperatures, but not over 70°F in winter, fresh, moist air, and a loam-based potting soil kept evenly moist. Make cuttings in the spring.

LYTHRACEAE. *Loosestrife Family.*

Shrubs, trees, and herbaceous plants characterized by whorled or alternate leaves and showy flowers. Two genera are of interest here, *Cuphea* and *Lagerstroemia.*

Cuphea hyssopifolia (elfin-herb) has wiry branches densely set with small leaves and starlike, purplish-rose flowers. It is easily kept under twelve inches as a pot plant, and an excellent candidate for bonsai or a miniature tree-form standard, or for fluorescent-light culture. There are also dwarf selections, one of which, 'Linda Downer', has white flowers—it's exceptional for bonsai. Likes a sunny to semisunny situation, average house temperatures, fresh, moist air, and loam-based potting soil kept evenly moist. Make cuttings in the spring.

Lagerstroemia indica, crape myrtle, in a miniature habit marketed as a "crape-myrtlette," is sometimes offered in seed or plant form. It is a low shrub to two or three feet and some plants may also display a cascading habit. The flowers, which may be white, pink, rose, lavender, or purple, appear in great abundance in summer. The growing season is spring and summer; the plants must be kept cool and on the dry side in fall and winter. They are best considered for the indoor/outdoor container garden.

MALVACEAE. *Mallow Family.*

Herbs, shrubs, and trees from all over the world. The alternate leaves are usually lobed, or deeply cut, and the flowers of most genera are showy. Of particular interest for houseplanting are *Abutilon, Anisodontea,* and *Hibiscus.*

Abutilon (flowering maple) is a genus of shrubby South American flowering plants from four to six feet tall that have attractive maple-shaped leaves and bell- or lantern-shaped nearly everblooming flowers in many colors, all pendant. Its habit tends to be stiffly upright or sufficiently lax to be readily trainable as espalier or exceptionally graceful standards. The leaves may be plain green to variegated with white or creamy yellow to gold. Give it a sunny to semisunny position, average house temperatures (at least ten degrees cooler by night in order to keep the flower buds coming), fresh, moist air, and a humus-rich, loam-based potting soil kept evenly moist. Whiteflies will inevitably appear on indoor abutilon; weekly insecticidal soap sprays will keep things under control. Ideal for indoor/outdoor and more fully explored in Chapter 8. Propagate from seeds or cuttings at any season.

Anisodontea hypomandarum, from Africa, grows to about three feet tall, and becomes covered with quarter-size vivid pink flowers haloed cranberry at the center. Grow from seeds or cuttings in winter or spring. This is an indoor/outdoor plant and it trains well into a two- to three-foot tall tree-form standard.

Hibiscus rosa-sinensis is the ever popular Chinese hibiscus that may be grown as an all-year houseplant or indoors/outdoors. The flower- and bud-covered Chinese hibiscus offered in small pots have often been treated with a growth retardant; as long as it lasts the effect will be a dwarf plant having an unusual number of large flowers. In succeeding seasons and with fresh potting soil the chemically dwarfed plant will revert to its normal size and spacing between leaves and flowers. Instead of growing only two feet tall, it may reach four to six feet. Give hibiscus a sunny to semisunny situation, average house temperatures, fresh, moist air, and a humus-rich, loam-based potting soil kept evenly moist. Make four-inch cut-

Hibiscus rosa-sinensis *'The Path'*.

Calathea ornata *'Roseo-lineata'*.

tings of half-ripened (see page 54) wood in spring or summer; to reduce wilting in the cuttings, cut off half or more of each of the largest leaves before planting.

MARANTACEAE. *Arrowroot Family.*

Herbs from tropical America with handsome foliage, many with tuberous roots. Showy bract flowers are also a possibility. Basal leaves narrow toward the stem to sheathe it, and the flowers, showy or not, are sheathed by bracts. The genera *Calathea* and *Maranta* are of interest for houseplanting.

Calathea, six inches to four feet tall, comprises a large group of highly decorative foliage plants from tropical America that are also surprisingly durable under the fairly constant stresses of low light and low humidity. The many calatheas we see in the marketplace today are propagated by tissue culturing the most beautiful specimens of the strongest plants the growers can find of a given species. The result is a tough houseplant looking like something that should never be let out of a greenhouse. Four different calatheas have been with me through thick and thin for twenty years. They grow best in warmth (65° to 80°F), with bright diffused light, fresh, moist air, and a humus-rich, loam-based potting soil that is kept evenly moist.

The most extraordinary calatheas I have seen were in the city parks conservatory in Cincinnati, Ohio, and in a display at the Montreal Botanical Garden. In each case I asked the grower if there was a secret and both times I was told "water on the leaves." When I am able to sprinkle or mist the leaves of my calatheas once or twice daily, the plants soon take on an extra glow.

Calatheas have rhizomatous roots, and the leaves arise from the crown in tufts. They sucker readily, and in time will fill a pot with foliage. The leaves of calatheas are long, broad, and pointed at the tip. The veins run diagonally from the main rib to the outer edge of the leaf, and most coloration follows this general direction. In some varieties, the leaf reverses are wine red.

A calathea that has perhaps been a bit neglected, or has overgrown its pot, and has a lot of dried up leaves or leaves died back from the tips among the healthy ones can be rejuvenated. Remove the plant from pot and cut back all growth to an inch or two from the soil. Transfer to a size or two larger pot and fill in with a humus-rich, loam-based potting soil. Place where temperatures are constantly warm (70° to 80°F) in bright diffused light. A strong, clean new plant will arise in two to three months. Propagate by division of the roots at repotting time, late winter–spring.

Maranta leuconeura kerchoveana (rabbit-track plant), eight to twelve inches, from Brazil, has broad, bright green leaves with rows of brownish to dark green blotches on either side of the midrib. At night the leaves fold upward like hands in prayer, hence its other common name, prayer plant. *Maranta leuconeura* var. *leuconeura* (formerly *massangeana*) is strikingly colored, with parallel stripes of silver and pink from the midrib to the leaf margins, the leaf surface feathered in silver along the main rib, shading into bright brown to blue-green at the edges. It likes a semisunny to semishady position with bright diffused light, average house temperatures, and fresh, moist air (but avoid all drafts). Pot in humus-rich, loam-based soil and keep it evenly moist. Divisions may be made at repotting time, late winter–spring.

MELASTOMACEAE. *Meadow-beauty Family.*

Tropical herbs, shrubs, and trees, frequently from the Amazon region, with showy opposite or whorled leaves. The decorative flowers sometimes have colorful bracts. Of interest here are *Bertolonia*, *Centradenia*, *Medinilla*, *Schizocentron*, *Sonerila*, and *Tibouchina*.

Bertolonia maculata, six to eight inches, from Brazil, has brown oval leaves margined in red, with red reverses that are sprinkled with silver along the midvein, and completely covered with long hairs. *Bertolonia pubescens*, five to seven inches, from Ecuador, another gem, has puckered oval leaves of green banded through the center with purple-brown, and shorter hairs. Other bertolonias may display clear carmine, bright white, or brilliant purple in the leaves, and distinctively colored veins and reverses. Small blossoms often are produced in summer atop erect stems just above the leaves. These are not easy plants. Give them bright diffused light to semishade and constantly warm and moist air; all drafts are anathema to bertolonia. Pot it in humus-rich, loam-based soil and keep evenly moist. If leaf tips turn brown, increase humidity; check to be sure the plant is constantly moist and not receiving too much direct sun. Propagate from cuttings in warmth and high humidity at any season.

Centradenia 'Starsprite' is a cultivar offered by Kartuz (see Resources) of a southern Mexico–Central American plant having slender, arching stems six to twelve inches tall, with one-inch-long willowy dark green leaves and starry half-inch pale lavender flowers all year. It does best

Maranta leuconeura *var.* leuconeura.

in a small container; may be treated as a bonsai. Excellent for a fluorescent-light garden. Care as for wax begonia, *Begonia semperflorens* (see page 100).

Schizocentron elegans (Spanish shawl), from Mexico, is a somewhat succulent, creeping plant which will root at each node if the reddish stems are in contact with damp soil. Its small, dark green, slightly hairy leaves, and large, summer-flowering magenta blossoms are especially effective cascading from a basket or shelf. Likes a sunny to semisunny situation, cool temperatures (40° to 60°F) in winter, and fresh, moist air. Pot it in humus-rich, loam-based soil and keep evenly moist, more so in spring and summer. Propagate by cuttings in warmth and high humdity at any time.

Medinilla magnifica is discussed on page 227. *Medinilla sedifolia*, six to twelve inches, is a rare species suited to terrarium culture or as a small hanging plant; a rainforest plant, it needs constant warmth and high humidity. Slow but spectacular, it bears one-inch waxy bright magenta-pink flowers in winter and spring. Its leaves are dark green, closely set, waxy. Care as for *Bertolonia* (see page 152).

Sonerila margaritacea 'Argentea' is a very showy small foliage plant native from Java to Burma. Purplish red and silver leaves foil rose-lavender flowers in summer. Care as for *Bertolonia* (see page 152); this is a fine terrarium plant, especially for a warm maxi light garden.

Tibouchina semidecandra, from southern Brazil, is a medium-size shrub with bronze green, hairy leaves that are intricately veined or quilted, and large royal purple flowers in summer and fall that have beguiling rosy pink reproductive parts. This is a quintessential indoor/outdoor plant; see page 228. It may be deployed outdoors as a low to tall shrub, or as a medium to tall tree-form standard, four to six feet.

MORACEAE. *Fig Family*.

Vines, shrubs, and trees of temperate as well as tropical origins, grown for their edible fruit or handsome foliage; rubber is derived from some. *Dorstenia* and *Ficus* are of interest as houseplants.

Dorstenia includes some 170 species of monoecious herbs and shrubs, one to two feet, from tropical Africa and America, with a few from Asia. Some are caudex (trunk) forming even as very young plants in thumb pots or mame bonsai pots. Others are leafy. The inflorescence

Sonerila margaritacea.

Dorstenia nova mecca.

is periscopelike, a sort of inside-out fig, and useful in teaching botany. The calcareous seeds, when ripe, are catapulted away from their receptacle at the slightest disturbance. *Dorstenia contrajerva*, with pinnately lobed, silver-marked leaves to eight inches long rising from a basal rosette, is from the Caribbean tropics and has naturalized in many gardens in the American South. It does make an interesting foliage plant and, when the curious flowers appear, children of all ages will want to come have a close look. Specialist growers who carry cacti and other succulents, Lauray of Salisbury, for example (see Resources), sometimes have the caudex-forming dorstenias such as *D. nova mecca* from Africa. The leafy species do well in semishade to shade while the caudex-forming species need sun to semisun, in average house temperatures, with good air circulation. Pot them in a loam-based soil. The leafy sorts need to be kept evenly moist. Those having caudexes need to dry out a little between waterings. Propagate by sowing the seeds or transplanting the volunteers that come up from self-sown seeds, at any time.

Ficus carica, common fig, from the Mediterranean region, makes a handsome foliage plant to eight feet in a large tub (fourteen-inch diameter or more) that also bears edible fruit; see Chapter 8. *Ficus diversifolia* (also *F. deltoidea*), from India, Java, and Malaya, is a twiggy, small plant, to six feet, with dark green leaves to two inches long, shaped like a fig fruit, and one-half-inch inedible yellow figs. *Ficus elastica*, to eight feet high and much more, from India and Malaya, and its varieties are the durable rubber plants, grown for bold-textured, sometimes variegated foliage. *Ficus lyrata (F. pandurata)*, to eight feet high and much more, from tropical west Africa, has large, shiny, leathery, wavy-edged leaves whose shape suggests its common name, fiddle-leaf fig. *F. triangularis* var. *variegatus* is rare and coveted for growing as a small indoor tree, to six feet or so.

Weeping fig, *Ficus benjamina*, to eight feet high and much more, is one of the best, and consequently most popular, of all indoor trees. The leaves, about two inches long, are shiny, bright to dark green, held on gracefully drooping branches. Sometimes three or more are planted

together and braided from a young age, so that eventually they fuse to become one large tree. Indian laurel, *F. retusa nitida*, is similar, except erect in habit and the leaves are more substantial, waxier, thicker. Both trees can be pruned and trained variously into casual or formal shapes.

The creeping figs, *Ficus pumila* (often called *F. repens*), from Australia, China, and Japan, and *F. radicans*, from the East Indies, are remarkably different from the upright kinds. They have small leaves, no more than two inches long, that may be plain green or variegated. They willl climb to indefinite lengths on any damp, rough surface. Another of these is *F. sagitata* 'Variegata', with gray-green and white lance-shaped leaves. It will make an exquisite wreath six inches in diameter in a maxi light garden.

Ficus triangularis *var.* variegatus.

Ficus sagitata 'Variegata'.

The ficus I have introduced represent only a sampling of the possibilities. As soon as you consider yourself beyond Houseplants 101, seek out the lesser-known ficus; ironically, some of the rarer kinds can make better houseplants than the ubiquitous ones we all know.

Ficus in general need all the sun that can be mustered indoors. Ficus trees often go to pieces when they are moved suddenly from a high light growing area into a low light house garden. Ficus trees in this kind of stressful situation are often also under- or overwatered and sometimes in desperation the neophyte may overdose the traumatized plant with fertilizer. Ficus will generally adapt if given time and no drastic measures. More details on ficus problems are covered in Chapter 9 (see page 231). The care is basically sunny to semisunny conditions, average house temperatures, fresh air (moist for the creep-ing types), and a humus-rich, loam-based potting soil kept evenly moist. Propagate by air-layering, from cuttings, or, rarely, from seeds in spring; propagation requires warmth and high humidity.

MUSACEAE. *Banana Family*.

The largest of all herbs, some tree-size, of tropical origin, cultivated for their edible fruit, showy flowers, or distinctive foliage. Considered here are *Heliconia*, *Musa*, *Orchidantha*, and *Strelitzia*.

Heliconia rostrata, to six feet, from Brazil, has bananalike leaves and exceedingly showy red bracts with yellow ends, which surround the flowers. Other species of interest include *H. aurantiaca*, *H. brasiliensis*, and *H. velutina*. Give a sunny to semisunny location, average house temperatures, fresh, moist air, and a humus-rich, loam-based potting soil kept evenly moist. Propagate by dividing roots in late winter–spring.

Musa coccinea, the red banana, to five feet, from Vietnam, has golden flowers and yellow-tipped scarlet bracts followed by ornamental orange fruit. *Musa nana* (or *M. cavendishii*), four to six feet, the dwarf ladyfinger banana from southern China, bears edible fruit over three inches long. *Musa rosacea*, eight to ten feet, from India, is grown for its bright green leaves, which have an iridescent purple-red midrib, and yellow flowers; its three-inch-long fruit is not edible. *Musa velutina*, three to six feet, from Assam, is probably the most dwarf species discussed here. It bears erect clusters of pale yellow or pinkish flowers in red bracts, and soft pink fruit. Give these plants a sunny to semisunny situation, average house temperatures, fresh, moist air, and a humus-rich, loam-based potting soil kept evenly moist. Biweekly fertilizing is important during spring and summer, along with lots of water in warm weather. Plant in large pots, at least twelve inches across. Propagate in late winter–early spring by removing suckers which form at the base of the parent; also by sowing seeds in warmth, moisture, and high humidity in winter and spring.

Orchidantha, sometimes listed as *Lowea*, is a relatively low-growing plant, two to three feet tall, resembling in leaf and habit the aspidistra. Orchidlike flowers, pale yellow and purple in *O. borneensis*, while in *O. maxillarioides*, from Malaya, a slightly taller plant, the blossoms are green-lipped, with purple variegation and a purple calyx. These are seldom offered plants that are not difficult to grow. Care as for *Musa*.

Strelitzia reginae, the bird-of-paradise flower, from South Africa, has become a favorite indoor/outdoor plant, familiar to almost everyone, at least through the commercially available cut flowers. Who is not entranced by the orange-petaled, blue-tongued blossoms that appear from a red-edged, green, boat-shaped bract? There is a dwarf form, to about eighteen inches tall, that is usually preferred for potting. *Strelitzia nicolai* (tree strelitzia), twelve feet tall or more, with blue-and-white flowers, is much larger in all its parts. Give strelitzia sunny to semi-sunny locations, average house temperatures (but not over 75°F in winter), and fresh, moist air. Pot in loam-based soil and keep evenly moist in spring and summer, a little on the dry side in fall and winter. Plant in a large pot or tub (ten- to fifteen-inch diameter) and do not disturb until the container is nearly bursting; this should bring on flowering, normally winter and spring, even from seedlings in four or five years. Propagate by removing offsets in the spring, or by sowing seeds in warmth and moisture at any time.

MYRSINACEAE. *Myrsine Family.*

Tropical trees and shrubs with opposite, evergreen, leathery leaves and not particularly showy flowers which are often followed by colorful, long-lasting berries. One genus is on the houseplant agenda, *Ardisia*.

Ardisia crispa (or *A. crenulata*), from China and Malaya, is often used for Christmas decoration because of its red, hollylike berries and unusually attractive evergreen foliage. The plant, called coralberry, makes a graceful small tree to three or four feet tall and must attain considerable maturity before it will produce the fragrant white or pinkish blossoms in spring which precede the berries. *Ardisia japonica* (marlberry) in its variety 'Hakubotan' has leathery leaves liberally splashed pink

Ardisia japonica.

and cream and white or pinkish flowers followed by long-lasting, bright, shiny red berries. They prefer a semisunny to semishady position, average house temperatures that are on the cool side in winter, fresh, moist air, and a loam-based potting soil kept evenly moist. These plants benefit especially from daily misting or showering in sunny winter weather. Propagate by air-layers, cuttings, or seeds in late winter–early summer.

MYRTACEAE. *Myrtle Family.*

Tropical shrubs and trees with aromatic foliage. Some bear showy flowers, others are cultivated for their foliage or edible fruit. Two genera are considered here: *Callistemon and Myrtus.*

Callistemon citrinus (synonym *C. lanceolatus*; crimson bottlebrush), to twenty-five feet, from New South

Myrtus communis microphylla *topiary at Logee's.*

Wales, is an open shrub with sparsely set leaves. The numerous small blossoms in summer and fall feature showy crimson stamens with golden anthers; they are arranged so as to suggest the plant's common name. Give a sunny situation, average house temperatures, and good air circulation. Pot in a loam-based soil and keep evenly moist in spring and summer, slightly less so in fall and winter. Propagate from air-layers, stem cuttings, or seeds in late winter–spring.

Myrtus communis, the Greek myrtle, resembles boxwood. It is cultivated for its fragrant foliage and is usually trained as topiary or clipped to a geometric shape. *Myrtus communis microphylla* has smaller leaves on a more compact plant and is available also in a form having variegated leaves. These make excellent houseplants, are ideal in an indoor-outdoor scheme, and the small-leaved sorts may be grown in a maxi light garden until they are too large. They prefer a sunny to semisunny location, average house temperatures that are on the cool side in fall and winter, fresh air, and a loam-based potting soil kept evenly moist. Be ever watchful for mealybugs and brown scale; if detected, treat at once by individually rubbing out the insects with cotton swabs dipped in denatured alcohol or by spraying or dipping with neem solution. I have found that myrtles react badly to soap sprays. Propagate by rooting cuttings of firm or partially ripened wood at any time (see pages 53–56).

NYCTAGINACEAE. *Four-o'clock Family.*

Herbs, trees, and shrubs, mostly from tropical America, with simple, smooth-edged leaves and showy flowers. *Bougainvillea* is the genus of interest as a houseplant, best managed indoor/outdoor; see pages 218–220.

OLEACEAE. *Olive Family.*

Evergreen and deciduous shrubs and trees from many parts of the world cultivated for ornament (lilac, for example) as well as food (the olive). Two genera, *Jasminum* and *Osmanthus* are of special interest here.

Jasminum is the genus for true jasmines. Those that are everblooming in warm weather, indoors or out, include:

Jasminum nitidum, royal jasmine, has glossy leaves and a constant show of starry white flowers the size of a half-dollar. I find the plant half shrubby, half vine and sometimes a bit of a challenge to decide how best to train. One success has been to set four bamboo stakes four feet long tepee-style in a twelve-inch pot, and to train the jasmine upward by gentle bending, tying, and occasional pruning back to size, which promotes new growth and more flowers.

Jasminum officinale 'Grandiflora', the French perfume or poet's jasmine, produces double white flowers on twining stems from spring to fall. It can be trained as a bush, a hanging plant, or upward on trellising.

Jasminum sambac 'Maid of Orleans' is the Arabian tea jasmine, used in the Far East for scented tea and in

Jasminum sambac 'Maid of Orleans'.

religious observances. It is perhaps the best of the lot for houseplant growers and can be had in bloom almost any day of the year.

Jasminum tortuosum is a vigorous climbing jasmine from South Africa that has pinnately compound leaves and clusters of snowy tubular flowers on the tips of new growth. It can be trained up on a bamboo stake tepee or on an eighteen-inch wire or dried vine wreath.

All the above-mentioned jasmines need up to a half day of direct sun, temperatures of 60° to 80°F, and lots of water. Apply fish emulsion or liquid seaweed every two weeks in spring and summer. If spider mites should appear, you are probably growing too dry; spray three times at weekly intervals with insecticidal soap and begin at once to water more generously. Grow in humus-rich, loam-based potting soil and keep evenly moist. Fresh, moist air circulation is a boon to jasmine. Propagate any time from cuttings of half-ripened wood. Prune to shape and size following a season of flowering.

Jasminum polyanthum is the species that has been widely commercialized in recent years as a hanging-basket plant for scented winter window gardens. It has sprays of small starry white blossoms that are blushed pink on the reverses, and blooms late winter–early spring, following a period of coolness in fall and early winter, 40° to 55° F. This jasmine is superb for a cool sun porch, home greenhouse, or frost-free winter garden of any sort. It needs to summer outdoors in part sun. *Polyanthum* will not flower well if the indoor garden is constantly warm in fall and early winter; in this case, *J. tortuosum* is a better choice.

Osmanthus fragrans, the sweet olive, has few peers among fragrant houseplants. The leaves are durable and leathery on twiggy to upright woody branches, reaching, after many years, to six feet, and occasionally seen as small trees, to twenty feet. Clusters of small, creamy blossoms appear from the leaf axils almost constantly from fall until spring, filling the sunny, airy, cool (40° to 65° F), moist atmosphere (which is to this plant's liking) with an intoxicating perfume, something on the order of a ripe apricot just picked from the tree on a warm, sunny day. During this long flowering season, maintain evenly moist soil to slightly dry at the surface. Sweet olive does well in a loam-based soil, with the addition of an extra portion of well-rotted leaf mold or compost. Established plants needn't be repotted every year but they will benefit in the intervening years if top-dressed in the spring with two or three inches of well-rotted compost or leaf mold.

Osmanthus fragrans.

Any pruning of sweet olive can be done in the spring, as flowering finishes. Healthy pieces of stem removed in the pruning process can be turned into cuttings; set them to root in a fifty-fifty mix of moistened peat moss and sand. Place in bright light but where hot sun will not shine directly on them. They are not easy to root unless you have an automatic misting system but if several are set, surely one or more will take root. If possible, move the plant outdoors in frost-free weather, where it can experience the more Mediterranean conditions of its forebears. There is also something of a "secret" for success with this plant, which is to give it ample phosphorus and potash, such as from a 10-20-20 fertilizer, in order to prevent leaf-tip dieback.

ONAGRACEAE. *Evening-primrose Family.*

Herbs from temperate as well as tropical parts of the world. Leaves may be alternate or opposite; the flowers are showy. *Fuchsia* is the genus of interest here.

Fuchsia triphylla 'Gartenmeister Bohnstedt', the honeysuckle fuchsia (for the shape and habit of the flowers; they are not scented) of West Indian heritage, is better suited as a houseplant than the hybrid sorts seen as summer container plants outdoors in climates where the weather isn't too hot (see page 224). 'Gartenmeister Bohnstedt', of upright bushy habit, two to four feet, can be an everblooming plant in a sunny window or maxi light garden, in average house temperatures, with fresh, moist air. Give it humus-rich, loam-based potting soil kept evenly moist. Whiteflies will appear in due course; spray weekly with insecticidal soap. Propagate from stem cuttings of half-ripened wood (see page 54), in late winter–spring.

ORCHIDACEAE. *Orchid Family.*

Epiphytic as well as terrestrial herbs from tropical and temperate parts of the world; more than thirty thousand species are known. The relatively recent innovation of meristemming or tissue culturing has revolutionized the orchid world, making possible almost overnight a dazzling array of orchids, untold numbers of which can be cultivated as houseplants or in the indoor/outdoor cycle described generally in Chapter 8.

Basic Culture

One of the major trends in gardening in recent years is the availability of potted orchid plants in bloom. A large percentage of the recipients of these plants are puzzled about what to do next. After flowering the plant usually needs time in conditions which encourage new growth—to replenish roots, pseudobulbs—bulblike moisture storers—if there are any, and the foliage. Several common mistakes are made with orchids. Basically they need fresh air; don't seal them in a glass or plastic case, terrarium-style. Orchids also need to be on a drench-and-dry cycle, not lingering at either extreme of wet or dry for more than a few hours, at least not during the season of rebuilding and serious regrowth.

Orchids also need repotting in a fresh medium such as fir-bark chips or osmunda fiber when—or ideally just

Fuchsia triphylla 'Gartenmeister Bohnstedt'.

before—the existing medium starts to decompose. This usually occurs within two years. When repotting, trim off all dead growth. In my collection I have started filling the bottom third of each pot with the plastic foam peanuts that are used as filler for packages. These constitute a waste problem, yet when placed in the bottom of an orchid pot they afford air circulation and help avoid a soggy state that could lead to rotted roots and declining orchid health. They also reduce the amount of expensive potting medium that must be purchased.

One more observation about orchids in general. They have a way of multiplying and increasing until, before you know it, you have a collection. And if you don't curtail the urge to coddle every offset and acquire every new eye-catcher, soon there will not be enough growing room.

The most important factor in growing orchids is the right amount of light.

High light means maximum brightness without scorching or bleaching the leaves—at or near a window that receives full sun for most of the day.

Medium light, such as a window facing southeast, south, or southwest, suits a wide variety of orchids—often even those from the high-light group.

Low light does not mean a dark corner—try an east or west window where African violets, begonias, and ferns thrive.

If you want to grow orchids with a variety of lighting needs, use four 40-watt fluorescent tubes (two warm white, two cool white) turned on for sixteen hours daily. Place orchids like cattleyas, laelias, and oncidiums in the center, where the light is strongest; low-light paphiopedilums and ludisias (jewel orchid) near either end; and medium-light phalaenopsis in between.

No matter whether an orchid's basic light needs are high, medium, or low, your plant's appearance and behavior are the best guides. Too much light yellows the leaves and may even cause unsightly burn spots. Too little light results in unnaturally dark green leaves, stunted growth, and no blooms.

In the cool North an orchid can take more direct sun than in the Sun Belt. Plants in a house garden need more

Cattleya *orchid and* Schlumbergera.

direct sun than those in a greenhouse, where they benefit from multidirectional lighting. All orchids can benefit from spending the summer outdoors, usually with protection at midday from direct sun even for those that are in the high-light category.

Temperature. The temperature needs of orchids are divided into cool, intermediate, and warm. But there is considerable overlapping, so you do not necessarily have to stick to just one category; you can, for example, grow cattleyas with phalaenopsis. And all can take slightly warmer temperatures in summer. Of primary importance is a drop of ten to fifteen degrees at night.

Cool. Around 50°F at night rising to a day range of 60° to 70°F; suitable for cymbidiums, odontoglossums, and certain paphiopedilums, in particular the plain green-leaved types.

Intermediate. Night temperatures of 55° to 60°F up to a range of 65° to 75°F by day. Countless orchids fall into

Vanda × rothschildiana.

this category, including cattleyas, some oncidiums, miltonias, and species such as *Coelogyne ochracea, Brassavola cucullata*, and *B. nodosa*.

Warm. 65° to 70°F at night, up to 80° to 85°F by day. Suitable for phalaenopsis, vandas, and the mottle leaf paphiopedilums.

Water/humidity. Err on the side of dryness if you must, for it takes ages to kill an orchid by drought, much less time by drowning. However, watering on a drench-and-dry cycle, with a brief lingering at either extreme, is usually the best policy. One way to give orchids the fifty percent or more humidity they need is to grow them in pots on a pebble tray filled with water and topped with wire hardware cloth. A humidifier also helps, especially in heated homes in winter. Most need a damp medium. Test it by touching with your fingers; if they tell you "dry," apply water.

Orchids need a fair amount of moisture in the air, ideally fifty percent or more. Because they also need air that can circulate freely, growers often place wire hardware cloth or plastic louver grids over a basin of water and set the orchid pots on top of this. More discussion of humidity and humidifiers is on pages 11–14.

If you have a tendency to crowd your plants, use a small fan to provide good air circulation. Avoid dank or stale air.

Potting mix. Favored growing mediums for the epiphytic orchids include osmunda fiber, shredded fir-bark, and tree fern. More terrestrial types, such as paphiopedilum and cymbidium, are grown in mixtures that may include those ingredients as well as coarse peat, redwood bark or fiber, perlite, and decayed oak leaves. As a beginning orchid grower your best bet is to purchase a medium or mix recommended specifically for the plant you wish to repot.

The cattleya and allied genera such as laelia and brassavola grow by means of a rhizome that creeps along the surface of the potting medium and may go over the edge of the pot and from there into eventual decline if not removed and given fresh medium. I grow these orchids in medium-size fir-bark chips, which can be obtained from local garden centers or ordered from the catalogs of orchid specialists. At Brooklyn Botanic Garden I was taught to add a handful of horticultural charcoal chips to about a quart of the fir-bark and mix this together before potting.

When ready, remove your orchid from its present container. Shake away all of the old growing medium, which may have begun to decompose in the bottom of the pot. Working in good light, examine the roots. Keep the living ones and cut off all the others. If some of the oldest growth, or backbulbs, turns out to have no roots re-

Paphiopedilum × maudiae.

maining, discard them as well. Each division needs at least one or two healthy backbulbs, the bulb which bloomed this year and the eye that promises flowers next time around. (This is the way most home growers propagate orchids, by dividing at repotting time and setting each division in its own pot. Orchids are also grown from seeds, an exacting process that must be done under sterile conditions. I once knew a retired night watchman in Florida who grew the most beautiful phalaenopsis orchids in the world from seeds under lights in the recreation room of his home, then the seedlings were transplanted to community pots in a small greenhouse just outside his back door.) Tissue culturing or meristemming is the cutting-edge way to propagate orchids, but the how-to is beyond the scope of this book. Details can be gotten from the American Orchid Society (see Resources for address).

In the bottom of the clean pot you have chosen, add a layer of broken clay potshards or plastic foam peanuts equal in depth to about one fourth to one third the height of the pot. Add fresh fir-bark and charcoal chip mix as you hold the orchid upright, with the oldest part against the wall of the pot and the new growth as far from the edge of the pot as possible. Position at about the same depth as before, never more than a half inch deeper. Stake the orchid in place so that it will remain in the same position until new roots take hold. Water well after the initial potting, then very lightly until the new roots are obviously making strong growth.

Generally, the epiphytes need to dry between waterings, while the terrestrials are kept moist but not wet. In the wild, epiphytic orchids grow in the crotches of trees or wherever they find a humusy lodging place. During a rain and immediately after they have an abundant water supply. However, as the sun comes out and the wind blows, the orchids' roots dry and remain so until the next rain. Although the roots may be dry, the atmosphere around them is not. This is an important point to remember in growing epiphytes, including bromeliads, many aroids, and gesneriads, as well as orchids.

Epiphytic orchids and bromeliads that are mounted on slabs of bark or tree fern will need to be given a new mounting after one to two years. The process is not that different from conventional repotting. All the dead parts are cut away. Remount on a fresh slab or bark or tree fern and tie in place with nylon cord. I have not been very successful in my apartment with epiphytes planted this way, because the air cannot be kept sufficiently humid. I do know home growers who succeed. They give the plants a sink shower or pail dunking every sunny day. Cloudy days they mist the plants in the morning, sometimes again in the evening. All of this takes more devotion than I was able to muster.

Fertilizer. During active growth, fertilize orchids with either a chemical or organic fertilizer diluted at the strength indicated on the label. Many growers alternate a chemical and an organic such as fish emulsion or liquid seaweed. Where orchids are concerned, no amount of fertilizing can take the place of fresh growing medium.

Good beginner orchids in *high light* are cattleya and the allied laelia, brassavola, sophronitis; in *medium light*, phalaenopsis; and in *low light* the mottle-leaf species paphiopedilums and jewel orchids such as ludisia (sometimes called haemaria). When you have had some success reblooming mature orchid plants, invest in some two- or three-year-old seedlings.

The *Miltonia*, or pansy orchid, is a recent love of mine that is worth trying if the moderate to high humidity it needs at all times can be provided. Any of the modern pansy orchid hybrids can be exciting to grow as well as the species of *Miltonia* that came originally from the lowlands of Brazil. Species from mountainous regions

Phalaenopsis *hybrid.*

need cooler temperatures than most of us can provide without special summer air conditioning. The miltonias have pronounced pseudobulbs, each usually with two grassy leaves. Despite the moisture-storing pseudobulbs, these have a softer appearance than cattleya, vanda, and many dendrobium orchids.

Miltonias do not have a pronounced dry and cold season as some orchids do, and to me this is one reason why they make promising houseplants. But fresh, moist air that circulates freely is a necessity, otherwise they are likely to vegetate indefinitely without ever coming into flower. And the flowers of a hybrid miltonia are something to behold. At first glance they bear an uncanny resemblance to a modern hybrid pansy. Closer inspection reveals a distinct and unique flower that is unmistakably that of an orchid.

Miltonias are increasingly available from orchid dealers, both locally and by mail. I've noticed among my friends who've been specializing in indoor gardening for many years that miltonia orchids seem to fit in with collections of gesneriads, begonias, bromeliads, ferns, and aroids.

In fact, if you are successfully growing phalaenopsis orchids, it is likely you will get on well, perhaps even better, with hybrid miltonias. I grow several of these in medium-size firbark. They are provided with timed-release fertilizer pellets (14-14-14) and from time to time receive a liquid fertilizer prepared with 30-10-10 or 15-30-15. There have never been any bug problems, but slugs have no trouble locating the buds on these orchids and no doubt consider them a delicacy.

I have recently learned a useful tip about keeping slugs away from emerging orchid flowers: Wrap a piece of cotton around the stem, below the bud or unfurling flower. The cotton is too scratchy to suit slugs and sends them to find supper at another table. If you find the cotton distracting, a nice piece of green woods moss can be used instead—just be sure that it is not already harboring a slug! As soon as the moss dries out, it becomes too scratchy to suit the slugs.

Orchid names, incidentally, are more complicated than those for other plants, and are being made ever-increasingly so by the tremendous amount of breeding that is going on. My most recent lesson had to do with a small orchid I acquired in bloom with only these words written on the label: *Onc. Carioca* 'Kosaki'. "Onc." is an abbreviation for the genus *Oncidium* and the rest of the name suggests the parentage, which orchid specialist Charles Marden Fitch looked up for me and says is Royal Claret × Whithorn. This still leaves me mostly in the dark, except Charles says the plant in question is one of the equitant hybrid oncidiums, which are excellent for indoor gardens. ("Equitant" describes leaves overlapping one another in two ranks, forming a fan, as in many iris.) This small orchid needs a sunny bright window, nighttime temperatures around 60° to 65°F, and the usual free air circulation. Equitant oncidiums are very small, and that is partly why they have become popular as houseplants where sunny window space is often limited. During warm, frost-free weather, these are plants that will thrive if placed in a shade tree where they can receive dappled sun and be hosed down once or twice daily unless it rains.

OXALIDACEAE. *Wood-sorrel Family*.

Bulbous or tuberous herbs, usually with palmately divided leaves, and small, showy, funnel-shaped flowers. Two genera are of interest here, *Biophytum* and *Oxalis*.

Biophytum sensitivum (life plant, miniature sensitive plant), ten to twelve inches tall, from tropical Africa and Asia, has very small trunks supporting palmlike configurations of pinnate leaves which fold when touched and at night. It bears tiny powderpuff blossoms intermittently, pink or yellow with yellow pollen. Give it a semisunny to semishady position, average house temperatures, fresh, moist air, and a humus-rich, loam-based potting soil kept evenly moist. Does well in a terrarium. Usually grown from seeds at almost any season and treated as an annual.

Oxalis is a highly variable genus that runs the gamut from weedy to wonderful. I pull up more oxalis than I grow, but there are certain species that are first-rate houseplants. *Oxalis regnellii*, for example, from South America, is nearly everblooming, with white flowers set among or slightly above square-cut leaflets of dark bronze green, flushed maroon beneath. Moreover, it will adapt and continue to bloom in suprisingly low light.

Oxalis alstonii (formerly *O. hedysaroides* 'Rubra'), from South America, has wiry stems to several inches tall set with small, delicate, wine red leaves, earning it the sobriquet "fire-fern." Under good culture it will bear a profusion of small yellow flowers at almost any season and for an extended period. *Oxalis bowieana*, to twelve inches, from South Africa, bears large rosy red flowers in summer and fall; *O. carnosa*, to four inches, from Chile and Peru, has yellow flowers in spring; and *O. cernua* (Bermuda buttercup), to twelve inches, from South Africa, has fragrant yellow flowers in spring. Its double-flowered form, *flore pleno*, is also known as 'Capri'. *Oxalis deppei*, to ten inches, from southern Mexico, has yellow-throated, rosy red flowers above attractive foliage, while *O. hirta*, from South Africa, grows semi-upright to eighteen inches and bears yellow-tubed, rose-colored flowers in winter. *Oxalis melanosticta*, from South Africa, forms a very compact rosette of leaves, four to six inches, covered by glistening, silvery hair; it bears yellow flowers in autumn. *Oxalis ortgiesii*, from the Andes of Peru, grows strongly upright to one-and-a-half feet or more, and is called tree oxalis. It has brownish red foliage and a never-ending display of small yellow flowers. *Oxalis rubra* (known often as *O. crassipes*), six to twelve inches, from Brazil, has generous clusters of rosy pink or white flowers borne above graceful mounds of bright green foliage; it is nearly everblooming. My Great Aunt Eulice got me started with a division from her pink-flowered one when I was five years old. I realize that this plant is often considered an out-and-out lawn weed—or worse. However, in the right place . . . *Oxalis variabilis*, eight to twelve inches, from the Cape of Good Hope, is the "Grand Duchess" of commerce, with vivid yellow-throated rose flowers, to over an inch across, in winter.

Oxalis do best in sunny to semisunny conditions, with average house temperatures and exposure to fresh air. Pot them in loam-based soil and keep evenly moist in any active growing season, dry or nearly dry for a season of

Oxalis alstonii.

rest. As a rule, winter-flowering species are dormant in summer, and vice versa. Everblooming kinds need re-potting annually, in summer or fall, and trimming back, which promotes new growth at the same time all im-perfect foliage is efficiently removed. Propagate by re-moving offsets at potting time, or by division of those kinds having rhizomes.

Palmaceae. *Palm Family*.

Tropical trees, sometimes bushlike, with tough, leath-ery leaves and relatively insignificant flowers. The family includes coconut, date, and oil palms, as well as an array of genera grown for ornament.

Caryota mitis, *C. plumosa*, and *C. urens*, twelve to forty feet, are known as "fishtail palms" owing to the unique shape of the fronds. Young plants make excellent container specimens. Give them a sunny to semisunny location, average house temperatures, fresh, moist air, and a loam-based potting soil kept evenly moist. Propagate by sowing seeds in moist soil and warmth (80° to 85°F) in spring.

Chamaedorea cataractarum, to eight feet, from Mexico, is dwarf, and showy indoors; the female plants bear scarlet fruits. *Chamaedorea costaricana*, to ten feet, from Costa Rica, forms clusters of bamboolike canes with elegant, graceful fronds. *Chamaedorea elegans*, to six feet, from Mexico, is known as the parlor palm, and *C. elegans bella*, from eastern Guatemala, is the everpresent miniature palm. *Chamaedorea seifritzii*, to ten feet, from Mexico, bears clusters of small, slender canes. It has an overall lacy appearance. These palms prefer a semisunny to semishady position, average house temperatures, fresh, moist air, and a loam-based potting soil kept evenly moist. Propagate as for *Caryota*.

Chamaerops humilis, to five feet, rarely to twenty feet, from southern Europe and North Africa, is the fan palm. It is dwarf enough to be cultivated indoors and has a distinct, bold appearance. Give it a sunny to semisunny situation, average house temperatures that are on the cool side in winter, 50° to 70°F, and fresh, moist air. Pot in loam-based soil and keep evenly moist to wet. Propagate as for *Caryota* (page 164).

Chrysalidocarpus lutescens, to thirty feet, from Madagascar, the butterfly or areca palm, has willowy, furrowed, yellow canes in a clump. It may form more than a dozen of these in one small pot, and thus serves as a showy container plant. Be careful when you purchase an areca; it is a very common and widely distributed plant that often winds up suffering all kinds of abuse, chilling or overheating, drying or drowning, and mechanical damage such as the tearing or bruising of the fronds. Care as for *Chamaedorea* (above); propagation as for *Caryota* (page 164).

Howea belmoreana and *H. fosteriana*, both from Lord Howe Island in the South Pacific, are sometimes known as the kentia palms. They are slow-growing, showy in containers, and among the better of large-size palms for houseplanting. They are usually more expensive than the more common and apparently faster propagating areca. In any case, all of these palms tend to come on the market when they are four to six feet tall, often with the greatest girth so that it will be right at eye level in a room. If this is a problem, lift the palm onto a pedestal, two to four feet tall, so that the fronds will spread over your head instead of right in your face. Care as for *Chamaedorea* (see page 165); propagation as for *Caryota* (see page 164)

Licuala spinosa, to fifteen feet, from Malaya to Java, has fan-shaped leaves, with the segments plaited and terminated as if they had been cut squarely with pinking shears. Care as for *Chamaedorea* (above), with extra emphasis on the moist air. Propagation as for *Caryota* (see page 164).

Livistona chinensis, to thirty feet, from China, is another fan palm (see also *Chamaerops*, above). Its individual leaves are sometimes more than five feet wide. This palm grows to a single stem, and makes an imposing container plant while young. Care as for *Chamaedorea* (above), with special care about moist, fresh air. Propagation as for *Caryota* (see page 164).

Phoenix roebelenii, to six feet, native from Assam to Vietnam, is the dwarf date palm. It is one of the showier, more graceful palms to grow indoors. Care as for *Chamaedorea* (above); propagation as for *Caryota* (see page 164).

Rhapis excelsa and *R. humilis*, five to ten feet, both from southern China, have bamboolike canes and fan-shaped leaves. They are outstanding houseplants and there are many different varieties, some dwarf (one to two feet), some having variegated leaves, sought after by collectors. Care as for *Chamaedorea* (above), except keep on the cool side in winter, preferably not over 70° F. Propagation as for *Caryota* (see page 164).

PANDANACEAE. *Screw-pine Family.*

Tropical trees and shrubs cultivated as foliage houseplants. In an outdoor habitat a mature screw pine will produce flowers that are followed by cones. Of interest here is *Pandanus*.

Pandanus veitchi, four to twenty feet, from Polynesia, and other screw pines are remarkable for the perfect spiral arrangement of their long, prickly margined, sword-shaped leaves, often white-variegated, and for the aerial

Rhapis excelsa *dwarf 'Koban'*.

roots which hang down to the soil, becoming in the right situation stout prop roots which, in habitat, steady the plants against mighty tropical windstorms. There are strains having smooth-edged leaves but for some reason those having thorns are more widely distributed. They can make great accent plants in the house but need placement off the beaten track so that no one will walk unwittingly into the prickly leaves. I find that screw pine plants also tend to work better in a room if they are lifted onto a forty-two-inch or similar height pedestal. That way the greatest girth of leaves is lifted into the air space overhead and doesn't take away human living room. Give them a sunny to semisunny location, average house temperatures, and fresh, moist air. Pot in humus-rich, loam-based soil, and keep evenly moist, except slightly less so in the fall and early winter. The most active growth occurs from midwinter to summer; repot at this time, if nec-

essary. Propagate by removing suckers at repotting time, or when one has some roots and can be handily separated from the parent.

PASSIFLORACEAE. *Passionflower Family*.

One genus containing succulent species, *Adenia*, is of interest to houseplanters, and *Passiflora* itself offers some challenges.

Adenia is newly popular for its succulent vines and shrubs. These natives of East Africa, Madagascar, and Union of Myanmar develop sculptural tubers—really thickened stems—and are in the habit of dying back for the winter. Adenia needs full sun, average house temperatures, and 5-10-10 or similar high-phosphorus, high-potash fertilizer during its season of active growth, which is summer. Water adenia generously from the time leaves appear in spring until early fall. Then one day you will notice that the leaves are starting to turn yellow. At that point, stop watering. All the leaves will soon fall and the thinner, twiggy branches can be cut back to the more swollen parts. Adenias do well with good air circulation but have no special needs for humidity. They can be propagated by stem cuttings in spring or early summer.

Adenia spinosa comes from Transvaal in South Africa. There it can have a bottle- or boulder-shaped base to four feet tall and eight feet in diameter. Potted specimens will do well almost indefinitely in an eight-inch pot. Adenias are relatively rare, but they are also easily cultivated and have a fascinating appearance. I have an unidentified species that has digitately lobed leaves with silver markings on the upper surface and tendril-climbing stems. The plant is especially meaningful to me because it was a gift from a Texas gardening friend who has been deceased for well over a decade. I also like the disappearing act this plant pulls in autumn, thus automatically changing the appearance of the garden in which it is trained up and around a thirty-inch wire wreath form that is suspended in the middle of the window. The effect is of a Chinese moon gate, and whether in or out of leaf, the sight always gives me pleasure. I'm almost ashamed to say it, but this plant has lived in the same eight-inch pot of soil for nearly ten years. This season it has been the best ever, so I would say this is definitely easily cultivated, about as carefree as any indoor plant can be.

Passiflora is a genus of vines that has fascinated me for as long as I can remember. I published a monograph on them by Florence Knock in the 1960s. In many ways it has been a genus waiting to happen, and now we are well into the "happening," thanks to the breeding efforts of Patrick Worley, John MacDougal at the Missouri Botanical Garden, and others. Some achievements are winter-hardy passifloras that come back from the roots in areas as cold as USDA zone 5 ('incense' is one), passifloras that grow vigorously and bloom heavily over a long season ('Coral Glow'), and passifloras that, in addition to their extraordinary flowers, produce edible fruit. Some of my choices as houseplants include *P. suberosa*, a miniature with tiny three-pointed leaves, perfect blossoms in proportion in spring and summer, followed by dark blue seedpods. *Passiflora vitifolia* has thick, three-lobed grapevinelike foliage and a profusion of red blossoms with white filaments in spring and summer; the Logees put me onto this crimson passionflower, a better performing houseplant than *P. coccinea*. There is more on the pas-

Assorted blossoms and leaves of Passiflora.

siflora as an indoor/outdoor plant on page 228. Indoors give it a sunny to semisunny location, average house temperatures, fresh, moist air, and humus-rich, loam-based potting soil kept evenly moist. Propagate from cuttings late winter to early summer. Train on a four-stake bamboo tepee four feet tall or on an eighteen-inch wreath form.

PHYTOLACCACEAE. *Pokeweed Family.*

Herbs, shrubs, and trees tending to weediness. One genus is of interest as a houseplant, *Rivina*.

Rivina humilis, from tropical America, is an erect plant two to three feet tall with spreading branches and slender-stalked, pointed-oval leaves. It is grown for its clusters of berrylike fruits which follow the small pink and white flowers. Rivina, the bloodberry or rouge plant, is related to the garden pokeweed, and the berries are just about as short-lived. Nevertheless, a seedling eight months old will make quite a nice show in a winter garden where every spot of color shines out. It prefers a sunny to semisunny situation, average house temperatures, fresh, moist air, and a loam-based potting soil kept evenly moist. Propagate by sowing seeds or making cuttings in any season when they can be given constant warmth and bright diffused light. Rivina grows and fruits nicely in a maxi light garden.

PINACEAE. *Pine Family.*

Cone-bearing evergreens from tropical as well as temperate parts of the world. Except for bonsai (Chapter 5), only *Araucaria* is of interest as a houseplant.

Araucaria heterophylla, the Norfolk Island pine, resembles a true pine tree. It has stiff needles, resinous sap, and is capable of forming woody cones. On its native island, this pine reaches a height of two hundred feet, but in captivity two to five feet is more likely. Juvenile specimens have long been houseplants, especially favored at Christmas, because of their symmetrical growth, and also because they stand a certain amount of abuse, such as being decorated for the holidays. Give it a sunny to semishady location, average house temperatures that are on the cool side in winter, fresh, moist air, and a loam-based potting soil kept evenly moist. Propagate from seeds, or root the top leader—twelve to eighteen inches—of an old plant (side shoots do not make well-shaped specimens). The cutting should include, besides the leader, at least one tier of branches, plus a lowermost tier that will be removed by pruning next to the main stem. Insert deep enough in the rooting medium to cover the part of the stem where the branches were removed. Moisten well and enclose in clear plastic. Place to root in bright light and moderate temperatures, around 65° to 75°F. After several weeks or months, new growth will indicate that roots have formed. Gradually remove the cover so as to accustom the delicate new growth to the open air.

PIPERACEAE. *Pepper Family*.

Tropical herbs and shrubs with fleshy, smooth-edged leaves and not particularly showy flowers. The genus *Piper* yields the common black pepper but also ornamental vines of interest to the houseplanter. There is also the large and variable genus *Peperomia*.

Peperomia includes a large number of potential houseplants. They range from vines with small foliage to erect bushes of large, heavy leaves. Foliage color may be almost black, green, reddish, silvery, buff, or bronze, quilted or pleated, shiny or hairy, or with blotches, bands, margins, or undersides of contrasting color. Those that form a basal rosette of leaves resembling the habit of an African violet are especially vulnerable to root and crown rot if left standing in water, especially when temperatures are cool and the weather is cloudy. Peperomias will adapt to light, from that found in a fluorescent-light garden to the full range of window light, from merely bright to full sun. They like average house temperatures, fresh air, and a loam-based potting soil kept evenly moist in spring and summer, and approaching dryness at the surface before watering in fall and winter. Propagate from leaf or stem cuttings. Kinds having highly variegated foliage may not come true from leaf cuttings, in which case those that are rosette-forming, like an African violet, can be divided. Those that grow upright can be propagated by stem or tip cuttings.

Piper ornatum, a twining vine from the Celebes, has heart-shaped leaves combining ochre, silver, pink, and matte green. It is suitable for training as a small wreath in a maxi light garden or in a semisunny to semishady window garden. It prefers average house temperatures, fresh, moist air (but no drafts), and a humus-rich, loam-based potting soil kept evenly moist. Root cuttings in late winter–spring in warmth and high humidity.

PITTOSPORACEAE. *Pittosporum Family*.

Trees and shrubs, sometimes vinelike, mostly from Australia, with thick, leathery, alternate leaves and showy flowers.

Peperomia clusiifolia 'Variegata'.

Coccoloba uvifera.

Pittosporum tobira, with its thick, shiny, leathery leaves arranged in whorls at the tips of branches, is a shrub that tends to grow in flat planes and is especially adapted to bonsai training; it is agreeable to pruning and shaping. A variegated form is also available, grayish green with creamy-margined leaves. Both bear in spring clusters of small white flowers that smell of orange blossoms. Give a semisunny to semishady location, average house temperatures that don't top 72°F in winter, fresh, moist air, and a loam-based potting soil kept evenly moist. Root cuttings of half-ripened wood (see page 54) in late winter or spring.

PODOCARPACEAE. *Podocarpus Family.*

Evergreen shrubs and trees cultivated outdoors in the South. One genus is seen as a houseplant.

Podocarpus macrophylla maki, from Japan, is a coniferous evergreen tree which remains small for many years when containerized. It has slender leaves spirally arranged along the stems. *Podocarpus nagi* has spreading branches and shiny green elliptic leaves. Both are trained as bonsai. They like a semisunny to semishady position, house temperatures that are cool in winter (not over 72°F), fresh, moist air, and a loam-based potting soil kept evenly moist. Frequent misting or showering of the leaves is beneficial, especially in winter. Propagate from seeds, or by rooting cuttings of almost ripened wood (see page 54) in late summer or autumn.

POLYGONACEAE. *Buckwheat Family.*

Herbs, shrubs, trees, and vines from all over the world. Some are foodstuffs and others are cultivated for their showy flowers or foliage. Two genera are of interest to the houseplanter, *Antigonon* and *Coccoloba*.

Antigonon leptopus, from Mexico, is a robust, tuber-forming vine. Coral vine, as it is known, climbs by tendrils. Racemes of bright rose-pink flowers, arising from the leaf axils, appear freely from early spring to fall. Give it a sunny location, average house temperatures, and fresh, moist air. Pot in loam-based soil, and keep evenly

moist in spring and summer, and dry for its fall-winter dormancy, during which time cooler temperatures are acceptable (50° to 60°F) and no fertilizer should be applied. Propagate by sowing seeds in winter or spring.

Coccoloba uvifera, the sea-grape from southern Florida and the West Indies, is a shrubby evergreen plant of leathery, rounded leaves with prominent red veins which change to white at maturity. A sport, *C. u. aurea*, has nearly stemless leaves that are generously splashed with creamy yellow. Give it sun to semisun, average house temperatures, fresh, moist air, and a loam-based potting soil kept evenly moist. Propagate by seeds or from cuttings of ripe wood (see page 54) in winter or spring, or by air-layering in spring or summer.

POLYPODIACEAE. *Fern Family.*

Most tender as well as hardy ferns belong to this family. Many genera are of interest to the houseplanter: *Adiantum*, *Asplenium*, *Cyrtomium*, *Davallia*, *Nephrolepis*, *Platycerium*, *Polypodium*, *Polystichum*, and *Pteris*.

Ferns in general do well in relatively small pots in a light, humusy growing medium. Packaged soilless mixes such as Pro-Mix and Baccto Professional Planting Mix produce excellent results. By this system the ferns will need watering nearly every day and fertilizing every two weeks, using fish emulsion, 30-10-10, or 23-21-17. Potted ferns do less well in large pots filled with dense, heavy growing medium. This situation invites overwatering. Fern roots need a constant supply of air and water, hence the need for a humus-rich medium. Indoor ferns also need protection from drafts, both hot and cold. They thrive on cool nights (55° to 65°F) and moderate days

(65° to 75°F). Moist air is also a boon and suggests setting the pots in pebble trays with water added as necessary to keep the level just below the base of the pot.

Adiantum is the genus name for the elegant, ever so delicate maidenhair ferns. Of these. *A. hispidulum* is tougher than most and does well in bright light, with little or no direct sun, moderate humidity, and a humus-rich potting mix kept nicely moist. Drying out to the point of withering the fronds is anathema to any adiantum, and can be caused by lack of water as well as placement so that a draft of hot, dry air blows on the plant. These extraordinarily beautiful ferns really need a cool, moist atmosphere, with fresh air that circulates freely.

Asplenium nidus is a bold foliage plant, not at all "ferny" in the usual sense. Larger fronds form a sort of vase, from the base of which new growth arises out of what appears to be a dark brown or nearly black bird's nest, hence its common name bird's-nest fern. It grows best in bright, diffused light, but in not much direct sun. Too much light bleaches or burns the broad fronds. If the light is too weak, they thin out and the plant will take on an overall spindly appearance.

Pot up bird's-nest fern in a humus-rich mix such as equal parts garden soil, peat moss, clean sand, and well-rotted leaf mold or compost. To each quart of this combination, add a handful of horticultural charcoal chips. Don't leave bird's-nest fern standing in water for more than a few hours. However, it is perhaps a worse offense if the growing medium is allowed to become so dry that the fronds wilt even slightly, especially in the presence of bright sun and warm temperatures.

Like other ferns, bird's-nest responds well to regular applications of fish emulsion fertilizer. Diluted liquid manure tea may also be applied and will be unusually effective in the spring as average temperatures and day length are on the increase. A typical problem with this fern is that the fronds die back from the tips and along the edges or the green parts are puckered irregularly. This is the result of letting the roots go dry between waterings.

Cyrtomium falcatum, or hollyleaf fern, is one of the toughest of all ferns and perhaps not surprising, a bit on the coarse side. The plant grows in rosette form, to twelve inches tall and as wide, with individual segments on the fronds an inch wide by twice as long and shaped something on the order of true holly leaves. It is a great plant for beginning gardeners; to be honest, hollyleaf was the first fern I was able to grow successfully. That experience gave me the confidence to try some of the more refined ones. This fern thrives in bright light but not much direct sun, with good air circulation and a humus-rich, loam-based soil kept evenly moist.

Davallia is the genus name for the rabbit's-foot ferns, so-called because of the furry creeping rhizomes from which the finely cut fronds arise. The davallias grow best during the longer days of spring and summer in temperatures above 60°F. They appreciate moist air that cir-

Asplenium nidus *(center, front) in arrangement at Dixon Gallery and Gardens, Memphis, Tennessee. The tall plants at back are* Camellia, *with* Spathiphyllum, *Narcissus,* Chamaedorea *(dwarf palm), and* Hedera *ivy.*

culates freely and probably do best in hanging containers. To my mind this is one of the tougher of the delicate-appearing ferns, a plant that "looks like a fern" but isn't all that fussy about the environment.

Nephrolepis exaltata 'Bostoniensis' is the ever-popular Boston fern, a plant that can become huge, to the size of several bushel baskets. A miniature variety, *N. e.* 'Dallasii' or Dallas fern is widely distributed and grows perfectly for me in its place on the living room floor about six feet back from a bright window, nestled next to a leg of the grand piano. It gets water nearly every morning and very diluted high-nitrogen fertilizer at least once a week. *Nephrolepis exaltata* 'Elzevir' is a miniature 'Fluffy Ruffles', with tiny, irregularly fringed fronds and a dense, congested habit; Kartuz says this is probably the best of the ferns for small terrariums.

Button fern, *Pellaea rotundifolia*, may look tough, but it is as delicate as any fern, short of the filmy ferns that require a special greenhouse to make their cultivation possible. It is native to New Zealand and cliff-brake is a more general common name applied to the genus as a whole, earned for its habit of living among rocks. Some species require limestone soil. Button fern has these needs:

1) A shaded or northern exposure.
2) Coolness, ideally a range of 50° to 70°F.
3) Ordinary all-purpose or African violet potting soil that is kept constantly moist. Avoid extremes!

If you provide these conditions unfailingly, button fern will give much pleasure. A four- to six-inch pot readily supports a button fern eight to twelve inches across. I have the best luck if the pot sits in a deep tray or saucer filled with pebbles or gravel and water, which helps maintain the humidity necessary for perfect fronds and vigorous plants. Trim off any dead tips or leaves from button fern. If it has an alarming number, try moving it to a cooler, shadier, moister spot.

Polypodium punctatum 'Grandiceps', fish-tail fern, is a proven trouper for houseplanting. It is a clustering form of *P. punctatum* or clumping birdsnest, native to New South Wales, Natal, Angola, and Guinea. It needs half

Pellaea rotundifolia *(foreground) in a basket planting with* Asparagus, Gerbera, Kalanchoe, Adiantum, *and* Hedera.

sun to half shade, warm temperatures, and moderate to high humidity. Propagate by division at repotting time in late winter or spring.

Pteris ensiformis 'Victoriae' is a silver-variegated Victorian table fern that grows easily to about eighteen inches tall and makes a beautiful specimen to place on a desk or table or in a floor arrangement with other plants in bright light but with not much direct sun. It looks beautiful and gets on well with African violets and most begonias.

PORTULACACEAE. *Purslane Family.*

Herbs and shrubs from temperate as well as tropical parts of the world, with fleshy leaves and often showy flowers. The genus *Portulacaria*, in the species *P. afra* and its variety *variegata*, is something of a miniature jade plant often displayed in a mame bonsai-style pot and

Polypodium punctatum 'Grandiceps'.

habit. The related *Portulaca* gives us the popular warm-weather rose moss that does exceptionally well in sunny, hot places with moist-to-dry, well-drained soil, and makes one of the better candidates for flowering hanging baskets in Sun Belt states.

PRIMULACEAE. *Primrose Family.*

Herbs from many parts of the world with attractive foliage and showy flowers. Two genera are of particular interest here, *Cyclamen* and *Primula*.

Cyclamen persicum giganteum, native from Greece to Syria, and its many hybrids have handsome rosettes, to twelve inches, of fleshy, heart-shaped leaves, often decorated impressively with silver, and colorful shooting-star flowers on individual stems, rising from the crown of the plant. All of this grows from a fleshy tuber, similar to that of the tuberous begonia and sinningia (florist gloxinia). Give it a semisunny to semishady position, cool house temperatures in winter (not over 70°F), and absolutely no drafts, just fresh, moist air. Pot in humus-rich, loam-based soil and keep evenly moist in fall through spring, and dry during its summer rest. Repot in early fall keeping the tuber at the same level at which it grew previously; keep barely moist until new growth shows. Seeds started in August will bloom in about four-teen to eighteen months. The miniature or "mini" cyclamen will bloom in ten to twelve months from seeds. Some cyclamen are quite fragrant as the morning sun warms the volatile oils.

Primula malacoides, the "fairy" or "baby" primrose, eight to twelve inches, is considered a choice houseplant. It has slender stalks bearing multitudes of small blossoms in tiers in winter and spring. *Primula sinensis*, Chinese primrose, eight to twelve inches, has lobed leaves and umbels of typical primrose flowers of many colors in winter and spring. *Primula obconica*, eight to twelve inches, has large, broad, rounded leaves with hairs that when touched to the skin lead to quite an uncomfortable rash in some individuals, hence its common name poison primrose. The flowers, in winter and spring, are borne in clusters atop stems eight to twelve inches tall, in glorious colors such as crushed raspberry, apricot, and periwinkle; they are offered as cut flowers in the Paris flower markets. Give it semisun to semishade, cool house temperatures—50° to 70°F—in fall and winter, fresh, moist air, and a humus-rich, loam-based potting soil kept evenly moist. Sow seeds in early spring or late summer. Mostly these primulas are treated as annuals, discarded at the end of their initial flowering. None is tolerant of freezing temperatures.

PROTEACEAE. *Protea Family.*

Mostly tropical trees and shrubs, there is one genus of interest for growing as a houseplant. Several of the flowering shrubs are grown for their spectacular and long-lasting cut flowers, the *Protea* itself, for example, and these are favorites for displaying in water among living houseplants.

Grevillea robusta, the silk oak, to 150 feet, has large seeds that sprout easily and grow quickly (three feet in one year is not uncommon). The leaves are fernlike in texture on upright stems. This can make a really nice houseplant tree in a hurry, and before it threatens to push the ceiling, just cut it back by a third or more, ideally in late winter or early spring. Give it a sunny to semisunny location, average house temperatures but not too hot (no more than 72°F) in fall and winter, fresh, moist air, and loam-based potting soil kept evenly moist. Propagate by sowing seeds in winter or spring.

PUNICACEAE. *Pomegranate Family.*

This family contains only one genus, *Punica*, a dwarf form of which makes an excellent houseplant and is often trained as a bonsai.

Punica granatum nana, to six feet, from southwestern Asia, has single red-orange flowers followed by small but showy (and edible) fruits on a dense, twiggy bush with narrow, shiny, apple green leaves. The variety 'Chico' has double flowers of many crepe-textured petals; it does not bear fruit. 'Party Dress' is also dwarf but has pink flowers and pink fruit. They prefer a sunny to semisunny location, average house temperatures, ideally not over 75°F in winter, and fresh, moist air. Pot in a loam-based soil, and keep evenly moist, somewhat less so in cool, cloudy, winter weather. Pruning is important to the development of a dwarf pomegranate for it to have a framework of basic branches that supports the form or shape desired—bush, tree-form standard, bonsai, or espalier—and many twigs of current growth on which the flowers are produced. Any pomegranate in a pot will be better off on the indoor/outdoor plan. Propagate by cuttings of half-ripe wood (see page 54) in spring or summer, many of which can be salvaged from the prunings or shearings done in spring and sometimes again in early summer, but not later than July 4, or the wood will not have time to harden sufficiently to bloom. When dwarf pomegranate is outdoors in the summer, with lots of sun and an occasional drying-out, followed by devoted watering and fertilizing, it will give an abundance of flowers through early fall. There may be some buds lingering to open indoors, after the plant has been brought in ahead of frost, and then there is the increasing show of the fruits as they begin to turn. I'm a romantic when it comes to this plant, completely supportive in times of sudden defoliation or habitation by well-meaning insects. I find it is also remarkably forgiving and the sort of plant with which one can expect to enjoy a long relationship.

Punica granatum nana.

RANUNCULACEAE. *Buttercup Family.*

Herbs, and sometimes shrubs, mostly from the North Temperate Zone. *Anemone* and *Ranunculus* are of interest to houseplanters, first as among the most alluring cut flowers money can buy and, second, as living plants. As we shall see, they are not houseplants in the sense of a trailing philodendron or corn plant dracaena, but rather seasonal accents that gardeners who have cool, sunny, airy winter gardens, outdoors or under glass, can also grow.

The florist's anemone is a hybridized form of *Anemone coronaria*, a tuberous species from the Mediterranean region. If the flowers are double it could be a cultivar 'Flore Pleno', or, if very double, 'Chrysanthemiflora'.

The florist's ranunculus is *Ranunculus asiaticus* in some configuration of the cultivar 'Superbissimus', a name that could cover a lot of territory. This tuberous-rooted species is also known as the Persian buttercup and it came from southeast Europe and southeast Asia.

The tubers of both anemone and ranunculus are planted in the fall and permitted a time of moderate temperatures (around 55°F) and even moisture to establish feeder roots. As leaves appear, give them more water, a semisunny to sunny position, and cool to moderate temperatures (40° to 70°F). They require fresh, moist air, and a loam-based potting soil kept evenly moist. Plant the tubers an inch deep and two inches apart. Be prepared to spray against green aphids that often show up on new growth. Flowering can begin in about twelve weeks from the time of planting, or midwinter, and continue until spring.

ROSACEAE. *Rose Family.*

Herbs, shrubs, and trees from many parts of the world, cultivated for garden ornament and as foodstuffs. Often divided into three tribes: the rose, apple, and peach. In addition to the dwarf fruit trees and *Pyracantha* which are of interest for bonsai work (see Chapter 5), two genera may be of interest for houseplanting.

Fragaria vesca, from Europe, has a variety *albo-marginata* called the variegated wild strawberry, because its small leaves are marked with creamy white and red. The white flowers, a great many in spring, but continuing in moderation all summer, are followed by slender, inch-long strawberries. Runnerless varieties, readily grown from seed to fruit in a few months, are also of interest. They include 'Baron Solemacher' and 'Harzland', with red fruit, and the golden-fruited 'Alpine Yellow'. Give them a sunny situation, cool temperatures (40° to 65°F) through fall and winter, fresh, moist air, and a loam-based potting soil kept evenly moist. Propagate by rooting stolons, or runners, when they appear, by division, or by sowing seeds winter through spring.

Rosa chinensis minima, or *R. roulettii*, from China, and other pygmy or miniature roses make interesting houseplants. They are perfect replicas of the large and cluster-flowered hybrid roses, though on a small scale. Available as seeds, bushes, and diminutive tree-form

standards, they like a sunny to semisunny location, average house temperatures, fresh, moist air, and a loam-based potting soil kept evenly moist. Be prepared to treat against spider mites, aphids, and possibly black spot or powdery mildew. Cuttings of half-ripened to hardwood (see page 54) growth can be rooted at any season in a maxi light garden, or when conditions conducive to rooting can be provided in window light or outdoors.

RUBIACEAE. *Madder Family.*

Herbs, shrubs, trees, and vines from temperate as well as tropical parts of the world, including genera cultivated for medicinal purposes, for fruit or showy flowers, typically very fragrant. The genera of interest to the houseplanter include *Coffea, Gardenia, Hoffmannia, Ixora, Manettia, Mitriostigma, Nertera,* and *Pentas.*

Coffea arabica, the coffee tree of commerce, has glossy, dark green leaves nearly identical to those of its relative, the gardenia. It requires thoughtful pruning in late winter or spring to make a shapely shrub or tree, four to eight feet tall. Fragrant white flowers in spring and summer are followed by bright red beans in winter. Give it a semisunny to semishady location, average house temperatures, fresh, moist air, and a humus-rich, loam-based potting soil kept evenly moist. Yellowing, chlorotic leaves indicate the need for more acid fertilizer such as fish emulsion or 30-10-10. Propagate by sowing fresh beans or from tip cuttings of half-ripened wood, in warmth and high humidity at any time.

Gardenia jasminoides 'Fortuniana', four to six feet, from China, has smaller leaves and flowers than the typical gardenia used by florists, but it is more easily cultivated as a houseplant and the most generous with flowering, possible intermittently year round. *Gardenia radicans floreplena*, from Japan, is dwarf in habit, easily kept to eighteen inches. Its leaves seldom exceed three inches in length, and the double flowers measure about two inches across. In general it can be said that gardenias are tender evergreen shrubs prized for their fragrant, double, velvety, white blossoms and dark green, glossy, ovate leaves. *Gardenia thunbergia*, however, can become a

Gardenia jasminoides.

large shrub to ten feet, or even a small tree (there is a specimen in the Virginia Robinson Garden, Beverly Hills, California; open to visitors by appointment) with single fragrant white flowers having a corolla three inches across, eight-lobed, with a slender tube to three inches long.

Gardenias are nearly as well known for dropping their buds as for the flowers they manage to produce. Bud drop is frequently the result of a change in environment, as from a greenhouse to a drafty, dry house. This causes leaves and new growth to turn black at the tips, or the plant may completely defoliate. To avoid this pathetic situation, provide a balanced supply of moisture—evenly moist soil—diffused sunlight, and temperatures that would be comfortable for yourself in at-home clothing, about 62° to 75°F. Gardenias need fresh, moist air and a humus-rich, loam-based potting soil; avoid extremes of wet and dry. Use acid fertilizers such as 30-10-10 or fish emulsion. Propagate from cuttings of half-ripened wood (see page 54) in late winter or spring, or at any time in a maxi light garden.

Hoffmannia refulgens, twelve to eighteen inches, from Chiapas, has closely set, parallel veins running from the midrib outward to the leaf margins depressed in such a way that they give a ribbed effect, leading to its common name corduroy plant. This and other species, such as *H. ghiesbreghtii* and *H. roezlii*, both from Mexico, are showy foliage plants characterized by unusual texture and vein patterns in the obovate leaves (the broad end away from the stalk). The upper leaf surfaces may be shaded green to copper or rose-purple, while reverses are usually a dark green. Veins may be light green, pinkish, or silvery. They prefer a semisunny to semishady position, average house temperatures, fresh, moist air, and a humus-rich, loam-based potting soil kept evenly moist. Propagate by rooting cuttings in warmth and high humidity at any time; a maxi light garden is ideal.

Ixora coccinea (flame of the woods), a shrub from the East Indies, to six feet, has clusters of scarlet, tubular flowers in great abundance. Recent hybrids range from pale yellow through orange to dark red, from pink to dark rose. Of these, 'Red Emperor' (possibly sold as 'Super-king') has exceptionally large heads of red, red flowers; recommended for greenhouse and maxi fluorescent-light gardens. *Ixora javanica* (jungle geranium), from south-eastern Asia, has bright orange-red flowers and performs well under semishady conditions. *Ixora stricta (I. chinensis)* is available as 'Dwarf Lemon' (a globe-shaped, compact plant with pale lemon flowers that fade to apri-

Hoffmannia refulgens.

cot) and 'Sunkist' (very congested habit with salmon orange star flowers); both are recommended for warm house gardens and for planting in small bonsai pots. Ixoras are evergreen and almost everblooming, with leathery leaves of glossy green and new growth that is often an attractive bronze-pink color. The bushy plants are amenable to pruning back after they have been flowering for an extended period. Give them a sunny to semisunny situation, average house temperatures, fresh, moist air, and a humus-rich, loam-based potting soil kept evenly moist. Be generous with an acid fertilizer such as 30-10-10 or fish emulsion whenever you want to promote lots of new growth and the flowers that accompany it. Propagate from cuttings in late winter–spring, each having four pairs of leaves; set in a sand-peat mixture, and keep warm and moist.

Manettia inflata (firecracker vine) from Brazil, is a fast-growing, free-blooming plant having tubular flowers, yellow-tipped scarlet, arising on short stems from the leaf axils in summer and fall. It manages well in a window situation trained on a twelve- to fifteen-inch wreath (see page 192). It prefers a sunny to semisunny location, average house temperatures but preferably on the cool side (50° to 70°F) in fall and winter, fresh, moist air, and a loam-based potting soil kept evenly moist. Propagate from cuttings in spring and early summer.

Mitriostigma axillare, the African gardenia, has a different but pleasing sweet perfume and it is considerably easier to grow and flower as a houseplant than the true gardenia. Clusters of single white, pink-tinged blooms appear in profusion from the leaf axils in warm, moist growing conditions, intermittently all year. Mitriostigma can be a small bushy plant, twelve to eighteen inches, or it can be trained upward tepee-style so that it becomes a shrub three to five feet tall by about half as wide. Give it a semisunny to semishady location, average house temperatures, fresh, moist air, and a humus-rich, loam-based potting soil kept evenly moist. Fertilize generously with fish emulsion or 30-10-10 in spring and summer, or at any time in a warm maxi light garden. Propagate from cuttings of half-ripened wood (see page 54) in warmth, high humidity, and bright diffused light at any time.

Pentas lanceolata '*California Pink*'.

Pentas lanceolata, from Arabia and tropical Africa, is a small bushy plant easily kept under two feet by frequent pruning. It yields white, lavender, pink, or rosy red flowers over a long season in upright, domed clusters; each flower is about the diameter of a dime, a five-pointed star. It likes a sunny to semisunny position, average house temperatures, fresh, moist air, and a humus-rich, loam-based potting soil kept evenly moist. After extended flowering, prune back sharply, or start fresh with cuttings of partly ripened wood (see page 54).

RUTACEAE. *Citrus Family*.

Mostly tropical trees and shrubs cultivated for fruit or ornament. The foliage is glossy and appealing, often aromatic when bruised lightly; frequently the flowers are deliciously fragrant. *Citrus* and *Correa* are of particular interest here.

Citrus aurantiifolia is a spiny, small tree, eight to fifteen feet, which bears small limes. *Citrus limon* 'Meyer', six to eighteen feet, from China, is known as the Meyer lemon. It is dwarf-growing, with relatively small leaves and branches and edible lemons of average size. *Citrus limon* 'Ponderosa', three to six feet, is an exciting tub plant which bears unbelievably large lemons, individual fruits weighing as much as two pounds. *Citrus mitis*, the popular calamondin, is now more properly called *Citrofortunella*, but I will discuss it here since the care is the same. It is easily kept under three feet by pruning in spring or early summer. The fragrant white flowers are followed by tart-juiced fruits which mature to a diameter of two inches and a bright orange color. *Citrus nobilis deliciosa*, the tangerine, is a nearly thornless tree with willowy leaves; its fruits are also known as Mandarin oranges. *Citrus taitensis*, the Otaheite orange, begins to bear plum-size, lemon-shaped (but inedible) fruit even when it's less than twelve inches tall. All of these plants prefer a sunny position, average house temperatures, fresh, moist air, and a humus-rich, loam-based soil kept evenly moist. Be generous with acid fertilizer during

Correa decumbens.

spring and summer. Citrus can be kept a little on the dry side in fall and early winter, provided the average temperatures are on the cool side, not over 60°F.

Correa decumbens, to two feet, is an Australian flowering shrub that is easily managed as a potted indoor/outdoor plant. It has small, tough, sandy-textured green leaves and in summer a profusion of bell-shaped, red flowers, from which the stamens protrude noticeably. Train it as a bush or a small tree-form standard (see page 189). Care and propagation as for *Citrus* (above).

SAXIFRAGACEAE. *Saxifrage Family.*

Herbs, shrubs, trees, and woody vines from many parts of the world cultivated for garden ornament. Three genera are of interest here, all capable of withstanding temperatures of 20°F, some much colder.

Hydrangea macrophylla, eighteen inches to three feet, the large-leaved or florist hydrangea, or hortensia, from Japan, has showy flowers that may be white, pink, or blue. The coloring of the pink and blue varieties is determined by the degree of soil acidity. A plant that is pink one year (in soil with a pH of 6.0 to not more than 6.2) can be made blue another year by changing the soil pH to a more acid range of 5.0 to 5.5. White-flowered hydrangeas have no coloring pigment and are little affected by the soil pH.

If you obtain a potted hydrangea in full bloom, be sure to give it lots of water, otherwise it will wilt, quickly becoming a "de-hydrangea." Flowering hydrangeas last longer in bright filtered light, but protected from direct rays of hot sun. They always need fresh, moist air circulation. After danger of spring frost, set potted hydrangeas outdoors in a partly shaded place, ideally receiving morning sun. When the blooms have faded, cut them off. Prune the shoots back about halfway, or to within two leaf joints from the soil. Repot, working the old soil away from the roots, and replanting in a humus-rich, loam-based potting soil. Keep the plants well watered and fertilized through the summer. The young growing tips may be pinched out until early July. This induces branching and ultimately a larger yield of flowers.

Before danger of hard freezes in autumn, put potted hydrangeas indoors in a cool, airy, sunny place, such as a pit greenhouse, where temperatures will be about 40° to 50°F. Keep quite dry and withhold fertilizer. After Christmas, and before late January, begin forcing the hydrangea into growth by providing minimum temperatures of 50° to 55°, up to 65°F maximum, in lots of moist air and sunny brightness. When the leaves are making active growth, the temperature may be increased slightly. At this time, begin biweekly fertilizings which should continue to the flowering stage. These consist of applying a solution made by dissolving 1 ounce ammonium sulfate and 1 ounce iron sulfate in 2 gallons water. To produce blue flowers, at two-week intervals after growth becomes active, make three to six applications of 1 teaspoon aluminum sulfate per six-inch pot, watering it in.

Saxifraga stolonifera (strawberry geranium, strawberry begonia), from China and Japan, has rounded, bristly leaves arranged in loose rosette form. The leaves are dark olive green, patterned with light gray areas along the veins, spotted purple beneath. The small white flowers in winter or spring are borne in airy clusters on tall, thin stalks, to eighteen inches. Baby plantlets are borne at the ends of thin, yarnlike runners. The variety 'Tricolor' has leaves variegated cream, pink, rose, or white. Give it a semisunny to semishady position, cool temperatures (not over 72°F in winter), fresh, moist air, and a humus-rich, loam-based potting soil kept evenly moist. Propagate by removing the young plantlets which form at the ends of bright rosy red runners. Saxifraga is used as a ground cover in gardens to zone 5.

Tolmiea menziesii, twelve to eighteen inches, native from the California coast to Alaska, is a lightly hairy, soft-leaved perennial which grows in an open rosette. Known as the piggyback plant or pickaback, it is notable for the development of baby plants at the base of mature leaves, on the surface at the sinus, where the leaf comes together and joins the petiole or leaf-stalk. Care and cold hardiness as for *Saxifraga*. Propagate by pinning the baby plants to damp soil until they root, then cut from the parent and move along separately.

Tolmiea menziesii *with foliar embryo.*

SCROPHULARIACEAE. *Figwort Family.*

Herbs, shrubs, trees, and vines from many parts of the world cultivated for their colorful flowers.

Asarina antirrhiniflora, from California, Texas, and Mexico, is a thin-stemmed perennial vine distinguished by its white-throated, purple, trumpetlike blossoms borne over a long period. A*sarina barclaiana*, from Mexico, is a strong climber with downy leaves and trumpet flowers, white through rose to purple, downy outside with a greenish tube. *Asarina erubescens*, from Mexico, has larger flowers than A. *barclaiana*, and their rose-red coloring and shape suggest a misleading common name, creeping gloxinia, although in the higher order of plants, the gesneriads and the scrophularias are allied. All asarinas may sometimes be listed as *Maurandia* or *Maurandya*. Give them a sunny to semisunny position, average house temperatures, fresh, moist air, and a humus-rich, loam-based potting soil kept evenly moist. Plant seeds or root cuttings in late winter–spring.

Calceolaria herbeohybrida (pocketbook plant), from species native to the cool Andes of Chile, has softly hairy, large leaves and terminal clusters of ballooned flowers often in vivid colors and combinations. These are principally annual plants, sold in bloom by florists. To prolong the display, keep cool (not over 70°F), moist, in plenty of fresh, moist air, protected from hot sun rays. When flowering ceases, add the plant to the compost. Propagate by sowing seeds in spring or early fall. The seeds require coolness in order to germinate and proceed properly.

Cymbalaria muralis (Kenilworth ivy), from Europe, is a small creeping perennial with rounded, scalloped

Calceolaria herbeohybrida.

leaves and, in spring, tiny, yellow-throated, lilac flowers which resemble miniature snapdragons. Give it a semisunny to semishady situation, house temperatures on the cool side in winter, fresh, moist air, and a humus-rich, loam-based potting soil kept evenly moist. Propagate by sowing seeds or by rooting stem cuttings at any time.

Tetranema roseum (synonym *Allophyton mexicanum*) is a beautiful small plant, short-stemmed, with long, broad, leathery, dark green leaves. The clusters of small, lavender (white in 'Alba' and 'Purity'), tubular flowers appear intermittently all year, borne on slender stems about four inches above the foliage. Each flower resembles a miniature foxglove with a large, lobed white lip and purple-violet throat, living up to its common name Mexican foxglove. The flowers are fragrant during the early morning hours. It prefers a semisunny to semishady location, moderate temperatures (not over 75°F in winter), fresh, moist air, and a humus-rich, loam-based potting soil kept evenly moist. Propagate by sowing seeds in late winter–spring.

SELAGINELLACEAE. *Selaginella Family*.

The annual and perennial herbs in this family belong to one genus, *Selaginella*, and all are mossy or fernlike.

Selaginellia emmeliana (sweat plant), from South America, forms a rosette of bright, lacy, fernlike fronds in constant high humidity. *Selaginella kraussiana*, from South Africa, is known as spreading clubmoss, and spread it does, by sending down roots at every node along the stems. The tiny leaves are bright green; in the variety *aurea* they are splashed with creamy white and in the dwarf, tuft-forming *brownii* they are emerald green. *Selaginella lepidophylla*, from Peru, Mexico, and Texas, is the resurrection plant that can be fully dried into a tight brownish ball, yet brought back to life by placing the roots in shallow water. *Selaginella uncinata*, from southern China, makes an iridescent blue-green ground cover for terrariums and bottle gardens. They all prefer a semishady to shady situation, average house temperatures, constant high humidity, and a humus-rich, loam-based potting soil kept evenly moist. Propagate at any time by rooting cuttings in warmth and high humidity.

SOLANACEAE. *Nightshade Family.*

Nearly all kinds of plants from tropical as well as temperate parts of the world make up this important family. They have alternate leaves and the flowers of most are regular. The genera of interest are *Browallia, Brugmansia, Brunfelsia, Capsicum, Cestrum, Solanum,* and *Streptosolen.*

Browallia speciosa major, twelve to eighteen inches, from Colombia, forms a bushy plant of bright to dark green leaves, set with innumerable white-throated violet-blue flowers, intermittently or as the seasons dictate. They can be covered with bloom outdoors all summer, provided temperatures are not constantly above 85°F, but winter flowering is also possible in a bright, cool spot. The so-called orange browallia is *Streptosolen,* see page 181. Browallia likes a semisunny to semishady location, cool house temperatures, not over 72°F in winter, fresh, moist air, and a humus-rich, loam-based potting soil kept evenly moist. Propagate by sowing seeds from midwinter to late spring, or by rooting cuttings in autumn or winter.

Brugmansia is the nightshade that dangles its fragrant angel-trumpet blossoms while the related *Datura* holds the angel-trumpets outward or upward. *Brugmansia candida* 'Double White' is described by Logee's as a " . . . stately bush that produces a marvelous display of flowers year around. Each dangling blossom is pure white and boasts a trumpet within a trumpet. Easily grown, free flowering." This is the sort of description I find irresistible, not to mention *B.* 'Charles Grimaldi', a "luminous salmon," or *B. versicolor,* a " . . . handsome hybrid that produces huge blossoms opening cream, evolving to apricot-peach." *B. suaveolens* is a pristine single white. Give these plants as large a pot as you have room for as they have an enthusiastic root system. They prefer sunny to semisunny situations, good air circulation, and a humus-rich, loam-based potting soil that is generously watered in warm, sunny weather. Fertilize regularly, alternating between an NPK that will encour-

Brugmansia suaveolens *flanked by* Schizanthus.

age vegetative growth (23-21-17, 30-10-10, or fish emulsion) and flowering (15-30-15 or 8-14-9). Propagate from tip cuttings of half-ripened wood (see page 54) at any time from late winter to early fall. Cut off up to two thirds of each of the larger leaves so as to prevent unnecessary loss of moisture during the rooting process.

Brunfelsia calycina floribunda, from Brazil, three to six feet, is a small evergreen shrub which bears showy tubular flowers from fall to spring. These open a dark lavender, fade to near-white by the third day, hence its common name yesterday-today-and-tomorrow plant. *Brunfelsia australis* is similar but has larger flowers that are sweet-scented and appear early spring to fall; *B. jamaicaensis* blooms also in warm weather, single, tubular white to cream blossoms that are deliciously evening-scented. Give them a sunny to semisunny position, average house temperatures, fresh, moist air, and a humus-rich, loam-based potting soil kept evenly moist. Prune back as necessary in spring or early summer to keep desired size. Propagate from cuttings in late winter–spring.

Capsicum annuum, six to eighteen inches, and its many varieties, originally from South America, make showy fruiting pot plants. They form small bushes of bright green leaves, first laden with starry white flowers, followed by chartreuse to purple to flaming scarlet peppers of various sizes and shapes. They are edible, but fiery hot; and do not confuse them with the related *Solanum pseudocapsicum* which bears poisonous fruit. They like a sunny to semisunny situation, average house temperatures, fresh, moist air, and a loam-based potting soil kept evenly moist. Propagate by sowing seeds in winter or spring. Seedlings kept outdoors during warm weather will set on more fruit than those kept inside. These peppers are generally treated as annuals, but they are in fact tender perennials and therefore fair game for keeping over if you have the space and inclination.

Cestrum diurnum, three to six feet, willow-leaved cestrum, bears in spring clusters of starry white fragrant flowers that open in the daytime. *Cestrum elegans* is favored for umbels of bright pink blossoms in winter; *C.*

Cestrum nocturnum.

nocturnum (night jessamine), three to twelve feet, from the West Indies, is a gangly evergreen shrub of bright green, willow-shaped leaves, with tubular greenish white flowers borne from the leaf axils in great bundles and giving off night fragrance that can be nearly overwhelming in a small, enclosed space. Give them a sunny to semisunny position, average house temperatures, and fresh, moist air. Pot in a humus-rich, loam-based potting soil and keep evenly moist spring through summer, on the dry side (excepting winter-blooming *C. elegans*) during its fall-winter semidormancy. Prune back sharply in spring, at the beginning of active growth. Propagate by rooting cuttings of half-mature wood (see page 54) in spring and summer.

Solanum pseudocapsicum, from Madeira, has pointed oval leaves with a strong pungent smell when disturbed and brightly colored globular fruit, usually bright scarlet-orange, often measuring about an inch in diameter; but "Jerusalem cherry" is not edible. Do not confuse with the related *Capsicum annuum*, some cultivars of which have been bred to mimic the Jerusalem cherry. Care and propagation as for *Capsicum* (page 180).

Streptosolen jamesonii, to six feet, from Andean Colombia and Ecuador, can be grown outdoors in USDA zones 9 to 11. It is cultivated primarily as an indoor/outdoor container plant for its winter-spring show of orange bellflowers on pendant stems. When you succeed with this plant, it is a joy. Ideal for bringing to bloom in a greenhouse or plant room that is on the cool side in fall and winter, gradually warming up as spring arrives and with it the need for more watering and fertilizing. Care as for *Capsicum* (page 180). Propagate from cuttings in summer.

TACCACEAE. *Tacca Family*.

A family comprised of a single genus, *Tacca*, which contains ten species of rhizomatous or tuberous perennial herbs from the tropics of the Old World and South America.

Tacca chantrieri and *C. integrifolia*, both called bat flower, have leaves to two feet long and ten inches wide

Streptosolen jamesonii.

Tacca chantrieri *at Fuqua Conservatory, Atlanta Botanical Garden.*

Fertilize regularly in spring and summer, none in fall and winter. Propagate by division at repotting time in late winter or early spring, or by planting seeds at any season in a warm maxi light garden.

THEACEAE. *Tea Family.*

Tropical shrubs and trees, mostly evergreen, cultivated for their showy flowers. *Thea sinensis* furnishes the tea leaves of commerce. *Camellia* is treated at length on pages 221–222.

TILIACEAE. *Linden Family.*

Herbs, shrubs, and trees from many parts of the world cultivated for fiber, ornament, or timber. *Dombeya* and *Sparmannia* are of interest here.

Dombeya, to thirty feet, is seldom grown but makes quite an astounding houseplant for a sunny, warm garden in winter. A potted specimen of *Dombeya tilacea* four or five feet tall may even flower, yielding a large dangling mass of white or pale pink flowers redolent of ripe tropical

on a petiole to sixteen inches long, and the flowers, up to thirty, appear on a scape to two feet tall, green to brown-purple, held by bracts that are green to brown-purple, also with long, dangling, threadlike, white, greenish, purple to dark brown bracts among the flowers. They are sometimes grown in pots as a curiosity, the active season for growing and flowering being spring through summer. Give them a semisunny to semishady position, constant high humidity, and a humus-rich, loam-based potting soil kept evenly moist. Dry off and store at moderate temperatures (around 60°F) in winter.

fruit. *Dombeya wallichii* bears dark pink or red flowers in winter. Care and propagation as for *Sparmannia*.

Sparmannia africana (African hemp, parlor linden), ten to twenty feet, from South Africa, is a fast-growing, lustrous-stemmed plant which resembles a linden tree in foliage. The leaves are large, soft, hairy, pale green, and lightly lobed. There is also a variegated form having white-splashed leaves. Unless the roots are restricted the plant may become treelike, developing many trunks or main stems. The flowers, in late winter and spring, are white and held in terminal clusters, with petals reflexed to expose yellow filaments. Give it a sunny to semisunny location, average house temperatures, fresh, moist air, and a humus-rich, loam-based potting soil kept evenly moist. Prune back in early spring. Pot up as the roots fill each container, until the desired basic size is reached. Tip cuttings root readily in spring in warmth and high humidity.

Sparmannia africana 'V*ariegatus*'.

TURNERACEAE. *Turnera Family*.

One genus is of interest as a houseplant, *Turnera*.

Turnera ulmifolia angustifolia (sage rose, yellow alder), six to thirty inches, from tropical America, has elm-shaped leaves that are aromatic and violet-eyed yellow flowers that are quite showy; there is also a white form. It likes a sunny to semisunny situation or a maxi light garden, average house temperatures, fresh, moist air, and a humus-rich, loam-based potting soil kept evenly moist. Propagate from cuttings in late winter–spring.

URTICACEAE. *Nettle Family*.

Tropical as well as temperate herbs, shrubs, and trees differing remarkably in their growth habits and appearances. Some of the genera have stinging hairs, but not those cultivated as houseplants, *Pellionia* and *Pilea*.

Pellionia daveauana, from Burma, Malaya, and southern Vietnam, has close-set pairs of silvered leaves edged brownish purple, with pink creeping stems. *Pellionia pulchra*, from Vietnam, has oval leaves of light greenish gray netted with black or brown veins. Both are good candidates for indoor baskets or ground covers in large planters. Give them a semisunny to semishady location, average house temperatures, fresh, moist air, and a humus-rich, loam-based potting soil kept evenly moist. Make tip cuttings winter through spring.

Pilea cadieri (aluminum plant), twelve to eighteen inches, from Vietnam, and its variety *minima*, six to eight inches, are succulent, well-branched upright plants of bright green, quilted leaves that are silver-marked. *Pilea involucrata* (panamiga, South American friendship plant), six to twelve inches, from Peru, has oval, deeply quilted leaves that are coppery red-brown and hairy and at almost any time tiny green flowers held in clusters at the axils of terminal leaves. *Pilea microphylla*, from the West Indies, has much-branched, fleshy, semiupright stems covered with bright green leaves not more than a quarter-inch across. Its common name, artillery plant, refers to the way ripe pollen is forcibly ejected from the

Pilea involucrata.

Pilea 'Silver Tree'.

plant. This pilea is best renewed yearly from cuttings in winter or spring. *Pilea nummularifolia*, from the West Indies to Peru, is a creeping plant with small, round, slightly hairy leaves and a tendency for the stems to root at each node. It is called creeping Charley, but this is not the garden weed/plant *Nepeta hederacea* or *Glechoma hederacea* of the same common name. Give them a semi-sunny to semishady situation, average house temperatures, fresh, moist air, and a loam-based soil kept evenly moist. Make cuttings late winter through spring.

VERBENACEAE. *Verbena Family.*

Mostly tropical herbs, shrubs, trees, and woody vines cultivated for showy flowers. *Clerodendrum* and *Lantana* are discussed on pages 223 and 225.

VIOLACEAE. *Violet Family.*

About eight hundred different herbs—perennial, shrubs, rarely trees, climbers—that are widely distributed. One is of special interest as a houseplant.

Viola hederacea (Australian violet, ivy-leaved violet, trailing violet), from Australia, is a stemless, tufted, stolon-forming plant with reniform to spatulate leaves and a great showing of blue and white flowers in winter and spring. It likes a sunny to semisunny location, average house temperatures that are on the cool side in fall and winter, fresh, moist air, and a humus-rich, loam-based potting soil kept evenly moist. Grow as a hanging basket or use as a ground cover for a large container plant. The flowering stems will spill over the sides. The fragrant English violets, V. *odorata*, are of interest in this context only if you have a sun-heated pit greenhouse that is quite chilly in winter.

VITACEAE. *Grape Family.*

Mostly woody vines from temperate as well as tropical parts of the world. They climb by means of tendrils, and the genera grown indoors are cultivated for their handsome foliage. *Cissus, Parthenocissus,* and *Rhoicissus* are of interest here.

Viola hederacea.

Of all cissus, *Cissus discolor* is perhaps the aristocrat, with dark red vines and quilted angel-wing leaves that combine moss green, silver, and red-purple in a manner reminiscent of the rex begonia. This cissus needs more moisture, warmth, and humidity, in less direct sunlight than the others. Quite dramatically different is *C. quadrangularis*, from Arabia, tropical Africa, India, and Moluccas, a succulent with square, segmented stems, an occasional three-lobed leaf, and stout tendrils by which it climbs. This cissus can stand full sun, cool temperatures in winter (60° to 70°F), and needs only enough water to keep the succulent stems from shriveling. Otherwise, cissus in general need semisunny to semishady lighting, average house temperatures, and fresh, moist air. Pot in a humus-rich, loam-based soil, and keep evenly moist to slightly dry at the surface. Propagate from cuttings in late winter and spring.

Parthenocissus henryana (starry woodbine), a vine from China, has palmate leaflets, olive patterned white, violet on the reverses. It grows exuberantly as the days become longer but goes into a decline in autumn and is nearly completely dormant in winter. When grown outdoors in USDA zones 8 to 11, blue berries are formed.

Cissus is the name for members of the grape family known variously as grape ivy (*C. rhombifolia*), kangaroo vine (*C. antarctica*), and rex-begonia vine (*C. discolor*). My choice is less known, the pink cissus, *C. adenopoda*. New growth is bright pink, while older leaves are a glowing rose-burgundy when backlighted by the sun, which is the way you will see your plant from inside during the daytime. Even rarer is *C. rotundifolia*, round-leaved Arabian wax cissus, with bright green leaves. It can be unruly indoors unless trained to a twelve- to eighteen-inch wreath form. If you break one of these rounded succulent leaves it will smell exactly like a freshly opened bottle of cod liver oil. Miniature grape ivy, *C. striata*, combines reddish shoots with bronzy green palmate leaves and a compact habit. It makes a beautiful desktop plant, adapting nicely to life within the circle of brightest light cast by a desk lamp burned twelve to sixteen hours daily.

Cissus discolor.

Parthenocissus henryana *(wreath) with flowering* Scadoxus multiflorus *in C. Z. Guest's greenhouse.*

I grow this vine on a wreath in order to accommodate it in my warm closet light garden. It is also a trouper, albeit an elegant one, in the indoor/outdoor container gardens at C. Z. Guest's Templeton.

Rhoicissus capensis (Cape grape), from South Africa, is a tuberous-rooted vine having leaves to eight inches across, brownish and woolly on the undersides and bearing red berries. *Rhoicissus thunbergii* (cinnamon wheels) has leathery oval leaflets in sets of three, mahogany on the top, cinnamon beneath, on clambering stems; it is also tuberous-rooted. Treat as for *Cissus.* The felting on the leaves suggests a need for lots of sun.

ZINGIBERACEAE. *Ginger Family.*

Aromatic tropical herbs cultivated for ornament and flavoring. Genera of special interest here, principally for their beautiful foliage or flowers, are *Alpinia, Amomum, Costus, Curcuma, Hedychium, Kaempferia, Nicolai,* and *Zingiber.*

The prevalence of exotic cut gingers in local flower shops has created much interest in growing the plants at home. Two of the showiest are *Alpinia purpurata* (red ginger) from the Pacific Islands and *Nicolai elatior* (torch ginger) from the Celebes and Java. The cut flowers themselves often originate in Hawaii. By now you may be getting the idea that these are tropicals from exotic lands where in nature they have more space, fresh air, humidity, and sun than can be mustered in northern window gardens. They are, however, fairly commonly grown in greenhouses and conservatories around the world. For either of these plants you will need at least a bushel-basket-size container filled with sandy but humus-rich soil and air space above of four feet square by four feet tall. In the fall and winter as much full, direct sun will be needed as is possible, and some shade through the hottest weather in spring and summer. Red and torch gingers also need constant high humidity and air that circulates freely. *Alpinia speciosa variegata,* with yellow-striped and splashed leaves, is a durable houseplant. Water these gingers generously in warm weather, presumably spring and summer, but keep them a little on the dry side in fall and winter. Propagate by division at repotting time in late winter or early spring.

There are some smaller gingers that aren't as spectacular, but fascinating to grow in smaller indoor gardens.

Amomum cardamomum, to about two feet in cultivation, from Java, sends up lance-shaped leaves of dark green from a creeping rootstock. The foliage yields a spicy aroma when bruised and, when good care is given, the plant puts up conelike spikes of yellow flowers among the leaves in late summer and early fall. Give it a semisunny to semishady position, average house temperatures, fresh, moist air, and a humus-rich, loam-based potting soil kept evenly moist. Propagate by division at repotting time in late winter–spring.

Costus igneus (spiral ginger), to three feet, from Brazil, has bright, shiny green leaves stained red beneath, and red stems. Its three-inch flowers in spring and summer are brilliant orange, and open flat to display the ragged petal edges. Numerous other species are treasured house and greenhouse plants for their foliage that winds up the stems like a spiral staircase; some are variegated. Care and propagation as for *Amomum.*

Curcuma roscoeana, from Burma, is a robust perennial which grows from a tuberous rootstock. It is noted for having in summer and early fall large spikes of concave or hooded orange bracts from which the yellow flowers scarcely emerge. It prefers a sunny to semishady location, average house temperatures, and fresh, moist air. Pot in humus-rich, loam-based potting soil, and keep evenly moist spring and summer, nearly dry fall and winter. Propagate by dividing the tubers at repotting time in spring.

Hedychium species, known as ginger-lilies, are tropical plants which are very ornamental in both foliage and flower. Although many are too large for indoors, some have canes less than six feet tall, and thus can be managed in tubs or large pots where space permits. *Hedychium flavum*, to five feet, from the Indian Himalayas, has highly fragrant light-yellow blossoms in summer and long, slender, smooth leaves. *Hedychium greenei*, to six feet, from Bhutan, has red-stained, long, heavy leaves and brilliant red flowers in summer. They like a sunny to semisunny situation, average house temperatures, and fresh, moist air. Pot in humus-rich, loam-based soil, and

Kaempferia roscoeana.

keep evenly moist to wet, except nearly dry for a few weeks immediately after flowering finishes. Propagate by dividing the tubers at the beginning of a growing season.

Kaempferia decora, to one and a half feet, from East Africa, has cannalike foliage and primrose yellow flowers two inches across. It is one of the showiest of summer-blooming potted plants. *Kaempferia roscoeana*, to one foot, from Burma, is called peacock plant because of the iridescent bronze overlay on the foliage. It bears one-and-a-half-inch violet-shaped, lavender flowers all summer. There are several other kaempferias which are fascinating for houseplanting. They include *K. galanga* from India, *K. gilbertii* from southern Burma, *K. grandiflora* from Kenya, *K. involucrata* from Sikkim, Assam, and upper Burma, and *K. rotunda* from the Himalayas, India, and Sri Lanka. They all like a semisunny to semishady location, average house temperatures, and fresh, moist air. Pot them in humus-rich, loam-based soil, and keep evenly moist in spring and summer, nearly dry fall and winter. Propagate by division at repotting time in late winter–early spring.

Zingiber officinalis, to four feet, is the true ginger, native from India to the Pacific Islands. It has slender, reedlike stems and narrow, glossy leaves. *Zingiber zerumbet*, from India, larger and with broader leaves, is noted for its spikes or cones of bracts which resemble pinecones and turn red in the fall. Its variety *darceyi* is a rare form with white-and-green leaves margined in pink. Give them a sunny to semishady situation, average house temperatures, fresh, moist air, and a humus-rich, loam-based potting soil kept evenly moist. Propagate by division of the clumps in spring.

chapter five

Discipline Is Freedom—the Trained Houseplant

The idea that backs up the title of this chapter is that you will make one decision—the shape of the finished plant—and keep this firmly in your mind's eye from the beginning. Everything you do henceforth is working toward that goal. In this dis-cipline there is freedom for both gardener and plant. There are important psychological benefits here, as well, for often a gardener whose personal life is out of control—someone, for example, who is the primary caretaker for a spouse or parent who is terminally ill—can find release

in training plants. I know a woman who grew spectacular potted topiaries, espaliers, and tree-form standards in the years leading up to her husband's death from Alzheimer's disease. Now that she has become self-reliant and is more in control of her life, her gardening interests have shifted to free-form planting beds outdoors and collecting woody plants. More details about gaining hours of patience from minutes of gardening are included in a discussion at the end of this chapter.

THE TREE-FORM STANDARD

One way to sharpen your pleasure in gardening is to train a shrubby, sprawly, or viny plant into a tree form, a process that requires staking and tying, constant pinching, and, if the plant is indoors, giving it a quarter turn in the same direction each time you water to assure even light distribution and symmetrical habit. Obviously, all of this takes devotion: It would be easier to pot up something like a coleus, water it routinely, and wait for nature to turn it into a beautiful foliage plant. But if you want an enormously satisfying experience, take that same coleus cutting or seedling and follow these steps:

1) Set a single-stemmed seedling or cutting, with a healthy growing tip, in a five- or six-inch pot. Insert alongside the stem a bamboo stake equal in length to the height of trunk you want your tree to have,

A professional propagator who worked at Shady Hill Gardens, Batavia, Illinois, trained these geraniums during her lunch hours as a means of stress reduction. They are, left to right, low, bushy Pelargonium *'Madame Salleron', a matched pair of single head tree-form standard and a single double in the center of* P. *'Prince Rupert Variegated', a pair of double head* P. crispum, *and finally a bush of silver leaf rose,* P. graveolens *var.* variegatum.

plus a few extra inches to anchor it in the pot of soil—perhaps thirty to forty-two inches total for a coleus tree. Use twist ties or strips of plastic plant tie to secure the stem to the stake. To do this, loop the tie loosely around the stem, so as to allow room for it to expand as it grows, then attach the tie firmly to the stake. Add another tie after every three to six inches of stem.

The gardener is taking the first steps toward growing a tree-form standard, here the rose geranium, Pelargonium graveolens. *Start with a strong, single-stem plant. Keep pinching and tying. A finished tree can take two years.*

Tree-form standard dwarf geranium Pelargonium 'Red Brookes Barnes' *grows eighteen inches tall in about that many months of training from a rooted cutting. A desirable size can be maintained by an annual sharp pruning in spring.*

2) As the main stem increases in length, remove any lateral branches as they appear, using your fingers or a pair of tweezers. Allow the primary leaves along the stem to remain until they mature and drop off naturally. After the branches begin to form the head of the tree, remove any leaves that are still remaining along the trunk.

3) When the stem reaches the top of the stake, pinch out the growing tip. In its place, two branches will grow. When these have two or three sets of leaves, pinch out the growing tip of each. Repeat this process over and over. Transfer to a larger pot as necessary, both to accommodate the roots and to give enough weight to balance that of the tree's head.

Although I have suggested coleus because it is one of the easiest bushy plants to train into a tree, you can apply the same one-two-three procedures to an almost endless variety of foliage and flowering plants. Generally speaking, the kinds that grow rapidly or have large leaves are best suited to training as trees three to six feet tall. Small-leaved and slow-growing types may be trained as shorter trees, perhaps with trunks only twelve to eighteen inches tall.

Besides coleus, some of my choices for training into trees include almost all geraniums, especially those with scented leaves, flowering maple (abutilon), Chinese hibiscus, gardenia, lantana, fuchsia, jasmine, brugmansia angel trumpet, and tibouchina.

Among herbs I particularly enjoy working with myrtle, sweet bay, rosemary, and lemon verbena. Small-leaved basil is also fun, aiming for a finished tree about fifteen inches tall, including an eight-inch trunk.

Vining plants, whether trailers or climbers, can also be trained as trees, but they require a little more doing. Take English ivy, for example, one with small to medium-size leaves. Instead of planting only one stem in the pot and training it as the trunk, you can plant three together and slowly, over a period of months, braid them to the top of the stake. (This can also be done with plants having woody upright stems, such as the weeping ficus and Chinese hibiscus.) At this point, secure a globe formed of chicken wire and stuffed with moistened, unmilled sphagnum moss on top of the stake. As the ivy grows, pin it into the moss; mist twice daily. In time, the ivy will root into the moss and give its entire surface a leafy cover. You may at your discretion remove the lower leaves to reveal the braided trunk which, with age, will become woody, gnarled, and full of character.

Another way to tailor a vine into a tree is to train it as I have described for English ivy, but also to add some kind of wire frame (perhaps an inverted wire hanging basket) at the top of the stake onto which you can train and tie the branches. As a rule I provide a moss-filled frame for a plant that typically trails and forms roots at any point where the stem touches moist earth— English ivy, pothos, trileaf wonder (*Syngonium podophyllum*), some philodendrons—but only wire for things that are not stem-rooting like hoya, dipladenia, stephanotis, and bleeding-heart vine (*Clerodendrum*).

My last suggestion for turning a vine into a tree is based on the training frames my gardening friend C. Z.

saw being used one summer in Newport and subsequently had fabricated for her own garden. Each of these is made of galvanized piping (which she has painted very dark green) and looks for all practical purposes like the driving wheel and steering column of an automobile. The column, with a circular plate welded to the bottom, is set in a large pot which is then filled with soil. Rooted cuttings of the vine are set around the base and trained up the column until finally they ascend between the spaces in the "steering wheel" and soon begin cascading all around. This technique works exceptionally well for orangeglow vine (*Senecio confusus*), a variety of jasmines such as *Jasminum polyanthum* and *J. tortuosum*, and almost any of the passifloras.

These triple rosemary topiaries each began several years before as a single rooted cutting of Rosmarinus officinalis. *They are in training at Logee's Danielson, Connecticut, greenhouses, spending summers outdoors and any freezing weather in a frost-free, solar-heated greenhouse.*

ESPALIER HOUSEPLANTS

Gardening on the vertical is a centuries-old practice you can be put to work indoors and out with all kinds of plants in containers. Use it to grow more in less space; to bring beauty in an unexpected place; as a stylish horticultural design element; or even to harvest more fruit earlier in a cold climate. A desire to grow fruit toward or beyond its northern limits is actually why the Europeans first trained trees with their branches flattened against south-facing walls. From this came the espalier (ess-PAL-yur or ess-PAL-yay), meaning a plant with height and width but very little depth.

Espaliers have been traditionally ground-planted fruit-bearing or ornamental trees or shrubs, but there is no reason not to borrow the pruning and training techniques for houseplants, outdoor container gardens, vines, herbs, even tomatoes. By inserting a suitable frame in a container, you can grow an espalier that can be kept indoors all year, or outdoors in warm weather.

Most classic espalier designs begin with a plant that has one main stem. At the point where branching is desired, cut off the top. Tie new growth that conforms

*'Prince Rupert Variegated' pelargonium is also called
'French Lace'. The branches of this favorite lemon geranium are pliable enough to espalier in any of the traditional patterns used for training fruit trees. The form used
is wire hardware cloth, anchored upright with bamboo
stakes.*

to the design to the trellis or frame. Continue tying desired growth and removing the rest while it is as young
as possible. After weeks or months the espalier will begin
to take form.

Espalier supports can be made of No. 9 or No. 12
galvanized wire for the frames, with No. 18 wire for the
joints. It is also possible to make them of redwood strips
or laths, bamboo plant stakes, or dead tree or shrub
branches pruned smooth; depending on the material,
secure the joints with screws, nails, staples, pieces of dark
green plastic, or strips of raffia.

Once the basic framework or trellis is completed and
anchored in a suitable container, all you have to do is
add a young plant with pliable stems, remove the unnecessary branches, and retain those that adapt to the
design. The design and strength of the support depend
on that of the plant you wish to train on it. A bamboo
frame can be made of smaller-size stakes for perhaps a
four- or six-inch pot, or of a larger size for a container
eight inches or more in diameter. On the smaller frame

you might train small-leaved English ivy or 'Prince Rupert Variegated' lemon geranium, on the larger, a variety
of English ivy or scented geranium having large leaves.

A trellis with closely spaced laths in a diagonal pattern
offers great freedom for creating living plant designs—
any classic espalier. It is also possible to use a piece of
quarter- or half-inch wire hardware cloth as an espalier
support. When the plant has grown into the desired
shape, use wirecutters to remove the excess wire backing.
This works well for miniature English ivy, creeping fig,
and most small-leaved geraniums.

The simplest espalier is the wreath or circle, shaped
from a wire clothes hanger, grape, or bittersweet vines,
or almost what-have-you? Use this system for open or
outline designs as well, such as a heart, a star, or an
animal—rabbits, cats, and dogs in profile being three
popular choices. Almost any plant having sufficiently
pliable stems can be trained as a wreath. Some likely

Firecracker vine (Manettia inflata) *twines nimbly around
a twelve-inch wreath form anchored upright in a six-inch
pot. This member of the Rubiaceae, from Paraguay and
Uruguay, flowers nearly every day of the year and in less
sun than many such plants.*

possibilities are asarina, manettia, morning glory (*Ipomoea*), thunbergia, passiflora, stephanotis, bougainvillea, scindapsus or pothos, *Hedera helix* ivies, *Jasminum tortuosum*, *Parthenocissus henryana*, *Cissus adenopoda*, and prostrate rosemary.

The *Hedera helix* ivies, available in a seemingly endless number of varieties, many having leaves that are noticeably variegated gold, white, or silver, seem made in horticultural heaven for training into the classic wreath shape. Success and pleasure in this venture depend first on growing healthy ivy, otherwise spider mites, mealybugs, and brown scale will spoil everything. Water and light are the key ingredients. Here's a system that works for me:

1) Feel the soil in each pot or hanging basket. Keep in touch. When your fingers feel a condition that could be described as "barely damp" or "approaching dryness," water generously. One hour later pour off any excess that still stands in the saucer. Ivies grown consistently too dry almost invariably fall prey to spider mites.

2) Shower the leaves clean, top and especially the bottom sides, using a fairly strong spray of lukewarm water. If you do this once each week the leaves will be dust-free and much less likely to host mites.

3) Each week after you shower English ivy, set it aside to drain. When dry, spray with rubbing alcohol, again being sure to wet all leaf surfaces as well as the leaf stems and vines. This discourages insects from getting established and leaves the ivy with a natural sheen. Spray only in a well-ventilated place, away from open flames and out of direct sun.

This three-step system is really designed to favor the needs of the ivy instead of the opportunistic insect predators. Presuming the light is strong enough in the daytime to read by, and the temperatures are in a range for human comfort, this simple, direct—and safe—routine will encourage long-lasting individual leaves that show an attractive sheen.

It also helps, of course, if the ivy is potted in an appropriate mix. I combine two parts well-rotted leaf mold or compost to one each of garden loam and clean, sharp sand. Regular fertilizer boosts growth, either fish emulsion, liquid seaweed, or a timed-release pellet such as 14-14-14. Ivy grows best indoors in half-shady to half-sunny situations where temperatures range from 60° to 75°F, in combination with lots of fresh air circulation. Weak light is the chief cause of color loss in the variegated varieties, although some such as 'Gold Heart' are more unstable and may revert to all-green even under the best of conditions.

Another plant that gives me a lot of pleasure when it is trained as a wreath is the 'Heavenly Blue' morning glory, which will perform amazingly well in any sunny window, with first blooms possible in only two months from sowing seeds. Here is the procedure:

1) Sow five seeds one half inch deep in a six-inch pot filled with all-purpose potting mix.

Varieties of Hedera helix *having small to medium-size leaves are best suited to training as topiaries. Use a purchased or homemade form. Keep the moss moist and the ivy will root into it. Other plants adapted to this treatment include the creeping figs and baby's-tears.*

2) When seedlings are up and the first true leaves begin to unfold, thin out, leaving only two or three.

3) From the time you sow the seeds, be sure to keep the soil nicely moist to the touch. If the roots become so thirsty that the leaves wilt, future growth will be thwarted and subject to spider mite attack.

4) By the time morning glories are a few weeks old, some kind of trellis is needed around which the stems can twine. Besides a circle of wire or grapevine, some possibilities are string, bamboo stakes, or twiggy growth pruned from outdoor trees or shrubs.

5) Position potted morning glories in the sunniest window garden possible where temperatures range from moderate to warm, 55° to 75°F. Fertilize regularly, using a blossom-booster formula such as 15-30-15. Fresh air circulation is important to encourage stocky growth and to discourage spider mites.

6) In the event morning glory leaves take on yellow or grayish flecking, spider mites are likely the cause. Mist the leaf undersides with rubbing alcohol every three days; apply this treatment only at night or in the cool of the day, not when the sun is shining on the plants. Promptly pick off any brown or discolored foliage.

M O R E   W A Y S   T O   T R A I N   H O U S E P L A N T S

Window frame. To border a window with twiners and climbers, outline the window with string, holding it in place with thumbtacks or small nails. Help the plants take hold by tying them loosely to the string support with additional string or twist ties. Possible subjects for this treatment when an abundance of sunlight is available are bleeding-heart vine *(Clerodendrum)*, bougainvillea, hoya, *Jasminum tortuosum*, mandevilla, morning glory *(Ipomoea)*, climbing nasturtium, passiflora, stephanotis, and black-eyed-Susan thunbergia. Vines adaptable to less

sun include cissus (the kangaroo vine *Cissus antarctica* and pink *C. adenopoda*), creeping fig, *Hedera helix* ivies, vining philodendron, and scindapsus and epipremnum (pothos).

Hanging basket. For beautiful baskets with full growth all around, hang them from swivel hooks so you can give the plants a quarter turn (always in the same direction) each time you water. Bend stiff branches into graceful cascades by tying lead fishing weights to the tips. In half sun to half shade you can grow trailing African violet, baby's-tears, begonias like 'Orange Rubra' and 'Wayne Newton', flame violet episcia, rabbit's-foot fern davallia and staghorn platycerium, phalaenopsis orchid, *Oxalis rubra*, a variety of peperomias, strawberry geranium saxifraga, and Cape primrose streptocarpus (especially the streptocarpella types). Possible plants for abundant sun include asparagus fern, bougainvillea, bromeliads, burro's-tail sedum, holiday cactus, coleus, columnea, apple-, nutmeg-, and allspice-scented geraniums, ivy geranium, hoya, lipstick vine, manettia, morning glory, nematanthus, passiflora, plumbago, purple passion gynura, rhipsalis, rosary vine, prostrate rosemary, miniature hanging rose, Swedish ivy, Tahitian bridal-veil, and wandering Jew. For shady conditions consider baby's-tears, grape ivy cissus, creeping fig, fittonia, *Hedera helix* ivies, Kenilworth ivy cymbalaria, pellionia, vining philodendron, piggyback tolmiea, pilea, and scindapsus and epipremnum (pothos).

Watering hanging baskets indoors takes special care, otherwise they will become too dry or the excess will spill onto furnishings and the floor. Determining the need for water is perhaps most reliably done by touching and pinching some of the surface soil with our fingers. Don't wait until leaves and blossoms are visibly wilted. Commercial hanging containers usually come with a saucer attached. If this is not provided or is in any way ineffectual, watering well without troublesome spillovers requires removing the container, dipping in a pail of water, soaking, then draining before returning to the hanging position.

Hanging gardens of Babylon. Envision a series of terraced plantings, just like the original "wonder of the

BONSAI AND PENJING: FAR EASTERN INFLUENCE

Green or dried twigs with pliability can be turned into to-piary and espalier frames like this one for sweet peas at the Chelsea Flower Show. Raffia and dried leaves from Beaucarnea recurvata *are examples of natural, durable tie materials; strips of green plastic or twist ties can also be used. Photograph by William C. Mulligan.*

world." Stack three or more soil-filled pots in successively smaller sizes, such as eight, six, and four inches. Fill with a small creeper such as baby's-tears or creeping fig, whose stems will spill down over the sides of the pots as they grow. (Unglazed clay pots are recommended.)

When bonsai were first displayed by the Japanese in London at the beginning of the twentieth century, they were dismayed to discover that the English saw tortured plants, not the epitome of worshiping nature through a living work of art. Moreover, when the Japanese bonsai masters ventured into English gardens they saw trees coppiced, pleached, pollarded, and espaliered, apparent Western ideas of plant torture. I like to think we have made some small progress in understanding Eastern and Western cultures in the last hundred years, at least "horticultures." Nevertheless, I have learned that my personal bent (no pun intended) is for the Western ways of training and that to understand the Eastern takes a different mindset. For a number of years the person who has been my interpreter in horticultural matters of the Far East has been Memphis gardener Bonny Martin, who with her very supportive husband, David, has one of the finest bonsai collections I have seen. Here in a greatly pared down version is Bonny's credo for bonsai:

Bonsai, pronounced bone-sigh with no particular emphasis on either syllable, translated literally means "tray planting." It originated centuries ago in Japan and before that in China as "penjing." It is the art of keeping a tree or shrub dwarfed by confining it to a small pot. Horticulturally, it is among the highest of art forms, blending artistic ability and horticultural expertise. Controlling the size of any bonsai is done by pruning the roots and branches at the time of planting. All its life it will be periodically unpotted, root-pruned, and repotted with additional soil to retain its size and shape. It will also demand constant pruning and pinching of new growth.

These plants are basically outdoor in nature, although bonsai can be done with tropicals and kept indoors all year. But even the hardy kinds of temperate climates must have protection when temperatures drop below 28°F, and must be shielded from wind and continuous freezing and thawing. Water is an important factor in growing bonsai. They must never be allowed to dry out; it will kill them

One bonsai has a way of leading to a collection, which spends summers outdoors on concrete-block supported shelves and winters in a cold greenhouse, 28°F minimum, as here at the home of Mr. and Mrs. David B. Martin in Memphis. Such an arrangement serves the needs of the temperate climate plants that have been traditionally trained as bonsai. Since World War II the idea has been expanded to include plants from the tropics so that the art can be practiced all year indoors.

instantly. In most places, this means watering them every day in the summer. If your soil mix is correct, they will never be overwatered.

There are five basic styles of bonsai: formal upright, informal upright, slanting, cascade, and semicascade. There are variations to these basic styles including forest and clump.

Bonsai pots come in all sizes and shapes. Each tree is styled and shaped and a bonsai pot is selected for that individual. The pots are unglazed inside and have large drainage holes which are covered with one-eighth-inch hardware cloth cut slightly larger than the holes and wired in place. This keeps the slugs from coming into the pot and the soil from washing out. Unglazed pots in brown, gray, or terra-cotta are generally used for evergreens while glazed pots are used for deciduous trees. The length of the pot should be approximately two thirds the height of the tree. Straight trunks are better in a rectangular pot while curved trunks look better in round or oval pots. Cascade pots are considerably taller than they are wide.

Always use new clean soil for bonsai. A good average mix is equal parts commercial potting soil (pasteurized),

peat moss, and a large to medium type aggregate (coarse sand, tiny pebbles, or finely crushed gravel). A rule of thumb is that the same amount of roots and foliage should be removed. Leave the small hairlike surface roots on the ball. Loosen the root ball and rake away most of the soil; then cut off one fourth, one third, or one half the root system, depending on how much has been cut off the top of the tree. If it has a taproot, cut it out and also remove old clumps of soil under the root. Place soil in the bottom of the container and fit in the tree, cutting the root to the size and shape of the pot. Straighten all the roots and finish potting, making certain there is soil under and around all the roots, with no air pockets. Use a chopstick or pencil to achieve this. The plant should be tied down with a long length of wire going through the bottom drainage holes and around the plant to secure it. Place the bonsai in a tub of water or sink filled to the brim of the container. When the soil is entirely wet, remove and place in a semishaded area for a week to ten days. Do not fertilize for a month or two. If new growth appears, pinch back continually. The plant should eventually be placed in full sun and watered daily. If the sun gets too hot, filtered sun is favored. Fertilize with bonsai fertilizer or any organic.

Some classic plants used as bonsai are:

EVERGREEN

Azalea, 'Satsuki' *(Rhododendron)*
Boxwood *(Buxus)*
Camellia
Cedar *(Cedrus)*
Chamaecyparis
Firethorn *(Pyracantha)*
Holly, Japanese *(Ilex crenata)*
Juniper, Japanese *(Juniperus rigida nipponica)*
Juniper, 'San Jose' *(J. chinensis* cv.*)*
Juniper, 'Shimpaku' *(J. chinensis* cv.*)*
Pine, five-needle *(Pinus)*
Pine, Japanese black *(P. thunbergii)*
Podocarpus
Spruce, dwarf Alberta *(Picea glauca* 'Albertiana Conica'*)*
Spruce, Norway *(P. abies)*

DECIDUOUS

Apricot, flowering (*Prunus mume*)
Barberry (*Berberis*)
Beech (*Fagus*)
Cotoneaster
Crab apple (*Malus*, any small-fruited species)
Cypress, bald (*Taxodium distichum*)
Elm (*Ulmus*)
Ginkgo (*Ginkgo biloba*)
Hackberry (*Celtis*)
Hawthorn (*Crataegus*)
Hornbeam (*Carpinus*)
Maple, Japanese (*Acer palmatum*)
Maple, red (*A. rubrum*)
Maple, Trident (*A. buergeranum*)
Oak (*Quercus*)
Privet (*Ligustrum*)
Quince, flowering (*Chaenomeles*)
Sweet gum (*Liquidambar styraciflua*)
Wisteria
Zelkova

INDOOR BONSAI

The Brooklyn Botanic Garden has pioneered the idea that classic bonsai training techniques can be applied to woody plants native to the tropics and subtropics as well as to those from temperate parts of the world. More recently the Indoor Gardening Society has given specific recommendations, including the following list of recommended subjects for sunny windows or maxi light gardens, from a newsletter issued by the Windy City (Chicago) Chapter of IGS:

Bucida spinosa (dwarf black olive). Shapes easily. Keep moist.

Buxus 'Kingsville' (Kingsville dwarf box). Outstanding for bonsai work.

Calliandra emarginata (powder puff). A good bloomer in sunlight.

Carissa grandiflora (Natal plum). Good-size foliage and fragrant flowers if grown in sun. Fruit is showy—and edible.

Cuphea hyssopifolia (false heather). Another bloomer in adequate light and readily trainable.

Eugenia uniflora (Surinam cherry). New foliage is red. Good light is needed for flowers and edible fruit.

Ficus benjamina (weeping fig). Readily available and stands pruning well. Excellent for practice.

Ficus retusa nitida (Banyan tree). A mini rubber tree.

Fortunella spp. (kumquat). A citrus with small orange fruits and fragrant flowers. Can be exceptionally showy in fruit.

Ilex vomitoria (yaupon holly). A species that can be grown indoors.

Lagerstroemia indica (crape myrtle). Flowers in bright light. Tolerates heavy pruning. Defoliates during short days of the year.

Ligustrum japonicum (Japanese privet). Another commonly available plant that is helpful for practice.

L. lucidum (glossy privet). Shiny foliage and fragrant flowers.

Lonicera nitida (box honeysuckle). Refined foliage and white flowers.

Malpighia coccigera (Singapore holly). Hollylike foliage, crepe-textured flower petals.

Olea europaea (olive). The true olive. Silvery green leaves. Makes wonderful romanticized tree.

Psidium cattleianum (strawberry guava). Likes water but not sopping wet.

Punica granatum nana (dwarf pomegranate). Needs humidity and cool temperatures in winter, lots of sun, and fresh air in summer. Beautiful flowers and showy, long-lasting fruit.

Serissa foetida. Many cultivars having white, pink, or lavender flowers, and various leaf variegations. Blooms in winter and can be likened to a quite miniature gardenia, to which it is related. (See also more extensive discussion following.)

Ulmus parvifolia sempervirens. An evergreen elm that can be managed indoors if kept cool in winter.

SERISSA BONSAI FOR HOUSE GARDENING

Serissas are naturally dwarf, bonsailike shrublets having small, rounded, evergreen, or variegated leaves and white or pink flowers, single or double, the latter resembling tiny gardenias.

While many of the plants we grow indoors have periods of dormancy or stand half resting for months at a time, the serissas are both evergrowing and everblooming, with peak blossoming in winter and spring. They are excellent for half-sunny windows and a few inches beneath the tubes in fluorescent-light gardens. Serissas are also growable outdoors in the Sun Belt, to 27°F, but seem best suited to intensive container gardening; otherwise such diminutive plants tend to get lost.

At least seven distinctive serissas presently in commerce are apparently derived from one species that hails from Southeast Asia, *Serissa foetida*. When the leaves are bruised or wayward branches clipped back, the specific name makes sense (and scents): There is a slightly offensive odor, but nothing to detract seriously from its charms.

If you have ever wanted to try your hand at bonsai, I can't imagine a better beginning plant than serissa, particularly 'Cherry Blossom', 'Kyoto', and 'Sapporo', all of which have compact habits by nature. If you grow one of these well, establish it in a small oriental pot, and keep any dead twigs clipped, the nearly automatic response will be a picturesque little tree.

Caring for a new bonsai. Many gardeners begin by purchasing a bonsai tree that is already established, or they receive one as a gift. Until you become acquainted with such a plant, avoid subjecting it to any extremes of light, temperature, or moisture. The first thing you need to know is the name of the plant so that its more precise cultural requirements can be looked up in a book. The second consideration is to be sure the growing medium and roots never dry out severely. Conifers—needle evergreens—are highly vulnerable to drying; any branches or needles that die prematurely will never grow back.

HOURS OF PATIENCE FROM MINUTES OF GARDENING

Gardening in general is a therapeutic activity but it is in the realm of plant training indoors that I have per-

sonally been the beneficiary and have observed others as well. The next time life demands the payment of more patience than you think you can negotiate, try this: Plant some seeds. Divide and repot. Begin one or more plant training projects. The idea is to reach out and embrace life: Take a sturdy cutting—or maybe one that isn't so sturdy—a rooted cutting, or any youthful plant that needs a home—and give it your best.

Since an embrace begins by reaching out, this gesture also suggests other ways to turn minutes of gardening into hours of patience:

1) Give some transplants to others who can benefit from the therapy inherent in plant parenthood.

2) Read everything you can get your hands on about an unfamiliar plant. This could be the one you just brought home, or something on order that will be at your door the minute weather permits shipping.

3) Bring order to some part of your life that is in disarray. Gardeners usually have pots and seed trays to clean and stack, not to mention a rat's nest, or at least a mouse's, of miscellany—stakes, ties, labels, fertilizers, and so on.

4) When there is nothing to do but be patient, an effective way to deal with the situation is not to think. Be busy—and thankful—for productive tasks; discipline your mind to concentrate on what you are doing. A lot of anguish can be scrubbed away while cleaning pots.

5) The need for extreme patience isn't necessarily short-term; its length may be measured in minutes, hours, days, months, or years. The more completely we let go and make the most of this very moment, the more successfully we generate patience. An involvement with plants—as with music or art or working with special children or adults—is a beneficial habit that can effectively dissipate anxiety.

chapter six

The Edible Houseplant

The point of growing a houseplant that can be eaten is not so much to reduce the food bills but to provide something that probably couldn't be purchased, or to produce a plant that is itself beautiful and fun to grow even if it were not among the edibles.

SPROUTS EVERYONE CAN GROW

The whole process of growing sprouts is uplifting and it's one kind of house gardening that doesn't depend on strong light. Sprouts are living food, vegetables vital to health and a sense of well-being. Sprouts let us be involved every day in the miracles of planting seeds without needing greenhouses or fields to accommodate the maturing seedlings.

The benefits of sprouts in salads, sandwiches, soups, homemade whole-grain breads, and stir-fry cooking are well known. They can also be eaten out of hand, a pick-me-up that won't let you down. Less known is that some individuals live on a sprout-centered diet, consuming six cups a day and more. There are lots of gardeners and farmers who can grow that quantity of vegetable matter

Edible wheat and bean sprouts make beautiful house gardens in petri dishes for cookbook creator James McNair.

outdoors all or a part of the year. A very few have greenhouses or other controlled environments to afford all-season production. But only in sprouts do we find a producible crop accessible to just about every living human—every day of the year.

Sprouts aren't all mung beans and alfalfa either. I have seen a chart in health-food stores that lists upwards of forty different kinds. As to practical how-to, here are the instructions from a packet of alfalfa seeds sold for sprouting by Erewhon, Inc., and purchased at a neighborhood health-food store:

"Wash ¼ cup alfalfa seeds and soak overnight. Drain off the water (use in cooking or to water a houseplant), put the seeds in a tea strainer, and set in a tea cup, cover loosely with a saucer. Keep sprouts moist in a warm, dark place. Sprouts will be ready to eat in three days. Yield: about 2 cups."

The method I have used is to put the soaked and rinsed seeds in a jar with a screw ring holding in place a piece of cheesecloth. This facilitates rinsing twice or more daily with fresh water. The rinsing oxygenates the germinating seeds and prevents the onset of fermentation. I have particularly enjoyed sprouting radish and mustard seeds. The sprouts have a peppery taste that gives a welcome kick to winter salads and sandwiches.

Edible flowers are another crop for the indoor gardener, the names of which I will list if you promise never to eat any flower unless you know for sure that it is not poisonous, either inherently or because it has been sprayed with a toxic pesticide. Some possibilities are begonias, calendulas or pot-marigolds, chrysanthemums, citrus blossoms, geraniums (species and varieties of *Pelargonium*), nasturtiums, roses, and tulips.

VEGETABLE HOUSEPLANTS

Not many vegetables are suited to growing as houseplants, although a cool place that receives plenty of sun or fluorescent light can be appropriated for growing leaf lettuce or the various salad crops that are mixed and offered as mesclun. Watercress will grow nicely in a large clay bulb pan or azalea pot that can be kept standing in a fairly deep saucer of water; it also needs cool temperatures and fresh, moist air circulation.

New Zealand spinach and Malabar spinach are vegetable leaf crops that may be attempted in the warm house garden. Both constitute attractive foliage plants. New Zealand spinach (*Tetragonia tetragonioides*) may be grown in a pot or hanging basket. Malabar spinach (*Basella alba* and the red-stemmed cultivar 'Rubra') is a vigorous vine that needs a bamboo stake tepee three or four feet tall, or try it as a fifteen-inch wreath.

Though most gardeners start tomato seeds indoors, a relative minuscule number actually grow fruiting tomato houseplants. It is possible, if appropriate cultivars are chosen and you are prepared to provide the necessary long-light days and warm daytime temperatures. At northern latitudes tomatoes make little progress during the darkest, shortest days of the year unless they are placed in a maxi light garden. The rest that I have to say about growing tomatoes indoors also applies to those planted in containers outdoors:

Look for determinate tomato cultivars that have been bred to perform well in small quarters. Two are 'Red Robin' (sweet cherry tomatoes on eight- to twelve-inch bushes) and 'Goldie Hybrid' (golden yellow "cherry" tomatoes on fourteen-inch bushes). Both of these bear over a long season and can be readily managed in any container gardening situation, indoors or out, where every inch of space counts.

Each dwarf cherry tomato plant needs a five-inch pot of soil or the equivalent in a community planting. Use an all-purpose potting mix that includes well-rotted compost. If whiteflies are detected, spray with insecticidal soap, working in the coolest part of the day when the insects are least active. Work gently and quietly so as not to disturb them. They cluster mostly on the leaf undersides. Spray every five to seven days until the flies are gone (which may be at the end of the tomato season).

If potted tomatoes dry out repeatedly between waterings the older leaves will shrivel and die prematurely, thus weakening the plant and making it all the more vulnerable to whiteflies and spider mites. Relatively small containers dry out quickly, especially outdoors in summer, and will require daily watering. This practice rapidly flushes away the nutrients, so it pays to fertilize at half the usual strength once a week.

FRUITING HOUSEPLANTS

Apart from an occasional strawberry from a pot of the runnerless *fraises des bois* type or those sold in seed packets such as 'Baron Solemacher', the citrus offer far and away the most rewarding houseplants that bear edible and showy fruits. Dwarf citrus offer glossy, dark, evergreen foliage; waxy, white, fragrant flowers; highly decorative, edible fruit. What more could a gardener want for a house garden?

The Ponderosa lemon makes the most spectacular show. Usually at least one lemon is on each plant at some stage of its maturity. By harvest, the golden fruit may weigh as much as two pounds, yet the plant on which it is growing may be hardly more than a foot tall. The Meyer lemon bears fruit similar to the size sold for eating and this ripens throughout the year. Like other citrus, the colors of the fruits at various stages of maturity are all beautiful.

The miniature orange or calamondin has become one of the popular commercial houseplants, readily obtain-

The calamondin of commerce, × Citrofortunella mitis, *fruits prodigiously and is often most colorful in the fall and winter. Here it chums with* Tropaeloum majus, *the edible nasturtium flower, in Zelma Clark's Westchester County, New York, home greenhouse.*

Ponderosa lemon is a naturally dwarf-growing citrus that produces relatively enormous edible fruits. The small trees have an affinity for large terra-cotta pots.

able from local and mail-order sources. The abundance of sweet white flowers on and off during the year is followed by small oranges that will practically cover a well-grown plant. They are too tart to eat raw, but their juice can be used for orangeade or in the making of marmalade. Another dwarf orange is the Otaheite, with plum-size, bright orange fruit and limelike juice.

There are also dwarf limes, tangerines or Mandarin oranges, and kumquats.

Dwarf citrus need full sun for as many hours as possible, at least half a day, in fall and winter. Partial shade is acceptable in spring and summer, but full sun all year is best. Young plants will thrive in a maxi light garden until they become too tall.

More specific care is given with the main discussion of citrus on page 176. Sometimes citrus foliage turns yellow and drops from the plant for no apparent reason. If this happens, be sure you are not over- or underwatering. Also, the soil may not be sufficiently acidic if you live in an area where the water is quite alkaline; in this case, water about twice yearly with a chelated iron product (available at the local nursery or garden center).

To assure pollination indoors, some growers use a camel's-hair brush to transfer citrus pollen from the anthers to the sticky pistil of the bloom. This can also be done by shaking the flower-filled branches at noontime on a sunny day, when the pollen is driest. There is no need for hand pollination if the plant is flowering outdoors.

A popular way to acquire citrus plants for container gardening is to plant the seeds collected from ripe fruit: orange, lemon, lime, tangerine, grapefruit, tangelo, kumquat. Rinse the seeds with water, then blot dry in a dish towel. Fill a good-size pot or bulb pan with a humus-rich, loam-based potting soil. Level the surface and scatter the seeds about an inch apart. Cover the seeds with a half inch of soil and press lightly in place with your fingers. Keep warm and moist in a sunny place or maxi light garden. Fresh seeds removed from fruit that was fairly ripe at the time it was picked give the best germination, in a couple of weeks.

Citrus seedlings make handsome foliage plants from the beginning, but the flowers may not appear for several years. The chances for quality fruit are slim. However, citrus seeds are definitely a source of no-cost plants that can be enjoyed as shrubs, trained into large trees, or dwarfed as bonsai.

HERBS for HOUSE GARDENING

Of all the herbs that can be grown indoors, basil is my all-time favorite. Bostonian Bessie Raymond Buxton in her book *The Window Garden*, published in 1936 by Orange Judd, observed, "The Greeks treasure and revere the basil, or Basilico, as they call it, *Ocimum basilicum*. Its use is so universal that if you see a pot or tub of basil at the window or on the steps, you may be quite sure that the house owner is a Greek." Funny, in my expe-

rience I'd have said Italian, but, come to think of it, the foremost expert I know on the subject happens to be a Polish-American, Marilyn Hampstead, the founder of Fox Hill Farm in Parma, Michigan, and author of *The Basil Book* (Long Shadow Books/Pocket Books/Simon & Schuster, Inc., New York, 1984). My interest in basil has grown steadily since the introduction of 'Dark Opal' in the 1950s and while this purple-leaved cultivar developed at the University of Connecticut has never grown particularly well for me, I do appreciate its distinct peppery flavor. Picked from the plant and chopped directly onto a hot baked potato, 'Dark Opal' can hardly be topped. (I have just consumed two baked potatoes that were first split open, fluffed with a fork and then topped with enough freshly cut 'Dwarf Bush' basil from my closet light garden to make the surface nearly solid green. Herbalists have taught for centuries that basil is beneficial to the upper respiratory system. Living in a city as I do seems to mandate eating lots of fresh basil.)

Thanks to Hampstead and others, there are now in cultivation at least two dozen varieties of basil, including those known as sweet, French fine leaf, lettuce leaf, the previously mentioned 'Dark Opal', 'Piccolo Verde Fino', lemon, *thrysiflora*, 'Nano Compatto Vero', 'Camphor', 'Licorice', 'Cinnamon', bush, "Tulasi" holy, and 'Genovese'. There is also African (noteworthy for its rosy purple stems and flower spikes, also small-leaved and suitable for indoors), 'Purple Ruffles', 'Green Ruffles', and 'Green Bouquet'. 'Spicy Globe', a recently popular cultivar with very small leaves and base-branching habit, has at this writing been sent back to the breeder for correction of "genetic drift."

I have noticed that wherever basils are grown in quantity with an abundance of sunlight and warmth, there seems to be a purple-leaved form of nearly all varieties, and some are green with purple splashings or vice versa.

The ideal place for growing basil during the fall and winter is about six inches directly beneath the tubes in a warm fluorescent-light garden where temperatures range from 65° to 80°F and sixteen-hour days can be maintained during even the shortest days and darkest weather of the year. A warm window garden is next best,

The hedge around a clump of miniature Narcissus *in C. Z. Guest's Long Island garden is 'Spicy Globe' basil, a naturally base-branching dwarf plant that grows into a ball shape. It can be sheared on occasion and the clippings eaten.*

with direct sun rays, weak though they may be, for several hours daily.

Small-leaved basils are best suited to indoor pot culture. I have kept some individual plants for several years by once or twice annual root pruning and repotting into fresh soil and by rigorously pruning the tops, both to use the leaves to eat and to train a strong plant. It is even possible to train twelve- to eighteen-inch tree-form standards, but only from the smaller-leaved sorts that are not insistently base-branching.

Basil comes with whiteflies—or didn't you know?—but these can be controlled by spraying weekly with insecticidal soap. (Before eating basil that has been sprayed with soap, rinse it lightly in tepid water.) Yellow sticky traps in the vicinity of the basil are also a helpful diversionary tactic. I once tried growing cherry tomatoes in pots along with the basil. Everything was going great until whiteflies found the picnic. What I learned is that they showed an overwhelming preference for the tomatoes—

which got quietly sacked in the cool of the night when whiteflies are least alert. Oh well, the Koreans around the corner have nice cherry and pear tomatoes from Holland or Israel every day of the year, sans whiteflies of course. I can usually provide the basil.

Rosemary has been often in my apartment garden, in various stages, from rooted cuttings to stylish eighteen-inch topiaries. Alas, the latter died suddenly, first one then the other, leaving me to wonder if I had somehow grossly mistreated them, unwittingly drowning, dehydrating, or overfertilizing. I have lately read that prostrate rosemary, *Rosmarinus officinalis* 'Prostratus', is one of the better choices for growing indoors. It works especially well for hanging in a window or cascading from a shelf, also for training in a variety of ways. I like to train young rooted cuttings into five- or six-inch wreaths, each anchored and rooted in a five-inch clay pot. These grow nicely in one season and, tied with a small bow, make welcome gifts.

Young herb plants can become a portable garden when they are combined in a single container such as this plastic bonsai tray. Included are sweet bay, chives, 'Dark Opal' basil, parsley, golden sage, and lemon thyme.

There are several mistakes made with rosemary, including 1) expecting it to live, if not forever, at least indefinitely; 2) having once lost a rosemary, never trying again; and 3) watering haphazardly, especially until soggy in cool winter conditions or waiting until it is bone-dry in summery heat (from furnace or otherwise). Basically rosemary needs Mediterranean conditions, "fat" in spring and summer (long days, lots of direct sun, fresh air, water to maintain a moist rootball with only slight drying at the surface between waterings), "lean" in fall and winter (considerably cooler temperatures on average, but not any serious freezing, less light, only enough water to maintain turgid leaves and dampness to slight dryness at the roots).

One reason I always have a pot of rosemary is the smell when it is brushed or clipped. Fresh rosemary leaves are always welcome in the kitchen, if not for eating, to simmer, often along with sage and thyme. As the big pot of water bubbles for hours in fall and winter, the moisture evaporating humidifies the air and gives it the bracing scent I associate with sagebrush and buffalograss pastureland following a shower in my native western Oklahoma.

Besides a cool to moderate sunny window with plenty of fresh air, rosemary needs well-drained soil with a pH of 6.0 (average acidic) to 7.5 (on the alkaline or "sweet" side). Avoid acid-type fertilizers (30-10-10) or fish emulsion) in fall and winter.

Rosemary plants indoors seem especially vulnerable to mealybugs. You can spray weekly with insecticidal soap, but I prefer to go over each stem and leaf with a magnifying glass and when a mealybuy is seen to remove it with a cotton swab dipped in denatured alcohol. This way snippets for flavoring food can be quickly rinsed in water and added to a dish without concern that there will be a lingering soap taste.

Rosemary will grow better in a soil-based potting mix rather than one of the soilless convenience products. I use a combination of similar portions each of clean garden loam (or packaged, all-purpose potting soil), sharp sand, and well-rotted compost.

If a rosemary plant seems lackluster despite what you believe are all the right conditions, it may be that the soil is too acidic. This can be corrected by a light top-dressing of oyster shells (available from a poultry supply store) or crushed eggshells.

Pericon, *Tagetes lucida*, is the newest edible addition to my indoor herb garden. It is a unique marigold from the south of Mexico that produces leaves having the exact and subtle flavor of the finest French tarragon. Pericon can be grown in any sunny window or light garden all winter long, something difficult if not impossible for true tarragon.

Unlike the tagetes species that are popular in gardens as African, French, or American marigolds, *lucida* has a narrow, entire leaf that, excepting serration along the edges, resembles very much that of true tarragon. To me, the taste is virtually identical. It may seem remarkable that two such apparently different plants could have leaves containing the same flavor but in fact both are members of the daisy or composite family. True tarragon is *Artemisia dracunculus*. Besides the attractive and flavorful leaves, *Tagetes lucida* also bears small yellow marigold flowers. I have seen it blooming in far northern greenhouses in the dead of winter, so presumably flowering as a houseplant is also possible. Seeds and plants are available from specialists in herbs and other edibles.

Parsley grows well indoors, either from seeds or purchased seedlings. Plants dug from the garden before frost, potted, and brought inside need extra coolness, moisture, and sunshine. The best I've seen were started from seeds around Labor Day, maybe a whole packet fairly evenly distributed over the moist soil held by one eight- to twelve-inch pot and covered to the depth of their own thickness with finely crumbled soil. Use a loam-based potting soil and keep nicely moist at all times in a bright or sunny window or six inches directly beneath the tubes in a light garden. This sowing will produce a small field of green in a month and leaves for the kitchen by Thanksgiving. Curly-leaved parsleys seem to grow better indoors than the flatleaf Italian and they look wonderful in hanging baskets as well as pots.

Chinese parsley, known also as cilantro, is grown from the seeds of coriander, *Coriandrum sativum*. A strain known as 'Santo' is slow to bolt into flower and seed production and therefore considered better for growing indoors for clippings of cilantro in fall and winter. This plant responds to the same conditions as described for parsley and under the best care has a life span of less than a year.

Sweet bay, *Laurus nobilis*, is an excellent indoor plant which can be shaped as a bush or trained into a tree-form standard. Seeds are almost never available, but rooted cuttings and young specimens are sold by herb specialists. An indoor/outdoor existence is ideal, but it is also possible to grow this broadleaf evergreen indoors all year. Since the leaves persist for years, often until picked for cooking, it is important to keep them rain-fresh by frequent water showers. The more sun the merrier, along with fresh air circulation, but bay will also adapt to part shade. Be on the watch for brown scale.

Chives, *Allium schoenoprasum*, is fun to grow from seeds sown in a pot at any season. The grassy leaves can be clipped beginning a couple of months later. Established chives can also be dug from the garden and potted. These will grow best indoors if first cut back and chilled for several weeks, either outdoors in a frame or inside in the bottom of the refrigerator. When brought to a warm sunny window and watered, growth occurs rapidly.

Hardy English lavender doesn't do at all well indoors, but some of its frost-tender relatives do nicely. Fringed or French lavender, *Lavandula dentata*, grows easily for me as a small bush in my closet light garden, also as a twenty-four-inch tree-form standard in a sunny window. The cut leaves give off a sweet, distinctive scent when brushed and vary in color from green to gray-green depending on light and temperatures. *Lavandula stoechas* has gray leaves more like those of English lavender and produces uniquely showy flowers over an extended season. It's best for a sunny window in winter, with moderate temperatures and great caution about overwatering. Treat this one more as if it belonged with the cacti and other succulents. Tovah Martin in *The Essence of Paradise* (Little, Brown, 1991) finds the aroma of *stoechas* ". . . reminiscent of fresh pine needles immediately following a thunderstorm."

Another herb of rather major interest to me is myrtle, *Myrtus communis*, particularly the dwarf varieties known variously as 'Compacta', 'Microphylla', 'Minima', and

Sweet bay (Laurus nobilis) *lends itself to being trained as a bush, a tree-form standard, or, as here in the Meadow-brook, Pennsylvania, garden of J. Liddon Pennock, Jr., a stylized cone or obelisk. Potted sweet bay does nicely indoors or out and makes a surprisingly durable houseplant.*

'Nana'. Among these there are also those having white-variegated leaves. One does not eat myrtle but I love the smell when it is clipped and a lot of this can be done since the little trees are readily trainable as bonsai, topiary, espalier, and tree-form standards. The dwarfs thrive in light gardens and larger specimens placed outdoors in summer can coast through winter in less than ideal light, although a half-sunny window is preferable. Watch out for brown scale, mealybugs, and aphids (the latter on new growth).

How far afield one can go indoors with herbs depends on individual tastes and the parameters of the growing space. Sun-heated pit greenhouses and frost-free sun porches are great places to winter over any of these plants, including all the thymes, sages, mints, oreganos, and so on. My dream space of this type would have its signature collection of *Pelargonium*, with emphasis on the scented and succulent species, fragrant heliotrope, and some potted old roses. Some "lesser" or one-of-a-kind herbs that I have enjoyed indoors include:

Pogostemon heyneanus, or patchouli. This leafy green plant reminds me of a bushy rather than trailing Swedish ivy (*Plectranthus australis*); both are members of the mint family. Patchouli is native to the East and West Indies and the scent it gives off is strongly associated with India, sometimes with the sixties counterculture. I always enjoy the smell given off when the plant is disturbed, but what I really like about it is its vigorous growth habit and generous leaf production, which suggest this herb does an extra-efficient job cleaning the air. Give it a sunny window, average house temperatures, evenly moist soil, and regular applications of organic fertilizer. If stressed or neglected, mites and mealybugs may appear.

Aloysia triphylla, or lemon verbena. Its willowlike leaves give off an intense lemon scent on a plant that can be trained as a bush or tree-form standard. The critical thing to know about lemon verbena is that it grows actively in spring and summer, then stops abruptly in autumn and may yellow and drop most of its leaves practically overnight. At this point apply no fertilizer and only enough water to keep the branches firm, but position in bright light to direct sun. Every insect known to the indoor garden picks on resting lemon verbena, so don't forget to spray it with insecticidal soap, being sure to coat throughly every part of the main trunk and branches. This is an ideal indoor/outdoor plant.

Coleus amboinicus, or Spanish thyme or Mexican oregano. Thick, broad, hairy leaves and succulent stems; some varieties have white, cream, silver, or gold variegation. This is said to be a popular herb for cooking certain Spanish dishes. I grow it for horticultural pleasure and to appreciate the scent. This herb will adapt to fairly low light but for best results, give it maximum sun and treat as for cacti and other succulents.

Helichrysum angustifolium 'Nana', or dwarf curry plant. When stroked its tiny needlelike leaves smell uncannily of culinary curry which is actually a mixture of herbs and spices, not something handily harvested from one plant. Dwarf curry is the sort of gray-leaved plant one automatically expects to grow in full sun but it has adapted well in a light garden and proved amenable to training into a ball-shaped topiary six inches in diameter. Water it well, then not again until the soil surface dries out a little.

Lippia dulcis, or sweet herb. This plant reminds me of a trailing lantana, except the blossoms are greenish and conelike. When the sun is shining and its essential oils are volatalizing, this herb may not smell so sweet but when one of the leaves is chewed, surprise! The taste is sweeter than saccharin. Joy Logee Martin put me onto this useful houseplant, the leaves of which she serves at teatime as an alternative to the more usual honey, sugar, or commercial sweetener. Grow the sweet herb in any sunny window or light garden, in average house temperatures, evenly moist soil, and provide regular applications of organic fertilizer.

Mentha, or mint. Pick a mint, any potted mint (peppermint, spearmint, orange mint, pennyroyal), and you can grow it in a half-sunny window or light garden. Mints need lots of water and a soil that quickly drains off any excess. They also benefit from regular fertilizing with fish emulsion or liquid seaweed. Avoid letting them dry to the point of wilting as this invites spider mites. Also protect from drafts of hot air but take care to provide plenty of fresh air circulation so that temperatures remain moderate.

chapter seven

Miniature Houseplants

L ess is more. Smaller is better. Welcome to the world of miniature horticulture. Despite writing a book on miniature plants in the 1960s (updated and reissued in the 1970s by M. Evans and Company and Popular Library as *Little Plants for Small Spaces*) and growing them most of my life, I was first introduced to "miniature horticulture" as a separate sphere of gardening activity by artist Louisa Rawle Tine of South Salem, New York. Tiny plants, Tom-Thumb size plantscapes, and dollhouse flower arrangements are fun for all and especially suited for maximizing the house gardening experience in small spaces and for immobilized gardeners. Because there are so many miniature plants, often species, varieties, or cultivars of large and familiar sorts, they are dispersed throughout the pages of this book, always accompanied by the word "miniature." In this chapter I will concentrate on various ways of utilizing miniature houseplants.

Louisa Tine's interest in things miniature began with childhood dollhouses which her father helped build and furnish. "When I grew up, my mother, along with some of her friends, started the miniature classes in horticulture at the Philadelphia Flower Show. When she died I reclaimed my old miniatures and have continued with the help of a magnifying glass and my husband, Hal, a set

designer." Together the Tines create a scale model of a complete garden setting in which living plants and flowers, fresh or dried, play all the roles we would expect them to if they were full-size. If a planting requires a ground bed to accommodate plant roots, a four-inch-deep container base is made of sheet metal and filled with an appropriate potting soil; the scale model rests on top. Garden tools include tweezers, toothpicks, demitasse spoons, eye droppers for watering, and manicure scissors for hedge clippers.

Since Louisa's miniature gardens are created to be exhibited, they usually have a theme. One called "The Wind in the Willows," inspired by the classic story of a mole and a river rat, measures two and a half feet wide by two feet deep by two and a half feet high. "We built a tree stump by the river and carved out rooms. It was enchanting." After the show, this garden was purchased by another miniature horticulturist, Kathy Pitney of Mendham, New Jersey, who adds tiny potted living plants and puts it on display when she is expecting company.

Another of Louisa's Lilliputian fantasies replicates the garden folly and knot gardens at Montecute, Somerset, England, as they existed at the beginning of the seventeenth century. The theme, "Lavender's Blue, Dilly Dilly, Lavender's Green," was realized with rooted tip

A plastic sweater storage box makes an ideal portable greenhouse or growth chamber for a dazzling variety of miniature plants. Featured, from a stroll through Kartuz Greenhouses, Vista, California, are orange Gesneria cuneifolia, *white, pink, rose, and lavender* Sinningia *species and cultivars,* Malpighia coccigera, *selaginellas in variety, a miniature* Begonia rex, *and a white streptocarpus.*

cuttings of different lavenders. The scale model of a period house and folly looks onto a garden of dried flowers—individual baby's-breath, statice, the solitary tip flower of a pink delphinium, sea lavender. Rooted cuttings of various sedums in green and gray are woven into three knot gardens, each framed by wattling woven from small weeping willow branches. The walkways are sand, to represent the gravel used by the Elizabethans. A hedge was shaped from camphor thyme, which can be clipped as it is naturally upright and bushy. For reduced-scale ground cover Louisa used woolly and Hall's creeping thymes. A turf bench was fashioned of living moss.

A scale model of Rockwood Conservatory, Wilmington, Delaware, is another Tine creation, with furnishings and plantings designed to fit the period 1851–57. "Braxton Payne of Atlanta makes clay pots only two millimeters in diameter that are in perfect scale." Louisa fills these with "grains of sand and sedum tip cuttings secured in the pots with Elmer's glue which the sedums seem to like. Air-dried branchlets of flowering leptospermum last remarkably and resemble roses. Rooted snippets of kalanchoe work well for the tiniest of flowering potted plants. My biggest coup was a four-inch tree-form standard of the fuchsia 'Isis', which has blossoms a sixteenth of an inch long."

Proving that miniature horticulture knows no cultural or geographical bounds, another Tine creation is a lap-size Japanese garden, complete with a "bamboo" fence made from broom straws tied in place the same as for a real bamboo fence. The "bonsai" tree set into this landscape is *Juniperus procumbens nana*. Also included is a crassula that looks like a tiny horsetail or equisetum planted by the water basin and lantern that Louisa made from modeling clay. Small water-polished black stones came from a bonsai dealer. Edging logs in the Japanese manner were cut from twigs of uniform size.

No matter the theme of the landscape, Louisa thinks of effect, not necessarily duplicating a large plant in miniature. A small peperomia can represent hosta, spider plant babies can be used as edging instead of liriope. A miniature "citrus" can be fashioned from dwarf myrtle treelets and glued-on dried berries or fruits such as pyracantha. *Erodium chamaedryoides roseum* makes a perfect hanging basket. Small sedges, *Carex morrowii albo-marginata*, for example, can be jewels when one takes the smallest of the small divisions. *Teucrium marum* makes hedging around "rose" bushes of cat thyme with flowers provided by glued-on dried micro-miniature roses. Creeping thymes, *Ficus pumila repens*, and Corsican mint *(Mentha requienii)* can be turned into vines or espaliers on little frames. Rooted cuttings of 'Prince Rupert Variegated' lemon geranium can be trained into very small tree-form standards.

Louisa does most of her growing in a three-tier fluorescent-light garden in the basement. Kathy Pitney does hers in a greenhouse. Miniature horticulture can also be practiced in any bright to sunny window garden. Here are some selected sources for thimble-size houseplants and herbs: Glasshouse Works Greenhouses, Grigsby Cactus Gardens, Kartuz Greenhouses, Lauray of Salisbury, and Logee's Greenhouses (see Resources for addresses).

The word bonsai *means tray planting and here we see how the elements that make full-size gardens can also be used to create tiny landscapes: earthen colors, rocks, moss, lichens, and a dwarf azalea in bloom. Photographed in the Bonsai Museum, the Steinhardt Conservatory, Brooklyn Botanic Garden.*

THE INCREDIBLE SHRINKING BEGONIA

To give you an idea of the possibilities for miniatures, here are six miniaturized versions of the old-fashioned (and usually very large) angel-wing or cane begonia:

'Crispie' has rounded, crinkled, glossy green leaves. The white flowers appear as lacy caps over the leaves.

'Guy Savard' has long lancelike leaves that are silvery pink with maroon on the reverse and forest green veins. It rarely exceeds twelve inches and is an outstanding choice for small-space indoor gardens.

'Marjorie Sibley' is a compact hybrid that fits into the smallest of spaces. Frosty pink flowers emphasize small, rounded, dark bronze leaves.

'Orange Dainty' is another compact hybrid. Sprays of delicate orange flowers contrast with long, pale green leaves.

'Swan Song' is a true miniature with an excellent self-branching habit. Dark, smooth leaves and graceful, pure white flowers combine to make a plant that is a proven winner.

'Tiny Gem' has thumb-size leaves and seemingly endless cascades of candy pink flowers in winter. It performs well under a variety of conditions and has become popular throughout the world of begonias.

PLEASANT UNDER GLASS

At the very moment when gardening has become our number-one leisure activity, the time to do it seems increasingly precious. One response is to design and plant gardens as self-reliant as possible, to turn minutes of gardening into hours of pleasure. This might well have been in the subconscious of actress Glenn Close when she purchased at auction a hundred-year-old Wardian case, attracted by the "opulence and architecture of the structure." Once this was ensconced in a corner of the Close living room it was my assignment to design and install an aesthically pleasing arrangement of plants.

Envision if you will the octagonal mahogany and glass case, with its domed, removable roof and dimensions of eighteen by twenty-four inches, large enough to accommodate a landscape of compatible plants, and standing in a corner of the living room where the light is bright all day, but little or no hot sun strikes directly. From empty case to completed garden, this is more or less the step-by-step progression I followed to create a unique natural microcosm:

Daydream about what might be—something gardeners always do. Gardens, no matter the size or number of plants, indoors or out, tend to be formal or informal, Eastern or Western. The West usually seeks balance in axial symmetry while the East finds resolution in asymmetry. For the Close project I thought first of English formal in miniature, or perhaps Chinese *penjing*, with an important creviced rock to support bonsai trees. Then the case's Victorian roots reminded me of its original purpose, to showcase and shelter exotics that might otherwise have perished in the gas-fumed and often chilly interiors of that period.

Plants suited to an enclosure, whether in a sizable Wardian case or in a smaller terrarium, are often grouped together in the shop. Choose what you like, but avoid cacti and other succulents, including soft-leaved wax begonias and fresh-air fiends such as geraniums. The ones I bought can be found in most garden centers, some even in five-and-dime stores. I avoided rampant growers such as philodendron, kinds prone to leaf yellowing and general defoliation, and everbloomers that might drop too many petals.

You will need small bags of horticultural charcoal chips, sandstone or similar pebbles, and florist or woods sheet moss. Also, one bag each of all-purpose potting soil, sphagnum peat moss (or coarsely screened well-rotted compost), and clean, sharp sand, mixed together in a pail.

When all the elements are assembled around the container, and while the plants are still individually potted, experiment with different arrangements. Based on what you have versus what you may have dreamed about, a plan will emerge. At this stage I could tell right away that the Close garden would be a slice of the rain forest, with plants that in their natural setting might catch hold and grow in bits of decomposing leaves cradled in crevices between tree branches. A ten-minute walk around the property netted exactly the right piece of wood, a small log with several broken-off, twiggy branches having the promising character of driftwood.

Start the actual planting by adding a half-inch layer of charcoal chips to the bottom, topped with another half-inch of pebbles. This serves to catch excess water and lets air reach the roots and soil. The Close case even has a built-in, galvanized tin-lined drawer at the bottom to catch water, a strong point in its design.

The major element goes into position first. In this case it is the tree log, which miraculously stood securely without any special rigging.

As for the plants, I started with clump-forming, almost grasslike types and a fern that might naturally emanate from the base of a tree trunk:

- *Guzmania,* a bromeliad from Colombia and Ecuador with a long-lasting orange flower bract.
- A miniature green-and-white-striped *Chlorophytum bichetii,* a spider plant from Gabon that does not send out new plantlets into the air in the manner of more common spider plants.
- A young holly fern, *Cyrtomium falcatum,* from Asia, South Africa, and Polynesia, which may need to be cut back to size after six months.
- An ornamental pepper vine, *Piper porphyrophyllum,* from the Malay Peninsula, with rose-pink spots, olive veins, and heart-shaped leaves set on a tough, malleable vine that twines up and around the log. (Note, perfectly healthy leaves of this plant develop bumps all over the undersides that appear to be a

Piper ornatum—*smaller but similar to* P. *porphyrophyllum—is the decorative Celebes pepper vine. It requires warmth, high humidity, and bright diffused light.*

dread attack of mites—or worse. Not to worry, they're only evidence of a plant that guttates, a way of easing moisture tensions within the leaf tissue without actually exploding, in which case the condition becomes edema.)

- A miniature ladyslipper orchid, *Paphiopedilum* 'Alba' from tropical Asia, is perched near the top of the log, with its roots and bark-chip medium wrapped in woods moss and nestled in a crevice between twigs. The exquisite pale-pink-spotted white flower lasts several weeks. Its mottled, dark green leaves will remain attractive until the next bloom in six months or so.
- A second ladyslipper orchid, whose parents hail from Thailand and Borneo, the *Paphiopedilum* 'Maudiae', is moss wrapped and set on a lower branch.
- A miniature fern from Asia, *Polystichum tsus-simense*, with moss-wrapped roots, is given a perch at the top of the log.

Begonia *'Buttercup' is a miniature developed by Michael Kartuz that produces a constant show of chrome yellow and orange flowers with distinct red striping. Grow this in long-fiber sphagnum moss in a terrarium under fluorescent lights. It will become a favorite plant.*

Now pause, walk around and see that the garden is pleasing from every angle. This is the time for adjustments. I filled the base of the container with about three inches of potting mix and added more plants. It is amazing how many can fit into a miniature garden.

- *Episcia cupreata*, flame violet, from Colombia, has showy leaves that are more silver than green. Extremely sensitive to cold drafts but thrives in terrarium conditions.
- Nerve plant, *Fittonia verschaffeltii*, from Colombia and Peru, carpets the ground with pink-veined, olive green leaves.
- Pink-variegated ti plant, *Cordyline terminalis* 'Tricolor', native to eastern Asia, a natural "tree" companion to the nerve plant.
- Maidenhair fern, *Adiantum cuneatum*, a filmy fern that languishes in the presence of gas fumes or smoke, prospers in a pollution-free terrarium.
- Jewel orchid, *Ludisia discolor*, from the Malay Archipelago, has satiny copper leaves with pink veins. It thrives on less light than most plants and makes a splendid ground cover.
- Three diminutive insectivorous plants with moss-wrapped roots—Venus flytrap *Dionaea* (from the Carolinas), *Darlingtonia* (from California and Oregon), and Mexican butterwort (*Pinguicula caudata*)—snuggle into crevices up and down the log and could conceivably eat any insect that might be living there.
- Creeping *Selaginella uncinata*, from the south of China, effects a moss carpet and in time will need clipping back.
- *Neanthe bella* gives a Victorian touch, the parlor palm in miniature.
- Extremely slow-growing *Pleomele thalioides*, native to Sri Lanka and tropical Africa, has leaves at right angles to the stalks, suggesting a Balinese dancer.
- One last empty space holds three rooted cuttings of *Begonia prismatocarpa*, a miniature rhizomatous type from Africa. It will form a small green clump with tiny yellow-orange blossoms that drop and disappear. In effect it is a self-cleaning plant.

Woods or florist sheet moss carpeting is laid down as a finishing touch, to hide all bare bits of earth. Strands of Spanish moss, an epiphytic bromeliad, *Tillandsia usneoides*, from the American subtropics, are trailed from the branch tips. About two cups lukewarm water is added to settle all newly disturbed roots. A few well-aimed sprays of water from a mister rinse away any specks of soil from the leaves and interior glass walls.

In caring for a terrarium, remember that when the exterior temperature falls below that inside, droplets of moisture will form, then run back into the planting medium. If you do not see this clouding effect as outside temperatures drop, add water, a few tablespoons at a time, taking also this opportunity to add fertilizer at one fourth the strength recommended on the label for regular potted plants. When leaves or flowers wither or die, clip them. If a plant outgrows the garden, prune it back or remove it. Your goal in planting a terrarium is to create an almost entirely self-sufficient microcosm, a world that can be very nearly held in your hands.

I did three very different small terrariums as a gift for Close, the sorts of nearly self-sufficient gardens that can be enjoyed in nearly every room, especially at the center of a dining table, on a kitchen or bath counter, or under a desk lamp: An eight-inch glazed clay bulb pan was planted with miniature African violets and a carpeting of miniature nerve plant, *Fittonia*. This was covered with a clear plastic dome. A large glass brandy snifter container was fitted with 'Pink Star' cryptanthus and two different species of *Tillandsia*, bromeliads all, with moss for ground cover. The third planting was based on an earth-toned bonsai tray about one inch deep by eight by fourteen inches. A miniature calathea planted in a tall Chinese clay pot was displayed under a clear glass globe toward one end of the tray on a bed of coarse sand and water, an expression of *shibui*—a Japanese word suggesting exquisiteness—in Lilliputian scale.

WARDIAN CASE DISCOVERY

The Victorian Wardian case purchased by Glenn Close harks back a couple of hundred years, to a time when English gardeners began to bring ferns and flowering potted plants indoors from their conservatories and glasshouses and enclose them individually in bell jars and other glass containers. The benefits were obvious. Delicate leaves and pampered flowers enjoyed a relatively warm and moist atmosphere in these enclosures. However, it was not until around 1829 when Nathaniel Ward, an Englishman variously described as botanist, surgeon, and scientist—all of which he may well have been—discovered that a little soil and some plants sealed in a glass container could exist, indeed thrive, indefinitely, forming a microcosm of nature. The discovery happened by accident. Dr. Ward enclosed a chrysalis with some garden soil in a jar. Since garden soil contains seeds and possibly other living plant matter, in time green growth appeared. What happened to the chrysalis we do not know, but Dr. Ward had the good sense to appreciate what was happening with the plants inside the jar and to document his findings in a scientific journal.

So it is that we honor Dr. Ward as the father of the Victorian Wardian case, which has, in the form of terrariums and bottle gardens, truly come of age. If we trace the development and early practical application of Dr. Ward's discovery, it is easily understood why the idea works so well for us today. Following that first sealed jar, he built large glass cases, which were used by early explorers to keep newly discovered plants alive during long sea voyages. (A life-size reproduction of one of these cases stands today just inside the door of an old glasshouse at the Chelsea Physic Garden in London. It looks uncannily like a scale-model I once constructed of my own home greenhouse for exhibit as a Future Farmer of America in the Beaver County, Oklahoma, Fair.) It was not long before these practical cases were made up into the ornate glass enclosures for exotic plants which we associate with the Victorian drawing room. Keeping tropicals in those drafty, chill rooms was hopeless until the Wardian case came along.

Wardian cases soon became popular in drawing rooms in the more genteel American homes. Presumably this practice continued until central heating arrived. Just how those elegant under-glass gardens evolved into the terrariums of today is not easily traced. Conjecture has it that teachers, wishing to recreate Dr. Ward's discovery for students, began to refer to the glass jars and other containers as terrariums—"*terra*" meaning "earth" and "*arium*" meaning "home." It was probably one of those students who decided once again that the time was right to try some small exotic plants in a glass enclosure and the old idea found new life.

The germ of the idea in all of this is that a glass or plastic enclosure makes it possible for one or more plants to have a constant and high degree of humidity. It is not necessary to possess a Wardian case proper or an elegantly designed terrarium. Glass jars, overturned drinking glasses, bubble bowls, large brandy snifters, and clear plastic beverage bottles are only a few of the possibilities for turning found objects and throwaways into working terrariums.

PLANTING BOTTLE GARDENS

Since you can't reach your hands into that small an opening to plant a bottle or other permanently closed container, you will need some special tools, most of which can be improvised from materials found around the house:

1) Bulb baster from the kitchen for watering.
2) A slender wood dowel or bamboo plant stake at least six inches longer than the height of the bottle, or a terrarium planting tool.
3) A length of wire clothes hanger, bent with a small loop on one end to hold and position plants and materials inside the bottle, with a handle by which to hold it bent on the other end.

Sinningia 'White Sprite' is a pure white sport of S. pusilla, *the tiny lavender-flowered miniature gloxinia. Provide terrarium culture, alone or in thoughtful combination with compatible plants, and these little sinningias will bloom nonstop.*

4) A second length of wire clothes hanger with a bottle cork stuck onto one end (the cork must be slightly smaller than the bottle neck) to use as a soil tamper to firm roots in place.

5) A second piece of wood dowel with a single-edge razor blade attached to one end, to use as a pruning instrument.

6) A funnel, or, instead, a piece of fairly stiff paper rolled into a funnel shape.

7) Finally, a mechanic's pickup tool can be extremely helpful in certain situations.

In addition to these bottle gardening tools, I sometimes tape a demitasse spoon on the end of a long wood dowel or bamboo stake to serve as a trowel. To remove particles of soil from the leaves, tape a small camel's-hair brush to the same kind of dowel or stake. To remove dead leaves and flowers and growth you have cut with your "pruning shears," the mechanic's pickup tool is a great help. Long, slender, wooden terrarium tongs are also a worthwhile investment. This is obviously the time to make haste with deliberate slowness.

After you assemble your tools, plants, gravel, charcoal, potting soil, moss for ground cover and any other finishing touches, clean the bottle. First rinse it out with warm water to which a little household detergent has been added. Stains may require soaking for a time in household bleach. Once the bottle is clean, rinse it several times with clean water, then set aside to dry in a warm place. If the inside walls are moist, every flying particle of planting medium will adhere to them. When dry, you will have to use a funnel to add layers of gravel, charcoal, and soil. After you add each layer, use a piece of dowel, bamboo stake, coat hanger with a loop, or stake with a demitasse spoon attached to shape the terrain.

Before you begin to place plants inside the bottle, set it on a piece of paper and, with a pencil, draw a line around it. Set the bottle aside and experiment with various arrangements of your plants inside the circle (or other shape) you have drawn. Once you have marked out an arrangement that is pleasing, proceed by inserting one plant at a time through the neck of the bottle and settling it in place as nearly as possible to the position it occupied on your paper pattern.

As you pick up each plant, remove it from the pot and gently work or rinse off in room-temperature water most of the old soil. Also check for signs of any insect infestation; if detected, treat accordingly before placing inside the bottle. Remove any discolored or damaged growth.

Depending on the size of the plants in relation to the size of the bottle opening, you may be able to lower them, within the loop of your wire clothes hanger tool, or you may have to coil the leaves gently around so that the plant alone slips through the neck and drops onto the soil surface. Once the plant is safely inside the bottle, use one or more of your long-handled tools to precisely position it and cover the roots with soil.

After all the plants are in place you can proceed to add moss ground cover, pebbles, or any other finishing touches. Next, use the camel's-hair brush to clean the foliage, flowers, and interior walls of any particles of earth. Finally, draw a little room-temperature water into the bulb baster and rinse down the walls and any leaves or flowers that may have particles of soil remaining. Be very careful about adding too much water to a bottle garden, however.

An interesting alternative to placing plants inside a bottle is to plant a few seeds of one kind of plant, or perhaps two or more compatibles. In a very small bottle you might, for example, drop a few seeds of *Sinningia pusilla* or any other miniature gloxinia. Then you'll have the fun of watching for them to sprout, grow, and eventually reach flowering size. In a gallon to five-gallon size bottle you might plant a few seeds of hybrid African violets, spores of miniature fern, or whatever small-growing plant appeals to you. The miniature green-and-white nerve plant fittonia will do beautifully for years in a bottle garden.

See also on page 242: Terrarium Trouble Signs—and What to Do.

chapter eight

Houseplants Indoors/ Outdoors

The old notion of houseplants outdoors was that the sturdier sorts were eased outside on a nice spring day, after danger of frost, and left in some protected spot until it was time to go inside in the fall, before frost. The new idea of indoor/outdoor sees in this the opportunity to grow well some of the world's most beautiful flowering plants, especially the woody sorts and flowering vines. None of the cast of characters here can withstand frost, but most if not all can be wintered over in any growing or holding area that can be kept above freezing—an unused guest bedroom, a sun porch, a home greenhouse, conservatory, or sun-heated pit.

Many houseplants benefit from a summer spent outdoors. Move them into open air when the weather is warm in spring or early summer, and bring indoors well ahead of frost in autumn. They need the same care as other plants in the garden. Provide routine pruning, regular spraying to prevent insect damage, watering, and biweekly or more frequent applications of fertilizer. It is easier to care for potted plants being summered outdoors if they are grouped together in one or two places rather than scattered over the yard.

Any location that receives protection from whipping winds and hard rains can be decorated with container plants. They are especially enjoyable near entranceways, on steps, terraces, patios, porches, walks, landing strips by driveways, tops of walls, sun decks, and rooftops. Many houseplants thrive in the summer under large trees, heavy-foliaged shrubs or beneath groups of perennials such as daylilies and hostas. (Such places are also favored by slugs and snails. Keep a watch out for them. If you find holes in leaves, chewed-off flowers, and telltale slimy trails, set out saucers of beer among your plants at night. The mollusks are so attracted by the smell they crawl in and drown.) Some houseplants do well in hanging baskets, window boxes, and large planters. For the ultimate in summer care of houseplants, use a lath or slat house, shaded cold frame, or air-conditioned greenhouse.

When plants growing in containers outdoors are kept moist and protected from searing winds, they are more tolerant of sunlight. Kinds that need sunny locations indoors (see pages 7–8) usually do well outdoors in sun-drenched places, but partial shade will also give pleasing results. Houseplants that need semisunny and semishady locations indoors (see lists on pages 5–8) thrive outdoors in the dapply shadows cast by tall trees, or on the north side of a building. True shade-loving plants (see page 8), can be summered outdoors in a shady, moist nook which receives little or no direct sun except possibly early or late in the day.

Outdoor steps, paved surfaces, the tops of garden walls—these are ideal places for grow-ing and showing container plantings during frost-free weather. Here are some of the treasured trained plants from the collection of Ernesta and Fred Ballard, Philadelphia, Pennsylvania: Blue agapanthus, numerous geraniums, citrus, shrimp plant, and king's crown.

HOW TO MOVE HOUSEPLANTS OUTDOORS

Moving day for houseplants may be scheduled for any convenient time after the average date of last frost in a given area. In the Northeast, we begin moving cool-loving houseplants outdoors in late April or early May. By the third weekend of May, most of the tropicals are situated for the season. Before setting plants into garden areas, harden them off a few days by placing them on a cool porch, under trees, or beneath overhanging eaves. This is to allow them time to harden or stiffen their stems,

and to firm up their foliage. Orchids and bromeliads do well hung from tree limbs or the roof of a lath or slat house.

African violets, florist gloxinias, and other hairy-leaved gesneriads such as streptocarpus will do best outdoors if they can be on a bright porch where there will be shield-ing from strong winds and rains. These are plants that ideally should never be rained on. Outdoor light often has a multidirectional quality that is rarely attainable indoors. Be respectful of this possibility as you position plants outdoors.

HOW TO MOVE HOUSEPLANTS INDOORS

Bring houseplants back inside well ahead of when frost is expected. Start with warmth-loving tropicals, then the subtropicals, finally the warm temperate sorts. Most of the plants discussed in this chapter belong to the warm temperate category. Plants that set buds in response to a little night chilling in autumn—holiday cactus and cymbidium orchids—can be left out until just before frost is predicted. Everything else will adapt better if brought in while the days are still warm enough for doors and windows to be open, before the heating system must be activated.

Houseplants that have spent the summer outdoors may harbor insects you'd rather not have indoors. It is a good idea to pick up and inspect each plant, groom it, and then to spray with insecticidal soap. Be sure to check under pot rims and all around for slugs.

When and how much to prune back plants being brought inside is a matter of choice for the individual gardener. Plants such as fuchsias, begonias, and geraniums that have been blooming all summer can be cut back up to a half or more before bringing inside. If the plant is still blooming attractively, I like to hold off cutting back until it stops, usually some days, weeks, or even months after moving indoors.

FAVORITE INDOOR/OUTDOOR HOUSEPLANTS

Abutilon or flowering maple is so-called because the leaves are reminiscent in shape to those of the true maple, but in a botanical sense this plant belongs to the mallow family, along with such popular plants as rose of Sharon or althea, hollyhock, Chinese hibiscus, and even the okra we—or some of us—eat.

Tip cuttings of abutilon will root quickly in pots of moist soil, and can be trained as bushes, into tree-form

standards, or tepee style. Some abutilons are infected with a harmless virus that renders the leaves mostly golden yellow between the green veins. It is the habit of some species and hybrids to grow strongly upright, as in the superior cultivar known as 'Moonchimes', while others are lax in habit and adapt well as hanging plants, as espaliers, or even trained wreath-style. Here is a three-step plan for growing abutilons having an attractive, compact habit and an abundance of hollyhocklike bellflowers:

1) In late winter or spring, remove the pot and, using your fingers or an old kitchen knife, remove about a third of the outermost roots, including especially those that may have circled around the bottom of the rootball.
2) Now cut back all of the branches by one third to one half their length. In the process you may cut off most of the leaves, but some of what is removed can be salvaged and rooted as cuttings. If any of the parts removed should have on them some open

Abutilons such as 'Clementine' flower on new growth and so may be had in bloom at almost any season. They make superb summer plants outdoors, especially when trained to bush or basket form or as standard trees.

flowers, use these for a small bouquet—the flow-ering maple was once treasured for its production of cut flowers.

3) Replant in the same pot or one a size or two larger, filling in with fresh potting mix. Add a portion of well-rotted compost if you have it. Set the newly potted abutilon to soak in a basin of water until beads of moisture show on the soil surface. Set aside to drain. Place to recover in a mostly shaded part of the garden. When new green shoots start to sprout from the old wood, move to a sunny place.

It also helps to fertilize abutilons every two weeks. Fish emulsion or liquid seaweed is effective for promoting new growth, with a switch after a month or six weeks to a blossom-booster such as 15-30-15. If you pinch out the tips of new shoots after they have five or six leaves, there will ultimately be twice as many flowers, that is if you give them half sun and enough water so that the leaves are never found in a dead wilt.

Allamanda. The yellow allamandas, for which the genus is best known, include the 'Williamsii' cultivar of *Allamanda cathartica* that becomes an enormous vine requiring strong trellising. There is a bushier, much smaller in all parts, oleander-leaved allamanda, A. *nerii-folia*, and A. *violacea* which has rose-pink to reddish purple blossoms and is said to grow best if grafted on a cultivar of A. *cathartica* such as 'Hendersonii' or 'Schottii'. The *cathartica* cultivar 'Nobilis' has a mag-nolialike fragrance and 'Stansill's Double' has double flowers.

Allamandas need lots of sun and temperatures mostly above 65°F. They wilt if allowed to become the least bit dry, so be sure to include moisture-holding humus such as peat moss or old, half-decomposed turf in extra por-tions at potting time, and also water freely. This is the sort of plant I place in a saucer even when it is outdoors, so that often there is water standing—by the next day, though, it will have been soaked up.

Allamandas also benefit from regular fertilizing in spring and summer. I use fish emulsion normally, but if a plant seems to be withholding blossoms despite all the right conditions, I make an application of 1-6-5.

Whether or not any of these can be grown as house-plants really depends on the individual gardener and the space. They can be kept quite dry and on the cool side in fall and winter, then cut back at repotting time in spring. As a group they are related to plumerias and, like them, are remarkably free of insect and disease problems and very free-flowering throughout the hottest summer months.

Bougainvillea. One late winter while I was photo-graphing in Key West, Florida, the bougainvillea was just beginning to bloom. The specimen I most enjoyed had climbed high into the branches of a tree in the garden next door. Other guests, less horticulturally inclined, kept asking what kind of tree it was. Frankly, I couldn't tell, but it was the bougainvillea they wanted to know about. What I did observe about the tree was that its branches were mostly leafless, a condition those of us who live in the North associate with frost and winter. In tropical and subtropical climates some trees also shed their leaves, more likely in response to seasonal drought and heat or relative coolness than actual freezing. In this instance the tree and the bougainvillea were synergizing impres-sively: While scantily clad in fall and winter, the tree allows maximum sun to warm the bougainvillea and bring on blooms. Late winter and spring rains, followed by tropical heat, turn the tree back into a leafy canopy, under which the bougainvillea reverts to leaf and stem preparatory to another season of bloom.

The more I have thought about this cycle, the more I have understood why bougainvillea can be grown as a houseplant even though most of us know it as a large, unruly, and sometimes spectacular woody vine. It is all of these things—with some needle-sharp thorns to boot—and more.

The most remarkable bougainvillea I have seen had been nurtured for more than twenty-five years in a bonsai tray. Its trunk was thicker than my wrist and as gnarled as a choice piece of driftwood. The branches and what-ever leaves they carried were all but obliterated by the Schiaparelli-pink flowers. The whole tree stood all of two feet tall, a living work of art.

Another bougainvillea I have known was perhaps just as remarakable, at least in my eyes. Of course, my having

Bougainvillea glabra *'Barbara Karst' is an example of the sort of plant that needs to bake outdoors in the sun in warm weather in order to give back a big flower show the following fall and winter indoors. By nature a clambering vine, this plant can be trained as a large wreath, an espalier, or hanging basket.*

served as nature's helper in turning it from a spindly rooted cutting in a handful of soil to a bushy flower-covered specimen in a six-inch pot may have glorified the memory. In any event, at a time when I had seemingly unlimited space in which to grow—a suburban house with sunny windows, a basement for light gardens, a greenhouse, and more lawns and flower beds than I knew what to do with—the one bougainvillea I grew made a lasting impression. A recent acquisition is a naturally miniature variety I plan to bonsai train.

Here is a plan for growing and training bougainvillea as an indoor/outdoor container plant:

1) Start with a rooted cutting of a choice cultivar or color, for example 'Barbara Karst' (rose-red), 'Apricot Praetorius' (a combination of apricot, bronze, orange, yellow, and shades of pink), 'Sterling Silver' (pale lilac with silvery sheen), or 'Crimson Lake' (dark red; cultivars 'San Diego' and 'Scarlet O'Hara' are the same or very similar).

2) Decide how you want to treat the plant, then pot up accordingly. Select a container which holds a minimum of five cups of soil, but be careful of overpotting bougainvillea lest its roots drown from excess water.

3) Use a potting mix of two parts well-rotted compost, leaf mold, and peat moss to one each of soil, coarse vermiculite, and clean, sharp sand.

4) Place in a sunny window or directly beneath the tubes in a maxi light garden. Set outdoors in partial to full sun during warm, frost-free weather.

5) From late winter until the end of summer keep the soil between evenly moist and slightly on the dry side. Apply flowering houseplant fertilizer on a regular basis.

6) From early fall until midwinter, keep the soil on the dry side and do not fertilize. Temperatures that are cool, 50° to 70°F, are recommended. Don't be surprised if most of the leaves drop during this period—that's perfectly natural. A sunny place is preferable.

7) Around the end of January begin to water slightly more and to apply flowering fertilizer. Provide light as specified in step 4 and temperatures between 60° and 80°F, 40 percent or more humidity, and fresh air circulation. Flowering should commence within a matter of weeks.

Pruning is an integral part of growing bougainvillea. Since it blooms on new wood, generally following a period of semidormancy induced by relatively dry soil and cooler temperatures, spring and summer are the usual times to prune. Exactly which branches and how much depends on the habit you are aiming for—shrub, standard tree, hanging, espalier (an eighteen-inch wreath for example), or bonsai.

Bougainvillea is a member of the four-o'clock family. The true flowers are small white trumpets. What we think of as the flowers are papery bracts, long-lasting and colorful. You can propagate bougainvillea in late spring or early summer from five-inch cuttings of mature or half-ripened wood (see page 54). The seeds, which sprout readily in warmth and moisture, are also listed in specialty catalogs.

This regimen for forcing bougainvillea for exhibition in twelve-inch-deep pots is from the Royal Horticultural Society:

1) After flowering, prune each plant heavily and fertilize with a high potassium (potash) fertilizer such as 12-12-17, one tablespoon per twelve-inch pot.
2) Water twice a day for two weeks.
3) Spray the new, rapidly growing foliage with a weak fertilizer solution once a week, and if any signs of disease appear, spray or treat accordingly.
4) After two weeks of heavy watering, gradually reduce the amount of water until the plants are watered only enough to keep them from seriously wilting.
5) Six to seven weeks after the plants are pruned and fertilized they should be in full flower. Fertilize the plants again with a high potassium fertilizer and foliar feed again.
6) Water heavily for two weeks to help the plants take up the fertilizer and then resume normal watering. It is not necessary to let the plants dry out as thoroughly as in step 4, where the severe watering schedule seems to promote flower bud initiation.
7) The plants should bloom for about six weeks before time to start the cycle again. Pot bougainvilleas in a rich organic soil that includes compost and some sphagnum peat moss. Good drainage is also essential. Since they are greedy feeders, top-dress the pots every three months.

Bouvardia, although not that familiar today, can be found in earlier books about gardening under glass. Those who now practice energy conservation can readily provide the cool night temperatures in fall and winter that it needs. Add a sunny window garden and it seems we have the potential in bouvardia for a really rewarding and everblooming indoor plant for fall and winter, the seasons when indoor blooms are usually most welcome.

Bouvardia is in the madder family, as is ixora, so the resemblance is more than incidental. Also related are the gardenia, coffee, and pentas. *Bouvardia longiflora* has white flowers that are intensely fragrant, while *B. ternifolia* blooms are pink. Kinds having orange and scarlet flowers are also cultivated.

Bouvardia is a subtropical American flowering shrub with terminal clusters of four-lobed flowers. Blooms appear most generously in fall and winter, after which time the plants are cut back by a third or more and rested by keeping cool, on the dry side, and withholding fertilizer until spring.

Repot bouvardia in the spring, using a mix of one part each of packaged all-purpose potting soil and clean, sharp sand (or perlite) to two parts sphagnum peat moss (or well-rotted compost). Set outdoors in warm, frost-free weather in a place that receives direct sun several hours daily. Water freely so as to keep the roots evenly moist; avoid extremes, wet or dry. Apply 30-10-10 fertilizer in spring, 20-20-20 or similar in summer, 15-30-15 in the fall, and 1-6-5 in the winter.

Bring bouvardia indoors to a sunny window garden or greenhouse when temperatures become chilly. Flower bud initiation occurs best in night temperatures of 50° to 55°F, the same as for holiday cacti and many orchids. In higher night temperatures the buds will set only with short light days (the same as for poinsettia and chrysanthemum).

Brunfelsia can be grown all year indoors but heavier flowering will occur if it can be moved outside in warm weather. This plant is a subtropical member of the tomato family (Solanaceae) that blooms naturally in winter and spring, but often in summer and fall as well. In cold weather give it a sunny window where night temperatures in fall and winter are on the cool side, about 50° to 55°F. During the spring and summer be generous with sunlight, warmth, water, and fertilizer. Pinch out the tips regularly until midsummer; this is to build a bushy plant

The blossoms of Brunfelsia australis, *from early spring until fall, carry a light lemony scent. Each flower goes through three stages of color, from blue-violet to nearly white, hence its common name yesterday-today-and-tomorrow plant.*

having many branch tips, from which the next season's flowers will be borne.

Brunfelsia thrives in compost-enriched, sandy soil; one recipe is to mix equal parts soil, well-rotted leaf mold, sand, and peat moss. Repot in spring to a slightly undersize pot as best bloom occurs on plants that have recently become rootbound.

There are several brunfelsias in cultivation, ranging from low shrubs to small trees. Fragrance is a common trait, and while references variously cite them as blooming in specific seasons, many have the pleasant habit of intermittent flowering. *Brunfelsia australis* placed in a warm, sunny greenhouse or plant room in autumn, watered generously, and top-dressed with 14-14-14 timed-release fertilizer pellets will rarely be out of bloom. While most brunfelsias have the habit of opening a dark lavender blue and fading to near white, hence the common name yesterday-today-and-tomorrow plant, there is also a showy, white-flowered species from the Blue

Mountains of Jamaica called *B. jamaicaensis*. Young plants from rooted cuttings are available from Logee's (see Resources). This species blooms normally from early spring until fall, with two-inch tubular flowers that are nocturnally fragrant.

Cacti and other succulents have been discussed by families and individuals in Chapter 4. Here I want to point out that sometimes they are the ideal choices for an outdoor container gardener who is extremely busy or must travel out of town frequently. If set in appropriately large pots that quickly drain off any excess water from rain or from your watering can, and where there is a half day or more of sun, there are an infinite number of cacti and other succulents that will grow beautifully, mostly without any help from you. Some of the choicest types for this treatment are succulent sedums, sempervivums, echeverias, aloes, aeoniums, and kalanchoes; and among the cacti, mammillaria, opuntia, rebutia, and notocactus.

Camellia is one of the flowers for which I have carried a torch longest—only now am I about to have a place where they can be grown indoors/outdoors. The nicest house-grown ones in memory are those on the unheated (but frost-free) sun porch of a friend in Kansas City. Beginning in autumn, the night temperatures are between 45° and 55°F. The porch faces east and receives some sun from the south. However, large deciduous trees provide a certain amount of shade, even in winter when they are leafless.

An acid soil that tests between pH 4.0 to 5.0 is used, and it is composed of two parts sphagnum peat moss to one each of well-rotted compost and clean, sharp sand. The porch has a relative humidity of fifty percent or more most of the year. This is maintained by growing other cool-loving plants set in trays of pebbles and water on the porch.

In addition to the pebble humidity trays, my friend mists the foliage and buds of the camellias once or twice a day with water until blooming begins. These tubbed camellias spend the summer outdoors under the shade of high-branched trees. They are hosed down daily with water in the absence of showers. A close watch is kept for mites, scale, and mealybugs. As necessary, insecticidal soap or neem sprays are applied weekly.

Repotting is done just before growth becomes active in spring. If a plant does not need repotting, some of the surface soil is removed and replaced with fresh. In spring and early summer, an acid fertilizer such as 30-10-10 is used. Pruning is also done in the spring, after flowering.

Here are some other success tips for camellias: Bud drop can be caused by high or fluctuating temperatures and drafts, or by letting the soil dry out. Aluminum sulfate may be applied to increase soil acidity, at the rate of one ounce per gallon of water. To get specimen blooms, pinch off all the buds except one in each cluster when the buds are still quite small. Applying gibberellic acid is another way to get a few extraordinary camellia blossoms; details are available from the American Camellia Society (see Resources).

One of the things about camellias that appeals to me, their beauty aside, is that there are so many, with natural flowering times from fall to spring. By careful selection it is possible to have a burst of bloom in winter with a scattering in other seasons, or some all along but no single crescendo. Another feature that appeals to me about camellias is that some are delightfully scented, especially found among *Camellia sasanqua*, *C. lutchuensis*, and recently introduced cultivars 'Fragrant Pink' and 'Scentuous'.

In order to have camellias that bloom profusely, proper pruning is a necessity. In fact, the late C. Norwood Hastie, Jr., of Magnolia Gardens, Johns Island, South Carolina, wrote " . . . once you understand the necessity for constant pruning and training of camellias, the appearance of the plants becomes as interesting and rewarding as the blossoms themselves." Here are some suggestions from an article he wrote for the American Camellia Society Yearbook and Journal:

1) The ideally pruned camellia is one with an interior completely hollow and free of twigs and foliage, with lower limbs pruned clear of the ground. Branches or foliage less than twelve inches from the ground may be considered too low.

2) Look into the interior near the soil; probably there will be a few entirely dead twigs on the main branch. Remove them, making the cut next to the trunk. Do not leave stubs.

3) Now look for twigs that are still alive but definitely detract from the plant. If you are in doubt as to whether or not a twig or branch ought to come off, comparing the one in question with vigorous shoots at the top will show you.

4) The control of scale is closely tied in with pruning. You can see how scale is favored on branches near the soil and seems to thrive on interior twigs. A plant badly infested with scale must be drastically pruned or much of your spraying effort will be in vain. Watch for and remove deformed, curled leaves; they harbor scale.

5) As a general rule cut out branches that tend to grow inward, for they will be shaded out in later years.

6) To prune an old camellia, which has perhaps become a mass of long, stringy, knotted branches, examine each branch from the outer end and follow it toward the main trunk. Usually, somewhere between the tip and the trunk there will be a vigorous shoot—perhaps small—starting out. Cut the branch off at this shoot, leaving the latter to break out and grow.

7) If a camellia is in such poor condition that good medial shoots cannot be found, remove a large proportion of the poor branches and wait to see which parts put out new growth. Portions that fail to respond must be then cut back further.

Chrysanthemums, at least of the florist type, we think of as seasonal flowering plants, and I have previously discussed them as such on page 39. Here I want to introduce the possibility of growing trained or extraordinarily flowered chrysanthemum cultivars as part of the indoor/outdoor garden. These plants can make marvelous container specimens that are fascinating to observe in a garden at nearly every stage of growth. Chrysanthemums do best when divided every spring. Replant only the strongest divisions from the perimeter of the clump. Discard the woodier parts from the center. Cuttings of tip growth three to five inches long root readily and also form vigorous new plants.

Besides annual division, chrysanthemums also need frequent pinching back from early in the season until midsummer. This causes many branches to form and results in a much more abundant flower show. Or you may wish to grow cascades, tree-form standards, or single-stemmed plants, each topped by a single perfect blossom.

Through the growing season it is vital that chrysanthemums have always an ample supply of water. If the leaves wilt regularly for lack of moisture, the older ones will die prematurely and the wood of the plant will harden nonproductively. It's best to set the plants in fairly large containers where soil moisture and temperatures can be stabilized. Situate where there is a half day or more of sun and apply liquid 15-30-15 fertilizer regularly, or top-dress with timed-release pellets. When brought indoors, these plants need an abundance of light and fresh, moist air that circulates freely.

Two *Chrysanthemum* species I have seen recently in large pots outdoors were *C. nipponicum* or Montauk daisy, and *C. pacificum*, which has silver-edged gray-green leaves that at the very end of the growing season are crowned by golden heads of tansylike flowers. The Boston daisy, known until recently as *Chrysanthemum frutescens*, has been given a new botanical name: *Argyranthemum frutescens chrysaster*. Culture remains the same as for chrysanthemum.

Clerodendrum. This genus gives us at least one flowering shrub that is winter-hardy to 0°F, *Clerodendrum trichotomum*, and a host of other species that make wonderful indoor/outdoor container plants. *Clerodendrum thomsoniae*, the bleeding-heart vine, is to me one of the loveliest of all flowering vines. It does need a trellis, or you can train it wreath-style around a circular wire or dried vine form about twenty to twenty-four inches in diameter, secured upright in a twelve-inch container.

Clerodendrum thomsoniae blooms on new growth and will benefit from generous amounts of humus matter in the soil, peat moss, well-rotted leaf mold, and compost as well, and regular applications of fertilizer high in ni-

trogen. It needs a half day of sun and thorough watering before the soil becomes dry enough to wilt the large quilted leaves.

Bleeding-heart vine can be grown indoors in a sunny window, or outdoors during frost-free weather. It can also be trained as a hanging-basket plant and will tend to bloom whenever temperatures are warm and there is adequate sun to promote new growth. Once or twice a year, after a period of heavy flowering, thin out the oldest wood and prune back any overly rampant growth. This encourages new flowering shoots and helps develop a compact, attractive habit.

Dwarf banana. *Ensete ventricosum*, also known as *Musa ensete* or Abyssinian banana, is a broad-leaved member of the banana family that is often grown as a tub plant, kept indoors in cold weather, outdoors if possible when the season is warm and frost-free. It needs a

Bleeding-heart vine, Clerodendrum thomsoniae, *which flowers most profusely after cutting back and repotting has fostered lots of exuberant new growth. Training to a large wreath shape or on some kind of trellising promotes the development of laterals on which still more flowering occurs.*

half day or more of sun, humus-rich, loam-based potting soil, and lots of water and fertilizer in warm weather.

Ficus is for figs. Trees that produce edible figs can also make exciting indoor/outdoor container plants. One of the plants I have helped care for on Long Island is a big 'Brown Turkey' fig that has been established several years in a two-foot-square Versailles tub. It gets top-dressed with an enriched soil every spring when the branches are pruned back by a third or more. Last season there were exactly ninety-nine figs, all of excellent quality. Before hard freezing, it is wheeled into a sun-heated pit greenhouse where the temperatures rarely fall below freezing and there it spends the cold season in a state of semi-dormancy.

Not only does this tubbed fig tree produce a harvest of edible fruit, it also provides summer shade and the bare ground around it in the planter is used for growing any number of smaller plants, even the likes of dwarf bush cherry and pear tomatoes, bush basil, rosemary, and thyme.

Incidentally, one fall day while visiting the Morris Arboretum in Philadelphia, I was given a tip cutting of a fruit-bearing fig with an unusually notched leaf. Back home I stuck it in a pot of moist soil in a warm, moist light garden and right away new leaves began to grow. Now, some three or four years later, this has become a tree nearly five feet tall that grows in a twelve-inch clay pot. This season there were at least two dozen perfect edible figs.

If a potted edible fig must be carried over winter in the house, situate it in a bright or sunny place where, ideally, temperatures are cool but frost-free. Keep the soil on the dry side, but never bone-dry, and do not fertilize.

Fuchsia. These handsome small shrubs or trees have simple, usually opposite leaves, and spectacular blossoms arising from the leaf axils on new growth. Fuchsia flowers are unusual in having brilliantly colored sepals instead of the inconspicuous green ones of many other flowers. The fuchsia sepals are elongated tubes with four widely flaring petallike parts which open to expose the pendent petals and extruding stamens. Petals may be four or five in number, often twice that in the double forms, and

may match or contrast with the sepals in coloring. The tones range from pure white through pale pink to rose, red, lavender, violet, purple, and blue in the hybrids, with hundreds of named cultivars from which to choose. Some are hanging basket or shelf plants, others grow as graceful upright shrubs. There are also tiny miniatures, 'Isis' for example, and the larger honeysuckle fuchsia, 'Gartenmeister Bohnstedt', that can be grown as houseplants.

Fuchsias need semisun to semishade, frost-free temperatures but coolness when possible, and fresh, moist air. They need a humus-rich, loam-based potting soil kept evenly moist spring-summer, on the dry side in fall and winter when the plants are semidormant. At the time they are brought indoors before frost in autumn, prune back by up to two thirds. Root cuttings in late winter or early spring.

In hotter climates, especially inland, summer heat can make fuchsias miserable. Hector Black, a Tennessee grower who has specialized in this plant, says, "I eliminate the ones that fail in hot weather. Also, if you want heat resistance, steer clear of the big doubles. Almost invariably the singles and smaller-flowered ones are the better choices for hot weather." Some fuchsia cultivars that have proven heat-resistant include, besides 'Gartenmeister Bohnstedt', 'Red Cardinal', 'New Fascination', 'Marinka', 'Hollydale', 'Rufus', 'Mephisto', and 'Mrs. L. Swisher'.

Impatiens. I will never forget my first encounter with impatiens as an eight-year-old on a midsummer day's journey with my parents to visit relatives. We stopped at a roadside vegetable stand and there were these tall juice cans in which were growing what seemed to me the most exotic plants in the world. I realize now they were the tall and graceful precursors of today's flower-smothered mounds that have become something of a cliché for color in shade gardens. Quite recently I have had the pleasure of seeing impatiens growing wild in the United States National Rain Forest, El Junque, in Puerto Rico. This magical place is a pleasant hour's drive into the country from San Juan and the only U.S. national forest located in a tropical climate. Since it is relatively close to home, a visit there is the most expeditious way to experience the rain-forest habitat which many of us try to approximate in our indoor gardens.

I have started impatiens seeds indoors, in my closet light garden, but otherwise I find them quite impossible to manage as houseplants owing to persistent and worsening attacks of spider mites. They are surprisingly adaptable and rewarding outdoors, especially if you venture beyond the dwarf hybrids and try some of the species or "wild" types. In any case, the facts of light have a great deal to do with success. The *Impatiens wallerana* types, the most familiar of the commercial types, tend to flower better in more light, not less. The New Guinea hybrids, with unusually large flowers and often colorfully variegated leaves, definitely need direct sun most of the time.

Impatiens grow ideally in slightly acid soil, pH 5.5 to 6.5. Many that we buy are started in peat-based growing mediums. These transplant most effectively into soil that has been enriched with sphagnum peat moss or other humus such as well-rotted oak leaves, and with sand added in the event of poor drainage.

To promote general growth and flowering, use a balanced fertilizer such as 20-20-20 or time-released 14-14-14. If well-formed bushes fail to bloom in adequate light, change to a low-nitrogen formula such as 1-6-5. Try not to let your impatiens get so dry that the leaves wilt. This reduces flowering and invites spider mites.

The species impatiens I have enjoyed growing in recent years is marketed as 'African Queen'. It produces clusters of orange-red and yellow one-inch flowers that remind me of candy corn. With a couple of deft pinches a young plant assumes the appearance of a miniature tree about fifteen inches tall. I haven't grown 'African King', but it is said to yield large cornucopia-shaped flowers of dark crimson in generous clusters among dark quilted leaves.

Iochroma is one of those violet-blue flowers that I find nearly irresistible. It is a member of the solanum family from tropical South America. Summer is its time for growth and bloom, outdoors, in direct sun. A space air conditioned for human comfort in hot weather will not do. One sees these plants as large shrubs in southern California gardens, and I marvel that we do not grow

them more in containers in summer gardens everywhere. They need weekly insecticidal soap sprays against whiteflies, lots of water, plenty of fertilizer, and sharp pruning back and repotting at the beginning of the season in spring. In winter, maintain indoors cool but frost-free, on the dry side, and do not fertilize. Spray as necessary against whiteflies.

Lantana. *Lantana camara*, from the West Indies, and its cultivars are shrubby, spreading perennials which will bloom the year round if they receive sufficient sunlight and moisture. The flowers are in dense heads, about two inches across, usually creamy yellow, or dark yellow aging to orange and red, although there are numerous other color selections, from nearly pure white to very dark pink-purple. *Lantana montevidensis*, from Uruguay, is less shrubby and, when planted in a hanging basket, makes a graceful cascade of green foliage and countless heads of lavender blossoms. There is a white-flowered form that I prefer. The secret with this species is constant pinching or shearing back in the early stages; then the multibranched plant can be permitted to come into flower.

Lantana, like basil, is almost always accompanied by whiteflies. Fortunately the control—weekly sprays with insecticidal soap or neem solution—is not difficult. Lantana leaves have a wonderful fragrance when they are disturbed and leaves of *Lantana camara* (yellow sage) are used for brewing a tea; the seeds, however, are poisonous.

Lantana, indoors or out, needs full sun and lots of fresh air; ideal growing temperatures are from 50° to 60°F at night up to 75° to 80°F by day. It needs a loam-based potting soil kept evenly moist in spring and summer and on the dry side fall through winter. Root cuttings late winter or spring. Readily trainable as tree-form standard, or treat as a bushy shrub or hanging plant.

Lonicera, the genus name for honeysuckle, is not necessarily synonymous with fragrance or everblooming habit. However, here are some that can be managed as indoor/outdoor plants for a long season of fragrant bloom and trainable growth habits.

Lonicera sempervirens 'Flava' is a relatively small-growing honeysuckle that has the pleasing habit of blooming intermittently over a long season. Though 'Flava' can be grown over a broad geographic range, with winter lows from 40° below zero to 40°F above, and summer highs to 90°F or more, it is not nearly as well-known as the rampant Hall's and Tatarian, both of which are also fragrant and bloom over a long season. 'Flava' can be grown in a ten-inch pot with a tepee trellis formed by three or four four-foot bamboo stakes placed equidistant around the pot perimeter and tied together at the top with a twist tie. This plant can then be brought inside at the beginning of winter to a frost-free sun space where

it will continue flowering. Provide a humus-rich, loam-based potting soil kept evenly moist in warm weather.

In gardens where winter means temperatures as low as minus 20°F, the winter honeysuckle, *Lonicera fragrantissima*, is a tempting species. It could make a splendid candidate for a large pot in a cool home greenhouse or sun porch, with sweet-smelling blossoms virtually every sunny day during the coldest weather of the year.

Mandevilla. Pale pink *Mandevilla sanderi* and its vivid dark pink cultivar 'Red Riding Hood' yield a profusion of three-inch trumpet flowers that appear nearly nonstop,

Mandevilla sanderi 'Red Riding Hood' blooms all year, more generously and in a much more vivid color than the species, itself no ugly duckling. This evergreen vine trains beautifully on a bamboo cane tepee, as a large wreath, on a trellis, or around a hanging basket.

month after month, season after season. These are small twining vines sometimes listed under the name *Dipladenia* that can be trained as bushes, as pillars on a bamboo tepee, or as wreaths. Mandevillas may be grown outdoors all year where temperatures stay above freezing. They are popular all across the Deep South and warm Southwest. Another named cultivar, 'Alice Du Pont', has larger flowers and leaves and makes a spectacular show on a trellis or pergola.

'Red Riding Hood' in particular makes a splendid houseplant and in this situation probably works best trained around a wire or vine wreath staked upright in an eight- to ten-inch pot. Water well, then not again until a pinch of the surface soil feels nearly dry. Avoid extremes or many leaves may yellow and fall. If there is any secret to growing mandevilla with an abundance of flowers it is to provide a "tight shoe." In other words, flowering is stimulated as the roots become slightly pot-bound. It also helps if the environment is sunny bright, warm, and moderately humid with fresh air circulation.

The only serious problem I've experienced with mandevilla is mealybugs. Rubbing off with alcohol and cotton swabs is a completely safe and effectual treatment, but you must be thorough and keep a sharp eye out for any new arrivals. Spraying with insecticidal soap is another means of control.

Medinilla, of all the plants one ever sees coddled in a container indoors/outdoors through all kinds of weather, is the treasure, one seldom seen except in conservatory collections of tropicals. The first I ever saw, and still the largest, was grown by the parks department of the city of Paris. The young gardener assigned as my host spoke little English and I little French but we had no trouble communicating about *Medinilla magnifica*. The specimen stood nearly four feet tall and as broad at the edge of an indoor pool, with many arching branches drooping panicles of purple-anthered carmine-red flowers set in showy pink bracts; all of this was reflected in the water. Definitely Medinilla the Magnificent.

During the seasons of active growth—from spring to early fall—medinilla needs warmth (70°F the nighttime minimum), strong light but not to the point of scorching the leaves, and an abundance of water. Fertilize frequently. In late fall and early winter provide cooler temperatures (50° to 55°F the minimum at night) and water less, but never let the roots get dry enough to wilt the leaves. Change from this lean regimen in late winter to warmer and wetter conditions with high humidity, and expect flowering soon afterward, into summer.

Repot medinilla and do any pruning to direct overall shape after flowering finishes, presumably by midsummer. Use a mix of two parts sphagnum peat moss to one each of packaged all-purpose potting soil and clean, sharp sand (or perlite). If you have well-rotted compost or oak leaf mold, add one to two parts. As new growth commences, pinch out the tips to encourage branching.

Medinilla can be propagated from cuttings of half-ripe wood (see page 54) in the late winter or early spring. Keep constantly moist and warm, around 80° to 85°F. Air-layering is also a possibility, beginning in the same time frame.

Apart from having an established plant in excellent health, flowering in medinilla is really dependent on the contrast between a growing season characterized by tropical warmth and humidity and a time of rest in autumn that is induced by shorter days, cooler temperatures, less water, and no fertilizer. Although medinilla may survive life in a window garden that is air conditioned in summer, don't expect blooms without real seasonal heat and high humidity.

Nerium oleander is the botanical name for oleander, a plant that is potentially nearly everblooming, fragrant, and able to withstand the driest of soils in the midst of high temperatures and heavy air pollution. It is no wonder this old-fashioned plant has become increasingly popular for landscaping outdoors in mild climates and growing in containers elsewhere. For winter a place that is frost-free and sunny is ideal. There are some dwarf cultivars, nice for pots and conservatories or plant rooms. When oleander is indoors in fall and winter, keep it in a bright, cool place, with soil on the dry side and no fertilizer.

Oleanders thrive on all the direct sun you can give them, warm days and moderate nights, 60° to 80°F. They need fertilizing with 30-10-10 or any high-nitrogen fertilizer from time to time to keep the leaves green and new shoots growing, and 20-20-20 or 15-30-15 alternated on a regular basis when there is ample light and warmth to nurture active flowering.

I cannot write about oleander without mentioning its poisonous nature. This plant is never to be chewed and prunings are best buried so that no unsuspecting person burns them and inhales the smoke, or chooses one for roasting a hot dog. On the brighter side, oleanders can be delightfully fragrant, they start blooming as rooted cuttings, and are readily trainable into small tree-form standards, to eight feet high, that look just right next to terrace and patio seating in warm weather.

Passiflora. There are perhaps five hundred different species of *Passiflora* and now uncounted hybrids, many of them from the efforts of breeder Patrick Worley, whose business is called The Plant Kingdom and is based in Lincoln Acres, California, and John MacDougal of the Missouri Botanical Garden. To my way of thinking these flowering vines offer all the potential of clematis, and some also produce edible fruits. The finest I have seen as container plants are those in the collection of C. Z. Guest on Long Island. Each large pot, about fifteen inches in diameter, is outfitted with a pipe four feet tall that has a metal plate welded on the bottom, which becomes buried and anchored in the soil, and on top there is a circle about twenty inches in diameter, sort of like a steering wheel. The passionvine shoots are first trained up the pipe, then through and around the top wheel. After about three months of training they droop, swoop, and send off shoots in all directions, with untold numbers of flowers.

C. Z.'s passifloras receive full sun, abundant watering, and ample fertilizing, alternating between 30-10-10 and 15-30-15, in very much the same program she uses with orchids, Chinese hibiscus, abutilons, begonias, and fuchsias. One of the nice bonuses about passiflora is that when the plants can be kept in a warm, sunny, moist, airy environment in winter, such as a heated sun porch or home greenhouse, they go on flowering intermittently. Even one of these flowers brings great joy on a cold winter day and a certain magic to a small vase of flowers set on the dining table or next to your bed.

Plumeria. Frangipani is another name for this elegant member of the dogbane family (Apocynaceae), the creamy or velvety flowers of which are synonymous with the Hawaiian lei. *Plumeria rubra* (red jasmine), ten to fifteen feet, from Mexico to Venezuela, has large leaves, to sixteen inches long and four inches wide. The highly fragrant summer flowers vary in color from pink to rosy purple, are about two inches long, and flare at the top to an equal width. There are also many other plumerias, some having the most subtle pastel colors to be found in the plant kingdom. Situate a young plumeria in a twelve- to fifteen-inch pot or tub and prune to convenient size each year immediately after the flowering season.

To me the plumeria is one of the choicest of plants that can be grown on the indoor/outdoor plan. After orchids, hardly anything is more thrilling or collectible for the serious amateur. Success at this pursuit might well begin by studying *The Handbook on Plumeria Culture* (Tropical Plant Specialists, 1991) by Richard and Mary Helen Eggenberger, who are also owners of a nursery called The Plumeria People (see Resources). There is also a Plumeria Society of America (see Resources).

An established potted plumeria can be rejuvenated without going through complete repotting. The Eggenbergers recommend removing the top two or three inches of old potting mix and replacing with fresh, then applying liquid manure tea. Position outdoors in full to part sun as soon as the weather is warm and settled and there is no possibility of freezing. Water generously and fertilize regularly. In autumn, before danger of frost, stop fertilizing, gradually reduce the amount of water, and bring the plumeria indoors. Maintain in semidormancy through winter, on the dry side, no fertilizer, in bright light to sun.

Tibouchina, also called Brazilian princess flower or glory bush, is to me one of the most beautiful plants in the indoor/outdoor crowd. I suppose it is flowered indoors but the best I've seen were spending the summer outdoors in half to full sun. There they burst into bloom around the Fourth of July; if constantly watered and fertilized

Plumeria obtusa *flowers in El Yunque, the rain forest in Puerto Rico. It makes a remarkably rewarding container plant requiring little in winter except a place that is frost-free.*

they will still be going full tilt at frost time. The flowers are large purple-blue with prominent pink filaments. The velvety leaves are uniquely quilted. Habit and size vary depending on what is needed and how it's trained. Tibouchinas grown from cuttings and trained as low bushes are becoming popular in summer bedding-out schemes, often seen in the company of purple pennisetum, an ornamental grass, purple-leaved *Oxalis regnellii*, and any of the vervains, such as *Verbena bonariensis* and V. *rigida* 'Polaris'.

The way I have grown tibouchinas is to treat them as large, multibranched shrubs, or as tree-form standards. They train beautifully because when the wood is cut back, many sprouts rise up, not just at those points where a leaf or twig might once have arisen. I learned this one spring when my tibouchinas got put outdoors too soon and suffered a severe freezing. When the frozen parts had all been removed, nothing was left but leafless sticks that showed enough green for me to have hope. "High-

nitrogen fertilizer" flashed in my mind, 30-10-10 for example. "Warm, humid atmosphere" came next, and, as activity became apparent, increasing and generous amounts of water. Lots of sun with air movement too.

Besides what I've said, the one other secret with tibouchina is to persevere with pinching in spring, or the first two months of active growth, when you are pushing with 30-10-10. As each shoot or branch produces one or two pairs of new leaves, remove the emerging or smallest pair. Four to six weeks after you stop pinching, and change to a blossom-booster fertilizer such as 15-30-15, flowering will begin.

Through summer and fall the tibouchinas in my care spend the summer outdoors in large clay containers on a very sunny terrace. They are watered nearly every day and fertilized on weekends, 15-30-15 for flowers, or 30-10-10 if I detect any yellowing in the leaves. Weekly spraying with insecticidal soap keeps bugs at bay, the most threatening being whiteflies.

When tibouchinas are moved to a sunny enclosure in autumn, before frost, they seem at their height of glory, but then we've been saying that already for months. Hardly any woody plant is as consistently showy for as long and it appears that gardeners all over North America are succeeding with tibouchina. With cool nights (between 40° and 50°F) and full sun the foliage and buds take on burnished rosy hues. It's almost too good to be true, but when the blooms finish they quietly disappear, self-cleaning themselves to the breezes.

Vireya rhododendrons are an exciting group of tropicals that can be carried over winter in a greenhouse or sun porch. I have not personally had any experience with them, but I have seen them growing in several gardens. At the Brooklyn Botanic Garden they are kept in hanging pots in the orchid house. I have seen them in breathtaking bloom growing in the ground at the Strybing Arboretum in San Francisco. As they are epiphytic in nature, vireyas need a loose, extremely well-drained planting mix. Some of the commercial orchid barks would probably work as a planting mix. The use of a very dilute liquid fertilizer monthly works well. Fish emulsion at half the recommended strength is satisfactory, according to a friend who

Vireya *is allied with the more familiar* Rhododendron *and is a shrubby plant from the Himalayas. Successful orchid growers often find the vireya is compatible and not too much of a stretch.*

grows vireyas. They also need to be on the dry side for a brief period before each thorough watering. If new growth is chlorotic and doesn't green up, add a little

ferrous sulfate to the mix. Situate in bright light but protect from hot, direct sun in warm weather.

Over twenty different rhododendrons of the vireya type are listed by specialist growers, making this a major and relatively new collectible on the American gardening scene. The late T. H. Everett noted that the vireyas were intolerant of both winter cold and extreme heat and suggested growing them in a greenhouse or other controlled environment with a minimum winter night temperature of 55° to 60°F, not higher than 65° to 70°F by day. In summer, night temperatures are best kept at 60° to 70°F, to as high as 80°F in the day, but always with fresh air that circulates freely.

I dare say that vireyas can be managed nicely in many parts of the country by keeping them outdoors in warmest weather, in a slat house or other partly shaded area, perhaps along with orchids, bromeliads, and epiphytic gesneriads such as columnea and aeschynanthus. Keep them cool in winter in almost any indoor garden, striving to maintain the growing medium on the dry side but never extremely dry. The air needs to be quite moist and to move freely, very much the same as for orchids. The vireyas to have a tendency to legginess, but the flowers are so uncommonly beautiful in form and color, who could care about a little gangliness?

chapter nine

Trouble in Paradise: Bugs, Blights, and Bloomless Dilemmas

Every active house garden has its share of predatory insects that chew and suck the vital juices from leaves and buds, not to mention an occasional slug or caterpillar that can do major damage in one evening. There are also leaf blights and root rots but mostly the problems have to do with some imbalance in the environment or perhaps some misunderstanding about the plant's needs.

Obviously, the healthier the plant, the less vulnerable it is to attack. Keeping leaves clean by using nothing more than fresh water is a considerable deterrent to insects such as spider mites and aphids. Spraying weekly with insecticidal soap or neem solution is the way to thoroughly clean up insect infestations but the old idea, to spray weekly whether or not there were insects damaging the plants, is no longer valid. I say concentrate on growing healthy plants and the rest will more or less take care of itself.

Some insects that attack houseplants are too small to be seen well with the naked eye, but sucking types such as aphids, mealybugs, whiteflies, and brown scale are detected fairly readily. These insects leave a sticky substance, called honeydew, which in turn acts as a host to sooty mold. Unless you have exceptionally sharp eyes, you'd better invest in a high quality magnifying glass.

Aphids. There are hundreds of different kinds of aphids or plant lice. They cluster on new growth, causing it to become discolored and malformed. Their presence can suggest excess nitrogen, but not necessarily. Wash off as many as you can in a stream of running water.

Aphids, here on a Chinese hibiscus, cluster on new shoots and flower buds.

Some can be dealt with directly, by squeezing them between your fingers. Insecticidal soap and neem sprays are also effective against aphids.

Cyclamen mites. This insect is difficult to control. It is an infinitesimal creature capable of rendering horrendous damage to plants, causing new leaves to emerge deformed and stunted. Mite damage is readily detected in African violets. The center leaves become thickly furred, petioles (leaf stalks) are visibly shortened, and buds have enlarged stems so dwarfed in length that the flowers seem to be opening near the soil. Dispose of badly infested plants and start new ones from fresh leaves. If the plants are irreplaceable, clean them up by cutting out the infested part, and spray the plant with a miticide such as insecticidal soap. Leaves and buds already damaged will not grow out to natural size, but following a weekly spray program, new growth should be normal. Keep cyclamen-mite-infested plants isolated. Wash your hands well before touching other plants, for these mites are easily carried from one place to another. Other gesneriads, begonias, and cyclamen are especially susceptible.

Earthworms. These necessary inhabitants in the outdoor garden aren't always as welcome in the house. There was a time when I suggested ridding pots of them by

Mealybugs and other scale insects can be removed by the gardener, using a cotton swab dipped in rubbing alcohol.

drenching the soil with malathion. I hope Mother Earth will forgive me for making such a blatantly stupid recommendation. Today I am sure there are some earthworms among my many plants, but they are no problem whatsoever. There was an article by Anne Raver in a recent issue of *The New York Times* about how John Ameroso, an agricultural extension agent who lives in Brooklyn, is using earthworms to make compost of vegetable waste matter under his kitchen sink.

Gnats. These gray to near-black insects are about one eighth of an inch long. The adults, while harmless to plants, are a nuisance to have around. They hatch from whitish maggots, about one fourth inch in length, which are likely to be in soils containing decaying plant materials. In concentrated numbers the maggots can be detrimental to roots. Otherwise my advice about gnats is to increase air circulation and ignore them.

Mealybugs. These are soft-scale insects covered with waxy powder. They are one of the most persistent insects where house gardens are concerned. They look like specks of cotton on a plant. If there are but a few (I question the possibility of a "few" mealybugs), remove them individually by using a cotton swab dipped in denatured (rubbing) alcohol. A more pervasive infestation can be treated by spraying weekly with insecticidal soap or neem solutions.

Spider mites. Too small to be seen easily with the naked eye, these tiny insects spin fine webs on the undersides of leaves, and in advanced stages around the growing tips. They suck plant juices until the leaves become nearly transparent. If you aren't sure of their presence, shake a branch of the plant over a sheet of paper. If dark specks fall to the surface and start moving around, get out your sprayer with insecticidal soap or neem solution. Spray weekly until the spider mites are gone. Spider mites are highly opportunistic, so when they appear, you know that something is stressing the plant. Treat the plant at once to stop the mites, then set about to give it better care and less stress.

Scale. Hard or soft scales are brown or black, round, slow-moving insects—but they do definitely move around, from leaf to leaf, plant to plant, and even room to room. Treat exactly as described for mealybugs.

Slugs. If you are an active house gardener, slugs will happen. They live around plants, under the rims of clay pots, in woods moss. Constant vigilance in plant sanitation is the best control measure.

Sowbugs (also called pillbugs). These insects have segmented, shell-like bodies. The sowbug is oval, up to one half of an inch long and usually gray. When you expose one at work (eating decaying organic matter and, rarely, tender plant parts), it runs for cover. Pillbugs roll up in a ball. I know these insects inhabit my houseplant collection but they have never been a problem.

Springtails. The near-microscopic insects which scurry on the surface of humusy, moist potting soil are called springtails. Sometimes they damage emerging seedlings. They are often confused with the harmless psocids that live in similar conditions, and which you may have seen between the leaves of old, slightly damp books or magazines. Increasing fresh air circulation is the only treatment needed.

Thrips. These small sucking insects feed on the juices of leaves and flowers. They rasp away the plant tissue, leaving thin papery scars. In the outdoor garden they

This slug is no doubt heading out to work, to chew holes in your most cherished buds (orchids of any kind are especially tasty) and leaves. Hand picking and beer traps are effective. Check pots for slugs (and snails) before bringing them in from outdoors.

Brown scale, here on an African gardenia (Mitriostigma axillare), *occurs mostly on the undersides of leaves and along the stems and stalks of the plant.*

favor gladiolus; indoors, florist gloxinia. Spray weekly with insecticidal soap or neem.

Whiteflies. These small flying insects cluster on the undersides of leaves, eventually turning them yellow and producing sufficient honeydew to host sooty mold. Spray weekly with insecticidal soap or neem. Be thorough. Be quick. Do your work very early in the day, or when temperatures are coolest; that is when the flies are least active and most likely to stay put on the leaf while you do them in.

Yellow sticky traps are used to catch adult whiteflies and also as a way of monitoring the population that could be building up in a collection of plants.

Certain plants seem destined to host at one time or another certain insects, the sign of which does not necessarily mean the plant is unduly stressed. However, a diet of weak light and haphazard watering will almost surely lead to insect problems.

BENEFICIAL INSECTS AND BIOLOGICAL CONTROLS

By social conscience or by law it has become a necessity for outdoor gardeners to learn about and practice IPM, for Integrated Pest Management. This requires among other things monitoring on a regular, routine basis insect populations in the garden and never using a lethal, one-application-kills-everything pesticide. In fact, the right combination of patience and "good" guys versus "bad" guys often means that the gardener needs to do nothing, just keep gardening so as to nurture the plants. The concept applies also to the new houseplant and numerous sources for beneficial insects and biological insect controls are listed in the back of this book (see Resources). Besides encouraging the plants by taking good care of them, it is often necessary that beneficial insects or biological controls be introduced to the indoor garden. Some specific possibilities are these:

Diatomaceous earth. A fine, powdery substance made from the cracked shells of one-celled sea plants called diatoms. When dusted on plant parts being chewed or sucked, or on the soil surface around a plant where slugs or snails are suspected, microscopic needles of silica puncture and discourage or kill a wide variety of "bad" guys.

Green lacewings. The larvae of *Chrysoperia carnea* eat aphids, mealybugs, immature scales and whiteflies, the eggs of many undesirable insects and mites, thrips, and spider mites. If there is high humidity, such as in a greenhouse, the related *Chrysoperia rufilabris* is more effective.

Lady beetles. Adults and larvae are predators of aphids and many other plant insect pests.

Mite predators. These are effective against the usual houseplant red and two-spotted spider mite, also many others. Three of these types, which may be sold in mixture, are *Phytoseiulus persimilis*, *Neoseiulus californicus*, and *Mesoseiulus longipes*. They live among the mites, consume them, and lay eggs, but cause no harm to the plant.

Parasitic wasp. The tiny *Encarsia formosa* is harmless to people, plants, and other insects, yet death to whiteflies.

Sticky traps. These are usually yellow and are hung among plants to catch flying insects such as aphids and whiteflies. They are also used to monitor the general population of flying insects.

"NATURAL" PESTICIDES NOT NECESSARILY SAFE

Perhaps least recognized about "natural" pesticides is that they are not necessarily safe. I read in an old book that cigar butts could be turned into a "safe but effective spray against plant insects." Never mind the procedure required to do this (who is going to smoke the cigars in the first place?), why not use a truly safe and effective spray of insecticidal soap and water?

The old remedy was to steep cigar butts in boiling water until it became the color of weak tea. Then cool, strain, and apply as a spray for plants attacked by the likes of aphids and whiteflies. While plant-derived pesticides such as pyrethrum are relatively safe, nicotine in solution is more toxic to people and pets than such chemicals as carbaryl, malathion, and methoxychlor.

The most recent entry into the field of botanically derived and safer pesticides is neem, the active ingredient being Azadirachtin, which is extracted from the seeds of the neem tree, *Azadirachta indica*, also known as margosa in India. It is a beautiful evergreen shade tree from the mahogany family whose origins lie in southern and southeastern Asia, but today it is also cultivated in Australia, parts of Africa, Central and South America, the Caribbean, Puerto Rico, and the Virgin Islands. Neem plantings in southern Florida are thriving, and field cultivation has begun in Oklahoma, southern California, and Arizona.

As of this writing neem insecticide concentrate is being marketed under two names, Bioneem and Neemisis, and it has been licensed for control of whiteflies, thrips, mealybugs, caterpillars, aphids, and gypsy moths on ornamentals, trees, and shrubs. The label precautions read like those on a petrochemical, so I take this to be another "natural" pesticide to treat with utmost respect.

If you don't want to spend money on insecticidal soap or neem solution that has been formulated for use on plants, here are some alternatives.

Besides healthy soil and proper care, one of the most effective, safe, and frugal means of insect control in the garden is to prune away and discard the leaves and stems that are infested. Then apply an 0.2 percent solution of soapy water, which can be made by adding 1 teaspoon liquid dishwashing detergent to 1 quart water. Ivory dishwashing liquid is the product often used, but it is not licensed for this purpose and strength presumably can vary enough to make a difference so far as delicate plants are concerned.

Do not spray plants when sunlight is shining directly on them. For greatest effectiveness you must be thorough, consistent (spray the affected plants weekly until they are clean), and vigilant in your watch for undesirable insects.

There is ever-mounting evidence that the stronger the pesticide, the greater the likelihood of resistence building up in the targeted insects. In a recent scientific study, soft brown scale actually showed a significant increase in reproductive capacity when exposed to a sublethal treatment of insecticide.

Alcohol is another ordinary household staple that can be used against insects. Use one pint rubbing alcohol to a gallon of water. Mix well and apply by dipping or spraying the affected areas. For best results, first wash the buggy plant in soapy water, rinse, and allow to dry. Then apply the alcohol treatment and keep the plant out of direct sun until dry. This is safe and effective against aphids, spider mites, mealybugs, scale, and whiteflies— but you must be persistent and thorough, the same as when using soap and water.

In case you like to experiment, try this recipe from organic gardeners Doc and Katy Abraham, reported in *Organic Gardening* magazine and effective against the same insects mentioned in the previous paragraph: Mix together 1 gallon water, 1 tablespoon Tabasco sauce, 1 tablespoon liquid dishwashing detergent, and 1 quart rubbing alcohol.

Malathion is a pesticide that has been around for a long time and at this writing is still available on garden center shelves and still recommended by some gardeners. In a clipping dated 1976 I see that I recommended malathion as a soil drench against the tiny black fungous gnats that sometimes appear among houseplants. Some years later I was informed that malathion comes out of the nerve-gas family and is, among other things, relatively unstable, having a shelf life of perhaps a year. I haven't recommended malathion for several years, but did use it myself in 1985 in a warm, closed greenhouse and without a mask. This sent me to bed for four days and taught me a lesson I hope not to learn again.

In the 1950s, when I was first writing about plants, a commonly recommended pesticide was DDT. Experts in the field said that it was safe and nothing short of miraculous in its ability to rid the garden of troublesome insects. Today I am alarmed at an old photograph that shows me dusting DDT on a gloxinia, again in a greenhouse, again without a mask or any protective clothing on my arms.

Another area where house gardeners need to be cautious is when mixing ingredients for potting soils. Dry perlite, for example, sends up a fine white dust in the air that is certain to set off a coughing spell. This is your body saying no, no, please don't do this to me. The wise gardener always dons a mask or ties a cotton handkerchief across the nose and mouth before commencing any potentially dusty activity. Where perlite is concerned, it's best to open a corner of the bag gently and spray some water inside, then proceed.

One potentially risky activity that is best avoided entirely is the spray painting of flowers, fresh or dried. Breathing any such particulates is risky. My view is that if we stay healthy, we will have plenty of time to appreciate the subtle and natural colorings of all kinds of plant materials.

DIAGNOSING SOME COMMON HOUSEPLANT MISHAPS

The longer I grow houseplants and treat them against such problems as insects and diseases, the more apparent it becomes that a healthy, clean, vigorous houseplant is the best if not only defense. By the time something has gone so wrong that it catches the gardener's attention, there are often several aspects about the plant, the care it receives, and the environment that need to be reviewed in order to decide proper treatment. In the text that follows, I will spell out some specific houseplant problems and give the suggested solutions. At the present time I am personally using only insecticidal soap and alcohol against insects, but plan to try neem the next time caterpillars invade.

COLLAPSED HANGING BASKET

When a houseplant goes to pieces and no insects on which to lay the blame can be found, then something is probably amiss with the care being given or the environment. Despite the strong constitution of the pothos or epipremnum, for instance, hanging basket plantings are often seen in great distress, especially in public places such as restaurants and office buildings. A typical scenario is that the plant has suddenly gotten a lot of yellow leaves, the green ones have gone into a permanent droop and the stems at the base, if checked, will reveal to have rotted off.

This is because the watering needs of hanging containers are obscured—it is hard to see what is going on without climbing up on a stepstool or ladder, or conversely, arranging to unhook and bring the plant down to eye level—and even if the container is reachable, some people just do not like the idea of reaching up and touching soil to feel what is going on. Pothos, for all its endurance, sufficient to be nicknamed "devil's ivy," does need well-drained soil; its roots rot off quickly if left standing in water. However, tip cuttings can be salvaged and set to root in a glass of water in bright light and average room temperatures.

Pothos will grow in almost any soil mix, plain old "dirt" included, if drainage is adequate. The plant can also be grown in nearly full sun or in light that is merely bright enough to read by. I am constantly surprised at where I find a runner of pothos growing in my living room from one of the two large wreaths that stand to the side at either end of the sofa. Some trail down and head for the windows, others for the nearest wall, and yesterday I found one headed under the sofa.

"MYSTERIOUS" FICUS DECLINE

It is impossible to pursue growing plants seriously and not eventually have one that inexplicably goes into decline. When this happened to my *Ficus benjamina*, which had been doing well for several years, I tried first one fertilizer then another, to no avail. Leaves continued to drop prematurely, with twigs and small branches dying as well.

Fortunately, spring house cleaning unearthed a soil pH meter, which it turns out makes quick and simple one of the gardener's most useful chores: soil testing to determine pH, whether acid (pH 4.0 to 7.0) or alkaline (7.0 to 9.0). Most cultivated soils will test betwen 4.5 and 7.5. Within a minute after sticking the two probes of the pH meter in the soil of the ficus tree I knew why it was ailing: Instead of the acidic 5.0 to 6.0 range needed by this genus it was extremely alkaline, slightly above pH 8. This change to strongly alkaline is a common occurrence when potted plants are raised on a regular diet of artificial fertilizer.

An old-fashioned way to correct such a condition is to water with a solution made by mixing one teaspoon cider vinegar with one quart water. Plantswoman Joy Logee Martin originally told me about this, and suggested it as a tonic for such acid-loving plants as Boston fern, Chinese hibiscus, dwarf citrus, ixora, and azalea. I can confirm it works, and since a soil pH meter allows constant monitoring, I know when to add more vinegar water, or, in case the condition becomes too acidic, when to flush out the excess by watering heavily several times within a short period.

It is also possible for a plant such as dwarf pomegranate or rosemary to go into decline, or simply to sit, because the soil has become too acidic. These types thrive in neutral to alkaline soil, 7.0 to 7.5, which is also termed "sweet" or limey. Boost such a plant by scratching a teaspoon or more Dolomite powdered limestone into the surface soil; do not use the "quick" or hydrated lime more commonly sold for lawns.

Without proper pH a plant is not able to assimilate nutrients from the soil, such as nitrogen, phosphorus, potash, and trace elements. Soil test kits, as well as meters, are available to judge the presence of these. Besides knowing the pH of the growing medium, you must also know the pH needs of each plant. A majority thrive between 5.6 and 6.5, but it pays to be sure. The pH requirements for a host of indoor garden plants are set forth in the accompanying chart.

pH Degrees for Indoor Plants

Botanical Name	Common Name	Preferred pH
Abutilon	Flowering maple	5.5–6.5
Acacia	Acacia	6.0–8.0
Acer palmatum	Japanese maple	6.0–8.0
Adiantum	Maidenhair fern	6.0–8.0
Aechmea	Bromeliad	5.0–5.5
Agave	Century plant	5.0–6.5
Aglaonema	Chinese evergreen	5.0–6.0
Allium schoenoprasum	Chives	6.0–7.0
Ananas	Pineapple	5.0–6.0
Anthurium	Flamingo flower	5.0–6.0
Araucaria heterophylla	Norfolk Island pine	5.0–6.0
Asparagus	Asparagus fern	6.0–8.0
Aspidistra	Cast-iron plant	5.5–6.5
Asplenium nidus	Bird's-nest fern	5.0–5.5
Bambusa	Bamboo	5.0–7.0
Begonia	Begonia	5.5–7.0
Billbergia	Bromeliad	5.0–6.0
Bougainvillea	Bougainvillea	5.5–7.5
Cactus	Cactus	4.5–6.0
Caladium	Caladium	6.0–7.5
Calceolaria herbeohybrida	Pocketbook plant	6.0–7.0
Callistemon	Bottlebrush	6.0–7.5
Camellia	Camellia	4.5–5.5
Chaenomeles	Flowering quince	6.0–7.0
Chrysalidocarpus	Palm	6.0–7.5
Chrysanthemum	Chrysanthemum	6.0–7.5
Cissus rhombifolia	Grape ivy	5.0–6.5
Citrofortunella	Kumquat	5.5–6.5
Citrus limon	Lemon	6.0–7.0
Clerodendrum	Bleeding-heart vine	5.0–6.0
Clivia	Kaffir lily	5.5–6.5
Coccoloba	Sea grape	5.0–6.5
Codiaeum	Croton	5.0–6.0
Coffea arabica	Coffee	5.0–6.0
Coleus	Coleus	6.0–7.0
Columnea	Columnea	4.5–5.5
Cuphea	False heather	6.0–7.5
Cyclamen	Cyclamen	6.0–7.0
Cyrtomium falcatum	Hollyleaf fern	4.5–6.0
Dieffenbachia	Dumbcane	5.0–6.0
Dionaea	Venus flytrap	4.0–5.0

pH Degrees for Indoor Plants

Botanical Name	Common Name	Preferred pH
Dizygotheca	False aralia	6.0–7.5
Dracaena	Dracaena	5.0–6.0
Episcia	Flame violet	6.0–7.0
Eucalyptus	Gum tree	6.0–7.0
Euonymus	Euonymus	5.5–7.0
Euphorbia milii 'Splendens'	Crown of thorns	6.0–7.5
E. pulcherrima	Poinsettia	6.0–7.5
Ficus	Fig	5.0–6.0
Fittonia	Nerve plant	5.5–6.5
Freesia	Freesia	6.0–7.5
Fuchsia	Fuchsia	5.5–6.5
Gardenia	Gardenia	5.0–6.0
Gerbera	Transvaal daisy	6.0–6.8
Grevillea robusta	Silk oak	5.5–6.5
Gynura	Purple passion	5.5–6.5
Hedera	English ivy	6.0–8.0
Heliotropium	Heliotrope	6.0–8.0
Hibiscus rosa-sinensis	Hibiscus, Chinese	6.0–7.0
Hippeastrum	Amaryllis	5.5–6.5
Hoya	Wax vine	5.0–6.5
Hyacinthus	Hyacinth	6.5–7.5
Hydrangea macrophylla	Blue florist's hydrangea	4.0–5.0
H. macrophylla	Pink florist's hydrangea	6.0–7.0
H. macrophylla	White florist's hydrangea	6.0–8.0
Impatiens	Impatiens	5.5–6.5
Ipomoea	Morning glory	6.0–7.5
Iresine	Iresine	5.0–6.5
Jasminum	Jasmine	5.5–7.0
Justicia brandegeana	Shrimp plant	5.5–6.5
Kalanchoe	Kalanchoe	6.0–7.5
Lagerstroemia indica	Crape myrtle	5.0–7.5
Lantana	Lantana	5.5–7.0
Laurus nobilis	Sweet bay	4.0–5.0
Lavandula	Lavender	6.5–7.5
Leptospermum	Tea tree	6.0–8.0
Ligustrum	Privet	5.0–7.5
Lilium	Lily, Easter	6.0–7.0
Litchi	Lychee	6.0–7.0
Mangifera	Mango	5.0–6.0
Mimosa	Sensitive plant	5.0–7.5
Monstera	Monstera	5.0–6.0

pH Degrees for Indoor Plants

Botanical Name	Common Name	Preferred pH
Musa	Banana	5.0–7.0
Myrtus	Myrtle	6.0–8.0
Narcissus	Daffodil	6.0–6.5
Narcissus tazetta	Paperwhite	6.0–7.5
Neomarica	Walking iris	5.5–6.5
Nephrolepis exaltata 'Bostoniensis'	Boston fern	5.5–6.5
Nerium	Oleander	6.0–7.5
Ocimum	Basil	5.5–6.5
Osmanthus fragrans	Sweet olive	5.5–6.5
Oxalis	Oxalis	6.0–8.0
Pandanus	Screw palm	5.0–6.0
Passiflora	Passionflower	6.0–7.0
Pelargonium	Geranium	6.0–8.0
Peperomia	Peperomia	5.0–6.0
Persea	Avocado	6.0–8.0
Petroselinum	Parsley	5.0–7.0
Philodendron	Philodendron	5.0–5.5
Pistacia	Pistachio	5.0–6.0
Pittosporum	Pittosporum	5.5–6.5
Plumbago	Plumbago	5.5–6.5
Podocarpus	Podocarpus	5.0–6.5
Polianthes	Tuberose	6.0–7.0
Portulacaria	Elephant bush	5.5–7.0
Primula malacoides	Fairy primrose	6.0–7.5
P. obconica	German primrose	5.5–6.5
Punica	Pomegranate	5.5–6.5
Pyracantha	Firethorn	5.0–6.0
Rhododendron	Azalea	4.5–6.0
Rosa rouletti	Miniature rose	5.5–7.0
Saintpaulia ionantha	African violet	5.5–7.5
Salvia officinalis	Edible sage	5.5–6.5
Sansevieria	Snake plant	4.5–7.0
Sarracenia	Pitcher plant	4.0–5.0
Scirpus	Sedge	7.0–8.2
Selaginella	Selaginella	6.0–7.0
Senecio	Cineraria	5.5–7.0
Sinningia	Gloxinia	5.5–6.5
Soleirolia	Baby's-tears	5.0–5.5
Strelitzia reginae	Bird of paradise	6.0–6.5
Syngonium	Nephthytis	4.5–5.5
Thunbergia	Black-eyed Susan vine	5.5–7.5

pH Degrees for Indoor Plants

Botanical Name	Common Name	Preferred pH
Thymus	Thyme	5.5–7.0
Tolmiea menziesii	Piggyback plant	5.0–6.0
Tropaeolum	Nasturtium	5.5–7.5
Viola	Violet	5.5–6.5
Wisteria	Wisteria	6.0–8.0
Yucca	Yucca	6.0–8.0
Zantedeschia	Calla lily	6.0–7.0
Zingiber	Ginger	6.0–8.0

HOUSEPLANTS DISEASES

Botrytis blight and numerous foliage diseases can attack houseplants that are in a warm, damp place where there is inadequate circulation of fresh air. This can be avoided or treated by spacing plants so that there is some air space between. Trees in the rain forest do this automatically, never quite growing together in the canopy. When large numbers of one kind of plant, African violet for example, are grown together and crowded, such as in a fluorescent-light garden, rots and powdery mildew can spread rapidly. It is imperative that every spent petal, flower, and leaf be promptly removed. If such diseases persist, it may be necessary to apply a houseplant or garden fungicide, and to operate an oscillating fan in the same room.

Root, tuber, bulb, and rhizome rots and basal stem rots occur when the growing medium is soggy or stands in water indefinitely. Roots must have oxygen. When a plant succumbs from too much water, there are often unaffected portions that can be salvaged, cleaned, dusted with a fungicide such as dusting sulfur, and then rooted.

Houseplant diseases, especially leaf rotting, spotting, or untimely yellowing, often occur during shipping. Plants that grow well indoors are in no less need of adequate fresh air and light than those grown outdoors.

BLOOMLESS DILEMMAS

One of the most frustrating things that happens to an indoor gardener is to lavish care and love on a plant and then to have it fail to bloom. Insufficient light is often the problem, especially for plants that have their origins in desert regions (cacti and other succulents), the Mediterranean, or South Africa (pelargoniums are a prime example, which we know mostly as geraniums). A common misunderstanding about orchids is that they are shade plants; in order to bloom, most need sunlight strong enough to make otherwise healthy leaves have an ever so slight yellowish cast about them. An orchid plant with dark green leaves will probably not bloom as expected.

Another frequent cause of nonbloom is growing a plant in temperatures that are fairly uniform day and night and from season to season. The flowering maple abutilon, for example, blooms best if night temperatures are at least ten degrees cooler than those by day. The clivia needs a time of chilling (but not freezing) and being quite dry at the roots (but not extremely dry or the leaves will die) in fall and early winter, otherwise it will not bloom spectacularly in the spring and early summer. The related hippeastrum, also known as amaryllis, will not bloom unless it has a season in which numerous full-size new leaves grow and reach maturity, followed by drying-off or at least being dry enough to harden the new growth and set buds, this in turn succeeded by an abrupt change from "lean" to "fat" conditions, the latter characterized by abundant water, warmth, humidity, light, and nutrients.

These calatheas are extremely dry, a prevailing state that results in premature dying of older leaves and in the curling or folding together of the younger ones. If the plants received less direct sun, they would not need as much water. However, under the existing lighting conditions evenly moist soil is required to support perfect foliage.

Lack of humidity keeps many plants from blooming lavishly as houseplants, especially those that came originally from the rain forest or other regions having relative humidity that is generally above fifty percent. This is true of African violets, florist gloxinias, and other gesneriads, also orchids, bromeliads, and a vast number of begonias.

Sometimes a plant does not flower because it has been fertilized improperly or is not able to assimilate nutrients that are in the soil. A fertilizer labeled for foliage plants, such as 23-21-17, often boosts lots of vegetative growth, but when flowers are wanted, it is necessary to switch to something on the order of 15-30-15. Sometimes the nutrients react as if locked up because the growing medium is permitted to dry out too much between waterings, or the medium is never thoroughly soaked through and through.

Day length also affects when some plants bloom. Especially among the summer bulbs—achimenes, caladiums, tuberous begonias—long days are necessary. Achimenes stop blooming at the onset of autumn and may even begin producing propagules—modified scaly rhizomes—in the leaf axils. Caladiums stop producing the colorful leaves for which they are grown and start sending up flowers that are at best interesting. Tuberous begonias change from the production of large, showy, double male flowers to those of the female which are typically single and smaller, subtending the ovaries. Short days bring on the blooms of poinsettia, many other euphorbias, kalanchoes, and holiday cacti, the latter also mightily affected by cooler temperatures, anything below 50° to 55°F being sufficient to set their buds regardless of day length.

TERRARIUM TROUBLE SIGNS— AND WHAT TO DO

If you do your homework well, more often than not a terrarium will be the most trouble-free of gardening endeavors. However, just in case something goes wrong, here are some symptoms and suggestions for what to do about them.

Plants tall, lanky, weak-stemmed; leaves frail or pale. The terrarium needs more light. The plants you are trying to grow may need more fresh air, or less water. Take this problem firmly in hand. Start over, either by removing the plants and cutting them back or by purchasing compact ones.

Walls of container constantly fogged over entirely with moisture. Too much water inside. Remove cork or cover until walls are clear, then replace. If they quickly cloud over again, repeat the procedure. Do this until they remain mostly clear, but not entirely. It is healthy for some moisture to condense on the walls and trickle back into the soil.

Leaves wilt and develop yellow or brown, burned spots. Too much hot sun shining directly through the walls of the terrarium onto tender leaves. Reduce amount of sun or switch to a fluorescent-light garden.

Leaves wilt or look pale; moss ground cover turns pale or brown. The terrarium is too dry. Add a little water and mist the foliage with a mister.

Water stands on the surface of the soil; soil and plants floating on water. You've watered too much. To solve this problem in an open terrarium, take a bulb baster and draw off the excess water. In a closed terrarium, such as a bottle garden, you may find it necessary to siphon off the water by using a length of rubber or plastic tubing.

Insects visible on leaves and stems. In an open terrarium you can treat this problem using the usual insecticidal soap and water sprays. Inside a bottle you can extend the usual cotton swab dipped in denatured alcohol by attaching it to the end of a wood dowel or bamboo stake.

Leaves or stems rotted off; mold or mildew in evidence. Too much moisture; lack of air circulation. Some plants are not suited to a terrarium that is always closed. Angel-wing and semperflorens begonias, for example, will develop powdery mildew in short order.

Leaves and stems fill the terrarium in a tangled mass of undefined growth. Complete replanting is in order. Clean out the terrarium and start over. Wash it in warm soapy water, rinse, and dry. Use fresh gravel, charcoal, and potting soil. Cut back old plants, make cuttings of them (which can be rooted directly in the terrarium) or use new plants.

One plant is growing rampantly, climbing over and crowding out the others. Cut it back drastically, or remove entirely and replace with a less assertive type.

Glossary

ALTERNATE LEAVES: Those appearing alternately along a stem.

ANNUAL: A plant which grows to maturity in one season, sets seeds, and dies.

ANTHER: Part of the *stamen* which bears pollen.

AXIL: The upper angle formed by a leaf or branch and the stem from which it grows.

BIENNIAL: Plant which requires two years in which to reach maturity, set seeds, and die.

BRACT: Modified leaf, often near or with a plant's flowers, and sometimes so colorful and showy as to be called a "flower." The bracts of poinsettia, justicia (shrimp plant), and cornus (dogwood) serve as familiar examples.

BULB: Term used to describe a swollen stem (usually underground) which is covered by much modified, food-storing leaves. Roots come from the bottom of the stem, and the scalelike leaves serve to protect the bud. A parchmentlike covering is usually present; tulips and onions are good examples.

CALYX: A term used when referring to all of the *sepals* of a flower, whether they are separate or united.

CLONE: (Sometimes spelled clon.) The name used to designate a number of plants, all of which have been derived from one original individual through vegetative propagation. They are genetically identical. Seed-grown plants may appear to be the same, but they are not genetically identical.

COMPOST: Decomposed vegetable matter of vital importance to the outdoor garden, and useful in potting mixes as "garden loam" if it is first put through a quarter- or half-inch screen and then pasteurized (see page 16).

COMPOUND LEAF: One composed of more than one *leaflet* per leaf stalk, as in the rose.

COROLLA: The unit formed by the petals of a flower. These may be separate, as in those of the garden geranium, or united, as in the morning glory.

CULTIVAR: Term used to describe a plant which is maintained only in cultivation.

CUTTING: Term used to describe some vegetative plant part removed for the purpose of growing another plant identical to the parent.

DECIDUOUS: Leaf-losing, a term which applies ultimately to all plants, but used commonly with reference to trees and shrubs which drop their leaves each autumn, or during a dry season.

DORMANT: Term applied to a plant which is not growing, either because of unfavorable conditions, or because it is resting at the end of a growth cycle.

ELLIPTICAL LEAVES: Those which are oval and narrowed at each end.

EPIPHYTE: A plant which in nature finds lodging on another, usually larger, plant but only for the purpose of being better situated to receive light, air, and moisture, and not for parasitic reasons. "Tree perching" is frequently used to describe this kind of plant. Many orchids and bromeliads are "tree perchers" in nature.

FAMILY: Term used in connection with taxonomic botany to indicate a grouping of plants according to their resemblance and similarity. This may be apparent only on careful study of all plant parts.

FLAT: Shallow box with drainage holes in the bottom, used for starting plants. The standard size is sixteen by twenty-two inches, with a depth of two to four inches, but any convenient dimensions may be used.

FORCE: To induce a plant to reach maturity out of season; spring-flowering daffodils blooming in the house in February, for example.

FROND: Always the leaf of a fern, but sometimes used with reference to those of a palm or cycad.

GENUS (genera, plural): The main subdivision of a plant *family*. For example, the genus *Saintpaulia* is part of the gesneriad family or Gesneriaceae. Each genus may be further divided into *species*, the species into *varieties*, *cultivars*, and minor groups.

GERMINATION: The point at which a seed sprouts and becomes a plant.

HERB: Commonly, a plant used for flavoring, fragrance, or medicinal purposes. Botanically, a plant of fleshy, not woody, stems.

HOSE-IN-HOSE: A term used when one flower appears to grow from within another. This occurs usually in natural doubling of the flower, or when the *calyx* and *corolla* are of the same color. Some azaleas have hose-in-hose flowers; also campanulas (the cup-and-saucer Canterbury bells).

HYBRID: The result of crossing two different plants.

INFERIOR OVARY: One which appears beneath the point at which the *calyx* is inserted; typical of amaryllis and rose families.

IRREGULAR FLOWER: One made unsymmetrical by parts of different sizes.

LEAF BLADE: The expanded or flat part of a leaf, as distinguished from its *petiole* (or leaf stalk).

LEAFLET: One segment of a *compound leaf*.

LEAF MOLD: Partially decayed or decomposed leaves, used in potting mixes after first being put through a quarter- or half-inch screen and pasteurized (page 16).

LEAF STALK: A *petiole*.

LOAM: A mellow soil, composed of about equal parts silt and sand and less than twenty percent clay. A handful of it moistened will form a sturdy ball, and even when nearly dry it holds together well.

MIDRIB: The main or central vein of a leaf.

NODE: The joints or swellings which occur at regular intervals along a plant stem. It is at these points that leaf and bud growth begins and, in some circumstances, rooting occurs.

OBOVATE LEAVES: Those of *ovate* shape, except attached to the stem at their narrow end.

OPPOSITE LEAVES: Those set directly across from each other along a stem.

OVATE LEAVES: Those which are egg-shaped, attached to the stem at their broad end.

PALMATE LEAF: One whose sections radiate from a common point; handlike.

PANICLE: A loose, open flower cluster which blooms from the bottom or center toward the top or edges.

PEAT MOSS: Partially or wholly decayed plant parts, derived chiefly from bog mosses; a valuable ingredient for potting mixtures. There are many peat mosses sold; German peat is choice but hard to get, Canadian sphagnum peat moss is excellent and available wherever plants are sold.

PEDUNCLE: The stalk of a solitary flower, or that of the main stalk which supports a flower cluster. Each flower in a cluster is held on a pedicel which is connected to the peduncle.

PELTATE: Term used to describe a leaf whose stalk is attached away from its margin, often in the center.

PERENNIAL: A plant which lives on and on, theoretically without end so long as its environment is favorable.

PERFECT FLOWER: One which bears both male and female organs of reproduction; one which includes *stamens* and a *pistil*.

PERLITE: An almost weightless, gritty, white substance used in gardening as a substitute for sand.

PETAL: The segment of a flower, sometimes separate from the others, sometimes joined together.

PETIOLE: The stalk of a leaf, by which it is attached to the plant's main stem, or branch.

PINCH: To remove with scissors, or nip out with the fingers, the young growing tip of a stem, thus inducing it to branch.

PINNATE: Term used to describe a *compound leaf* whose *leaflets* appear opposite each other along a common axis; featherlike.

PISTIL: The *ovary, style,* and *stigma* of a flower's female reproductive parts.

PLUNGE: To set a plant container in water for the purpose of moistening the soil. Also, to set a plant pot up to its rim in a bed of soil or mulch.

POT-BOUND: Term used when the roots of a pot plant circle endlessly around and through the soil, filling it to the point of being unable to progress further.

RACEME: Term used to describe an elongated flower cluster, which blooms from the bottom upward.

RAY: The flat, marginal flower in the head of a member of the Compositae, or daisy, family.

REGULAR FLOWER: One whose parts are of equal size, regularly and symmetrically arranged.

RHIZOME: A thickened, fleshy, rootlike stem, occurring underground, or creeping along the soil's surface.

ROSETTE: A cluster of leaves radiating symmetrically from a central stem. These occur usually at or near the soil's surface, but are sometimes at the top of a tall stem.

RUNNER: Name given to a prostrate shoot from a plant which runs along the ground, rooting at each joint as in strawberries.

SEPAL: An individual part of the *calyx.*

SIMPLE LEAF: One which has only one blade attached to the main leaf stalk.

SPECIES: Term used to designate a major subdivision in a plant *family.* First the *genus,* as *Saintpaulia* in the family Gesneriaceae, second the species, as *Saintpaulia ionantha.* Species occur in nature and consist of plants which share distinctive characteristics.

SPHAGNUM MOSS: Gray or tan bog mosses dried and used as a planting medium for many kinds of plants. A handful, moistened and wrapped around the base of a cutting, will encourage rooting. Sometimes this type of moss, also called long-strand, is contaminated with a fungus that can cause sporotrichosis in humans (see page 24). Milled sphagnum moss is sterile and fine-textured, of value especially for starting dust-size seeds.

SPIKE: Term used to describe a racemelike cluster of flowers, except each is stalkless or nearly so.

STAMEN: The male reproductive parts of a flower, including the stalk, or filament, and the *anther* containing the pollen.

STIGMA: Termination of the *style* and *ovary,* the point at which pollen is received.

STOLON: Term used to describe a creeping, trailing, or horizontal stem, the tip of which terminates in a new plant; often called a "runner."

SUCCULENT: Term which refers to plants made drought-resistant by special water-storing powers. Some kinds actually store moisture in leaves, stems, and roots; others, through their physiological makeup, are able to exist through long seasons of dryness.

SUPERIOR OVARY: One which appears above that point at which the *calyx* is inserted.

TENDER: Unable to survive cold; usually applied to plants which are harmed by temperatures at or below 32°F.

TENDRIL: A threadlike prolongation of stem or leaf by which climbing plants cling to their means of support.

TUBER: A fleshy stem, mostly underground, with small leaf structures from which buds are borne; the tuber of a potato is a good example.

TUBEROUS-ROOTED: This term refers to a swollen root, as in the dahlia and sweet potato, distinguished from a tuber, which is a swollen underground stem.

UMBEL: A flower cluster, either flat or round, in which the individual flower stalks arise from one point; Queen Anne's lace (of the carrot family), and hoya or wax plant (of the milkweed family) serve as good examples.

VARIETY: A subdivision in a plant *family*, used to designate a natural variation in a *species*; this contrasts with the term *cultivar* which designates a new plant brought about in cultivation.

VERMICULITE: A sterile planting medium, expanded mica, used for rooting cuttings; frequently combined with loam and peat moss as a means of giving the mix a certain desirable friability.

WHORL: Three or more leaves, flowers, twigs, or other plant parts arranged in a circle and radiating from one point.

Resources

Plants, Supplies, Tools, Equipment, Furniture

Abbey Garden, 462 Carpinteria Avenue, Carpinteria, CA 93013; cacti and other succulents, also bromeliads. Catalog $2.

Alberts & Merkel Bros., Inc., 2210 S. Federal Highway, Boynton Beach, FL 33453-7799. Orchids and tropicals. List $1.

Allgrove Farm, P.O. Box 459, Wilmington, MA 01887; time-honored source for terrariums.

All Pest Control, 6030 Grenville Lane, Lansing, MI 48911; natural pest controls.

Alternative Garden Supply, Mail Order Dept., 108 N. Barrington Road, Streamwood, IL 60107; hydroponics; predatory mites and organisms.

Amaryllis Inc., P.O. Box 318, Baton Rouge, LA 70821. Complete listing of cultivars from South Africa and the Netherlands, also some species and older types.

Aqua-10, P.O. Box 818, Beaufort, NC 28516; seaweed concentrate fertilizer supplement.

Associates Insectary, P.O. Box 969, Santa Paula, CA 93060; beneficial organisms.

Banana Tree, 715 Northampton Street, Easton, PA 18042; large and enticing collection of tropical and subtropical plants from seeds; banana plants. Catalog $3.

Beneficial Insectary, 14751 Oak Run Road, Oak Run, CA 96069; beneficial insects and biological insect controls.

Biofac, Box 87, Mathis, TX 78368; pest control with beneficial insects. SASE for list.

Bio Insect Control, 710 S. Columbia, Plainview, TX 78368; beneficial organisms.

Breck's, 6523 N. Galena Road, Peoria, IL 61632; bulbs including precooled Dutch for easy forcing as houseplants.

Bricker's Organic Farms, Inc., 824 Sandbar Ferry Road, Augusta, GA 30901; Kricket Krap organic fertilizer.

Brudy, John, Exotics 3411 Westfield Drive, Brandon, FL 33511; large selection of tropical and subtropical seeds. Catalog $2.

Buell's Greenhouses, Weeks Road, Eastford, CT 06242; African violets, Buell Hybrid florist gloxinias, and other gesneriads; list 50 cents.

W. Atlee Burpee Co., Warminster, PA 18974; seeds, bulbs, nursery stock, perennials, tools, supplies. Free catalog.

Caprilands Herb Farm, 534 Silver Street, Coventry, CT 06238; a foremost American garden of herbs and herbal products; 203-742-7244.

Carroll Gardens, 444 E. Main Street, Box 310, Westminster, MD 21157; perennials, summer bulbs, roses, scented geraniums, herbs, vines, shrubs, conifers, and trees; catalog $2.

Catnip Acres Farm, 67 Christian Street, Oxford, CT 06483; herbs; catalog $2.

Charley's Greenhouse Supplies, 1596 Memorial Highway, Mt. Vernon, WA 98273; catalog $2.

Chicago Indoor Garden Supply, 297 N. Barrington Road, Streamwood, IL 60107; hydroponics and organics.

Clapper Company, 1124 Washington Street, Newton, MA 02165; garden tools.

The Cook's Garden, Box 65, Londonderry, VT 05148; only the best in salad and other vegetable seeds; catalog $1.

Cricket Hill Herb Farm, Glen Street, Rowley, Ma 01969; herbs; catalog $1.

The Cummins Garden, 22 Robertsville Road, Marlborough, NJ 07746; hard-to-find dwarf conifers, Texbury and Knaphill azaleas, small-leaf rhododendrons, and native ground covers; catalog $1. Mail-order only.

Daffodil Mart, Rt. 3, Box 794, Gloucester, VA 23061; all kinds of bulbs; specialists in paperwhite and related narcissus.

P. de Jager & Sons, Box 2010, South Hamilton, MA 01982; bulbs, corms, and tubers.

Earlee, 2002 Highway 62, Jeffersonville, IN 47130-3556; organic fertilizers, soil amendments, biological controls; send SASE for list.

Earthgro, Inc., Lebanon, CT 06249; organic and mineral fertilizers.

Earthly Goods Farm & Garden Supply, P. O. Box 4164, Tulsa, OK 74159-1164; soil and plant supplements, tools.

East Coast Hydroponics, 432 Castleton Avenue, Staten Island, NY 10301; hydroponics and lighting.

The English Garden, Inc., 652 Glenbrook Road, Stamford, CT 06906; trellises, gazebos, pavilions, seats, birdhouses, planters.

Fischer Greenhouses, Poplar Avenue & Blackman Road, Linwood, NJ 08221. Color catalog 50 cents.

Florentine Craftsmen, 46-24 28th Street. Long Island City, NY 11101; fountains, statues, sundials, urns.

Florist Products, Inc., 2242 N. Palmer Drive, Schaumburg, IL 60173; indoor gardening supplies.

Fountain's Sierra Bug Co., P.O. Box 114, Rough and Ready, CA 95975; ladybugs.

Four Winds Growers, P.O. Box 3538, Mission San Jose District, Fremont, CA 94539. Dwarf citrus. (Cannot ship to FL, TX, LA, AZ.) SASE for price list.

Fox Hill Farm, Box 7, Parma, MI 49269; herbs; catalog $1.

The Fragrant Path, P.O. Box 328, Fort Calhoun, NE 68023.

Howard B. French, Route 100, Pittsfield, VT 05762; bulbs, corms, and tubers.

Gardener's Eden, Box 7307, San Francisco, CA 94120; tools, accessories, outdoor garden furniture for indoor gardens.

Gardener's Supply, 128 Intervale Road, Burlington, VT 05401. Organic fertilizers and pesticides, soil amendments, seeds for green manures, supplies, tools, prefabricated greenhouses.

Gesneriads, Home-Grown, David and Colleen Turley, P.O. Box 8417, Fredericksburg, VA 22404; catalog $2.

Glasshouse Works Greenhouses, Church Street, P.O. Box 97, Stewart, OH 45778-0097. One of the most complete listings of houseplants available; highly praised resource.

Gothic Arch Greenhouses, P.O. Box 1564, Mobile, AL 36633. Prefabricated arched greenhouses.

Greenhouse Builders' Supply, Rt. 3 Box 80, Epping, NH 03042; parts and how-to for building a greenhouse.

Grigsby Cactus Gardens, 2354 Bella Vista Drive, Vista, CA 92084; extraordinary selection of cacti and other succulents, all originally seed-propagated and correctly named. Catalog $2.

The Guano Co., 3562 E. 80th Street, Cleveland, OH 44105; bat and seabird guano for natural fertilizers and soil amendment.

Halcyon Gardens, Box 124, Gibsonia, PA 15044; herbs; catalog $1.

Hamm, Robert B., P.O. Box 161361, Sacramento, CA 95816-1361; house plants for indoors/outdoors; list $2.

Hen-Feathers and Co., 10 Balligomingo Road, Gulph Mills, PA 19428; containers, birdbaths, sundials, benches, tools.

Hermitage Garden Pools, Box 361, Canastota, NY 13032; fiberglass garden pools and water features; catalog $1.

High Altitude Gardens, Box 4238C, Ketchum, ID 83340; grass seeds for topping bulb flats; soluble seaweed powder.

Holiday Cactus, 101 County Line Road, Griffin, GA 30223. Christmas and other holiday cacti. Catalog $2.

Home Harvest Garden Supply, 13624 Jefferson Davis Highway, Woodbridge, VA 22191; fertilizers, soil amendments, hydroponics, indoor gardening supplies. Catalog $2.

Horne, Jerry, 10195 S.W. 70th Street, Miami, FL 33173. Tropicals.

Hortica Gardens, Box 308, Placerville, CA 95667; bonsai.

Hurov's Tropical Seeds, P.O. Box 1596, Chula Vista, CA 92012. Edible, medicinal, and ornamental tropical seeds. List 50 cents.

Hydrofarm, 3135 Kerner Boulevard, San Rafael, CA 904901; hydroponics and lighting.

Indoor Gardening Supplies, P. O. Box 40567, Detroit, MI 48240; lighting and indoor growing supplies.

Integrated Pest Management, 305 Agostino Road, San Gabriel, CA 91776; beneficial organisms.

International Growers Exchange, Inc., P. O. Box 52248, Livonia, MI 48152; wide selection of bulbs, some extremely rare, but be patient! Catalog $5.

IPM Labs, Main Street, Locke, NY 13092-0099; beneficial insects plus monitoring tools.

Irving & Jones, Village Center, Colebrook, CT 06021; fine garden furnishings; brochure $2.

Janco Greenhouses, 9390 Davis Avenue, Laurel, MD 20707; catalog $5.

K. & L. Cactus and Succulent Nursery, 12712 Stockton Boulevard, Galt, CA 95632. Large selection. Catalog $2.

Kartuz Greenhouses, 1408 Sunset Drive, Vista, CA 92083; begonias, gesneriads, many outstanding miniatures and plants for indoor/outdoor container growing. Catalog $2.

Kemp Co., 160 Koser Road, Lititz, PA 17543; compost shredder/chippers.

Kinsman Co., River Road, Point Pleasant, PA 18950; cold frames, cloches, arches, baskets, and birdhouses; also compost bins and electric chipper/shredders.

Krieger, Albert G., 1063 Cranbrook Drive, Jackson, MI 49201; streptocarpus specialist; list $1.

Lauray of Salisbury, 432 Undermountain Road, Route 41, Salisbury, CT 06068; cacti, orchids, begonias, gesneriads, succulents. Catalog $2.

Le Jardin du Gourmet, Box 85, West Danville, VT 05873; herbs and gourmet vegetables; catalog 50 cents.

Lilypons Water Gardens, 6800 Lilypons Road, Box 10, Lilypons, MD 21717-0010; aquatics and pool supplies; catalog $4.

Livos Plantchemistry, 614 Agua Fria Street, Santa Fe, NM 87501; "natural and nontoxic" finishes, stains, lacquers, paints, spackles, glues, wood preservatives.

Logee's Greenhouses, 141 North Street, Danielson, CT 06239; a primary source for container plants and herbs; catalog $3.

Lord & Burnham Greenhouses, Under Glass Mfg. Co., P. O. Box 323, Wappingers Falls, NY 12540.

Kenneth Lynch & Sons, Box 488, Wilton, CT 06897; gates, statuary, fountains, pools, benches, sundials.

Machin Designs, Inc., 557 Danbury Road, Route 7, Wilton, CT 06877; conservatories.

Mantis Mfg. Co., 458 County Line Road, Huntingdon Valley, PA 19006; compost chipper/shredder.

McKinney's Glasshouse, P.O. Box 782282, Wichita, KS 67278-2282. Catalog $2. Large selection of different houseplants.

McLure & Zimmerman, 108 W. Winnebago, P.O. Box 368, Friesland, WI 53935; all kinds of bulbs for forcing, also one of the first suppliers of the newer miniature Dutch amaryllis.

Meadowbrook Farms, 1633 Washington Lane, Meadowbrook, PA 19046; one of the finest small, retail garden centers in the Northeast; by calling in advance, 215-887-5900, organized garden groups may arrange to visit the adjoining private gardens of Mr. and Mrs. J. Liddon Pennock, Jr.

Meadowbrook Herb Gardens, Route 138, Wyoming, RI 02898; herbs; catalog $1.

Merry Gardens, Camden, ME 04843; herbs, geraniums, ivies; catalog $1.

Messelaar Bulb Co., Box 269, Ipswich, MA 01938; bulbs.

Natural Gardening Research Center, Gardens Alive!, P.O. Box 149, Sunman, IN 47041; natural control of pests and diseases.

Natural Pest Controls, 8864 Little Creek Drive, Orangevale, CA 95662; praying mantis and sixteen other types.

Necessary Trading Co., P.O. Box 305, New Castle, VA 24127; fertilizers, pest controls, soil amendments. The source for an excellent all natural foliar plant fertilizer. Catalog $2.

Walt Nicke Co., Box 433, Topsfield, MA 01983; quality pruning shears and other gardening tools.

Nor'East Miniature Roses, 58 Hammond, Rowley, MA 01969; miniature roses.

Ohio Indoor Gardening, 4967 N. High, Columbus, OH 43214; hydroponics and lighting.

Orcon, 5132 Venice Boulevard, Los Angeles, CA 90019; beneficial insects and monitoring tools. SASE for list.

Organic Pest Management, P.O. Box 55267, Seattle, WA 98155; biological organisms, predators, organic botanicals.

Paradise Water Gardens, 14 May Street, Whitman, MA 02382; aquatic plants and pool supplies; catalog $2.

George W. Park Seed Co., Greenwood, SC 29647; all manner of garden and houseplant seeds, bulbs, supplies, tools, and equipment. Free catalog.

Peter Paul's Nurseries, Canandaigua, NY 14424. Insectivorous plants, supplies, books. Brochure free.

Plants International, 2635 Noble Road, Cleveland Heights, OH 44121; ingeniously designed ceramic self-watering pots.

The Plumeria People, P.O. Box 820014, Houston, TX 77282-0014; color catalog shows plumerias and other tropical plant specialties, $2.

Deborah Reich & Associates, Ltd., 466 Washington St., #8E, New York, NY 10013; 212-219-0873; topiary and supplies.

Otto Richter & Sons, Box 26, Goodwood, Ontario, Canada L0C 1A0; herbs; catalog $2.50.

Rincon-Vitova Insectaries, P.O. Box 95, Oak View, CA 93022; eleven types of beneficial insects.

Ringer, 9959 Valley View Road, Eden Prairie, MN 55344; bio-organic products for lawns, gardens, and house plants.

The Rosemary House, 120 S. Market Street, Mechanicsburg, PA 17055; herbs; catalog $2.

John Scheepers, Inc., 63 Wall Street, New York, NY 10005; bulbs, corms, and tubers.

Schultz Co., 14090 Riverport Drive, Maryland Heights, MO 63043; fertilizers and pesticides for houseplants.

Sequoia Nursery, 2519 E. Noble Avenue, Visalia, CA 93277; miniature roses.

Seventh Generation, Colchester, VT 05446-1672; composters, storage bins, useful home products. Catalog $2.

Shady Hill Gardens, 821 Walnut Street, Batavia, IL 60510; the largest selection of geraniums (*Pelargonium*) available from any single source. Catalog $2.

Singer's Growing Things, 17806 Plummer Street, Northridge, CA 91325; especially impressive collection of euphorbias. Catalog $2.

Smith & Hawken, 25 Corte Madera, Mill Valley, CA 94941; tools, some indoor plants, outdoor garden furniture for indoors.

Solar Components Corp., 121 Valley Street, Manchester, NH 03103; components for building attached or free-standing greenhouses. Catalog $2.

Sturdi-Built Manufacturing Co., 11304 S.W. Boone's Ferry Road, Portland, OR 97219; prefabricated home greenhouses.

Sunnybrook Farms Nursery, P.O. Box 6, 9448 Mayfield Road, Chesterland, OH 44026. Herbs, houseplants, Catalog $1.

Superior Growers Supply, 4870 Dawn Avenue, East Lansing, MI 48823; hydroponics and lighting.

Taylor's Herb Gardens, 1535 Lone Oak Road, Vista, CA 92084; plants and seeds. Catalog $1.

Texas Greenhouse Co., 2524 White Settlement Road, Fort Worth, TX 76107; prefabricated home greenhouses.

Thompson & Morgan, Box 1308, Jackson, NJ 08527; flower and vegetable seeds, many rare and unusual. Free catalog.

Tinari Greenhouse, 2325 Valley Road, Huntingdon Valley, PA 19006; African violets and other gesneriads. Catalog $2.

Tropical Seeds, P.O. Box 11122, Honolulu, HI 96828. Large selection of seeds from the tropics.

Troy-Bilt Mfg. Co., 102nd Street and 9th Avenue, Troy, NY 12180; rotary tillers and chipper/shredders.

Turner Greenhouse, P.O. Box 1260, Goldsboro, NC 27530; prefabricated and do-it-yourself greenhouses. Catalog $1.

Unco Industries/Wiggle Worm Haven, 7802 Old Spring Street, Racine, WI 53406; worm castings, night crawlers.

Van Bourgondien Bros., Box A, Babylon, NY 11702; bulbs, corms, and tubers; free catalog.

Van Engelen, Inc., Stillbrook Farm, 313 Maple Street, Litchfield, CT 06759; excellent bulbs for forcing.

Van Ness Water Gardens, 2560 N. Euclid Avenue, Upland, CA 91786-1199; large selections of aquatics and supplies for growing. Catalog $6.

Mary Mattison Van Schaik, Cavendish, VT 05142; bulbs, corms, and tubers; catalog 50 cents.

Vegetable Factory, Inc., Box 2235, New York, NY 10163; prefabricated greenhouses and porch enclosures; catalog $2.

Violet Creations, Jo Anne Martinez, 809 Taray de Avila, Tampa, FL 33613; African violets and gesneriads; supplies.

Walker, Mary, Bulb Co., P.O. Box 256, Omega, GA 31775; crinum lilies are a specialty; unusual bulbs.

Walpole Woodworkers, 767 East Street, Walpole, MA 02081; furniture, swings, picnic sets, weather vanes.

Waterford Gardens, 74 East Allendale Road, Saddle River, NJ 07458; aquatic plants and pool supplies; catalog $4.

Wayside Gardens, Hodges, SC 29695-0001; perennials, shrubs, vines, "new" old roses, bulbs; catalog $1.

Well-Sweep Herb Farm, 317 Mt. Bethel Road, Port Murray, NJ 07865; herbs; catalog $1.

White Flower Farm, Litchfield, CT 06759-0050; perennials, shrubs, bulbs; catalog $5.

Wicklein's Water Gardens, 1820 Cromwell Bridge Road, Baltimore, MD 21234; water lilies, lotus, bog plants, pool liners; catalog $3.

Wolfman-Gold & Good Co., 484 Broome Street, New York, NY 10013; statuary, garden furniture, latticework, window boxes, planters.

Wood Classics, High Falls, NY 12440; 914-255-7871; teak and mahogany outdoor furniture, kits or assembled.

Worms Way (for hydroponics and organic gardening supplies) as follows: 5311 56th Commerce Park, Tampa, FL 33610; 4620 S. State Road 446, Bloomington, IN 47401; 1200 Millbury, Suite 8G, Worcester, MA 01607; 12156 Lackland Road, St. Louis, MO 63146.

Wyrttun Ward, 18 Beach Street, Middleboro, MA 02346; herbs, catalog $1.

Yucca Do Nursery, P.O. Box 655, Waller, TX 77484; Mexican natives for indoors/outdoors; catalog $3.

Plant Societies, Botanical Gardens, Arboreta, Horticultural Societies, Periodicals

African Violet Society of America, Box 3609, Beaumont, TX 77704.

American Begonia Society, 8922 Conway Drive, Riverside, CA 92503.

American Bonsai Society, 1363 W. Sixth Street, Erie, PA 16505.

American Camellia Society, Box 1217, Fort Valley, GA 31030.

American Fern Society, Dr. Les Hickok, Botany Department, University of Tennessee, Knoxville, TN 37916.

American Fuchsia Society, Hall of Flowers, Golden Gate Park, 9th Avenue and Lincoln Way, San Francisco, CA 94122.

American Ginger Society, Box 100, Archer, FL 32618.

American Gloxinia and Gesneriad Society, Box 493, Beverly Farms, MA 01915.

American Hibiscus Society, Drawer 1540, Cocoa Beach, FL 32931.

American Horticultural Society, 7931 E. Boulevard Drive, Alexandra, VA 22308.

American Ivy Society, Box 520, West Carrollton, OH 45449.

American Orchid Society, 6000 S. Olive Avenue, West Palm Beach, FL 33405.

American Plant Life Society, Box 985, National City, CA 92050; amaryllids and other bulbous plants.

Arnold Arboretum, The, Jamaica Plain, MA 02130.

Atlanta Botanical Garden in Piedmont Park, P.O. Box 77246, Atlanta, GA 30357.

Bartlett Arboretum, The, Box 39, Belle Plaine, KS 67103.

Bartlett Arboretum, The University of Connecticut, 151 Brookdale Road, Stamford, CT 06903.

Berkshire Botanical Garden, Corner of Routes 102 and 183, Stockbridge, MA 01262.

Birmingham Botanical Gardens, 2612 Lane Park Road, Birmingham, AL 35223.

Blithewold Gardens & Arboretum, 101 Ferry Road, Bristol, RI 02809.

Boerner Botanical Gardens, 5879 S. 92nd Street, Hales Corner, WI 53130.

Bonsai Clubs International, Box 2098, Sunnyvale, CA 94087.

Botanic Garden of Georgia State, 2450 S. Millegde Avenue, Athens, GA 30605.

Botanica, The Wichita Gardens, 701 Amidon, Wichita, KS 67203.

The Bromeliad Society, 2488 E. 49 Street, Tulsa, OK 74105.

Brooklyn Botanic Garden, 1000 Washington Avenue, Brooklyn, NY 11225; fifty-two acres of visitor-friendly gardens and displays of plants arranged according to their botanical relationships; extensive under-glass plantings in the Steinhardt Conservatory, and a Bonsai Museum; 718-622-4433.

Brookside Gardens, 1500 Glenallen Avenue, Wheaton, MD 20902.

Cactus and Succulent Society of America, Box 3010, Santa Barbara, CA 93130.

Callaway Gardens, Highway 27, Pine Mountain, GA 31822.

Chicago Botanic Garden, Lake Cook Road, Glencoe, IL 60022.

Cleveland, The Garden Center of Greater, 11030 East Boulevard, Cleveland, OH 44106.

Clyburn Arboretum & Park, 4915 Greenspring Avenue, Baltimore, MD 21209.

The Cryptanthus Society, Kathleen Stucker, Secretary, 3629 Bordeaux Court, Arlington, TX 76016; $3 for sample of *Journal*.

The Cycad Society, 1161 Phyllis Court, Mountain View, CA 94040.

Cymbidium Society of America, 6881 Wheeler Avenue, Westminster, CA 92683.

Dallas Arboretum & Botanical Garden, 8617 Garland Road, Dallas, TX 75218.

Deep Cut Park Horticultural Center (including Elvin McDonald Horticultural Library), 352 Red Hill Road, Middletown NJ 07748.

Denver Botanic Gardens, 909 York Street, Denver, CO 80206.

Desert Botanic Garden, 1201 N. Galvin Parkway, Phoenix, AZ 85008.

Des Moines Botanical Center, 909 E. River Drive, Des Moines, IA 50316.

Dubuque Arboretum & Botanical Gardens, 3125 W. 32nd Street, Dubuque, IA 52001.

Epiphyllum Society of America, Box 1395, Monrovia, CA 91016.

Fairchild Tropical Garden, 10901 Old Cutler Road, Miami, FL 33156.

Fernwood Botanic Gardens, 13988 Rangeline Road, Niles, MI 49120.

Fine Gardening, bimonthly magazine, The Taunton Press, 63 S. Main Street, Box 355, Newtown, CT 06470; $22 yearly.

Flower & Garden, bimonthly magazine, 4251 Pennsylvania Avenue, Kansas City, MO 64111; $8 yearly.

Fort Worth Botanic Garden, 3220 Botanic Garden Drive, Ft. Worth, TX 76107.

Frelinghuysen Arboretum, 53 E. Hanover Avenue, Morristown, NJ 07960.

Garden Design magazine, 4401 Connecticut Avenue N.W., Suite 500, Washington, DC 20008-2302; $20 yearly.

Isabella Stewart Gardner Museum, 2 Palace Road, Boston, MA 02115; Fenway Court, an indoor courtyard filled with plants, is something of a mecca among gardeners; 617-566-1401.

Gesneriad Society International, Membership Coordinator, 1109 Putnam Boulevard, Wallingford, PA 19086.

Ginter, Lewis, Botanical Garden, 1800 Lakeside Ave., P.O. Box 28246, Richmond, VA 23228-4610.

Green Scene, published bimonthly by the Pennsylvania Horticultural Society, 325 Walnut Street, Philadelphia, PA 19106; $9.75 yearly, exclusive of PHS membership.

Garden Education Center of Greenwich, Bible St., Cos Cob, CT 068070.

Greenwich Garden Education Center of, Bible St., Cos Cob, CT 068070

Heliconia Society International, Flamingo Gardens, 3750 Flamingo, Ft. Lauderdale, FL 33330.

Hobby Greenhouse Association, 8 Glen Terrace, Bedford, MA 01730.

The Holden Arboretum, 9500 Sperry Road, Mentor, OH 44060.

Horticulture, The Magazine of American Gardening, 20 Park Plaza, Suite 1220, Boston, MA 02116; monthly; $24 yearly.

Houseplant Forum, HortiCom Inc., P.O. Box 128, Radisson, WI 54867-0128; $2 for sample copy of bimonthly newsletter.

Houston Civic Garden Center, 1500 Hermann Drive, Houston, TX 77004.

Hoya Society International, Box 54271, Atlanta, GA 30308.

Huntington Botanical Gardens, 1151 N. Oxford Road, San Marino, CA 91108.

Indoor Gardening Society of America, 128 W. 58 Street, New York, NY 10019.

Indoor Gardening Society of Canada, 16 Edgar Woods Road, Willowdale, Ontario M2H 2Y7.

International Aroid Society, Box 43-1853, South Miami, FL 33143.

International Carnivorous Plant Society, Fullerton Arboretum, Fullerton, CA 92634.

International Geranium Society, William McKilligan, 1442 N. Gordon Street, Hollywood, CA 90028.

International Palm Society, Box 27, Forestville, CA 95436.

Jackson State University Botanical Garden, 1400 John R. Lynch Street, Jackson, MS 39209.

Leu, H.P., Botanical Gardens, 1730 N. Forest Avenue, Orlando, FL 32803.

Longwood Gardens, Box 501, Kennett Square, PA 19348; 350 acres of formal and informal gardens, with more than three and a half acres under glass; seasonal displays; extensive education program and lecture series; 215-388-6741.

Los Angeles International Fern Society, 14895 Gardenhill Drive, La Mirada, CA 90638.

Los Angeles State and County Arboretum, 301 N. Baldwin Avenue, Arcadia, CA 91006.

Matthaei Botanical Garden, University of Michigan, 1800 N. Dixboro Road, Ann Arbor, MI 48105.

Memphis Botanic Garden, 750 Cherry Road, Memphis, TN 38117.

Mercer Arboretum and Botanical Garden, 22306 Aldine-Westfield Road, Humble, TX 77338.

Minnesota Landscape Arboretum, 3675 Arboretum Drive, Chanhassen, MN 55317.

Missouri Botanical Garden, 4344 Shaw Boulevard, St. Louis, MO 63110.

Montreal Botanical Garden, 4101 Sherbrooke Street E., Montreal, Quebec H1X 2B2; an extraordinary collection of some 26,000 different plants; 514-872-1454.

Morris Arboretum of the University of Pennsylvania, 9414 Meadowbrook Avenue, Chestnut Hill, Philadelphia, PA 19118.

Morton Arboretum, Rt. 53, Lisle, IL 60532.

National Fuchsia Society, 2892 Crown View Drive, Rancho Palos Verdes, CA 90274.

National Oleander Society, Mrs. E. Koehler, Box 3431, Galveston, TX 77552.

New Orleans Botanical Garden, Victory Avenue City Park, New Orleans, LA 70119.

The New York Botanical Garden, Bronx, NY 10458; 250 acres with extraordinary displays in the Enid A. Haupt Conservatory, and extensive plantings on the grounds; 212-220-8700.

Norfolk Botanical Gardens, Airport Road, Norfolk, VA 23518.

North Carolina Botanical Garden, UNC-CH Totten Center 457A, Chapel Hill, NC 27514.

Olbrich Botanical Society, 3330 Atwood Avenue, Madison, WI 53704.

Palm Society, Box 368, Lawrence, KS 66044.

Peperomia Society International, 5240 W. 20 Street, Vero Beach, FL 32960.

Phipps Conservatory, City of Pittsburgh, Schenley Park, Pittsburgh, PA 15213; thirteen connected greenhouses display more than two acres under glass; 412-255-2376.

Planting Fields Arboretum, Planting Fields Road, Oyster Bay, NY 11771; four hundred acres of formal and informal gardens featuring more than six thousand kinds of plants; camellia house contains one of the best collections in America; 516-922-9201.

Plumeria Society of America, Elizabeth Thornton, 1014 Riverglyn, Houston, TX 77063.

Powell Gardens, Rt. 1, Kingsville, MO 64061.

San Antonio Botanical Gardens, 555 Funston Place, San Antonio, TX 78209.

Selby, Marie, Botanical Gardens, 811 S. Palm Avenue, Sarasota, FL 34236.

Seymour Botanical Conservatory, 316 S. G Street, Tacoma, WA 98405.

Skylands Botanical Garden, Sloatsburg Road, Ringwood, NJ 07456.

State Fair Park Arboretum, 1800 State Fair Park Drive, Lincoln, NE 68510.

Strybing Arboretum & Botanical Gardens, Golden Gate Park, 9th Avenue at Lincoln Way, San Francisco, CA 94122.

Toledo Botanic Gardens, 5403 Elmer Drive, Toledo, OH 43615.

U.S. Botanic Garden, 245 First Street S.W., Washington, DC 20024.

U.S. National Arboretum, 3501 New York Avenue N.E., Washington, DC 20002.

University of California Botanical Garden, Centennial Drive, Berkeley, CA 94720.

University of Massachusetts, Durfee Conservatory, French Hall, Amherst, MA 01003.

University of Wisconsin Arboretum, 1207 Seminole Highway, Madison, WI 57311.

Utah Botanical Garden, 1817 N. Main, Farmington, UT 84025.

Waimea Arboretum and Botanical Garden, Waimea Falls Park, 59-864 Kamehameha Highway, Haleiwa, HI 96712.

Washington Park Arboretum, University of Washington (XDD-10), Seattle, WA 98195.

Wave Hill, 675 W. 252nd Street, Bronx, NY 10471.

Will Rogers Horticultural Center, 3500 N.W. 36th Street, Oklahoma City, OK 73112.

Index

Numerals in *italics* indicate illustrations.